AL JOLSON

Al Jolson as Pierrot (in 1910s). Permission of The George Eastman House.

AL JOLSON

A Bio-Bibliography

JAMES FISHER

Bio-Bibliographies in the Performing Arts, Number 48
James Robert Parish, Series Adviser

GREENWOOD PRESS
Westport, Connecticut • London

Library of Congress Cataloging-in-Publication Data

Fisher, James.
    Al Jolson : a bio-bibliography / James Fisher.
      p.   cm. — (Bio-bibliographies in the performing arts, ISSN
0892-5550 ; no. 48)
    Filmography: p.
    Discography: p.
    Includes indexes.
    ISBN 0-313-28620-5 (alk. paper)
    1. Jolson, Al, d. 1950 — Bibliography. 2. Jolson, Al. d. 1950 —
Discography. 3. Jolson, Al, d. 1950.   I. Title. II. Series.
ML134.5.J65F57 1994
782.42164'092 — dc20
[B]   93-37192

British Library Cataloguing in Publication Data is available.

Library of Congress Catalog Card Number: 93-37192
ISBN: 0-313-28620-5
ISSN: 0892-5550

First published in 1994

Greenwood Press, 88 Post Road West, Westport, CT 06881
An imprint of Greenwood Publishing Group, Inc.

Printed in the United States of America

The paper used in this book complies with the
Permanent Paper Standard issued by the National
Information Standards Organization (Z39.48-1984).

10 9 8 7 6 5 4 3 2 1

For my father and mother

Contents

Illustrations	ix
Preface	xi
Acknowledgements	xiii
1 Biography	1
2 Chronology	39
3 Stage	49
4 Film	83
5 Discography	129
6 Radio and Television	151
7 Sheet Music	177
8 Bibliography	209
Books	209
Periodicals/Magazines	245
New York Times	255
Variety	261
Appendix A: Stage Shows Based on Jolson's Life	269
Appendix B: Newsreels	273
Appendix C: Cartoons	279
Appendix D: Awards	283
Appendix E: Endorsements	287
Title Index	289
Name Index	307

Illustrations

A studio portrait of a dapper Al Jolson in the
early days of his Broadway career (1910s).   xvi

Al Jolson -- "The Singing Fool" (1928).   38

Al Jolson in *Big Boy* (1923).   47

Al Jolson singing on NBC radio in the mid-1930s.   48

Eugenie Besserer, Al Jolson, and Warner Oland
in *The Jazz Singer* (1927).   82

Davey Lee and Al Jolson in the deathbed scene from
The Singing Fool (1928).   128

A montage photo of Ruby Keeler and Al Jolson in costume
for *Go Into Your Dance* (1935).   150

Al Jolson and announcer Ken Carpenter at a rehearsal for
the Kraft Music Hall, late 1940s.   176

A studio portrait of Al Jolson in the later days of his
career (1940s).   286

Preface

As the length of the bibliography section of this book will surely suggest, much has been written about the life and career of Al Jolson. Few performers in his day were as well known or successful in as many aspects of the entertainment field as Jolson -- and few lasted as long. No single book has ever done complete justice to Jolson's life and career -- most have only attempted to penetrate the myths and gossip surrounding his private life. This book begins with a biographical overview stressing his career achievements, and will, in subsequent sections, illuminate the major aspects of Jolson's extraordinary and prolific participation in virtually all mediums of American show business in the first half of the twentieth century.

The major sections of this book include:

(1) *Biography* -- a biographical essay on Jolson's life and career, featuring commentary from spouses, co-workers, and noted critics and admirers.

(2) *Chronology* -- a detailed listing of the major dates and events in Jolson's life and career.

(3) *Stage* -- a complete listing of Jolson's major live stage appearances in circus, vaudeville, minstrel shows, concert stages, and musical comedy beginning in 1897. Each listing is preceded by the letter "S." Information in the entries includes opening and closing dates, tours, cast and production staff, a plot synopsis, listing of songs, critical reviews, and commentary.

(4) *Film* -- a complete listing of Jolson's films, both features and shorts. Each listing is preceded by the letter "F." Information in the entries includes producing studio, release dates, cast and production staff, a plot synopsis, listing of songs, critical reviews, and commentary. Feature length movies are listed first, followed by Jolson's involvement in short films.

(5) *Discography* -- a complete listing of Jolson's recording sessions. Each listing is preceded by the letter "D." Information in entries includes recording companies, dates of recordings, orchestra, songs recorded, composers, and lyricists,

recording numbers and commentary regarding the popular success of individual recordings.

(6) *Radio and Television* -- a detailed listing of Jolson's radio appearances. Includes entries on Jolson's own various radio series and his guest appearances on other radio programs. Each listing is preceded by the letter "R." For Jolson's radio series, entries include information on sponsors, dates of broadcasts, individual episodes, songs performed by Jolson, guests, and critical reviews. For Jolson's guest appearances on radio, entries include name of show, date of broadcast, and a listing of songs performed by Jolson. A complete listing of Jolson's few television appearances, along with entries on television programs about Jolson or featuring material on him. Each listing is preceded by the letter "T." Entries include information on sponsors, dates of broadcasts, credits, and commentary.

(7) *Sheet Music* -- a detailed listing of Jolson sheet music. Each listing is preceded by the letters "SM." Entries include the name of the song, composer, lyricist, and publisher, along with the size and date of the sheet.

(8) *Bibliography* -- a comprehensive bibliography including lists of books on Jolson, his films and books on various aspects of the arts with significant discussion of Jolson and his work. Each book listing is preceded by the letter "B." Book entries are annotated with commentary and brief quotes where appropriate. A bibliography of periodical and magazine articles follows the book bibliography, and each listing in this section is preceded by the letters "PM." Following periodicals and magazines is a listing of *New York Times* articles (not critical reviews, which are listed with the appropriate stage show, film, or radio program). These entries are preceded by the letters "NYT." The last bibliographical section is a listing of Jolson-related articles from *Variety* (again, critical reviews are listed with the appropriate stage show, film, or radio program). These entries are preceded by the letter "V."

Finally, appendices are included on stage shows based on Jolson's life and career (each entry is preceded by the letters "SS"), newsreels of Jolson (each entry is preceded by the letter "N"), cartoons featuring Jolson caricatures (each entry is preceded by the letter "C"), awards presented to Jolson (each entry is preceded by the letter "A"), and Jolson product endorsements (each entry is preceded by the letter "E"). Two indices are included: a title index (stage show, film, and song titles) and a name index. Each of these refers to the entry numbers with the exception of the biography which is indexed by page number.

The information in this book is complete as of August 1, 1993. Any additions or corrections for future editions may be sent to the author in care of Greenwood Press.

Acknowledgements

With gratitude, I would like to acknowledge the assistance and support of the following individuals: Michael S. Abbott, Barrie Anderton, Clive and Lenore Baldwin, Patrick Beidelman, Richard D. Bonesteel, Charles Bowles, Robert Brunet, Dennis W. Crow, William B. Davies, the late Lillian Gish, Herbert G. Goldman, Art Hatem, the late Lem Heneger, Tim Hollis, Dick Judge, Teresa Kaplan, Les Kaye, the late Ruby Keeler, Kenneth Kloth, Carolyn Breen Kolibaba, Dolores Kontowicz, Kaizaad Navroze Kotwal, Frankie Laine, John W. Landon, Jack Langdon (personal assistant to George Burns), Barbara Launer, Davey Lee, Erminie Leonardis, Glenn Loney, Otis R. Lowe, Wayne L. Martin, Tim Masal, Doug McClelland, Ann V. McKee, Don Muncie, John Newton, Mike Pitts, Owen L. Pomeroy, Max O. Preeo, Barbara Schwarz, Janet Slobodien, Fred Sopher, John Sonneborn, Ray Staruch, Charles Stillwagon, John C. Swan, Laura Wagner, Dwight Watson, and Bruce Wexler. Various members of the International Al Jolson Society, and the society's officers and services, provided considerable help as well.

Among those who knew or worked with Al Jolson, I am most particularly indebted to five talented ladies: Carol Bruce, one of the great singers of the Broadway and West End musical stages, who was a regular on Jolson's Colgate radio show; the incomparable Hildegarde, whose long successful career as a chanteuse allowed her professional path to cross with Jolson's during World War II; Sybil Jason, who performed as a child with Jolson in *The Singing Kid*, and knew him as a friend for the rest of his life; Evelyn Keyes, one of the brightest stars of the golden age of Hollywood, who memorably played "Julie Benson" in *The Jolson Story* and has written some of the finest memoirs of that fabulous era; and Betty Garrett, one of M.G.M.'s beloved musical comedy ladies, who was married to the screen's "Al Jolson," the late Larry Parks. Each of these talented women shared memories and opinions with candor and humor, illuminating the complex personality of "The World's Greatest Entertainer."

Erle Krasna, Al Jolson's widow, offered encouragement and a few helpful comments for which I am most grateful. I also wish to especially thank John and May Treasure, long-time Jolson admirers, for their generosity in sharing their vast collection of Jolson memorabilia, and for their encouragement and friendship.

Greenwood editors Marilyn Brownstein, Lynn Taylor, and George F. Butler have been considerate and helpful throughout the process, and James Robert

Parish, series editor of Greenwood's bio-bibliography volumes in the performing arts, was a valuable source of advice, encouragement, and assistance.

A considerable number of libraries, museums, and archives were of significant help: Alderman Library at the University of Virginia, American Library of Radio and Television at the Thousand Oaks Library, American Museum of the Moving Image, American University Library, Billy Rose Theatre Collection of the New York Public Library, Bing Crosby Historical Society, Boston Public Library, Buffalo and Erie County Public Library, Butler Library at Columbia University, California State University at Long Beach Library, Cinemathèque Canada, City College of the City University of New York Library, Cornell University Library, Delaware State Museums, Emerson College Library, Film Collections of the George Eastman House, Goodspeed Opera House, Harry Ransom Humanities Research Center at the University of Texas at Austin, Harvard Theatre Collection, Hearst Entertainment, Hofstra University Library, Howard University Library, International Theatre Institute of the United States, Inc., J. Walter Thompson Company Archives at Duke University, Jerome Lawrence and Robert E. Lee Theatre Research Institute at The Ohio State University, Jewish Museum, John Hay Library at Brown University, Lilly Library at Indiana University, Motion Picture, Broadcasting and Recorded Sound Division of the Library of Congress, Lockwood Memorial Library at the State University of New York at Buffalo, Los Angeles Public Library, Mugar Memorial Library at Boston University, Museum of Modern Art, Museum of Television and Radio, National Film Information Service at the Academy of Motion Picture Arts and Sciences, Newberry Library, Newsfilm Library of the University of South Carolina, Pacific Film Archive, Performing and Creative Arts Department at the College of Staten Island, Purdue University Library, Record Research, Rhode Island School of Design Library, Rodgers and Hammerstein Archives of Recorded Sound at the New York Public Library for the Performing Arts, San Francisco Performing Arts Library and Museum, Sherman Grinberg Film Libraries, Inc., Shubert Archive, Stanford University Libraries, Theatre Arts Library at UCLA, Theatre Collection of the Museum of the City of New York, Theatre Museum, Turner Entertainment Co., UCLA Film and Television Archive, University Library at San Diego State University, University of Miami Library, University of Oregon Library, University of Washington Library, Will Rogers Memorial, Williams/Watson Theatre Collection at Dartmouth College, Wisconsin Center for Film and Theater Research, Wolper Organization, Inc., Yale School of Drama Library, and Yale University Library.

The staff of Wabash College's Lilly Library have been helpful in a variety of ways, but I particularly wish to thank Debbie Polley for her many kindnesses and good will, and Bruce Brinkley for his thoughtful assistance. I am also grateful to my friend Diane Enenbach who contributed considerable energy and expertise in the bibliographic area, unearthing hard-to-find Jolson-related articles and reviews. Diane's daughters, Anne and Elisabeth, also assisted in library research, which I appreciate very much. I am indebted to Marjorie Jackson, secretary for the Wabash College Fine Arts Departments, who contributed mightily to the process of preparing the text for publication. My friend and Wabash College colleague Warren Rosenberg read and insightfully criticized part of the text, for which I am grateful.

During the preparation of this book, my wife Dana Kay Warner, and my children Daniel and Anna, endured repeated showings of Jolson's films, as well as the relentless playing of Jolson recordings, with relatively few complaints -- I love them very much.

My initial encounter with Al Jolson was as a child. Although I was born sixteen days after Al Jolson's death, I found his extraordinary voice first through my mother's Decca 78's, and subsequently being permitted to watch multiple showings of *The Jolson Story* on WOR-TV's "Million Dollar Movie." For their love and support, I dedicate this book to my parents.

James Fisher
1993

A studio portrait of a dapper Al Jolson in the early days of his Broadway career (1910s). Permission of The International Al Jolson Society.

1

Biography

"The World's Greatest Entertainer"

I confess I'm fond of that Mendelssohn--rag
    But not of Liszt's Rhapsody Hungarian
Which sounds to me like a musical jag
    (You see I am but a rank barbarian).
The long-haired high-brows call me "vulgarian"
When the "Great Big Beautiful Doll" I croon
    For I'm strong for the music that's real American
And the joy of my heart is a rag time tune.

You can't swing in the maze of the Turkey Trot
    To the strains of a Chopin symphony
Or the horrible noise that Wagner wrote
    Or chaotic nocturnes of Tschaikowsky
    Such spasms are much too deep for me
And I pine mid the all-pervading gloom
    To hear that song 'bout the Robert E. Lee
For the joy of my heart is a rag time tune.

-- Eugene O'Neill[1]

On October 16, 1951, the now legendary Judy Garland appeared for the first performance in an unprecedented nineteen week run as headliner of a two-a-day vaudeville bill at New York's show business mecca, the famed Palace Theatre. Her Palace engagement marked one of the most extraordinary comebacks in entertainment history -- both for Garland and for the spirit of vaudeville. As the last great singer created in the vaudeville tradition -- starting at the age of two in a musical sister act -- Garland came to symbolize and embody vaudeville's time-worn traditions and much-loved past entertainers, thanks both to her movies, which often evoked the era, and her own extraordinary versatility. A recent book by John Fricke celebrating her remarkable career is titled *Judy Garland. World's Greatest Entertainer*. The title was certainly deserved -- but there was an earlier "World's Greatest Entertainer," and Garland paid a humble tribute to him during performances of her 1951-52 vaudeville run. At each performance, after singing her herculean "Judy at the Palace," a musical tribute to stars like Nora Bayes,

Sophie Tucker, Fanny Brice, Eva Tanguay, and other great women who had headlined at the Palace Theatre in its heyday, Garland stepped into a spotlight and said "I'd like to do the next song, ladies and gentleman, not only because its such a good song -- great song -- one of my favorites, but because it's so associated with a man whom we all adored, we still adore him, I know we always will -- I think you'll recognize the song and the man." The orchestra struck up the opening chords and Garland sang, "Rock-A-Bye Your Baby With a Dixie Melody." The man, of course, was Al Jolson, who, curiously enough, had never played the Palace.

It was fitting that Garland should make such a tribute, and make it slightly less than a year following Jolson's passing. She was the sole entertainer of her generation to sing the songs of his generation -- songs forever associated with Al Jolson -- "Rock-A-Bye Your Baby With a Dixie Melody," "Swanee," "April Showers," "You Made Me Love You," "Carolina in the Morning," "For Me and My Gal" -- and to achieve something of his impact in singing them. The torch had been passed -- Garland, in her way, was saying that Jolson's music would live on long after the man himself.

Despite the passage of time and profound changes in musical tastes and cultural values, the name Al Jolson remains synonymous with the golden age of popular entertainment in America. During those burgeoning years of show business, from just before World War I to the decade following World War II, Jolson dominated -- and pioneered innovations -- in minstrel shows, vaudeville, Broadway musicals, the concert stage, recordings, motion pictures, radio, and television. Many artists have achieved success in one or two of these areas -- virtually none but Jolson excelled in all of them. A complex and difficult man to know and understand offstage, Jolson led an extraordinary life onstage. He tirelessly entertained American servicemen and women in three wars, appeared at numerous benefits, and bequeathed much of his vast personal fortune to a wide variety of charities. He was imitated frequently, but seldom equalled, and his trademark stage boast, "You ain't heard nothin' yet!," has become firmly entrenched in the cultural lexicon.

As Judy Garland knew, he had truly earned his billing -- Al Jolson, "The World's Greatest Entertainer."

An Introduction to Al Jolson

He was the most impressive entertainer on the American stage, a black-faced minstrel with a loud baritone voice, telling banal jokes and singing sentimental songs. Whatever he sang, he brought you up or down to his level; even his ridiculous song "Mammy" enthralled everyone. Only a shadow of himself appeared in films, but in 1918 he was at the height of his fame and electrified an audience. He had a strange appeal, with his lithe body, large head and sunken, piercing eyes. When he sang such songs as "There's a Rainbow Round My Shoulder" and "When I Leave the World Behind," he lifted the audience by unadulterated compulsion. He personified the poetry of Broadway, its vitality and vulgarity, its aims and dreams.[2]

-- Charlie Chaplin

From the early days of his stage career in the decades before World War I through his unparalleled comeback after World War II, Al Jolson was billed as "The World's Greatest Entertainer." During his own life, Jolson's volcanic singing and inspired clowning elevated both his onstage and offstage lives to mythical proportions. In a 1988 biography of Jolson, Herbert G. Goldman has suggested that "the genius of Al Jolson has been lost."[3] In actuality, Jolson has been an elusive figure. His relatively few films are rarely shown on television or in revival houses, and his greatest stage successes date from long before the days of original cast recordings and living memory. Film critics have generally ignored Jolson's movies with the exception of the historically significant first partial-talkie, *The Jazz Singer* (1927), which made Jolson a major film star, ushered in the sound era, and saved Warner Bros. Studio from almost certain bankruptcy. It would be an exaggeration to suggest that Jolson's work has been consciously suppressed, but for an artist who achieved so much acclaim and popularity for so long, and whose contributions and innovations in the entertainment field have been so conspicuous, it is unfortunate that his identification with the blackface tradition has led to a lack of acknowledgement today.

Few performers of his time -- or any other era -- demonstrated such an unbridled love of performing or cast such a spell over an audience. Beginning with his first Broadway stage success, *La Belle Paree* (1911), through his last, *Hold On to Your Hats* (1940), Jolson dominated the musical theatre, the recording industry, and, ultimately, films and radio. He pioneered innovations in show business in diverse ways: as the first major musical comedy headliner to tour widely, as the star of "the first talking picture," as the major performer of the first commercial television transmission, as the first million-selling recording artist, and as a tireless entertainer during wartime for American troops. Few performers before or since Jolson have achieved as much or wielded such influence in popular culture.

Clearly, Jolson's fellow artists looked to him as a model and responded to him as most audiences did. Among his contemporaries, friendly rival Eddie Cantor wrote that from "the very first time I saw Al Jolson, he was it for me. He was the King -- and the King could do no wrong."[4] Their mutual friend George Jessel proclaimed that Jolson "gave majesty to the popular song,"[5] and comic Jimmy Durante recalled that Jolson "put over a song [with] a lot of heart."[6] French boulevardier Maurice Chevalier noted that Jolson "was more than an entertainer, he was a great popular singer and something much more"[7]; and black entertainer Ethel Waters admired the fact that "Jolie was never a slacker. Until he died, and for good reason, they called him *the world's greatest entertainer*."[8] Among the survivors of Jolson's era, comedian Milton Berle has observed that "Audiences loved Jolson. He was a spellbinder, a superstar of his day, and he gave his audiences their money's worth,"[9] and George Burns remembers that "Nobody ever dominated a theater like Jolson."[10] Performers of subsequent generations were similarly admiring. Judy Garland, Frank Sinatra, Elvis Presley, Frankie Laine, Eddie Fisher, among many others, have all pointedly sung songs identified with Jolson and have publicly acknowledged his inspiration. Even rock-and-roll bad boy Jerry Lee Lewis has said: "I loved Al Jolson, I still got all of his records. Even back when I was a kid I listened to him all the time."[11] At the time of Jolson's death, Bing Crosby, whose popularity as a singer seriously rivalled Jolson's in the 1930's, perhaps best assessed Jolson's significance:

The personal magnetism of Jolie and the excitement he created in his audience had a tremendous and lasting effect on me. I had heard all of his records and naturally was a great Jolson fan. [. . .] No singer in the history of the American theater ever had such influence on other singers as Al Jolson, especially on their styles and delivery.[12]

Although Jolson's performing style is generally thought of as outmoded today, his recordings have remained available and popular for the forty-three years since his death, and they are now appearing with regularity on the latest entertainment innovation, compact discs.

Memories of his dynamic performing and timeless singing are clouded by several problems. Jolson made only two appearances on television, and there is comparatively little film footage of him in action. Jolson and most of his musical comedy contemporaries failed to make comfortable transitions from stage to screen, although his forceful presence in *The Jazz Singer* (1927), and its phenomenally successful follow-up film, *The Singing Fool* (1928), helped to make sound movies the dominant artistic and entertainment medium of the twentieth century. The best Jolson films were made during the Stone Age of talkies and, as such, they are rarely seen today. Although Jolson films turn up with some frequency on nostalgia channels, it is impossible to see him in his true medium, the live stage. Modern society has unfortunately lost much of its appreciation for what live stage performance is or used to be -- it has become saturated by state-of-the-art technology on stages, computer-generated trickery on film, and the quick musical "sound bites" of MTV. Today's audience is unaccustomed to seeing a popular singer or dancer *au natural*, without the benefit of a stage full of lights, sound equipment, and varied multimedia gimmicks. The great artists of popular song worked without a net; at their best, the Judy Garlands, Ella Fitzgeralds, Frank Sinatras, Bing Crosbys, and Jolsons required nothing but their own unique talents to thrill their audience.

The most difficult problem of all in regard to the memory of Al Jolson is that as the last well-known entertainer to perform with regularity in blackface, Jolson has come, in more enlightened and sophisticated times, to represent an odious racial stereotype. This is somewhat unfortunate and unfair, especially in view of Jolson's significant achievements on stage and film, as well as the charm his recordings retain even today. At the height of his career, Jolson was considered an artist of the first rank; at present, he seems to have fallen from grace largely due to his identification with the blackface tradition -- many have equated Jolson's blackface image with white America's condescending view of African-Americans. Although it is difficult to imagine that anyone today would seriously advocate the use of blackface, in his time Jolson was simply employing a widespread and well-worn stage convention used liberally by both black and white performers from the early nineteenth century. One legend suggests that it was a black performer who first suggested the use of burnt cork to Jolson as a way of covering his stage fright in his earliest vaudeville days. And, probably because he was the finest performer of the tradition, Jolson is today taking the blame for its proliferation and its obvious racial insensitivity. Virtually every musical performer of his day, and a fair number since, have at some time or other performed in blackface -- even some of the most beloved icons of the musical stage and screen: Eddie Cantor, Bert

Williams, Shirley Temple, Irene Dunne, Fred Astaire, George Murphy, Judy Garland, Bing Crosby, Donald O'Connor, among many others, appeared in blackface at some time -- even as late as 1980 Neil Diamond wore it briefly in the dismal remake of Jolson's classic film, *The Jazz Singer*.

For Jolson, blackface was a stage mask -- no more, no less; it gave license to his onstage persona "Gus" comparable only to *commedia dell'arte's* Arlecchino, the outrageous comic servant of the Renaissance stage. Arlecchino, at the lowest end of the social spectrum of his day, ultimately ruled his stage world through his wit, ingenuity, basic goodness, and his mistrust of power and pomposity. This was equally true of Jolson's "Gus"; his audience knew that blacks held the lowest position in American society at that time and they were entertained by this safely symbolic uprising, despite the fact that the oppressed themselves could not always play their own role. The striking parallel between this ancient theatrical tradition and Jolson's art was noted as early as 1923, when Gilbert Seldes wrote that "Jolson has re-created an ancient type, the scalawag servant with his surface dulness[sic] and hidden cleverness, a creation as real as Sganarelle or the figure behind all of Chaplin's variations, the one the French call Charlot."[13] Jolson's "Gus," descending from these earlier traditions, punctured the pomposities and inequities of modern life, as his predecessors had in their own times -- and as Chaplin's "Little Tramp" did on silent film screens, while he dominated Broadway's musical comedy stages.

Jolson's theatrical peers, Fanny Brice, Eddie Cantor, W.C. Fields, Will Rogers, and Sophie Tucker, all similarly found their own highly individual masks based on various ethnic or social stereotypes, and, as a result, all of them were liberated from reality and were thus able to ascend heights of vocal emotion and comic lunacy more naturalistic images would not have allowed. Viewers of the surviving evidence of these performers may often find the stereotyping offensive or ridiculous, but certainly this was not the intention of the performers themselves. Fanny Brice, for example, was herself a Jew whose wildly exaggerated Yiddish dialect evolved from her own heritage -- she amused her audience, also largely Jewish, through her ability to demonstrate the universal human qualities represented by the stereotype, thus transcending ethnic difference. Certainly, the performers of this time did not aim to give offense to any racial, religious, or ethnic group, even though their characterizations were drawn from the insecurities of unaccepted groups and the social inequities they often faced. George Burns, perhaps the only survivor from that era whose fame approaches that of Jolson, Brice, and the others, recalls that

> Working in "black," covering your skin with burnt cork and painting
> on wide white lips, was an important part of vaudeville. [. . .] It had
> no racial meaning at all, even great black stars like Bert Williams put
> on blackface. Performers wearing black didn't imitate blacks, most
> of them spoke in their ordinary voices. The only thing blackface
> meant was that the person wearing it was working in show
> business.[14]

Burns' recollection does not complete the picture; black performers of his era, like Williams, saw blackface as a necessary evil -- something that gave them otherwise forbidden access to the white theatrical world. Film critic Gene Siskel interviewed Sammy Davis, Jr. near the end of the versatile entertainer's life about many things.

When asked to comment on Jolson and the blackface issue, Davis replied, "No, it didn't bother me that he used blackface, . . .A lot of black performers at the same time were using cork, too [to exaggerate the color of their faces]. Guys like Pigmeat Markham. It was the vaudeville style."[15] Perhaps Davis was not offended because Jolson's "Gus" was no shuffling, slow-witted stereotype in the Stepin Fetchit mode; instead, Jolson could be said to have reinvented blackface by turning the stereotype inside out -- by ruling the stage from behind a mask which neither he nor his audience viewed realistically. Jolson's "Gus" was an American folk hero rising out of various oppressions to rule his imaginary world through Jolson's unique dynamism and command of the audience. His blackface mask became a pure theatrical confection belonging to no particular race, gender, time, or place. Although many of Jolson's early musical comedies were set on the inevitable plantation in the "Old South," and although he sang about "Swanee," "Alabama," and his ever-present "Mammy," any attempt at reality of situation or location was casual and purely gratuitous. His stage world was largely a fantasy place, and he and his audience knew it. It served as little more than a pleasant *mise-en-scène* within which Jolson could function most effectively. Observe the "on-stage" blackface scenes in *The Jazz Singer* or *The Singing Fool*, for example, and note that Jolson does not employ an exaggerated black dialect when in blackface. Similarly, observe him singing "Mammy, I'll Sing About You" in *Go Into Your Dance* (1935). Here, singing a traditional minstrel song in whiteface, it is obvious that there is no difference between Jolson's style in blackface or whiteface. Indeed, Jolson's stage presence was so monumental that issues of race, creed, or gender never truly figured in the symbiotic relationship between audience and artist that was unrivalled in its time. Perhaps these issues should have figured more centrally in the dialectic of his time, but Jolson, like most of his contemporaries, simply ignored them and worked as best they could within existing conditions. Near the end of Jolson's stage career, critic John Hutchens believed the same when he observed that Jolson could raise this tradition to unique heights:

> A "mammy song," as he sang it, could lose its ridiculous sentimentality and acquire suddenly the quality and importance of a folk ballad; and it is [. . .] a tribute to Jolson's individual style that the songs whose popularity he made, which might otherwise have been forgotten as swiftly as all popular songs, live on in a way from year to year because of his association with them.[16]

In short, it should be possible to appreciate Jolson's unique talents while we also acknowledge his historic role in the maintenance of stereotypes that are now outmoded. Jolson's predominance as a performer in his own time can hardly be exaggerated -- it is well-documented in stage, screen, radio and recording reviews, in box-office records and, less tangibly, in the manner in which his persona has become ingrained in American popular culture and in the performing styles of subsequent generations of entertainers, all of whom have a touch of Jolson in them. Surely he was the first performer of the vaudeville and popular music realm in America to be considered by critics, fellow performers, and audiences alike as a true artist of the first rank.

While his stature as a performer is undisputed, Jolson the man remains something of an enigma. His personal life and personality are filled with puzzling contradictions, and Jolson's biographers have largely tended to base their assessment of his private life on enduring myths (some of which may be patently untrue or broadly exaggerated) or a few witnesses, like George Jessel, whose own agenda based on equal parts jealousy and grudging admiration is often painfully evident in recollections of his longtime friend and sometime nemesis. Jolson's biographers, however, are not truly at fault. The first substantive biography, Pearl Sieben's *The Immortal Jolson*, was published in 1962, twelve years after Jolson's death. Sieben knew Jolson in his later years, but could hardly be considered a true "insider" in his private life. Even when Sieben published her book, there were few survivors with any real knowledge of Jolson's earliest years willing to talk. In 1952, Harry Jolson, Al's elder brother, had published a memoir of their early vaudeville days, *Mistah Jolson*, but his view is often self-serving in its contention that his own musical career was held in check by Al's predominance and ego. Compounding the problem, Jolson's wives have generally refused to speak of him in depth. The recently deceased Ruby Keeler, wife number three, and Jolson's fourth wife, Erle Krasna, both offered good wishes, but refused to be interviewed in depth for this book, as they have refused all others in the past. Keeler clearly harbored bitterness about her years as Mrs. Jolson, yet aside from some remarks about Jolson's ego and possessiveness, she never presented any significant substantiation for her grievances. In fact, on one of the rare occasions she did speak of him, at the time when a 1985 BBC-TV documentary included suggestions that Jolson drank too much and was known as a womanizer, Keeler spoke out vehemently in his defense: "It's just garbage -- how anybody can believe it I don't know. Al hardly ever drank. He was no angel, but wasn't an egotistical maniac, either. And he was no skirt-chaser during the 11 years we were married. I'd have known about it." Erle Krasna similarly leaped to Jolson's defense: "He never chased girls, and he was an incredibly generous man. He even left all his money to charity."[17]

Part of the problem is that the two highly successful biographical films, *The Jolson Story* (1946) and *Jolson Sings Again* (1949), are almost completely fictional and entirely complimentary. The public in general, as well as many biographers, have often accepted the films as telling the real and true Jolson story. Regarding the existing published biographies of Jolson, Erle Krasna writes in a letter dated August 4, 1992 that "most of them rewrite *The Jolson Story*," which, she states emphatically, "was pure fiction." There is no question that these films capture the essence of a performer driven by his love of an audience, but most plot details are indeed pure fiction. Certainly such fictionalizing was not unique for show business film biographies of that era (the best of them, *Yankee Doodle Dandy* [1942], an acclaimed account of theatrical great George M. Cohan's life, similarly eliminated any less than complimentary aspects). But as a result of the image of near human perfection created by these films, serious Jolson biographers have often tended to swing the pendulum the other way, crafting exposés of Jolson's "dark side." Other Jolson books tend to be mere celebrations of his greatness by devoted fans. Both approaches inevitably lead to distortions; one creates the myth of an out-of-control egomaniac while the others offer an alternate myth of a misunderstood genius who, for some unknown reason, is being unfairly villified.

So how to find the true Jolson? Perhaps the fairest approach is a recounting of the events of his life with a clear understanding that he is, and will undoubtedly always remain, an enigma. A few things about Al Jolson do seem certain. He loved to perform for an audience to the point that his life in the spotlight was more important to him than anything else. As a result, relationships with wives, friends, and co-workers were generally less significant to him and, as a result, were often characterized by unhappiness and rifts. Although virtually all of his fellow performers acknowledge his brilliance as a singer and comedian while also proclaiming his predominance in the entertainment field, some have made harsh criticisms of Jolson personally. These emerge frequently enough that they must be addressed -- some suggest that he was insatiably egotistical, even by the standards of a field of endeavor not known for its modesty; others speak of his toughness in business dealings; still others report, as the BBC-TV documentary did, of his womanizing and a fundamental insecurity which tended to manifest itself unpleasantly. In contrast to these views are those of many others who remember him as easy-going, down-to-earth, and even self-effacing; generous to a fault, both to individuals and to a wide range of charities and philanthropic works; and supportive of theatrical colleagues, particularly younger performers on their way up and out-of-work performers on their way down. On the positive side, too, Jolson entertained American troops (often at his own expense) during two world wars and in Korea, where, against doctors orders, he performed tirelessly leading to a fatal heart attack a few weeks after his return to the States. The problems posed by the complexities and contradictions of Al Jolson's unique personality are inevitable in search of a life spent in a very bright spotlight.

A Life of Al Jolson

What care I who makes the laws of a nation;
Let those who will take care of its rights and wrongs,
What care I who cares for the world's affairs,
As long as I can sing its popular songs.
Let me sing a funny song with crazy words that roll along,
And if my song can start you laughing, I'm happy. . .happy.
Let me sing a sad refrain of broken hearts who love in vain,
And if my song can start you crying, I'm happy.

-- Irving Berlin[18]

Contradictions about the life of Al Jolson start at the beginning -- with his birthdate and name. Born in poverty as Asa Yoelson in Seredzius, Lithuania, he was the fifth child of Rabbi Moshe Reuben and Naomi (Cantor) Yoelson. The exact date and year of his birth remain uncertain -- the year could be anywhere between 1879 and 1888, although 1885 or 1886 remain the most likely possibilities. He would later choose May 26th as his official birthday, although all he knew for sure was that he was born in the spring. It has been suggested (including by one Jolson relative, the late Maurice Jolson) that the family did not spell their last name "Yoelson" -- but it is impossible to verify that this spelling commonly used in Jolson biographies -- including *The Jolson Story* (thus suggesting Jolson's concurrence) -- is incorrect and that the accurate spelling is Joelson.

Around 1890, Asa's father left Seredzius for America to seek a position in an American synagogue. Unable to afford fares for the entire family, he left them behind in Seredzius promising to send for them all when he had secured a position and saved enough money for their fares. It took four years, but Rabbi Yoelson became head of the Talmud Torah Congregation in Washington, D.C., an impoverished synagogue, and he was finally able to send for the family. They sailed from Europe on the Umbria and arrived at Ellis Island on April 9, 1894, and shortly thereafter the family was reunited in Washington. The joy of the family's togetherness was to be tragically short-lived -- within less than a year, on February 6, 1895, Naomi died in childbirth. This devastating event was particularly shattering to young Asa, his mother's particular favorite, and when barely a year later Moshe married Chyesa "Hessi" Yoels on March 29, 1896, Asa began to pull away from the family. Not long after, Asa, now calling himself Al, and his older brother Hirsch, now Harry (1882-1953), Americanized their surname to Joelson (presuming the change was required), and frequently could be found performing on Washington, D.C. streets to earn pennies. Al's other siblings, Rose, Gertrude, Etta and half-brother George, unlike Al and Harry, were apparently not drawn toward the intoxicating rhythms of American show business.

Harry left home in 1897 and encouraged Al to join him in New York City. Over the next few years, Harry and Al attempted to find opportunities to perform, both together and separately. For a time in 1897, Al is thought to have worked with Rich & Hoppe's Big Company of Fun Makers, a small-time vaudeville troupe playing tank towns. When jobs were scarce the brothers both returned to Washington and the family, but when another theatrical opportunity arose they ran off once again. On one return home they performed at Fort Myer for soldiers at the outbreak of the Spanish-American War -- beginning a Jolson tradition that would continue through the Korean War. When Al left home again in 1898 he became a mascot for the Fifteenth Pennsylvania volunteers. At the war's end, Al, driven to perform, briefly joined the Walter L. Main Circus on a short tour. Following his few weeks with the circus, Al went to Baltimore and sang for pennies in a saloon before being apprehended by Gerry Society officers who put him in the custody of the St. Mary's Industrial School for Boys in Baltimore, where young George Herman ("Babe") Ruth also resided.

Shortly thereafter, Al once again returned home -- but only briefly. It is thought that he sang from the audience during Eddie Leonard's vaudeville act, and that he might have toured for a time with the Villanova Burlesque Company. Apparently neither of these opportunities lasted long, for beginning on September 18, 1899, he was appearing as an extra in a crowd scene at Washington's National Theatre during the out-of-town tryout run of Israel Zangwill's drama of contemporary Jewish life, *Children of the Ghetto*. He only participated in three performances before being removed from the cast by his father before the production moved on to a successful Broadway run. Not long after, the final break came with his family -- his father disapproved of his theatrical ambitions, but young Al was not to be stopped.

In October 1900, Al joined the Victoria Burlesquers as a foil in the act of Aggie Behler. Provincial reviews suggest that he occasionally made a small impression in the musical portions of the act. In 1901, Al teamed up with Fred E. Moore, and as Joelson & Moore they played in vaudeville, occasionally rejoining the Victoria Burlesquers company. Vaudeville at the turn-of-the-century was a hurly-burly and fertile proving ground for aspiring performers, and throughout his career, Jolson continued to make occasional forays onto the vaudeville stage, as Will Rogers (1879-1935), also a veteran of those ranks, recalled:

the loss of old vaudeville was more than just the loss of seeing the show. Taking away vaudeville was just like taking the high school away, and wanting the pupil to jump from grammar school to college. Then too, too many actors made the mistake of playing just on Broadway. They not only wore themselves out there, but they meant nothing on the road. No one knew them. That's how Jolson became so popular in the old days. Al was smart. He would always duck out of New York and play everywhere he could. He played many a one-nighter in the very height of his tremendous popularity. He would draw anywhere.[19]

Joelson & Moore joined forces with Al Reeves' Famous Big Company in March 1902. Reeves had a profound influence on Al's developing performance style and, as occasional reviews make clear, he began to make much more of an impression on audiences from about this time. In September of the same year, Joelson & Moore appeared with Lawrence Weber's Dainty Duchess Company, touring entensively throughout the east and midwest.

After parting company with Moore, Al began working again with his brother Harry. They billed themselves as The Joelson Brothers in an act called "The Hebrew and the Cadet," with Harry playing a comic Hasidic Jew and Al acting as his straight man. They met with some minor success, but in October 1904 they decided to team up with vaudevillian Joe Palmer in an act called Joelson, Palmer & Joelson. Sometime during this era the "e" disappeared from Joelson, and the name "Al Jolson" could be found on theatre marquees for the first time. Jolson also began performing in blackface during this era. There are several legends about how Jolson was introduced to this time-worn tradition, including an anecdote suggesting that one or another fellow performer suggested burnt cork as a method of hiding his chronic nervousness.

Harry abruptly quit the act in November 1905 to work on his own, and Jolson & Palmer continued in vaudeville as a team -- trouping on the treadmill of one-nighters and provincial tours. Not long after, in June 1906, Jolson began working occasionally as a single, becoming increasingly successful and confident in himself as a performer. He finally ended his partnership with Palmer, and launched himself as a single. At this time, while performing on the west coast, Jolson met Henrietta Keller (1888-1967), and they were married on September 20, 1907. Although the marriage seemed to be a happy one initially, Jolson was an eternally restless being -- and, as a promising young entertainer on the rise, he clearly had little real interest in a traditional home life or a spouse outside the profession. Their marriage would be a series of dizzying ups and downs, until Henrietta could no longer tolerate being left behind in the wake of the whirlwind of Jolson's life.

In November 1907, Jolson temporarily became a member of Walter Sanford's Players, a stock company in residence at the Globe Theatre in San Francisco, but his most important break finally came in August 1908 when he joined the celebrated Lew Dockstader's (1856-1924) Minstrels. Dockstader's troupe was a prosperous one, so Jolson now had the opportunity to work steadily with a solid group of seasoned professionals. In a sense, Jolson's time with Dockstader completed his theatrical education; Dockstader's Minstrels toured the United States and Canada in a relentless schedule of one-nighters and split weeks until late 1909. On rare breaks Jolson continued to play single dates for increasingly enthusiastic responses. He undoubtedly found himself as a performer during this era, as critics began to take significant notice of him in the Dockstader troupe and in his solo performances. He rose in prominence in the company until his popularity with audiences began to rival that of Dockstader himself. When the troupe played New York City in February 1909, Jolson was favorably reviewed by *Variety* for the first time:

> Dressing neatly in evening clothes of faultless cut and of the new color called "taupe," Jolson offers a quiet quarter of an hour of smooth entertainment. As a singer of "coon" songs Jolson has a method of his own by which lyrics and melody are given their full value. His talk moves along nicely and is kept within proper proportion to the rest of the act. Throughout the talk Jolson introduces little tricks of speech and for a finish has an odd, eccentric vocal performance in which he sings with a peculiar buzzing note. Of course, it's flagrant trick work, but it brings him back for a sure fire encore. [. . .] As it stands now Jolson's offering is capable of holding down a place in any vaudeville show. He is now in the next to closing position in the olio of Dockstader's Minstrels, following Lew Dockstader and Neil O'Brien among others, and Jolson is making a good mile.[20]

Following a tiff with Dockstader, Jolson briefly joined the rival I.P Wilkerson's "Minstrels of Today" in April and May 1909 before rejoining Dockstader, although his days as a member of the minstrel troupe were numbered. At about this time, with the guidance of manager Arthur Klein, Jolson managed to secure a release from his contract with Dockstader and he began to command a top salary as a single, making as much as $2,500 a week. Jolson is believed to have made his first recordings for the Edison Company in February 1910, although these recordings apparently have not survived. More importantly, he signed a contract with the prestigious theatrical entrepreneurs, the Shubert Brothers, Jacob J. (1880-1963), Sam S. (1876-1905), and Lee (1875-1953), and a few months later he made his debut in a Broadway musical revue, *La Belle Paree* (1911), a loosely constructed hodge podge presented at the Shubert's new Winter Garden Theatre. Jolson did not make much of an impression on opening night since his spot was scheduled so late in the proceedings that most critics and much of the audience had already departed. At the third performance, with his spot moved to an earlier time, he began to make a significant impression -- Al Jolson had arrived. The Shuberts would produce all of his musical shows until the mid-1920's, and Jolson's theatrical home would remain their lush Winter Garden. The nominal star of *La Belle Paree*, as well as Jolson's next show, *Vera Violetta* (1911), was the French charmer Gaby Deslys (1884-1920). She must have resented the rapid rise of Jolson's star in the Shubert heavens, but could hardly compete with his burgeoning talents, as her biographer has written:

> Despite her dislike of him, she watched Jolson's performance, and noted with awe his remarkable ability to seduce the audience. Even though his big, powerful voice had no difficulty in reaching the furthest seats in the auditorium, even before microphones were

invented, he would make sure that everyone got to hear him by leaping off the stage and running up and down the aisles, singing and clowning all the way.[21]

It should be remembered that although he had extraordinarily successful careers on screen and in radio beginning in the late 1920's, and a phenomenal comeback after World War II, Jolson's true golden age was as a stage performer between 1911 and 1925. The live theatre was his metier, and from *La Belle Paree* to his last Shubert show, *The Wonder Bar* (1931), he dominated the Broadway musical comedy stage in a string of remarkably similar musicals constructed to showcase his talents. At the height of Jolson's popularity, Gilbert Seldes wrote that "He is the great master of the one-man show because he gives so much while he is on that the audience remains content while he is off -- and his electrical energy almost always develops activity in those about him." On the critical side, Seldes points out a distaste for "Mammy" songs, but finds Jolson their finest exemplar, noting that "he leans on the second-rate sentiment of these songs, until they are forced to render up the little that is real in them." Seldes also objected to "a few very cheap jokes and a few sly remarks about sexual perversions" in Jolson's routine, but resolved that he "is driven by a power beyond himself. One sees that he knows what he is doing, but one sees that he doesn't half realize the power and intensity with which he is doing it. In these moments I cannot help thinking of him as a genius."[22]

During this era, Jolson also became a recording artist in earnest, first with Victor Records from 1911 to 1914, and later through a ten-year association with Columbia Records (Jolson also recorded for Brunswick Records from January 1924, and through the mid-1930's; he made his last series of recordings for Decca Records beginning in 1945). He also turned up with regularity on sheet music covers, both as a singer and as a collaborator. There has been much controversy surrounding Jolson's actual contributions to the songwriting process in any of these collaborations, but it is clear that his interpretation of a song led to its almost certain commercial success. It was not uncommon in Jolson's era for the few singers approaching his stature (Eddie Cantor, Fanny Brice, etc.) to command authorship credit for their ability to "put a song over."

Following *La Belle Paree* and *Vera Violetta*, Jolson's other pre-World War I shows included *The Whirl of Society* (1912), *The Honeymoon Express* (1913), *Dancing Around* (1914), and *Robinson Crusoe, Jr.* (1916), all initially presented at the Winter Garden followed by extensive national tours at the end of which Jolson would begin rehearsals for the next show. These productions were all cut from the same cloth, allowing Jolson, in his finely-honed comic persona as the blackfaced "Gus," free range as a comic. His improvisatory skills were showcased by these light-weight vehicles, and his supporting casts learned to take a back seat to Jolson in all circumstances. The shows each had individual scores, but they were loose enough in their construction to permit the easy interpolation of new songs, including tunes that would become Jolson standards: "Waiting for the Robert E. Lee" (*The Whirl of Society*), "The Spaniard That Blighted My Life" and "Who Paid the Rent for Mrs. Rip Van Winkle?"(*The Honeymoon Express*), "When I Leave the World Behind" (*Dancing Around*), "Where Did Robinson Crusoe Go With Friday on Saturday Night?" and "Where the Black-Eyed Susans Grow" (*Robinson Crusoe, Jr.*). On a good night, Jolson would sing well past the show's scheduled ending time, and, as many witnesses and critics recall, the audience would be left still wanting more. Critical reaction to *Robinson Crusoe, Jr.*, the most quintessentially Jolsonesque of these early shows, was typical of the response he came to expect in the pre-World War I era:

> As usual, Jolson is piloting the show to what success it attains, for Jolson's presence has a tendency to dispel any evidence of monotony and in a few instances where the book threatened to wabble[sic] he speedily came to the rescue and directed proceedings to the proper tension of joy. [. . .] His delivery of a song is a work of genuine art and he clears up as much of the mystery surrounding the musical publisher's activity during the Winter Garden premieres for in this respect Jolson has no equal. He is quick to take advantage of every comedy opening and knows the shortest route to laughs through the application of appropriate "business" as a substitute for dialogue. In this particular production Jolson is the life of the party, and if "Robinson Crusoe, Jr." establishes itself as a Winter Garden success, the bulk of the credit should go to the individual efforts of its star.[23]

In the midst of World War I, with Jolson in active and public support of the war effort through many appearances at bond rallys, army camps, and military hospitals, he opened in yet another Shubert-produced musical, *Sinbad* (1918). During the highly successful run of this show, Jolson interpolated a particularly rich vein of songs, all of which would remain forever in his repertoire: "Rock-A-Bye Your Baby With a Dixie Melody," "Swanee," "Avalon," and "My Mammy." By this time, he had built a repertoire of sure-fire songs, and his ownership of the stage and his audience was complete. Of Jolson's impact at this time, George Burns (b. 1896) recalls:

> I'll never forget a World War I bond rally. It was the biggest show ever put together. Every star you could think of was on it. Finally, Enrico Caruso, the opera sensation of his time, came on. He sang an aria from *Pagliacci*, and then he introduced a new war song written by George M. Cohan, called "Over There." He brought the house down. Then out came Jolson. He walked to the center of the stage, looked at the audience and said, "You ain't heard nothin' yet!" Can I tell you something, he was right.[24]

Playwright and drama critic George S. Kaufman wrote of Jolson's mystique at the time of *Sinbad*: "The show doesn't matter. *Sinbad*, for example, is an indifferent entertainment at best, but Jolson is now winding up his third season in it, and the production will have earned nearly a million and a half dollars when it is finally packed away this summer."[25] Jolson's domination of an evening's performance was so complete that often he could, and did, dismiss the rest of the cast part way through a show to the delight of the audience who, in fact, preferred to hear and see Jolson "in one." Since his earliest Shubert shows, he often appeared in their Sunday night concerts with performers from other Shubert productions also on the bill. Jolson inevitably dominated these evenings as he did his own current show.

With Jolson in high gear, *Sinbad* toured the country from 1919 through the first half of 1921. That same year, Henrietta Keller, typically left behind at home, divorced him following several unsuccessful attempts at reconciliation. When the

Sinbad tour concluded, Jolson immediately went into yet another Shubert opus, *Bombo* (1921), which opened at Jolson's 59th Street Theatre, a new Shubert house named for their most valuable star. *Bombo* was another triumph for Jolson, and during its run he introduced several songs which would become staples of his repertoire, including "April Showers," "Toot, Toot, Tootsie," and "California, Here I Come." Response to Jolson was uniformly ecstatic:

> Jolson is the show at the Jolson. That was expected and the first-nighters reveled with him and of him. "Bombo" as a show was not up to expectations. [. . .] His singing of "Whenever April Showers Come Along" was a splendid effort. He tried with it vocally, proving that he has a real voice. The lyric of "April Showers" is exceptionally fine and in Jolson's care was the prettiest of numbers. That the star liked it too was indicated by his repetition at the finale. [. . .] When Jolson first appeared the sustained welcome brought tears to his eyes and he dabbed at them with his gloved fingers. It was his work, his songs, his personality that carried "Bombo" along. [. . .] Jolson is as great an entertainer as he ever was -- greater, in fact.[26]

Like this critic, most observers of the popular American stage of the 1910's and 1920's place Jolson at the pinnacle of show business greatness. His theatrical "rivals", particularly Eddie Cantor and George Jessel, were widely applauded, but deemed inferior to Jolson who was considered in a class of his own by most critics and fellow-performers. There were certainly singers with more attractive voices (most musical comedy leading men could technically sing as well or better than Jolson) or those who could emote with equal fervor (Fanny Brice, for instance, whose heart-rending delivery of "My Man" and other torch songs, coupled with her singular comedic skill, made her a legend). Comedians like W.C. Fields, Will Rogers, Bert Williams, and later, Burns and Allen, were undoubtedly more consistently amusing than Jolson, and his few eccentric dance steps hardly placed him in a class with such dancers as Fred and Adele Astaire or Marilyn Miller. But with Jolson, the whole package was unique and on a stage he became totally irresistable. His love of (and need for) the audience -- his vitality, his need to please, his stage courage and inventiveness -- made him one-of-a-kind.

Before beginning the inevitable national tour of *Bombo*, Jolson married vaudevillian Ethel Delmar (real name: Alma Osborne [1900-1976]) on July 22, 1922. This marriage, too, would be troubled from nearly the beginning -- Jolson's work was his all-consuming passion, a wife would always come in second. In a July 28, 1992 telephone interview with the author, Teresa Kaplan, daughter of Jolson's sister Rose, remembers her uncle in this era as a "magnetic person, but I think he was a lonely man." As a child, she occasionally attended performances of Jolson shows, and she recalled being frightened during a visit to his theatre dressing room when she walked in to discover him in the act of blacking up.

Big Boy (1925), Jolson's next show, and his final stage appearance as "Gus," opened January 7, 1925 at the Winter Garden to typically enthusiastic notices. Numerous interpolations in its score included two new Jolson standards, "Keep Smiling at Trouble" and "It All Depends on You." Distinguished critic George Jean Nathan most eloquently assessed Jolson's gifts:

The power of Jolson over an audience I have seldom seen equalled. There are actors who, backed up by the great dramatists, can clutch an audience in the hollow of their hands and squeeze out its emotions as they choose. There are singers who, backed up by great composers, can do the same. And there are performers of divers sorts who, aided by external means of one kind or another, can do the same. But I know of none like this Jolson -- or, at best, very few -- who, with lines of a pre-war vintage and melodies of the cheapest tin-piano variety, can lay hold of an audience the moment he comes on the stage and never let go for a second thereafter. Possessed of an immensely electrical personality, a rare sense of comedy, considerable histrionic ability, a most unusual music show versatility in the way of song and dance, and, above all, a gift for delivering lines to the full of their effect, he so far outdistances his rivals that they seem like the wrong ends of so many opera-glasses. His present background is called "Big Boy." It is the usual thing of its kind made into a merry theatrical evening by this king among clowns.[27]

Big Boy closed abruptly on March 14, 1925 due to a severe respiratory ailment which forced Jolson to miss a number of performances. A few months later, the show was revived at New York's 44th Street Theatre before it began a lengthy, and highly profitable, national tour continuing on and off into December 1927. During an interruption of the *Big Boy* tour in late March 1926, Jolson appeared as a well-paid "guest star" for a four-week stint in the long-running Shubert revue, *Artists and Models* (1925), celebrating the fifteenth anniversary of the opening of the Winter Garden. Sadly, but inevitably, Ethel Delmar divorced Jolson in August 1926 -- she had taken to drink as a result of Jolson's continual absences and inattention.

In June 1923, Jolson had made a false start toward the next major stage of his career. Although he had previously appeared in some insignificant special short films in 1913, 1914, and 1918, his first serious foray into motion pictures was *Black Magic*, a film under the direction of D.W. Griffith (1875-1948). After a few days work, Jolson saw some of the dailies and was appalled -- uncomfortable about his own acting and Griffith's vision, he abruptly withdrew and sailed for Europe. Griffith sued, but Jolson did not return to continue work and the film was abandoned. His next attempt was more significant -- Jolson appeared in a short called *April Showers* (or *Al Jolson in a Plantation Act*) (1926) produced by the Warner Bros.-Vitaphone Corporation, and filmed at New York's Manhattan Opera House on September 6, 1926. Appearing in blackface in an obvious stage setting, Jolson sang three of his standards: "Rock-A-Bye Your Baby With a Dixie Melody," "April Showers," and "When the Red, Red Robin Comes Bob, Bob Bobbin' Along." The short premiered on October 7, 1926 at the Colony Theatre, New York, as part of a program featuring similar shorts capturing Elsie Janis, George Jessel, opera star Giovanni Martinelli, and others. These were all part of an on-going series of experiments by the Warners aimed at popularizing Western Electric's Vitaphone sound process. The shorts were well-received and the Warners proceeded with plans to make a film version of *The Jazz Singer* (1927), a play based on a Samson Raphaelson short story, "The Day of Atonement," which had starred George Jessel on Broadway and was, at the time, still touring the country. Warner Bros. had offered the lead role in the movie to Jessel, but he held out for a huge salary, and

Eddie Cantor also turned down the role fearing that the new sound process might not succeed.

The Warners, Jack L. (1894-1981), Sam (1888-1927), and Harry (1881-1958), then approached Jolson, who agreed to appear in the film. According to Warner Bros. documents, Jolson would receive $75,000 plus an additional sum of $2,500 for counsel fees for his work on *The Jazz Singer*. A letter to Jolson from Harry Warner, dated May 26, 1927, touches on several general artistic decisions regarding the film:

> We hereby engage you to sing and enact the sole star role in a motion picture production based upon the stage play "The Jazz Singer." Incidental to such production you will be required to sing and record in syncronization with such picture not exceeding six (6) songs, such six songs being entitled "Kol Nidre," "Mammie"[sic], "When I Lost You," "Yes, Sir, That's My Baby," "Mighty Lak A Rose" and "An Everything"[sic].

Most of these six songs were ultimately changed, and when Jolson ad-libbed a few lines prior to singing in one of the scenes during filming it was decided to incorporate some bits of dialogue in what was actually a silent film with sound intended only for musical sequences. The part-sound, part-silent film opened October 6, 1927 at the Warner Theatre in New York. Its subsequent popularity was a major step toward the abandonment of silent movies in favor of sound.

Jolson's earliest films are flawed in various ways, and the later ones often repeat tired formulas established in his earlier ones. However, there are still considerable pleasures to be had in viewing them, and, most importantly, for the opportunity they provide to catch glimpses of the Jolson of theatrical legend. One survivor from the set of *The Jazz Singer*, screen great Myrna Loy (b. 1905), who had one of her earliest roles in the film playing a sarcastic chorus girl, recalls Jolson's magic:

> My few scenes in *The Jazz Singer* were silent, but I heard Al Jolson. Stars, extras -- all of us left our own sets to watch that first talking sequence being shot. It must have been a very costly day. We all stood on the sidelines just listening to him sing. He was really magnetic, one of those rare entertainers that reach out to you with their voice, their eyes, their arms, everything. We knew they were recording his voice, and there was a certain excitement about it, of course, but we were mainly just pleased to have some time off and hear Al Jolson sing. Nobody realized that we had entered a whole new age.[28]

Raphaelson (1896-1983) was thrilled to have Jolson in the role (although he was not completely satisfied with some of the liberties the Warners took with his story), and he recalled that onstage Jolson's voice "hurtled through the house like a swift electrical lariat with a twist that swept the audience right to the edge of that runway."[29] In a study of popular music, *Can't Help Singing*, Gerald Mast praises Jolson's performance in *The Jazz Singer*, noting that he "acted through his singing and sang as he acted -- moving from song to talk and back to song again without breaking the mental thread of a whole performance. For the first time, a film audience witnessed the performance power a Jolson represented -- not of gesture alone, nor facial reaction, nor charmingly articulate speech, nor enthusiastic delivery, but the whole package together, of a single piece."[30]

This admixture of sound and silent sequences in *The Jazz Singer* seems odd at first, but to some extent, the film makes the most of the best aspects of both techniques. As a movie actor, Jolson often tended to be too broad and emphatic in his later all-sound films, but in a largely silent movie such an approach is rather effectively showcased by the silent dramatic sequences -- the vocal emoting is saved for the musical sound scenes. Jolson is vividly photographed and gives an earnest performance in *The Jazz Singer* -- and, as in most of his films, this one jolts to life whenever he sings. The musical sequences were not pre-recorded in those early Vitaphone days, as would become the accepted technique by the mid-1930's. Jolson was never comfortable with miming to his pre-recorded songs, and it showed in stiff movement and uneasy expression in the later films, so in *The Jazz Singer* and his other early films his explosive and uninhibited style is stunningly preserved. In the first musical sequence set at "Coffee Dan's" café, Jolson sings "Dirty Hands, Dirty Face" and "Toot, Toot, Tootsie." In the latter, Jolson becomes a singing dervish bound only by the confines of the screen. In the most legendary scene, he is seated at a piano singing "Blue Skies" to his mother -- his few ad-libs in this and the earlier café scene brought real talk to the screen while also offering additional flashes of the Jolson magic. Later in *The Jazz Singer* there is one thrillingly theatrical moment as Jolson, seated at his dressing table, applies burnt cork as "My Mammy" throbs insistently in the background. When his makeup is complete, Jolson turns and flashes an impish grin. This moment captures the essence of Jolson's mystique and the power of the blackface mask in liberating him as a performer -- coincidentally, it is a moment so effective that it was repeated in some form in virtually all of his Warner Bros. films. Near the movie's conclusion, Jolson adds one more unforgettable moment as he sings "My Mammy" and impetuously claps his hands at one point as if he can barely stand the wait for the next note. Here the driving, compulsive performer of legend is in striking evidence.

Despite its melodramatic embellishments, *The Jazz Singer* retains considerable emotional power through its depiction of a clash between the traditional values of an older generation and the liberated ways of modern society, and in its effectively detailed depiction of backstage and street life of the period. But it is Jolson's performance that makes the film a classic. Although *The Jazz Singer* was not, as has often been assumed, the story of Jolson's life, he stated that the character of Jakie Rabinowitz was the role that appealed to him the most among his films because "I was reliving part of my life -- my early environment and bringing up, my refusal to follow in my father's footsteps and become a rabbi, my unbreakable preoccupation with singing and acting. As I made the picture, I could see my father standing in the pulpit; he was a silent partner as I worked."[31]

It is common to think of *The Jazz Singer* as the apex of Jolson's career and as the movie that forced Hollywood to make the transition to sound, but it was actually the runaway success of Jolson's second feature film, *The Singing Fool* (1928), that made sound inevitable while also making Jolson the highest paid movie star of the era. He averaged an income estimated at $500,000 a film resulting from his salary and share of the profits. In a Warner Bros. document dated January 7,

1928, Jolson's salary for *The Singing Fool* is listed as $150,000; on August 7, 1928 a new Warner Bros. contract with Jolson called for him to make three films following *The Singing Fool* at $225,000 a picture and 10% of the gross film rentals in excess of $1,000,000. These three films would be *Say It With Songs* (1929), *Mammy* (1930), and *Big Boy* (1930).

The Singing Fool opened September 19, 1928 at Jolson's theatrical stomping grounds, the Winter Garden. Despite the fact that it was the biggest box office success of its era (finally eclipsed a decade later by the popularity of *Snow White and the Seven Dwarfs* [1937] and *Gone With the Wind* [1939]), *The Singing Fool* has been one of the least seen of all the Jolson films in recent years. Like *The Jazz Singer*, it is a silent film with Vitaphone sound sequences inserted; its story traces Jolson's affection for his young son, played by four-year-old Davey Lee, and exemplified by the De Sylva, Brown, and Henderson song "Sonny Boy." Jolson's recording of it became the first million-selling record despite its heavy-handed sentimentality, increased by the fact that Jolson reprised it at the climax of the film following the little boy's death. Today, Davey Lee (b. 1925) remembers Jolson fondly, writing to the author on September 6, 1992 that "he wasn't much of an actor, but the minute he started to sing, who cared!"

Dynamic Jolsonesque moments can be found throughout *The Singing Fool.* Despite a maudlin second half, the film boasts a prime Jolson score featuring "Sonny Boy," but also including such Jolson evergreens as "There's a Rainbow 'Round My Shoulder," "I'm Sitting on Top of the World," "Golden Gate," "It All Depends on You," and "Keep Smiling at Trouble." In most of these numbers Jolson is seen to advantage, especially in the film's better first half that particularly showcases the daemonic Jolson familiar to stage audiences -- in "I'm Sitting on Top of the World" and "There's a Rainbow 'Round My Shoulder" the quintessential Jolson emerges as he builds each song with impromptu eccentric dance steps and inflated gestures and expressions. He somewhat overdramatizes "It All Depends on You" and "Keep Smiling at Trouble," but the clichéd "Sonny Boy" is delivered with moving simplicity the first two times he performs it -- as he puts Sonny Boy to bed and, later, at the child's deathbed. The final rendition, following Sonny Boy's death, is offered on stage in blackface with the unabashed, full-tilt emotion which became characteristic of Jolson's films -- such emoting was also a significant factor in the decline of his movie career, as the public's tastes changed. But at the time, the film garnered rave reviews for Jolson:

> Whether Al Jolson was created for the Vitaphone, or the Vitaphone for Al Jolson, is a problem that I shan't attempt to solve. But there is no question that the two of them work incredibly well together and combine to provide entertainment the like of which has never before been known. When the Vitaphone is recording Al Jolson's songs, or even his most casual utterances, it forgets that it is still in the experimental stage and approximates perfection.[32]

In March and early April of 1928, Jolson appeared for four weeks as a "guest star" in the Chicago production of the long-running Shubert musical revue, *A Night in Spain* (1927), filling in for the ailing lead, Phil Baker. That same year, Jolson met Broadway and nightclub dancer Ruby Keeler (1909-1993), who would become the third Mrs. Jolson on September 21, 1928. Keeler, who began dancing in Tex Guinan's nightclub as a thirteen-year-old, had also danced in the chorus of a George M. Cohan musical and had, more recently, starred in two Florenz Ziegfeld productions, *Bye, Bye, Bonnie* (1927) and *The Streets of New York* (1927). She was also reputed to be the girlfriend of New York City mobster Johnny "Irish" Costello. Jolson had seen her in *The Streets of New York*, and when she came to California to make some stage appearances, he met her at the train station where he had come to greet Fanny Brice, arriving on the same train to make her Vitaphone debut. The smitten Jolson swept Keeler off her feet and took an interest in her career as well. She was scheduled to appear in Ziegfeld's musical *Whoopee* (1928) opposite Eddie Cantor, but withdrew to be with Jolson on the west coast where he was filming *Little Pal* (subsequently titled *Say It With Songs*).

Following the making of the film, the Jolsons went east where Keeler was to co-star with Clayton, Jackson, and Durante in another Ziegfeld musical, *Show Girl* (1929). On opening night, June 25, 1929, Jolson rose from his seat in the audience and sang "Liza" to Keeler as she danced. There are many versions of this legendary story, including the intimation that it was plotted in advance by Jolson and producer Ziegfeld as a publicity stunt. It has also been suggested that Jolson continued to do this for a week or more of the run, but Keeler has insisted that it happened only on opening night and that it was a typically spontaneous Jolson moment -- he was eager to be part of her big evening. It is hard to imagine that Keeler's co-stars were pleased with his intrusion, despite the publicity it generated for the show. Keeler left the cast of *Show Girl* after several weeks, again to be with Jolson on the west coast.

Jolson's stock as a film actor was at its height, and while in New York he saw a new play, *Penny Arcade* (1929), starring two young performers, Joan Blondell and James Cagney. Although the play flopped, as Cagney (1899-1987) later recalled, Jolson "liked it, and took an option on it for pictures. This was the beginning of Hollywood for me, and for Joan too, because on Jolson's recommendation we were given an offer from Warner Bros. to re-create our original roles."[33] Aside from making the Warners a fortune at the box office with his own films, Jolson now gave them two of their brightest young stars.

While in the east, Jolson appeared on an experimental color television broadcast for the Bell Telephone Company on June 29, 1929. It was reported at the time that he sang "Sonny Boy," but whether it was a live performance or footage from *The Singing Fool* has not been ascertained. Several weeks later, *Say It With Songs* opened on August 6, 1929 at New York's Warner Theatre. It was Jolson's first all-talkie, and it scrupulously followed the melodramatic formula of his two earlier films. However, repetition proved to be a bad idea: *Say It With Songs* was neither a popular nor a critical success to the surprise of Jolson and the Warners. Audiences apparently found the sentimentalized elements of *The Singing Fool* appealing, but in the weakly written *Say It With Songs*, which so obviously recycles its predecessor's key elements, they had apparently had enough. Aside from "I'm in Seventh Heaven" and "Used to You," the score of *Say It With Songs* is as weak as the plotting and limpid direction by Lloyd Bacon. *Say It With Songs* also frankly exposes and amplifies the flaws in Jolson's film acting technique, and without a brighter score, the movie has few delights to offer. Jolson is still effective in the musical moments, and he even manages to breath life into "Little Pal," an ill-advised attempt to replicate the runaway success of "Sonny Boy," but the viewer waits in vain for a typically Jolsonesque breakthrough moment.

Quickly following the failure of *Say It With Songs*, Jolson began filming *Mammy* in September 1929. It, too, has melodramatic elements, but focuses more attention on Jolson's strengths as a comic and singer in its account of life behind the scenes in a second-rate minstrel troupe. The film is helped by its visually atmospheric quality, and also benefits from some vintage musical interpolations into Irving Berlin's pleasant score. Berlin's best song, "Let Me Sing and I'm Happy," would serve sixteen years later as the thematic emblem of Jolson's film biography. Despite a gratuitous scene of sentimentalized mother love opposite Louise Dresser, Jolson is generally fine in this film, especially in the on-stage minstrel scenes. One number, an outrageous operatic parody of "Yes, We Have No Bananas," vividly captures the sort of grotesque parodies typical of Jolson's early stage shows. He also belts out "Why Do They All Take the Night Boat to Albany" and "Who Paid the Rent For Mrs. Rip Van Winkle?" in the high-voltage style critics of his stage shows have consistently described. The best number, of course, is "Let Me Sing and I'm Happy," and the filmmakers obviously know it -- Jolson sings it three times, most effectively in an "on-stage" plantation scene.

While awaiting the premiere of *Mammy*, Jolson gave a series of concerts in the south from January 18 through January 30, 1930, starting in El Paso, Texas, and closing in New Orleans -- he could never stray far from a live audience. *Mammy* opened on March 26, 1930 at New York's Warner Theatre and garnered a largely positive response from audiences and reviewers, as best exemplified by the critic from *Time*: "It is strange but inescapably true that Al Jolson can sometimes make his kind of song -- intrinsically tawdry though it is -- sound like a folk-tune a thousand years old and that he can be funny as well as sentimental."[34]

Within months of the release of *Mammy*, the Warners presented Jolson's next movie, *Big Boy*, a fairly faithful screen adaptation of his 1925 stage hit. Like *Mammy*, it is another return to Jolson's theatrical roots -- it is also the strangest of his movies since he appears throughout as "Gus." The oddness is exaggerated since he plays in blackface alongside a cast of actual black actors. From an historical point of view, however, the use of Jolson's burnt cork stage mask offers a unique opportunity to see some further evidence of the stage Jolson. It is not surprising that he seems generally more comfortable and at ease in this film than in virtually any other -- he is obviously at home playing "Gus," and freed from the need to enact a realistic character. Although the plot is complete nonsense and the jokes are tired even by the standards of 1930, Jolson handily dominates the film. Unfortunately, the original stage score has been jettisoned for a new one which does not include any Jolson standard. The opening number, "Liza Lee," is entertaining, but only the oft-repeated "Tomorrow Is Another Day" is at all memorable. In the highlight of the movie, a tacked-on epilogue, Jolson appears without blackface in a theatrical curtain call, replete with an audience and the film's entire cast. Offering to sing for the audience in the theatre, Jolson asks for requests. A cast member calls upon him to do "Sonny Boy," which sets off a mass exodus by the audience. Jolson convinces them to stay by promising not to reprise his over-exposed musical chestnut and instead energetically launches into a chorus of "Tomorrow Is Another Day" at the final fadeout. *Big Boy* opened September 11, 1930 at the Winter Garden to generally positive reviews, but with some nagging intimations that Jolson's movies had become predictably formulaic: "Mr. Jolson avails himself of chances to sing, even when he appears from under a table. There are a few amusing episodes, but it is hardly up to the standard of Mr. Jolson's other productions."[35]

Less than satisfied with his most recent movies, Jolson returned to the Shuberts for an untypical vehicle. On March 17, 1931, he opened triumphantly, sans blackface, in *The Wonder Bar* (1931) at New York's Nora Bayes Theatre. Based on a successful Viennese production, *The Wonder Bar* featured a new score by Irving Caesar and Robert Katscher, and its nightclub setting permitted Jolson the kind of flexibility that served his talents well. Jolson sang one song, "Oh, Donna Clara," in German and French as well as English, and also performed "Cantor on the Sabbath" in Yiddish. With comedienne Patsy Kelly in the cast there was also ample support for outrageous clowning; audiences and critics alike welcomed Jolson's return to the stage: ". . .the premiere audience applauded for Jolson upon his entrance until he stopped them and they did the same thing at the finish. In between when he sang or gagged, they laughed or applauded again, [. . .] What a break for the Shuberts to get Al Jolson."[36] Other critics noted that he seemed nervous and that the old magic, presumably spurred in the past by Jolson's "Gus," was missed. *The Wonder Bar* closed on May 30, 1931 after a brief Broadway run, but Jolson took it out on a well-received national tour that began in September 1931 and continued through April 1932.

Dissatisfied in general with his Warner Bros. vehicles, Jolson signed a contract with producer Joseph Schenck (1878-1961) of United Artists to make three films. He actually only made one movie for Schenck, *Hallelujah, I'm a Bum* (1932), which featured a score by Richard Rodgers and Lorenz Hart with a screenplay by S. N. Behrman from a story by Ben Hecht (based on a short story by Floyd Dell) about the vagabond leader (Jolson) of a community of bums (including silent screen great Harry Langdon) living in Central Park. A bittersweet love triangle permitted Jolson the opportunity of singing "You Are Too Beautiful," certainly the loveliest ballad written for any of his films -- he also shined in the title song and "I Gotta Get Back to New York." *Hallelujah, I'm a Bum*, under the direction of Lewis Milestone, was a significant departure for Jolson from the routine and formulaic scripts he had been given at Warner Bros., but perhaps the change was attempted too late. Although it showcases Jolson in one of his finest performances, and despite the fact that contemporary film critics and historians now consider it a classic, *Hallelujah, I'm a Bum* was neither critically nor commercially successful when it opened February 8, 1932 at New York's Rivoli Theatre.

Later that year, on November 18, 1932, Jolson moved in a new direction. He began his first radio series, *Presenting Al Jolson*, on the NBC Red Network. Although he had performed on radio from as early as 1922, Jolson was uneasy and nervous on this new series and the first program was not well received by critics. Despite his discomfort with a medium he rightly believed hindered his free-wheeling style, Jolson almost immediately returned to radio when he signed on as the first host of the new *Kraft Music Hall* following a successful two-hour special broadcast on June 26, 1933. The first regular one-hour program was broadcast on August 3, 1933 on the NBC Red Network and it featured Jolson in dramatic scenes as well as musical numbers. When he learned that Jolson was planning an edited radio version of his play *The Emperor Jones* for the *Kraft Music Hall*, distinguished

American dramatist Eugene O'Neill wrote to a friend: "It will be amusing to hear what he [Jolson] does with it. I hope Brutus Jones won't burst into *Mammy!*"[37]

While preparing for the *Kraft Music Hall*, Jolson made front page news around the country when he punched columnist Walter Winchell on July 21, 1933 while attending a prizefight. Winchell had recently completed a screenplay titled *Broadway Through a Keyhole* which he was attempting to sell to various movie studios. It depicted an egotistical Broadway performer and his wife, who had formerly been the girlfriend of a gangster. The similarities to the lives of Jolson and Keeler were obvious, and Keeler became upset about the script being turned into a film. Jolson hit Winchell following an exchange of angry words, and the fracas continued on front pages with Winchell threatening to sue Jolson. It was ultimately settled amicably, and Winchell and Jolson, who had appeared together in Dockstader's Minstrels years before, remained friendly.

During this time, Jolson's film career seemed to have stalled while Keeler's was on the rise. She had made a bright debut in *42nd Street* (1932), choreographed by Busby Berkeley at Warners, and, within a short space of time she had become one of the screen's most popular musical stars. Keeler subsequently made a series of movies for the Warners following *42nd Street*, including *Gold Diggers of 1933* (1932); *Footlight Parade* (1933), with James Cagney; *Dames* (1934); *Flirtation Walk* (1934); *Go Into Your Dance* (1935), her only feature opposite Jolson; *Shipmates Forever* (1935); *Colleen* (1936); *Ready Willing and Able* (1937); *Mother Carey's Chickens* (1938), on a loan-out to RKO Studios; and, *Sweetheart of the Campus* (1941).

Jolson returned to Warner Bros. to make *Wonder Bar* (1934), an all-star extravaganza based on his recent stage vehicle. The movie's strong cast and lavish production values are further bolstered by Busby Berkeley's inventive choreography. As with *Big Boy*, most of the original stage score was abandoned, and some lesser roles were built up for Jolson's co-stars, including Dolores Del Rio, Dick Powell, Ricardo Cortez, and Kay Francis. *Wonder Bar* features Jolson's most assured performance as an actor, although he is hampered by having few significant musical opportunities. He toned down the exaggerated histrionics typical of his earlier performances, and the film is fast-paced and entertaining as a whole. The major drawback for audiences today is the central musical sequence, an elaborate production number, "Goin' to Heaven on a Mule," staged by Berkeley and featuring Jolson in blackface. In typical Berkeley fashion, there is a stylish multiplication of images, but, unfortunately in this case, the number becomes an outrageous compendium of flagrant racial stereotypes. Jolson is featured as a black poor farmer who sings to a small child about one day riding his old mule to heaven. Subsequently, he is carried aloft to a minstrel paradise where he meets Old Black Joe, Uncle Tom, The Emperor Jones, and a rotund St. Peter, who gives him a tour of fried chicken machines, trees sprouting pork chops, and an astral Cotton Club where winged tap dancer Hal LeRoy bursts forth from oversized slices of watermelon manipulated by blackfaced chorines. It is truly unfortunate that Jolson's only encounter with Berkeley's imaginative staging produced a number that has now become virtually unwatchable. Jolson also performs a couple of brief novelty songs in foreign languages, as he had on stage in *The Wonder Bar*, but the viewer keeps hoping in vain for him to burst forth with one of his classic songs. The inclusion of an array of Warner stars along with popular and familiar character actors, including Guy Kibbee, Louise Fazenda, Ruth Donnelly, and Hugh Herbert, made it clear that the Warners felt the Jolson name was no longer sufficient to guarantee a film's success. *Wonder Bar* premiered on February 28, 1934 at New York's Strand Theatre to a mixed critical reaction, although most reviewers praised Jolson's performance: "The story, dealing with the killing of a wicked gigolo by his dance partner, is of little help, but the vitality of Al Jolson is of considerable assistance."[38]

In the mid-1930's, Jolson had to face the fact that his career was, for the first time, in some serious trouble. He had been the pioneer performer of sound films, but he was ill-equipped as a movie actor to compete with such early thirties movie stars as James Cagney, Edward G. Robinson, Clark Gable, Spencer Tracy, Franchot Tone, and many others. His appeal as a musical performer was undeniable, but other singers and dancers had appeared who were better able to conform their theatrical experience to the demands of the screen. Jolson's stage "rival", Eddie Cantor, made a string of successful movie musicals lavishly produced by Samuel Goldwyn during the 1930's, and other stage luminaries like Maurice Chevalier and Fred Astaire became charming and accomplished film stars. Pushing Jolson further back in line were such newcomers as Bing Crosby, Dick Powell, Nelson Eddy, and a score of others. Jolson similarly failed to dominate radio, where his theatrical peers, like Jack Benny, Burns and Allen, Ed Wynn, and others, excelled. Worse yet, he had reached an age where his options seemed to shrink. Movies and radio were seeking younger performers, and the musical stage no longer belonged to the performer alone. Composers, lyricists, and librettists were pushing the musical comedy form to new heights of sophistication, expecting actors to perform the text as written, so even the stage -- Mother Earth to Jolson -- was no longer a welcoming place for his singular improvisatory style. Biographers have tended to view the mid-to-late 1930's as a period of decline for Jolson, despite the fact that he worked continually in all mediums during this era. But in one sense, it was a period of decline -- Jolson had yet to find his way through the profound changes evolving in the world of entertainment. If he lost his footing during these days, it was only because he, and prospective employers of his talents, failed to have sufficient confidence in his uniqueness and failed to find the appropriate showcase for it. It would take some years before the "new Jolson" would emerge, so in the meantime he continued to promote the "old Jolson" with diminishing results he could only find disheartening.

On April 24, 1934, Jack Warner signed an agreement with Jolson to make two additional films, *Go Into Your Dance* (1935) and *The Singing Kid* (1936). Jolson would receive $60,000 per picture and 10% of the gross exceeding $800,000. The contract also stipulated that these films would be "special" pictures. On March 22, 1935, Warner amended Jolson's contract for the second of the two movies (*The Singing Kid*), for which Jolson would receive $70,000 provided he agreed to extend his contract for additional films. These additional films would never be made, and Jolson, unhappy with the quality of material coming his way, terminated his contract with Warners on May 20, 1937, insisting that Keeler do the same. The termination brought him the sum of $20,000, but Al Jolson would never be the sole star of a motion picture again.

Jolson was well-presented in *Go Into Your Dance*, in which he co-starred for the first and only time with Ruby Keeler. It was rumored at the time that Jolson was given the role only because Keeler insisted. This is unlikely, however, as the film seems tailor-made for Jolson. *Go Into Your Dance* mixes elements of musical comedy with the fast-paced, wise-cracking melodramatic formula typical of the Warner studio in that period. Archie Mayo's crisp direction, and Bobby Connolly's choreography, borrowing heavily on the Berkeley style, showcase Jolson and Keeler. They make a bright team, with her naive sweetness serving as an effective balance for his brashness. The film's score by Harry Warren and Al Dubin is one of the finest original scores for any Jolson film -- the two best songs, "About a Quarter to Nine" and "She's a Latin From Manhattan," are both elaborately staged as production numbers, and Jolson effectively delivers the neglected "Mammy, I'll Sing About You" and sings "Celito Lindo" in Spanish. Legendary torch-singer Helen Morgan is wasted in an ill-conceived secondary role, although she performs "The Little Things You Used to Do" in her trademark fashion; the riotous Patsy Kelly plays an out-of-work vaudevillian in a couple of brisk comic interludes with Jolson -- but the film is all Jolson's, despite the fact that his age was beginning to show. His scenes with Keeler have a genuine chemistry and charm that could easily have made them a perennial team, but their screen partnership was never to be repeated in a feature length film, although they appeared together in a brief cameo in the 1937 short, *A Day at Santa Anita*, and in a delightful 1936 *Lux Radio Theatre* performance of *Burlesque*, which might have made a fine screen vehicle for them. *Go Into Your Dance* opened May 2, 1935 at New York's Capitol Theatre, and it proved to be one of Jolson's most popular films, as reviewers noted: "Jolson may black his face, and he may sing a Mammy song, and he may get outrageously sentimental now and then, but few will gainsay that he is a grand entertainer. He breezes through this picture as though he were enjoying a holiday instead of working extremely hard."[39]

Shortly after completing *Go Into Your Dance*, Jolson's new *Shell Chateau* radio series began on April 6, 1935 on the NBC Red Network. It featured several guests per week, ranging from Amelia Earhart and Babe Ruth to George Jessel and Cab Calloway, as well as dramatic scenes, although this time without Jolson acting in them. On the home front, Jolson and Keeler adopted a little boy, called Al, Jr. (or "Sonny Boy"), and they moved into an estate in Encino, California, where Jolson was elected Honorary Mayor and President of the Encino Chamber of Commerce on December 28, 1935. He also made his final starring film for Warner Bros., *The Singing Kid*. It is a competent programmer of its period, but aside from the lively opening number, "I Love to Sing-A," the Harold Arlen and E.Y. "Yip" Harburg score is uninspired. It is hardly the "special picture" stipulated by Jolson's contract. The most memorable segment of all is the brief opening sequence leading into "I Love to Sing-A," which features a montage of Jolson performing snippets of his best known songs, "My Mammy," "Swanee," "Rock-A-Bye Your Baby With a Dixie Melody," "California, Here I Come," "April Showers," "About a Quarter to Nine," and "Sonny Boy." The film does bring Jolson together with a youthful Cab Calloway for a couple of lively numbers, but *The Singing Kid* is only a modest effort and a sadly lame conclusion to Jolson's career as a movie star.

Also appearing in *The Singing Kid* was child actress Sybil Jason (b. 1929). In a letter to the author dated September 1, 1992, Jason recalls Jolson with great fondness. When he found out she was filming on her birthday, Jolson gave her a bicycle and, as Jason remembers, during location shooting for the "You're the Cure For What Ails Me" number,

Jolie had catered a whole birthday party for me with cake, ice cream, birthday favors, balloons, birthday hats, lollipops, a big box of imported chocolates, a gold charm and some "toys of the day." Mr. Jolson always had a gang of his friends around him and they were all very nice gentlemen except for the fact that they all looked and dressed like something out of *Guys and Dolls*. It was so funny to see these men wearing funny birthday hats, some of them with lollipops in their mouths and in general really enjoying themselves. The reason might possibly be that the liquid in my punch bowl was perhaps slightly different than the liquid they were imbibing at their table! But thanks to Jolie and his generous heart I did have a birthday party on my actual birthday.

Even as a child, Jason realized that Jolson was not comfortable as a film actor, but she recalls that when Jack Warner visited *The Singing Kid* set he behaved more like a Jolson fan than his employer. Undoubtedly as a favor to both Jason and Warner, Jolson and Keeler made cameo appearances in Jason's starring short, *A Day at Santa Anita*, and Jason remained warm friends with Jolson until his death. In recalling him, she states emphatically that

I cringe every time his ego is mentioned. Yes, once and for all, he had an ego but any performer's career would not last too long without some form of ego. Jolie's was always blown way out of proportion and every now and again I would like to hear about his generosity that was in direct proportion to his ego. Of course, I may be prejudiced in this direction because he was always so very good to me, but I was witness to many examples of his thoughtfulness to others.

The Singing Kid opened April 3, 1936 at the Strand Theatre in New York. It was a modest success, at best, and did little to generate interest in any new Jolson films. On December 22, 1936, Jolson appeared in the first episode of a new radio series, *The Al Jolson Lifebuoy/Rinso Show* on CBS. He kept busy in radio for a time, and after some negotiation, signed to make three movies for Twentieth Century-Fox. In the first and best of his Fox films, *Rose of Washington Square* (1939), Jolson received third billing after stars Alice Faye and Tyrone Power. The plot fictionalizes the troubled off-stage life of Ziegfeld comedienne Fanny Brice (who sued Fox for invasion of privacy), with Jolson virtually playing himself in the atmospheric film -- the highlights of which were effectively staged scenes of him singing several of his standards, including "Pretty Baby," "Rock-A-Bye Your Baby With a Dixie Melody," "Toot, Toot, Tootsie," "California, Here I Come," and the inevitable "My Mammy." When *Rose of Washington Square* opened on May 5, 1939 at New York's Roxy Theatre, Jolson won strong reviews noting that "he's the singin' fool of the Winter Garden days of old, and so acknowledged by a pretty wise first night audience at the Roxy with intermittent applause. But remembered or not, the singer's blackface specialties are consistently socko."[40]

Jolson next filmed a cameo recreating the "Kol Nidre" scene from *The Jazz Singer* for Fox's *Hollywood Cavalcade* (1939), a technicolor extravaganza celebrating the early days of the film industry, starring Alice Faye and Don Ameche. It opened October 13, 1939, again at the Roxy, and although his appearance was brief, Jolson received some respectful mentions from critics. His final Fox film, *Swanee River* (1939), a poorly scripted fictionalization of the life of nineteenth century composer Stephen Foster, and starring Don Ameche and Andrea Leeds, featured Jolson again with third billing as minstrel man E.P. Christy. He gave a good performance and impressively sang several of Foster's most memorable songs, including "Oh! Susanna," "The Old Folks at Home," and the title song. When the film opened at the Roxy on December 29, 1939, the critic for *Variety* wrote that "Jolson gives out here as in the old days at the Winter Garden on Broadway."[41] However, *Swanee River* received generally unenthusiastic reviews -- for all intents and purposes, Jolson's film career was over.

During 1939, Jolson's rocky marriage to Ruby Keeler also drew to a close. They separated, but made several attempts at reconciliation in 1939 and 1940. A new Jolson Broadway musical, *Hold On to Your Hats* (1940), with a score by E.Y. "Yip" Harburg and Burton Lane, was one of Jolson's most obvious attempts at saving the marriage.   The show, co-starring Keeler, Martha Raye, and Parkyakarkus, began an out-of-town tryout in Detroit on June 30, 1940, but continued strains between Jolson and Keeler led to her withdrawal from the cast on July 27, 1940 during the Chicago out-of-town run. At a low professional and personal ebb, Jolson opened in *Hold On to Your Hats* on September 11, 1940 at New York's Sam S. Shubert Theatre. The reviews for his stage return were, as in days of yore, rapturous -- Alexander King, in *Stage*, wrote:

> what remains most poignantly in one's memory is Al Jolson's cast-iron poise which has suffered nothing in the years of his voluntary exile. Abandoning his role, the book, and all the traditions of play-acting, he takes complete command of his audience whenever the spirit so moves him, and he raises the art of entertaining effrontery to stratospheric heights. And finally, when he has them eating out of his hands, when the most grudging adolescent in the audience has found himself unexpectedly guffawing, he sings, of all things -- *Sonny Boy*. The song, which has been lampooned for a decade, is listened to in reverent silence, and when he is finished, the tears in his eyes may very well be real, for it culminates in the most deafening applause that has ever come to vindicate a man's faith in himself.[42]

Jolson's divorce from Keeler became final on December 27, 1940. Shortly thereafter, she married businessman John Lowe and disappeared from show business to raise a family, making only rare appearances until Lowe's death in 1969. In 1970, she agreed to star in a Broadway revival of the 1925 musical, *No, No, Nanette*. Although she was then in her early sixties, Keeler scored a phenomenal success in the revival and spent a few years back in the show business spotlight. However, after surgery for a brain embolism in the mid-1970's, Keeler's activities were curtailed, although she occasionally appeared at film festivals and on talk shows. She rarely and only reluctantly spoke of Jolson until her death in early 1993.

Dispirited following his divorce from Keeler, Jolson continued on in *Hold On to Your Hats* until February 1, 1941, before closing down the production citing illness. After a lengthy rest in Florida, he took the show out on an acclaimed national tour that concluded in November 1941 -- Al Jolson's Broadway career ended with the last performances of the *Hold On to Your Hats* tour in Columbus, Ohio.

Jolson could hardly have known that at this low point, seemingly the end of his professional career, that his life was about to undergo a major transition. With America's entry into World War II, Jolson was among the first stars to perform for U.S. servicemen. On January 21, 1942, he made the first of what would be an impressive series of tours with an appearance at the Jacksonville Naval Air Station in Florida. During the war he performed throughout the United States, Alaska, England, South America, North Africa, and Italy, perilously testing his physical strength, but also finding a new and younger audience. Jolson was delighted by the response to his shows, and on a return home from Africa and Sicily, he told *Time* magazine that the young soldiers and nurses "don't want Shakespeare. They're kids, they're babies -- they want light stuff, but no legitimate ham."[43] His interest in these performances seem to have given him a new lease on life.

Between military tours, both in the States and abroad, Jolson began a new radio series on October 6, 1942. *The Al Jolson Colgate Show* on the CBS Network followed the usual Jolson radio formula of a healthy dose of songs and some comic banter. Carol Bruce (b. 1919), at that time a promising young singer at the start of her career, was a regular on the Colgate show. Like Sybil Jason, Bruce wrote in a letter to the author on August 6, 1992 that she has little but fond memories of Jolson. She recalls that

> Working with "Al" was one of the highlights of my life. Just being privileged to watch him, was an education in the art of performing. I consider him one of the great entertainers of all time, along with Judy Garland, Danny Kaye, and just a few others! [. . .] He *loved* my long dark hair and often said he'd love to run barefoot thru it (but he was never anything less than a gentleman where I was concerned.) When he escorted me out on the town it was red carpet treatment for "Al" all the way!! (and I loved every minute of it). I was *very young.*

Bruce also joined Jolson to play some army camp dates, remembering that "the magic he performed for those servicemen topped even the lure of the pin-up gals! When he said *You ain't heard nothin' yet* he wasn't kidding." Bruce went on to become a bright musical comedy star on Broadway and in London's West End, but she has never forgotten her brief apprenticeship with Jolson.

The moderately successful Colgate show and, more importantly, the performances for American soldiers during the war, were the beginning of an extraordinary Jolson renaissance. In March, 1943, the first in a series of discussions were held about making a film of Jolson's life and career. Most studio moguls regarded Jolson as a back number, but the success of Warner Bros. *Yankee Doodle Dandy* (1942), a fictionalized musical biography of theatrical legend George M. Cohan, kept talk of a Jolson film alive. In 1943, Jolson returned to Warner Bros. to film a brief appearance playing himself in his Winter Garden heyday introducing "Swanee" in *Rhapsody in Blue* (1945), a film biography of George Gershwin. Film audiences were treated to a lavishly staged number, but they undoubtedly also noticed the effect of advancing years on the older and heavier Jolson. The opening of the film, delayed for over a year, finally came on June 27, 1945 at New York's Hollywood Theatre, with critics respectfully acknowledging Jolson's performance. His attention, however, remained on his appearances for the troops until a virulent recurrence of malaria led to emergency surgery for the removal of part of his left lung and two ribs on January 16, 1945. He remained in critical condition for some time, and Columbia Pictures studio head Harry Cohn (1891-1958), who had agreed to film a Jolson biography, had good reason to fear that Jolson might not live to record the soundtrack. Jolson not only recovered, but on March 23, 1945, in Quartzite, Arizona, he married Erle Galbraith (b. 1923), an X-ray technician nearly forty years his junior whom he had met in Arkansas on a tour of military hospitals. By all accounts, Jolson and his fourth wife had a happy marriage. They adopted a son, Asa, Jr., and were considering the adoption of a daughter at the time of Jolson's sudden death in 1950.

In August, 1945, Jolson made his first new recordings in several years for Decca Records demonstrating a deeper, more resonant voice, the result of his surgery and advancing years. He also returned to the microphone to record most of his repertoire of songs for use in the forthcoming movie biography of his life to be called *The Jolson Story* (1946). Filming began in black-and-white, but producer Cohn was so impressed with the initial scenes that production began all over again in color and with an expanded budget. The cast was headed by a young Columbia contract player, Larry Parks (1914-1975), who would play Jolson from youth to middle age, miming the musical sequences to Jolson's newly-recorded vocals. *The Jolson Story* could almost be thought of as the first music video in that it features the mellow later-day Jolson voice channeled through the youthful and handsome Parks. Jolson's vocals are superbly showcased within the film's pleasing visuals; and, at the very least, it is certainly the case that the superb Jolson recordings and the charming performance by Parks are the film's most substantial assets. In a letter to the author dated August 14, 1992, Parks' widow, musical comedy veteran Betty Garrett (b. 1919), cleared up some popular misconceptions about the making of the film:

> Contrary to popular belief Larry and Jolson did *not* have much contact -- we were at one dinner party at Harry Cohn's and Larry did do a radio broadcast with Jolson -- after the picture's release. They did some publicity stories and pictures together, but during the shooting Jolson was in Florida -- He really wanted a *big star* to portray him and didn't dream the picture would be such a success.

Garrett also remembers that Warner Bros. refused to loan any of Jolson's own films to Columbia, so Parks, who had never seen Jolson perform live, had little concrete evidence to go on in his creation of the character. This may well have been for the best, since Parks succeeded in creating his own appealing concept of how Jolson moved and sang, as Garrett explains:

> Larry had to prepare by simply listening to Jolson's soundtracks which were made before the picture was shot. Larry had the studio set up a rehearsal hall with *huge* speakers and a large mirror (the sound literally blasted in your ears). There he worked hours and hours with a play back man (Truck Krone) who worked the record

machine and Audrene Bryer a dance-choreographer. There they set the numbers as they *imagined* Jolson must have done them.

Garrett recalls that in an effort to help Parks prepare for the role, "Jolson did have one session with Larry which wasn't very helpful," as Parks himself once amusingly described:

> As I finished one of his songs, he said, "No, no, that's not it, son. Don't you remember how I used to do that?" I told him I'd never seen him perform, which didn't thrill him. Then he said, "Well, you're doing too much." To show me how to put the number across, he sang it. He almost wrecked the room. He practically hung from the chandelier. When he finished the song, perspiration was dripping from his forehead. "There," he said. "You see? I didn't move a muscle."[44]

Parks' own feelings about the Jolson films are summed up by Garrett who believes that he "loved making the Jolson pictures. Larry always said *When you can be in a movie that reaches millions of people and makes $10,000,000 you can't knock it!*" Contrary to some accounts included in earlier Jolson biographies, Garrett believes there was no particular friction between Jolson and Parks, although she points out that "you must remember Jolson didn't want Larry to play the part so he didn't go out of his way to make Larry's task easier."

Also adding significantly to the overall quality of *The Jolson Story* were the expert performances of Ludwig Donath and Tamara Shayne as Jolson's parents, and William Demarest as Steve Martin, a fictional amalgam of aspects of at least a dozen individuals from Jolson's life, ranging from his brother Harry and vaudevillian Al Reeves to Jolson's long-time personal manager, Louis "Eppy" Epstein, and his perennial valet, Frank "Pansy" Holmes. Demarest (1892-1983) once described his pleasure in making the film: "I like the idea that Steve Martin grew more sympathetic as he grew older. The whole picture took me back to my days in vaudeville. I was barnstorming at the same time Jolson was, playing the same towns, and on the set we often swapped memories."[45]

Columbia contract player Evelyn Keyes (b. 1919) gave one of the finest performances of her long career as "Julie Benson," the pseudonym applied to Ruby Keeler in the film. Keeler, long retired from the screen and raising a family with her second husband, was not pleased to learn that the film would include her relationship with Jolson. She ultimately agreed to allow the broad outlines of her life with Jolson to be included, but not if her name was used. Cohn paid Keeler $25,000 to avoid any potential legal ramifications.

Supporting the recollections of Parks and Garrett, in a letter to the author dated August 14, 1992, Keyes confirms that aside from recording the vocals, Jolson was not much involved in the making of the film and rarely visited the set:

> He probably made Larry nervous, don't you imagine, since Jolson wanted to play Jolson, himself? He never worked with Larry. Larry learned to do all that Jolson singing and movement himself, working around the clock to Jolson records, and watching Jolson on film. (I

saw Jolson squirming in Harry Cohn's projection room when Larry's test in blackface was being shown).

Keyes also remembers one particular day when Jolson recorded songs for the soundtrack: "I went on the recording stage to listen to him do it. It was a truly moving experience. Even there, in a sound booth, with head phones over his ears, he had it. (With one lung, too.)" Like many individuals who came into contact with Jolson, even toward the end of his life, Keyes observed "his forever on-going energy. He seemed to always be slightly bouncing whenever and wherever you came across him. As if the soles of his feet were only brushing the ground and that the impact would send them -- and the man they supported -- up into the air again. His eyes, too, danced and sparkled along in that same aura of energy." Keyes also recalls seeing Jolson sing on occasion at Hollywood social events during the making of the film, including one memorable party in Cohn's living room: "I remember seeing -- and hearing -- him sing *Sonny Boy* this way. With great humor, too, making fun of himself. He knew his style was old-fashioned by then; that the sentiment of the song was of another era. And he performed accordingly."

While filming of *The Jolson Story* proceeded, Jolson's father died in Washington, D.C. on December 23, 1945. Remembered by Jolson's niece Teresa Kaplan as "a remarkable man," Moshe Yoelson had lived to see his son become a show business legend, although he probably never truly understood or accepted the life his son had chosen. On October 1, 1946, only nine days before the New York premiere of *The Jolson Story*, a lavish testimonial dinner honoring Jolson for his war work was given at the Hotel Astor in New York. The most popular stars of the day appeared on radio hook-ups from several cities in tribute to Jolson -- among the celebrities were George Jessel and former New York City Mayor James J. Walker serving as masters of ceremonies, Frank Sinatra, Martha Raye, Perry Como, Dinah Shore, Bob Hope, Burns and Allen, Eddie Cantor, and the incomparable Hildegarde, who performed Jolson's evergreen, "April Showers." In a July 28, 1992 telephone interview with the author, Hildegarde (b. 1906) recalled having seen Jolson perform live at the Davidson Theatre in Milwaukee. She remembers him as a "dynamic performer, so giving of himself. He used his whole body -- arms, hands, everything -- he was wonderful." During World War II, Hildegarde made a couple of army camp appearances with Jolson in Miami, Florida, and found him to be "kind, outgoing, amusing, and charming," both on-stage and off. Before working with him, she had heard that Jolson was a difficult man to deal with, but after appearing with him she felt that some of his reputation undoubtedly came from the fact that Jolson "took his success seriously" and that he was an exacting professional. In this she compares herself to Jolson, pointing out that their performing styles were similar in their need to work before a live audience. She believes Jolson "was intimidated" by appearing in film and radio, and that he needed to "feel the audience." She stresses the power of his "charisma and his rapport with the audience" in recalling Jolson live on a stage, and remembers with amusement that when she and Jolson did the army camp shows that he "insisted on having his picture taken with me sitting on his lap!"

When *The Jolson Story* opened on October 10, 1946 at Radio City Music Hall, it quickly became Columbia Pictures' top-grossing film of all time, and it skyrocketed Jolson back to the first rank of show business in what was undoubtedly the most extraordinary comeback in entertainment history. Although a few critics carped at the obvious fictionalization of Jolson's life and personality in the film, such an approach was certainly not novel for Hollywood screen biographies. Otherwise, reviewers praised the film extravagantly, with particular kudos for Parks' performance and Jolson's singing:

> Larry Parks is a prettier Al than Al. He is also an astonishingly capable mimic. And consanguine with his image is the great Jolson voice, a voice whose dynamics seem to have lost nothing through the withering years. Mr. Parks' skill and the magic of movie technique have made possible an astounding fusion of two people to create a memorable portrait. Even Al Jolson should be pleased with *The Jolson Story*.[46]

During 1947, Jolson threw himself into a heavy schedule of guest spots on radio, including appearances with Burns and Allen, Joan Davis, Edgar Bergen and Charlie McCarthy, Jack Benny, and, in a series of delightful pairings, Bing Crosby. The two most popular singers of their respective days rollicked through duets of both vintage and contemporary songs, and hilariously indulged in competitive ad-libbing and comic banter. The results led to high ratings -- and more demands for Jolson guest spots. Shortly after Jolson's death, Crosby (1903-1977) recalled that Jolson was "indefatigable. If you'd let him, he'd sing all night."[47] The Jolson-Crosby chemistry was so potent that they made Decca recordings of a couple of their radio duets. Also at Decca, Jolson made many new recordings from his canon of classic songs, along with some new tunes. As a result, by 1948 record sales and radio ratings proved that Jolson was again the top singer in America despite the fact that he was then in his mid-sixties and his career had begun well over forty years before. The effect of this remarkable comeback on Jolson is clear from his statement to *Time* magazine: "If there weren't such a thing as years nobody would think I'm old. I may not be alive in ten seconds, but I feel better than I have in 20 years."[48]

Jolson returned to series radio on October 2, 1947 in CBS's *Kraft Music Hall*. It was a particularly sweet moment for Jolson who had asked to host the program a couple of years before, but had been turned down flat. When *The Jolson Story* resurrected his career, the sponsor did a complete reversal, wooing Jolson to take over the show. Jolson told *Time* magazine: "I didn't wanna do it. I didn't wanna do it! [. . .] I was swindled into it by this tremendous ego of mine."[49] With celebrated concert pianist Oscar Levant as his radio sidekick, the show followed the familiar format of Jolson's few previous series. He worked well with the acerbic Levant, and when he sang or bantered with an interesting guest the results were always pleasing. In the two years of the series, guests included Bing Crosby, Judy Garland, Humphrey Bogart, Cary Grant, Ezio Pinza, Charles Boyer, Groucho Marx, Burns and Allen, George Jessel, Victor Moore, Red Skelton and, in one particularly enjoyable episode, Jolson's screen alter-ego, Larry Parks.

Jolson also kept up a busy schedule of guest appearances on other radio shows. Although radio had been a medium that seemed to restrain and hinder Jolson's natural appeal in the 1930's and early 1940's, his own confidence and the affection of audiences was so high in the late 1940's that many of his guest appearances were memorable. Jolson continued to work well with Bing Crosby, but he also obviously enjoyed his guest spots with his old friends Jimmy Durante, Burns and Allen, Jack Benny, Eddie Cantor, and he seemed in top form playing himself on *Lux Radio Theatre* adaptations of *The Jolson Story* (1948) and *Jolson Sings Again* (1950). As a result of these appearances, and his weekly appearances on the *Kraft Music Hall*, interest in new Jolson recordings remained high, and he continued recording until virtually the end of his life.

Box office returns for *The Jolson Story* almost immediately inspired plans for a sequel. On September 27, 1948, Jolson filmed what many consider to be a "screen test" at Columbia, presumably in hopes of playing himself in the new film to be called *Jolson Sings Again* (1949). Whether or not this footage was a screen test or intended as a practice film for Larry Parks remains unclear, but when shooting commenced, Parks was once more impersonating Jolson. Betty Garrett points out that Parks "always thought the script of *Jolson Sings Again* was better written, but of course they had used up the greatest songs in the first picture." The cast again included Demarest, Donath, and Shayne, and newcomer Barbara Hale appeared as Jolson's fourth wife, Erle, given the movie pseudonym Ellen Clark. *Jolson Sings Again* includes a liberal dollop of clips from *The Jolson Story*, and, once more channeled through Parks' winning performance, Jolson's voice was again captured in a variety of songs long associated with him. Critics were generally approving: "The appeal of the Jolson sequel is only a matter of degree. In many respects it even shades the sock boxoffice champ of 1946."[50] Jolson's career continued on the ascendant, but although Parks was nominated for a Best Actor Academy Award for his performance in *The Jolson Story*, his promising career was ruined by blacklisting resulting from his testimony before the House Un-American Activities Committee investigation into reputed Communists in the entertainment industry. Parks continued to act periodically on the stage and in television, but returned to the screen only twice: in a British film, *Tiger By the Tail* (1955), and in a supporting role in John Huston's film, *Freud* (1962). Following a national tour in Neil Simon's play *Plaza Suite*, opposite Betty Garrett, Parks died of a heart attack.

Despite the fact that Parks was once again playing Jolson, New York movie audiences had the opportunity to see the genuine article when Jolson made a series of widely heralded live appearances to promote the film when *Jolson Sings Again* opened August 10, 1949 at New York's Loew's State Theatre. Making several stops per night at New York area theatres, Jolson's "iron-man" demonstration impressed audiences and critics alike. After his three days of personal appearances with *Jolson Sings Again* in New York, Jolson performed in Chicago at the Oriental Theatre and at the Chicagoland Music Festival at Soldier's Field on August 20, 1949. His appearance at the latter was broadcast on local television, only his second TV appearance ever -- twenty years after his first. Jolson was considering offers for network television appearances at this time, but although he signed with CBS-TV for some appearances planned for 1951, he seemed a bit hesitant about a jump into the new medium.

Flying high on the wings of this renewed professional popularity, Jolson's friends believed that his personal life was never happier than during these last years. At the height of his new success, Jolson was particularly generous with his energies in performing for various charities and good works. Hilliard Marks, Jack Benny's manager, recalled Jolson's chronic nervousness before one such benefit. Benny suggested that to make himself more comfortable, that Jolson might put on his trademark blackface makeup for the performance. Marks remembered that

Jolson's power over the audience remained undiminished:

> When it was time for Al to go on, Jack and I stood in the wings
> watching. Jolson strutted on stage and began his whole medley:
> "Swanee". . ."Waiting for the Robert E. Lee". . "Dixie". . .and
> "Mammy," sung on bended knee. Midway through, I looked at Jack
> and he looked at me. Both of us had tears streaming down our
> cheeks. It was a moment I'll never forget.[51]

Sybil Jason again encountered Jolson during this time. Attempting to get her own
career off the ground again following the interruption of World War II, Jason
recalls visiting Jolson in his dressing room before a radio broadcast. He offered
her some realistic advice.

> I will never forget his words. "Baby, don't lettum get t'ya! Just a
> short while ago ole Jolie couldn't even get on a benefit show but
> look at me now. I outlasted 'em all!" He sure did! [. . .] Besides his
> very great talent as a singer/performer he loved what he was doing
> and the people that he was doing it for! You can't fool an audience
> and they felt his emotion toward them. [. . .] His singing style was
> unique and no matter what era, the audience recognizes the energy
> and life behind the voice.

With the outbreak of the Korean conflict, Jolson again turned his attention to
singing for American soldiers. On September 11, 1950, he began a whirlwind tour
performing for U.S. servicemen in Japan and Korea at the start of the Korean
conflict. Struggling with a severe bronchial infection, Jolson managed despite that
and his age, to give over forty performances in various outposts in little more than
two weeks. He met with General Douglas MacArthur, who gratefully
acknowledged Jolson's commitment to entertaining the armed services. Surviving
newsreel footage of his appearances suggest that Jolson was, as usual, giving his all;
however, the films also demonstrate the severe toll it was taking on him.

When he returned to the United States in October 1950, Jolson began
discussions for a film tentatively titled *Stars and Stripes* to be produced by Norman
Krasna and Jerry Wald at RKO Studios. This time Jolson would play himself in
a movie tribute to the USO. Shortly thereafter, Jolson left his Encino home for
San Francisco to record another radio appearance with Bing Crosby. While playing
cards with friends at the St. Francis Hotel on October 23, 1950, the night before
he was to tape the broadcast, Jolson was suddenly stricken with a fatal heart attack.
His unexpected death was front page news around the country, and his funeral,
held at Hollywood's Temple Israel on October 26, 1950, was one of the largest in
Hollywood history. George Jessel delivered the eulogy celebrating the life of "the
sweet singer of Israel" before a congregation filled with several generations of
luminaries from stage and screen. For most of them, the passing of Jolson was
unimaginable -- truly the end of an era. He had set the tone for popular
entertainers for half a century -- now new models would have to be found.
Changes in the entertainment field had been so profound since Jolson had started
his career at the turn-of-the-century that it would be virtually impossible for any
performer to ever again hold sway over all aspects of the field as Jolson had done
for so long. Judy Garland might become a concert legend, Elvis Presley would

popularize rock-and-roll, the Beatles would symbolize a generation and an era, Milton Berle, Lucille Ball, and Jackie Gleason would own early television, and many stars would come to the fore on the movie screen, but no performer would ever again have the opportunity to pioneer and dominate as many aspects of show business as Jolson had done.

After setting up a trust fund for his widow and young son, Jolson left the remainder of his vast estate to a variety of charities and philanthropic organizations. As he had in life, Jolson continued to contribute to the welfare of his audience even after his death. It was to be nearly a year after his death before Jolson was laid to permanent rest in an elaborate memorial featuring a tall circular columned structure with a statue of Jolson on bended knee with his arms outstretched beside a cascading waterfall constructed at Hillside Cemetery in Los Angeles on September 23, 1951 with Jack Benny delivering a eulogy. The real Jolson story had ended.

Or perhaps it was only beginning. Of course, it is impossible to see Al Jolson cavorting on a stage again, and his movie performances are but mere flickering shadows of his theatrical greatness, but as poet Edna St. Vincent Millay wrote, the unforgettable Jolson voice will remain a unique part of American culture:

> . . .Blessed ones
> of this -- and every other -- succeeding generation
> who can, do, and shall discover
> for their first time
> the Voice of Jolson
> and who'll thrill to It
> and who, hence, will love him.[52]

NOTES

1. Eugene O'Neill. "Ballad of the Modern Music Lover," *New London Telegraph*, September 17, 1912.

2. Charles Chaplin. *My Autobiography*. New York: Simon and Schuster, 1964, p. 260.

3. Herbert G. Goldman. *Jolson. The Legend Comes to Life*. Oxford: Oxford University Press, 1988, p. 306.

4. Eddie Cantor. *As I Remember Them*. New York: Duell, Sloan and Pearce, 1963, p. 42.

5. Larry Wilde. *The Great Comedians Talk About Comedy*. New York: The Citadel Press, 1968, p. 292.

6. Ibid., p. 245.

7. Ibid., p. 194.

8. Ethel Waters. *His Eye Is On the Sparrow*. With Charles Samuels. New York: Doubleday, 1951, p. 217.

9. Milton Berle. *An Autobiography*. With Haskel Frankel. New York: Delacorte Press, 1974, p. 80.

10. George Burns. *All My Best Friends*. Written with David Fisher. New York: Putnam, 1989, p. 13.

11. Cited in Gary Giddins. *Riding on a Blue Note: Jazz and American Pop*. New York, 1981, pp. 33-34.

12. Bing Crosby. "*Jolie* Influenced Bing." *Los Angeles Examiner*, October 25, 1950.

13. Gilbert Seldes. "The Daemonic in the American Theatre, *Dial*, September 1923, p. 308.

14. Burns. *All My Best Friends*, pp. 35-36.

15. Gene Siskel. "Jolie: The Greatest Was Legend in His Own Mind." *Chicago Tribune*, May 3, 1987.

16. John Hutchens. "Al Jolson and Others," *Theatre Arts Monthly*, XV, No. 2, May 1931, p. 366.

17. Keeler and Krasna quoted in John Bell. "Outcry Over Claims That Al Jolson Was a Terror With the Women." *The Globe*, October 22, 1985.

18. Irving Berlin. "Let Me Sing and I'm Happy." Irving Berlin Inc., 1929.

19. Will Rogers. "Broadway Ain't What She Used to Be." *Will Rogers Weekly Articles. Vol. 6, The Roosevelt Years, 1933-35*. Oklahoma State University Press,

1982, pp. 21-22.

20. *Variety*, March 6, 1909, p. 14.

21. J. Gardiner. *Gaby Deslys. A Fatal Attraction*. London: Sidgwick & Jackson, 1986, p. 59.

22. Seldes. "The Daemonic in the American Theatre." *Dial*, p. 306.

23. *Variety*, February 18, 1916, p. 19.

24. George Burns. *Dear George. Advice and Answers From America's Leading Expert on Everything From A to B*. New York: Putnam, 1985, pp. 125-126.

25. George S. Kaufman. "The Other Side of Al Jolson." *Everybody's Magazine*, Vol. 44, April 1921, p. 16.

26. Ibee., *Variety*, October 16, 1921, p. 18.

27. George Jean Nathan. "Appreciation." *American Mercury*, March 1925, Vol. 4, p. 376.

28. Myrna Loy and James Kotsilibas-Davis. *Myrna Loy. Being and Becoming*. New York: Alfred A. Knopf, Inc., 1987, p. 52.

29. Samson Raphaelson. "Article." *American Hebrew*, October 14, 1927, p. 812.

30. Gerald Mast. *Can't Help Singin'. The American Musical on Stage and Screen*. Woodstock, New York: Overlook Press, 1987, p. 88.

31. Al Jolson. "The Role I Liked Best." *Saturday Evening Post*, August 31, 1946.

32. R.E. Sherwood, *Life*, October 5, 1928, p. 28.

33. James Cagney. *Cagney on Cagney*. Garden City, New York: Doubleday & Co., Inc., 1976, pp. 37-38.

34. *Time*, April 7, 1930, p. 69.

35. *New York Times*, September 13, 1930, p. 9.

36. Sime., *Variety*, March 25, 1931, p. 62.

37. Eugene O'Neill. *The Selected Letters of Eugene O'Neill*. Edited by Travis Bogard and Jackson R. Bryer. New Haven and London: Yale University Press, 1988, p. 431.

38. Argus, "On the Current Screen," *Literary Digest*, March 17, 1934, p. 37.

39. John Gammie, "What--And What Not--To See." *Film Weekly*, August 23, 1935.

40. Abel., *Variety*, May 10, 1939, p. 14.

41. *Variety*, December 21, 1939, p. 12.

42. Alexander King. "Native's Return." *Stage*, Vol. I, No. 1, November 1940, p. 39.

43. "Al Jolson." *Time*, October 11, 1943, p. 39.

44. Larry Parks quoted in Doug McClelland. *Forties Film Talk. Oral Histories of Hollywood, with 120 Lobby Posters*. Jefferson, North Carolina and London: McFarland & Co., 1992, p. 204.

45. William Demarest quoted in McClelland. *Forties Film Talk. Oral Histories of Hollywood, with 120 Lobby Posters,* p. 196.

46. Arthur Beach. *New Movies*, November-December 1945, Vol. 21, No. 11-12, pp. 5-6.

47. Bing Crosby. *Call Me Lucky*. As told to Pete Martin. New York: Simon and Schuster, 1953, pp. 153-154.

48. *Time*, May 26, 1947, p. 53.

49. "The Switcheroo." *Time*, October 6, 1947, p. 78.

50. Abel., *Variety*, August 1949, p. 8.

51. Mary Livingstone Benny and Hilliard Marks, with Marcia Borie. *Jack Benny*. Garden City, New York: Doubleday & Co., Inc., 1978, p. 175.

52. Cited in Harry M. Geduld. *The Birth of the Talkies. From Edison to Jolson*. Bloomington, Indiana/London: Indiana University Press, 1975, p. 144.

Al Jolson—"The Singing Fool" (1928). Permission of Turner Entertainment.

2

Chronology

1886   **May 26:** Asa Yoelson is born in Seredzius, Lithuania, the fifth child of Moshe Reuben and Naomi (Cantor) Yoelson. Although the exact date of his birth is not certain (the year may have been 1885), he would later claim May 26 as his birthday. Four years after his birth, Asa's father, a rabbi, departs for America to seek a position with a synagogue, leaving the family behind in Seredzius.

1894   **April 9:** Asa, his mother and his siblings arrive at Ellis Island, on their way to join Rabbi Yoelson who has secured a position as head of the Talmud Torah Congregation in Washington, D.C.

1895   **February 6:** Naomi Yoelson dies in Washington, D.C.

1896   **March 29:** Moshe Yoelson marries Chyesa "Hessi" Yoels in Washington, D.C. Asa, and his brother, Hirsch, altering their surname to Joelson, begin performing on Washington, D.C. streets to make money. Within months, Hirsch, now calling himself Harry, leaves home and encourages Asa, now Al, to join him in New York City.

1897   Al performs with Rich & Hoppe's Big Company of Fun Makers. Al and Harry eventually return to Washington, D.C., where they perform for soldiers during the Spanish-American War at Fort Myer. Al becomes a mascot for the Fifteenth Pennsylvania volunteers.

1898   **October:** Al joins the Walter L. Main Circus, touring Pennsylvania, Maryland, West Virginia, and Ohio with the troupe. Following his few weeks with the circus, Al goes to Baltimore and sings in a bar before he is taken by Gerry Society officers to St. Mary's Industrial School for Boys.

1899   **September 18:** Al appears as an extra at the National Theatre, Washington, D.C., in three tryout performances of Israel Zangwill's play, *Children of the Ghetto*.

        October 16: *Children of the Ghetto* opens at the Herald Square Theatre, New York, without Jolson, who is removed from the cast in Washington by his disapproving father. It is thought that during this era Al sings from the audience during the act of Eddie Leonard in a Washington D.C. theatre, and that he may have toured with the Villanova Burlesque Company.

1900   **October:** Al joins the Victoria Burlesquers in Chicago as a foil for Aggie Behler.

1901   **June 17:** Al gives his first performance in partnership with Fred E. Moore, and, as Joelson & Moore, they play in vaudeville during 1901 and 1902, occasionally rejoining the Victoria Burlesquers.

1902   **March 17:** Joelson & Moore join Al Reeves' Famous Big Company in Newark, New Jersey.

September 29: Joelson & Moore give their first performances with the Dainty Duchess Company in Philadelphia, and then tour the east and midwest with the troupe.

1903   **August 10:** Al begins working with his brother Harry, as The Joelson Brothers, at Rockaway, New York, in an act called "The Hebrew and the Cadet."

1904   **October 31:** Al and Harry team up for their first performance with Joe Palmer in an act called Joelson, Palmer & Joelson in Brooklyn, New York. During this era, the "e" is dropped from Joelson, and the name "Al Jolson" is created. Also, Jolson begins performing in blackface.

1905   **November 11:** Harry gives his last performance with the act in New Orleans, and Al and Joe Palmer continue in vaudeville as a team.

1906   **June 4:** Jolson begins working regularly as a single in Detroit, becoming increasingly successful in vaudeville throughout the next year.

1907   **September 20:** Henrietta Keller and Jolson marry in Oakland, California.

November 11: Jolson acts in a stock company, Walter Sanford's Players in San Francisco for a few weeks.

1908   **August 10:** Jolson gives his first performance as a member of Lew Dockstader's Minstrels in Plainfield, New Jersey.

1909   **February:** While Dockstader's Minstrels play New York City, Jolson appears in an olio act and is favorably reviewed by *Variety* for the first time.

April 25: Jolson performs briefly with I.P. Wilkerson's "Minstrels of Today" in San Francisco before rejoining Dockstader.

July 19: While continuing to perform with Dockstader, Jolson begins playing solo vaudeville dates in New York.

1910   **February 9:** It is believed that Jolson makes his first recordings for Edison Records in New York.

December 18: With the guidance of manager Arthur Klein, Jolson manages to secure a release from his contract with Dockstader.

1911   **March 20:** Jolson makes his Broadway debut in the Shubert musical, *La Belle Paree*, at the new Winter Garden Theatre, New York.

November 20: Jolson appears in *Vera Violetta*, at the Winter Garden, New York.

December 22: Jolson makes his first recordings for Victor Records in Camden, New Jersey.

1912   **March 5:** Jolson, continuing with the Shuberts, appears in *The Whirl of Society*, at the Winter Garden, New York.

June 29: *The Whirl of Society* closes, followed by a tour that continues into January 1913.

1913   **February 6:** Jolson becomes a major star in *The Honeymoon Express* at the Winter Garden, New York.

June 14: *The Honeymoon Express* closes, followed by a tour that continues through May 1914.

June 4: Jolson begins recording for Columbia Records in New York.

1914   **April 6-11:** Jolson makes a short silent film, *Hunting the Ferocious and Extinct Cuckoo*, to be shown exclusively in the California Building of the Panama-Pacific International Exposition.

October 10: Jolson opens in *Dancing Around* at the Winter Garden, New York.

1915   **February 13:** *Dancing Around* closes, followed by a national tour that continues through early December.

December 3: Jolson meets President Woodrow Wilson, who attends a performance of *Dancing Around* in Washington, D.C.

1916   **February 17:** Jolson continues in an unbroken string of successful musical comedies with *Robinson Crusoe, Jr.* at the Winter Garden, New York.

June 10: *Robinson Crusoe, Jr.* closes, followed by an extensive national tour that continues until mid-November 1917.

1918   **February 14:** Another Shubert-produced Jolson musical, *Sinbad*, opens at the Winter Garden, New York.

July 6: *Sinbad* closes.

September 2: *Sinbad* reopens (continuing through March 29, 1919 at the following New York locations: Century Theatre, Casino Theatre, Winter Garden Theatre, and the 44th Street Theatre).

May 6 and 9: Jolson films a short untitled silent movie for the New York Patrolmen's Benevolent Association in New York.

1919   March 30: Jolson begins a tour in *Sinbad* which continues through the first half of 1921.

1920   July 8: Henrietta Keller divorces Jolson.

1921   October 6: *Bombo*, opens at Jolson's 59th Street Theatre, New York, a new Shubert house named for their most valuable star.

1922   February 5: Jolson makes his first known radio appearance from Newark, New Jersey.

April 8: *Bombo* closes, followed by a national tour beginning in September and continuing, on and off through mid-1924.

July 22: Jolson marries vaudevillian Ethel Delmar at a resort in Maine.

1923   May 14: *Bombo* is revived on Broadway at the Winter Garden, New York.

June: Jolson begins work on *Black Magic*, a film directed by D.W. Griffith, but withdraws when he is unsatisfied with the footage he is shown. Griffith sues Jolson.

1924   January 17: Jolson begins making recordings for Brunswick Records in Chicago.

1925   January 7: *Big Boy* opens at the Winter Garden, New York, to unanimous critical praise for Jolson.

March 14: *Big Boy* closes abruptly due to a respiratory ailment which forces Jolson to miss a number of performances.

August 24: *Big Boy* is revived at the 44th Street Theatre, New York, before beginning a lengthy national tour that continues, on and off, into December 1927.

1926   March 20: Jolson begins performing as a "guest star" for a four week run in the Shubert production, *Artists and Models*, at the Winter Garden, New York.

August: Ethel Delmar divorces Jolson.

October 7: Jolson's first sound film, a short called *April Showers* (or *Al Jolson in a Plantation Act*) produced by the Warner Bros.-Vitaphone Corporation, premieres at the Colony Theatre, New York.

1927 **October 6:** Jolson makes screen history in *The Jazz Singer*, produced by the Warner Bros.-Vitaphone Corporation. The part-sound, part-silent film opens at the Warner Theatre, New York.

1928 **March 11:** Jolson begins performing for four weeks as a "guest star" in *A Night in Spain*, a Shubert production at the Four Cohans Theatre, Chicago.

September 19: *The Singing Fool*, produced by the Warner Bros.-Vitaphone Corporation, opens at the Winter Garden, New York. It proves to be the most popular film of its day, and remains the top-grossing movie for ten years.

September 21: Jolson marries dancer Ruby Keeler in Westchester County, New York.

December: Jolson films a short, *Theatre Opening*, to promote the Vitaphone sound film process.

1929 **June 25:** Ruby Keeler Jolson opens in the Florenz Ziegfeld, Jr. production of *Show Girl*, at the Ziegfeld Theatre, New York. During the performance, Jolson rises from his seat in the audience and sings George Gershwin's song, "Liza," as Keeler dances.

June 29: Jolson appears on an experimental television broadcast in color for the Bell Telephone Company.

August 6: *Say It With Songs*, a Warner Bros.-Vitaphone Corporation film, opens at the Warner Theatre, New York.

1930 **January 18:** Jolson begins a series of concerts in the south, beginning in El Paso, Texas, and ending in New Orleans on January 30.

March 26: *Mammy*, a Warner Bros.-Vitaphone Corporation production, opens at the Warner Theatre, New York.

September 11: *Big Boy*, a Warner Bros.-Vitaphone Corporation film based on Jolson's stage hit, at the Winter Garden, New York.

1931 **March 17:** Jolson returns to the Broadway stage, sans blackface, in *The Wonder Bar*, at the Nora Bayes Theatre, New York.

May 30: *The Wonder Bar* closes, followed by a tour beginning in September that continues through the spring of 1932.

1932 **February 8:** *Hallelujah, I'm a Bum*, a United Artists film featuring a score by Rodgers and Hart and starring Jolson, opens at the Rivoli

Theatre, New York.

November 18: Jolson begins his first radio series, *Presenting Al Jolson*, on the NBC Red Network from San Francisco.

1933   **June 26:** Jolson is selected as the first host of the *Kraft Music Hall* radio series following a successful two-hour special broadcast. The first regular program is broadcast on August 3 on the NBC Red Network from New York.

1934   **February 28:** *Wonder Bar*, a First National-Warner Bros. all-star film based on Jolson's stage hit, opens at the Strand Theatre, New York.

1935   **April 6:** Jolson's *Shell Chateau* radio series begins on the NBC Red Network from New York.

May 2: *Go Into Your Dance*, a First National-Warner Bros. film, starring Jolson and his wife, Ruby Keeler, opens at the Capitol Theatre, New York.

December 28: Jolson is elected Honorary Mayor of Encino, California (and President of the Encino Chamber of Commerce).

1936   **April 3:** *The Singing Kid*, a First National-Warner Bros. film, and Jolson's last starring vehicle for the Warners, opens at the Strand Theatre, New York.

December 22: Jolson begins a new radio series, *The Al Jolson Lifebuoy/Rinso Show* on the CBS Network from Los Angeles.

1937   Jolson and Keeler appear together in cameo roles in a Warner Bros.-Vitaphone short, *A Day at Santa Anita*. Shortly thereafter, they both terminate their contracts with Warner Bros.

1939   **May 5:** Jolson's first of three films for Twentieth Century-Fox, *Rose of Washington Square*, starring Alice Faye and Tyrone Power, with Jolson receiving third billing, opens at the Roxy Theatre, New York.

October 13: *Hollywood Cavalcade*, Jolson's second film for Twentieth Century-Fox, starring Alice Faye and Don Ameche, opens at the Roxy Theatre, New York.

December 29: Jolson's final Twentieth Century-Fox film, *Swanee River*, starring Don Ameche and Andrea Leeds, opens at the Roxy Theatre, New York.

1940   **June 30:** A new Jolson show, *Hold On to Your Hats*, with a score by E.Y. "Yip" Harburg and Burton Lane, co-starring Ruby Keeler and Martha Raye, begins out-of-town performances in Detroit. Strains between Jolson and Keeler, lead to her withdrawal from the cast on July 27 in Chicago.

September 11: *Hold On to Your Hats* opens at the Sam S. Shubert Theatre, New York.

December 27: Ruby Keeler obtains a divorce from Jolson.

1941   **February 1:** *Hold On to Your Hats* closes, followed by a tour that concludes in November.

1942   **January 21:** Jolson begins his first tour performing for U.S. servicemen during World War II at the Jacksonville Naval Air Station in Florida. During the war he will perform throughout the United States, Alaska, England, South America, North Africa, and Italy.

October 6: Jolson begins a new radio series, *The Al Jolson Colgate Show*, on the CBS Network from New York.

1945   **January 16:** Jolson undergoes emergency surgery at Cedars of Lebanon Hospital, Los Angeles, for the removal of part of left lung and two ribs. He is in critical condition for some time.

March 23: Jolson marries Erle Galbraith in Quartzite, Arizona.

June 27: *Rhapsody in Blue*, a Warner Bros. film biography of George Gershwin, opens at the Hollywood Theatre, New York. Jolson plays himself in a brief segment showing him introducing Gershwin's song, "Swanee."

August 10: Jolson begins recording for Decca Records in Los Angeles.

December 23: Jolson's father, Moshe, dies in Washington, D.C.

1946   **October 1:** A lavish testimonial dinner honoring Jolson for his war work, is given at the Hotel Astor, New York.

October 10: *The Jolson Story*, a Columbia Pictures film biography, featuring Jolson's vocals on the soundtrack, opens at Radio City Music Hall, New York. It becomes Columbia's top-grossing film of all time, and revitalizes Jolson's career.

1947   **October 2:** Jolson returns to series radio in the *Kraft Music Hall* on CBS from Los Angeles. Until his death, Jolson appears consistently as a guest on numerous radio programs as well.

1948   **September 27:** Jolson films a "screen test" at Columbia Studios in Hollywood.

1949   **August 10:** *Jolson Sings Again*, a Columbia Pictures sequel to *The Jolson Story*, opens at Loew's State Theatre, New York. Jolson makes several promotional appearances a night in New York with the film on August 10, 11 and 12, performing live for enthusiastic audiences.

August 20: Jolson appears at the Chicagoland Music Festival at Soldier's Field, Chicago. His performance is broadcast on local television.

1950   **September 11:** Jolson begins a tour performing for U.S. servicemen in Japan and Korea at the start of the Korean War. Following his return, Jolson is involved in discussions at RKO for a film tentatively titled *Stars and Stripes* in which he would play himself.

October 23: Jolson dies of a heart attack in the St. Francis Hotel, San Francisco, where he has gone to appear on a Bing Crosby radio show.

October 26: Jolson's funeral is held at the Temple Israel in Hollywood. The eulogy is delivered by George Jessel.

December 6: In Washington, D.C., Erle Jolson, and the Jolson's adopted son, Asa, Jr., accept the Civilian Order of Merit for Jolson's war work.

1951   **September 23:** Jack Benny gives a eulogy at Hillside Cemetery, Los Angeles, where Jolson is laid to rest permanently in an elaborate memorial.

December 7: Erle Jolson marries Norman Krasna.

1953   **April 26:** Harry Jolson dies.

1963   **October 28:** The NBC-TV series *Hollywood and the Stars* presents an episode called "The Immortal Jolson."

1967   Henrietta Keller dies in San Luis Obispo, California.

1976   Ethel Delmar dies in Islip, New York.

1986   **May 4:** England's *The South Bank Show* on ITV presents a documentary, "The Real Al Jolson Story."

1993   **February 28:** Ruby Keeler dies in Rancho Mirage, California.

Al Jolson in *Big Boy* (1923). Permission of The Shubert Archive.

Al Jolson singing on NBC radio in the mid-1930s. Permission of The International Al Jolson Society.

3

Stage

Al Jolson's stage career began in circuses, vaudeville, stock companies, and minstrel shows, all of which subsequently led to his legendary success in musical comedy. His major stage work prior to his Broadway debut in *La Belle Paree* is listed. After beginning in musical theatre in 1911, Jolson continued to make sporadic appearances in vaudeville (for example, in St. Louis in early 1928) and on the concert stage (in Texas, Oklahoma, and Louisiana in January 1930), along with personal appearances to promote his films (in January 1933 he appeared with great fanfare in Chicago to plug *Hallelujah, I'm a Bum*, and from August 10-12, 1949 he made several highly publicized appearances a night in New York area movie theatres to promote *Jolson Sings Again*, following this with similar promotional appearances in Philadelphia, Baltimore, and Washington, D.C.) and various and sundry benefits (such as a gala Christmas benefit at the Shrine Auditorium in Los Angeles, California, on December 14, 1934, and a show business benefit for Eddie Cantor on May 1, 1935 in New York), fetes (including one for President Franklin Roosevelt on January 20, 1943 at the Mayflower Hotel in New York), and roasts (Jolson made a memorable blackface appearance at a Friar's Club roast for George Jessel on October 23, 1948). He also made a one night (July 21, 1931) appearance in the Heywood Broun revue, *Shoot the Works*, at the George M. Cohan Theatre in New York. Along with all of this, Jolson made many appearances in army camps and hospitals, both in the states and overseas, during World Wars I and II and during the early days of the Korean War. All of these are far too numerous to list individually, but his other major stage appearances are included. Where possible, entries contain details about performances and pertinent quotes from reviews, along with a listing of selected other reviews. A detailed listing of Jolson's stage tours can be found in Herbert G. Goldman's *Jolson. The Legend Comes to Life* (see B4).

S1 *RICH AND HOPPE'S BIG COMPANY OF FUN MAKERS*

Al Jolson is alleged to have appeared with this troupe sometime in 1897. Locations of performances are unknown.

S2 *WALTER L. MAIN CIRCUS*

Jolson worked with this circus from October 3-22, 1898 at stops in Pennsylvania, Maryland, West Virginia, and Ohio.

S3   *CHILDREN OF THE GHETTO*

Opened: October 16, 1899 (Herald Square, New York) 49 performances.

Credits

A play by Israel Zangwill, from his own book of sketches. Director: James A. Herne. Produced by Liebler and Company. Scenery: Frank E. Gates, E.A. Morange.

Cast

Wilton Lackaye ("Reb" Shemuel), Frank Worthing (David Brandon), William Norris (Melchitsedek Pinchas), Adolphe Lestina (Moses Ansell), Gus Frankel (Simon Wolf), Emil Hoch (Michael Birnbaum), Frank Cornell (Ephraim Phillips), Fred Lotto (Sam Levine), Charles Stanley (Sugarman), Richard Carle (Shosshi Shmendrik), Phineas Leach (Father Sol), Mathilde Cottrelly (Mrs. Belcovitch), Ada Curry (Becky), Louise Muldener (Mrs. Jacobs), Ada Dwyer (Malka), Laura Almosnino (Milly Phillips), Rosabel Morrison (Leah), Sadie Stringham (Widow Finglestein), Mabel Taliaferro (Esther Ansell), Blanche Bates (Hannah Jacobs).

Synopsis

A sprawling dramatization of nineteenth century Jewish ghetto life focusing on the Jews own questions about Talmudic law.

Reviews

"It has none of the faults generally thought inseparable from the dramatization of novels, and is perfectly intelligible to the spectator who has never read Zangwill's book, and almost equally so to one who knows nothing of Jewish home life and the manners and customs of the Children of Israel who conform strictly to the letter of rabbinical law."(*New York Times*, October 17, 1899, p. 7)

Commentary

Jolson did not appear in the New York production of the play, as has often been reported. He appeared for three performances beginning September 18, 1899 at the National Theatre during the Washington, D.C. engagement in a crowd scene. His father pulled him out of the play before it moved on to its New York engagement.

S4   *VICTORIA BURLESQUERS*

Jolson toured with this troupe from October 8, 1900 through March 8, 1902. Sometimes he appeared in partnership with Fred E. Moore.

Reviews

"The specialty performers who do well are Aggie Behler, well known at this house, Reid and Gilbert, Leroy and Lernnion, Markey and Stewart, the Harpers and Joelson and Moore, all in singing, dancing, shouting, athletic and other acts."("Star -

-Victoria Burlesquers." *Milwaukee Journal*, January 21, 1901)

"Miss Gladys St. John has a strong alto voice, and Master Harry Johnson[sic; Jolson was using his brother's name at this time], whose name does not appear on the program, are the only two in the company who can sing."("The Empire -- Burlesque." *Indianapolis News*, March 15, 1901, p. 8)

"Among the specialties is one by Aggie Behler, a singer, who is assisted by Master Jeelson[sic], a boy with a good tenor voice, who appears afterward in illustrated songs."("The Empire -- Burlesque." *Indianapolis News*, December 31, 1901, p. 12)

S5   MASTER JOELSON & FRED E. MOORE

While appearing with the Virginia Burlesquers and Al Reeves' Famous Big Company, Jolson and Moore also made some appearances on their own in vaudeville in the summers of 1901 (June 17-29) and 1902 (June 2-21).

S6   AL REEVES' FAMOUS BIG COMPANY

Jolson and Fred E. Moore toured with this company in New York, New Jersey, and Pennsylvania from March 17 through April 26, 1902.

S7   J.W. GORMAN SPECIALTY COMPANY

Jolson and Fred E. Moore toured New York and Massachusetts with this company from June 30 through August 9, 1902.

S8   THE DAINTY DUCHESS

Jolson and Fred E. Moore toured Pennsylvania, Maryland, Washington, D.C., Ohio, Kentucky, Indiana, Illinois, Missouri. Wisconsin, Minnesota, Michigan, New York, Rhode Island, and Massachusetts with this company from September 29, 1902 until April 18, 1903.

Reviews

"Lawrence Weber's Dainty Duchess company began its annual engagment at Sam T. Jack's with the Sunday matinee. The company offers two clever burlesques, *The Duchess at Home* and *Harum Scarum*. The vaudeville olio includes numbers by Tenley and Simonds, popular comedians; Joelson and Moore, with new ballads and illustrated songs; the Hollands, daring acrobats; Washburn and Topack, in a comic sketch; Nellie Sylvester, with new songs; Lester and Anger, the German senators and the DeGraff sisters, soubrettes."("Notes on Amusements." *Chicago Daily News*, December 23, 1902, p. 10)

S9   THE JOELSON BROTHERS

Jolson and his brother Harry toured in this act alone (beginning August 10, 1903) and with the companies The Mayflowers (August 29-October 3, 1903), the Little Egypt London Gaiety Girls (February 8-June 4, 1904), and Dixon and Bernstein's Turkey Burlesque Show (probably during the summer 1904). The tour, which began in the late summer of 1903 and continued through most of 1904, played dates in New York, Pennsylvania, New Jersey, Massachusetts, Maryland, Connecticut, and Canada.

S10   *JOLSON, PALMER AND JOLSON*

Jolson toured with his brother Harry and Joe Palmer in this act from October 31, 1904 through November 11, 1905. They appeared in theatres in New York, Pennsylvania, Connecticut, Massachusetts, New Jersey, Ohio, Illinois, Minnesota, Colorado, California, Nebraska, Missouri, and Louisiana.

Reviews

"Jolson, Palmer & Jolson. . .Three men, singing and talking comedy sketch. Comedy and singing just fair. Got by with a little applause in the opening spot. Fair act. 18 mins."(Report filed with the Keith-Albee office by H.A. Daniels, Manager of Keith's Theatre, Philadelphia, Pennsylvania, for the week of November 28, 1904)

S11   *PALMER AND JOLSON*

Jolson toured with Joe Palmer in this act from November 20, 1905 through June 2, 1906. They appeared at theatres in Indiana, Ohio, Kentucky, Illinois, Missouri, Iowa, and Michigan.

Reviews

". . .Palmer and Jolson, the singing comedians, have many humorous parodies."(Mollie Morris, "Stage for Next Week." *Chicago Daily News*, April 21, 1906, p. 7)

S12   *AL JOLSON*

Jolson worked in vaudeville as a single from the June 4, 1906 through May 2, 1908. He played theatres in Michigan, Montana, Washington, Canada, Oregon, California, Texas, Nebraska, Iowa, Wisconsin, Minnesota, North Dakota, Colorado, Tennessee, Alabama, and Arkansas.

Commentary

The following item appeared on page 20 of the *New York Dramatic Mirror* on September 1, 1906: "Al Jolson, Armstrong and Holly, the Girdellas, Maude Beatty and the Fern Children are reported to have arrived in Seattle, from Everett, Wash., with a grievance, having played almost a week in an Everett vaudeville theatre without seeing any sign of the salaries that had been agreed upon."

S13   WALTER SANFORD'S PLAYERS

Jolson appeared with this stock company at the Globe Theatre, San Francisco, California, from November 11 through December 21, 1907 in the following productions: *Behind the Mask, His Terrible Secret, The Great Wall Street Mystery, On the Bridge at Midnight,* and *The Factory Girl.*

S14   LEW DOCKSTADER'S MINSTRELS

Jolson toured widely with this noted minstrel troupe from August 10, 1908 through December 18, 1909. He began as a member of the company, working his way up to a solo spot that rivalled Dockstader's popularity.

Reviews

"Mr. Dockstader, Neil O'Brien and Al Jolson also appeared in this part of the entertainment and that they made a hit goes without saying."("English's -- Dockstader's Minstrels." *Indianapolis News,* November 7, 1908, p. 12)

"Al Jolson (New Brighton) scored the big laughing hit of the bill at that house, and his monologue and songs were laughed at and applauded with remarkable generosity from start to finish. He rendered *You Ain't Talkin' To Me, Every One But Me,* a very funny number and one which was hugely enjoyed, and *I Was Born in Virginia.* His burlesque on grand opera was such a laugh producer that many women acted as if they were going into hysterics."(*New York Dramatic Mirror,* August 7, 1909, p. 19)

"Towards the end of the entertainment Al Jolson gets the opportunity of showing his qualifications and almost breaks the speed limit in one of the best features of the big show. Jolson is funny, whether he wants to be or not, and his creation of wit and melody was one of the parts of the show put in late in the evening, so as to leave a pleasant taste in the mouth of one after enjoying a sumptuous meal."(C.W.R. "In and Out of the Theatres." *Columbus Evening Dispatch,* November 16, 1909, p. 14)

"By far the best of the lot is Al Jolson, a most versatile and entertaining comedian. He quite puts the star of the evening in the shade, and his monologue and songs in the last part form the hit of the whole piece. He sings, dances, talks and whistles with equal facility, and is always interesting. He is decidedly worth seeing."("At the Theatres." *Ohio State Journal,* November 16, 1909, p. 7)

> **Additional Reviews:** *Chicago Daily News,* September 28, 1909, p. 12; *Ohio State Journal,* November 19, 1908, p. 9; *Variety,* March 6, 1909, p. 14.

S15   I.P. WILKERSON'S "MINSTRELS OF TODAY"

Jolson appeared briefly with this troupe from April 25-May 9, 1909 at the American Theatre, San Francisco, California.

S16   AL JOLSON

>Jolson again toured as a single in vaudeville sporadically from July 19, 1909 through August 6, 1911.

Reviews

"Al Jolson. 15 min. in one. There is certainly lots of life and ginger in Jolson's act. He sings new and clever songs with big dash, and his line of talk is immense. The crowd would not let him go this afternoon, and whether he told stories, sang, imitated or whistled, he was a big hit; in fact, this man will simply carry the evening audiences off their feet. He is beyond question the best blackface entertainer that has come on the Circuit in recent years."(Report filed with the Keith-Albee office by C.E. Barns, Manager of Keith's Theatre, Philadelphia, Pennsylvania, for the week of August 9, 1909)

"There are many reasons why Jolson is a sure hit in vaudeville, principally in that he does something. In his talk Jolson has many little facial expressions, and above all a happy liveliness in delivery. An excellent singing voice and unusual delivery as a whistler also send the blackface single along. Jolson upon his re-entry in vaudeville immediately takes place in the front rank with single entertainers."(Dash., *Variety*, January 1, 1910, p. 17)

"Al Jolson started the first real enthusiasm of the night with his classy blackface specialty. The applause developed as his first number progressed and he pulled down something close to a riot of appreciation for his final song. In this Harry von Tilzer and William Dillon have written about a girl who was *Hip, hip, hip-noa-tized* and unless all signs fail it will be one of the comic songs of the period. Jolson handled it just right, and retired under a fire of insistent applause."(Walt., *Variety*, January 22, 1910, p. 21)

"Al Jolson. 19 minutes in 1. Jolson was quite refreshing this afternoon after about 2 minutes got the audience for fair and they would not let him off."(Report filed with the Keith-Albee office by R.G. Larsen, Manager of Keith's Theatre, Boston, Massachusetts, for the week of February 14, 1910)

"Al Jolson. Blackface comedian. The unquestionable hit of the show. 15 min. in One."(Report filed with the Keith-Albee office by Charles Lovenberg, Manager of Keith's Theatre, Providence, Rhode Island, for the week of February 21, 1910)

"Al Jolson, the former minstrel star, is the big hit at Shea's Theater this week, and at both performances yesterday he was compelled to answer so many encores that he was finally obliged to beg off. As a burnt-cork entertainer Jolson tops the list, and his monologue, singing, impromptu witticisms and whistling imitations were enjoyed to the limit. His mimicry of one of the foreign artists on this week's programme created a great deal of merriment."("Vaudeville at Shea's." *Buffalo Courier*, March 8, 1910)

"Al Jolson, late of Dockstader's Minstels, left the Majestic stage Monday night long before the audience had had enough of his act. That wasn't true of all others on the bill."("Stageland." *Milwaukee Journal*, December 21, 1910)

"Al Jolson was presented with as much applause as the aggregate of several acts before and after him."(Otis Colburn, "The New Year in Chicago." *New York Dramatic Mirror*, January 4, 1911, p. 4)

"The Orpheum has a big hit in Al Jolson."(A.T. Barnett, "San Francisco." *New York Dramatic Mirror*, July 19, 1911, p. 14)

Additional Reviews: *Billboard*, December 26, 1910; *Indianapolis News*, January 3, 1911, p. 5; *New York Dramatic Mirror*, January 11, 1911, p. 18; *New York Dramatic Mirror*, January 18, 1911, p. 18.

Commentary

Among those with whom Jolson appeared in these performances were Louise Dresser (who, in 1930, would play his mother in the film *Mammy*), Billy B. Van, and Loie Fuller's Barefoot Dancers, among many others.

S17 LA BELLE PAREE

Opened: March 20, 1911 (Winter Garden, New York) 104 performances

Toured: September 11, 1911 (Winter Garden, New York) through November 4, 1911 (Lyric, Philadelphia, Pennsylvania).

Credits

A Jumble of Jollity in two acts and eleven scenes. Staging: J.C. Huffman, William J. Wilson. Producers: The Shuberts. Book: Edgar Smith. Lyrics: Edward Madden. Music: Jerome Kern, Frank Tours.

Cast

(in order of appearance) Harry Fisher (George Ramsbotham), Stella Mayhew (Eczema Johnson), Dorothy Jardon (La Duchesse), Mitzi Hajos (Fifi Montmarte), Mlle. Dazie (La Sylphide), Edgar Atchison-Ely (Henri Dauber), Kitty Gordon (Lady Guff Jordan), Paul Nicholson (Jack Ralston), Barney Bernard (Isadore Cohen), Lee Harrison (Ike Skinheimer), Florence Tempest (Toots Horner), Marion Sunshine (Susie Jenkins), Miss Ray Cox (Susan Brown), Yvette (A Violinist), Arthur Cunningham (Bridgeeta McShane), Al Jolson (Erastus Sparkler), Hess Sisters (Russian Dancers), Harold A. Robe (The Marquis de Champignon), Jean Aylwin (Madame Clarice), Grace Studdiford (Mimi), Violet Bowers (Fifine, a model), Bessie Frewen (Margot, a model), Grace Washburn (Marcelle, a model), Katherine McDonald (Fifine), May Allen (Juliette), Sylvia Clark (A flower girl), Ida Kramer (A Grisette), Ray Dodge (Buck Lyons), Lew Guinn (A "Cook" Guide), Milberry Ryder (A Cocher).

Synopsis

A revue described in the program as a Cook's tour through vaudeville with a contemporary Parisian landscape. The plot, as such, virtually defies description, but involves a wealthy Irish-American widow Bridgeeta McShane (played in drag by Arthur Cunningham) travelling in Paris with her maid, Eczema Johnson (Stella Mayhew). Jolson played Erastus Sparkler, "a colored aristocrat from San Juan

Hill." The outrageous characters and ridiculous plot easily permitted the insertion of vaudeville turns of various kinds, including ragtime songs by Mayhew, Russian dances by the Hess Sisters, Kitty Gordon's sex appeal and Jolson's singing and clowning.

Songs

"I'm the Human Brush," "Pretty Little Milliners," "The Edinboro Wriggle," "Sing Trovatore," "The Goblins' Glide." Jolson's songs: "Paris is a Paradise for Coons," "That Lovin' Traumerai." On tour, Jolson also performed "Dat Lovin' Touch."

Reviews

"Among the very best features were those provided by the two unctuous ragtime comedians, Miss Stella Mayhew and Mr. Al Jolson, both of whom had good songs and the dialects and the acting ability to deliver every bit of good that was in them."(Adolph Klauber, *New York Times*, March 21, 1911)

"Harry Fisher, Al Jolson, Barney Bernard and the other comedians look out well for the fun of the revue, which is here for an indefinite stay."(Jay Benton, "Theatre Events in Boston." *New York Dramatic Mirror*, October 4, 1911, p. 16)

"Stella Mayhew and Al Jolson scored as blackface entertainers."(J. Solis Cohen, Jr., *New York Dramatic Mirror*, November 1, 1911, p. 32)

> **Additional Reviews:** *Blue Book*, August 1911, pp. 700-702; *New York Dramatic Mirror*, March 22, 1911, Vol. LXV, No. 1683, p. 7; *New York Dramatic Mirror*, September 27, 1911, p. 14; *New York Herald*, March 21, 1911; *New York World*, March 21, 1911.

Commentary

Among the collaborators on the score for *La Belle Paree* was Jerome Kern, who would later achieve theatrical immortality with his score for the Florenz Ziegfeld-produced musical drama based on Edna Ferber's novel, *Show Boat* (1927), and numerous other stage musicals and movies. Throughout his career, Jolson often sang Kern songs. *La Belle Paree* was an overweighted revue featuring too many acts and too many well-known performers than one evening's entertainment could comfortably support. Jolson made little impression at the first performance of this, his Broadway debut, because his appearance was scheduled so late in the long evening's program. Most of the critics, and a considerable portion of the audience, had left the theatre before he sang. At the third performance, on the evening of March 21, 1911, Jolson was spotted earlier in the performance and he scored a hit at the lush new Winter Garden Theatre, which would be his theatrical home for most of his stage career.

S18   *VERA VIOLETTA*

Opened: November 20, 1911 (Winter Garden, New York) 112 performances

Tryout performances: November 13-15, 1911 (Harmanus Bleecker Hall, Albany, New York), November 16, 1911 (Court Square, Springfield, Massachusetts), November 17-18, 1911 (Hyperion, New Haven, Connecticut)

Credits

A Musical Entertainment in two scenes. Staging: Lewis Morton, William J. Wilson, Joseph C. Smith. Producers: The Shuberts. Book: Leonard Liebling, Harold Atteridge, adapted from the German of Leo Stein. Lyrics: Harold Atteridge. Music: Edmund Eysler.

Cast

(in order of appearance) Edward Cutler (Manager of a Skating Rink), Al Jolson (Claude, a waiter), Doris Cameron (Margot), Van Rensselaer Wheeler (Aristide de St. Cloche), Ernest Hare (Pierre, a waiter), James B. Carson (Prof. Otto von Gruenberg), Mae West (Mlle. Angelique), Barney Bernard (Morris Cohen), Billee Taylor (A Rounder), Florence Douglas (La Duchesse), José Collins (Mme. von Gruenberg), Melville Ellis (Paul Voissen), Gaby Deslys (Mme. Adelle de. St. Cloche), Stella Mayhew (Mme. Elise), Harry Pilcer (Andrew Mason), Harry Fischer (M. Berton), Clarence Harvey (Marquis de Tivoli), Maidie Berker (Ninon), Florence Douglas (Lulu), Jane Laurence (Susanne), Lew Quinn (Count de Mokins), Mel Ryder (Signor de Skate). Mae West left the cast and was replaced by Kathleen Clifford prior to the Broadway opening.

Synopsis

Jolson played Claude, a waiter, and wandered in and out of what was essentially a revue set in a modern day skating rink, presumably in New York, making impromptu remarks and bursting into song at the least provocation. The minimal plot involved a professor's wife who flirts with the husband of the professor's old girlfriend.

Songs

"Paree, Gay Paree," "Olga from the Volga," "Vera Violetta," "Come Back to Me," "My Lou," "I Wonder If It's True." Jolson's songs: "Rum Tum Tiddle," "That Haunting Melody."

Reviews

"Al Jolson contributed his usual share of fun and scored very definitely in *That Haunting Melody* and *Rum Tum Tiddle*."(*New York Dramatic Mirror*, November 22, 1911, Vol. LXVI, No. 1718, p. 7)

"[Jolson] succeeded in rousing the audience into its first enthusiasm of the evening, and kept them enthusiastic much of the time afterwards."(Adolph Klauber, *New York Times*, November 21, 1911)

Additional Review: *Green Book*, February, 1912, pp. 232-236.

Commentary

Jolson moved to the forefront in this Shubert entertainment, proving that his successful spot in *La Belle Paree* had not been a fluke. His popularity with audiences in *Vera Violetta* rivalled that of the nominal star, French charmer Gaby Deslys. During the run of the show, he made his first recordings for Victor Records, capturing his performances of "Rum Tum Tiddle" and "That Haunting Melody" which he performed in the show (see D2). Jolson performed "Rum Tum Tiddle" racing up and down the center aisle of the theatre.

S19   THE WHIRL OF SOCIETY, PRECEDED BY A NIGHT WITH THE PIERROTS

Opened: March 5, 1912 (Winter Garden, New York) 136 performances

Tryout performances: March 1-2, 1912 (Harmanus Bleecker Hall, Albany, New York). Toured: September 1, 1912 (Lyric, Chicago, Illinois) through January 25, 1913 (Majestic, Brooklyn, New York).

Credits

A musical satire of up-to-date society. Staging: J.C. Huffman. Staging of musical numbers: William J. Wilson. Producers: The Shuberts. Book: Harrison Rhodes. Lyrics: Harold Atteridge. Music: Louis A. Hirsch.

Cast (*A Night With the Pierrots*)

Prologue: Al Jolson (The Humpback), Stella Mayhew (Sumurun). *A Night With the Pierrots*: Billee Taylor (Interlocutor), Al Jolson (Bones), Barney Bernard (Tambo), Stella Mayhew, José Collins, Blossom Seeley, Kathleen Clifford, Mildred Elaine, George White, Melissa Tan Eyck, Laura Hamilton, Courtney Sisters, Doris Cameron, Clarence Harvey, Ernest Hare, Edward Cutler, Cecil Ryan, Barney Thornton, Harry Wardell, Martin Brown, Florence Cable. The following departed the cast at various times: Kathleen Clifford (March 9), Blossom Seeley (March 16), Barney Bernard (April 1), George White (May 13), Melissa Ten Eyck (May 13), Billee Taylor (May 27), Eugene Howard (June 17). The following joined the cast at various times: Willie and Eugene Howard (April 8), Irene Claire (May 6), James Davis (May 13), Laura Hamilton (May 13), Violet Colby (June 24).

Cast (*The Whirl of Society*)

(in order of appearance) Stella Mayhew (Mrs. Dean), Clarence Harvey (Mr. Dean), Jose Collins (Angela, their daughter), Al Jolson (Gus, their butler), Lawrence D'Orsay (Archduke Frederich), Mildred Elaine (Archduchess), Melville Ellis (Harry Courtfield), Martin Brown (Franklyn Copeland), Doris Cameron (Mrs. Vandercrief), Florence Cable (Mrs. Tatters), Dolle Dalnert (Mlle. Eclatante), Barney Bernard (Baron de Shine).

Synopsis

Jolson appears as blackfaced servant, Gus, a stage character he would play for virtually his entire stage career. The minimal plot, satirizing the recent American visit of the Duke and Duchess of Connaught, involves a party thrown by Long Island society doyen Mrs. Dean, allowing for various revue-style turns by various members of the cast.

Songs

"Hard Luck in Society," "Which Shall I Choose?," "Cinderella Waltz." Jolson's songs: "Snap Your Fingers," "Row, Row, Row," "Waiting for the Robert E. Lee."

Reviews

". . .Mr. Jolson, who from start to finish is the life of the party."(*New York Times*, March 6, 1912, p. 11)

"Stella Mayhew and Al Jolson do most of the work, because their talents fit them for it."(*New York Dramatic Mirror*, March 13, 1912, Vol. LXVII, No. 1734, p. 6)

"Ada Lewis, Fannie Brice, Al Jolson, Lawrence D'Orsay, Fay Courtney, and others won applause well merited."(*New York Dramatic Mirror*, October 9, 1912, p. 18)

"Al Jolson with his droll mimicry was the biggest hit of all. His good humor is extremely contagious."(J. Solis-Cohen, Jr., "Gaby Deslys Unpopular With the Press." *New York Dramatic Mirror*, December 4, 1912, p. 15)

"Al Jolson proved to be the hit of the show."(J. LeRoy Drug, "Brooklyn." *New York Dramatic Mirror*, January 29, 1913, p. 18)

> **Additional Reviews:** *Blue Book,* August 1912, pp. 697-700; *Buffalo Courier,* January 14, 1913; *New York Dramatic Mirror,* October 23, 1912, p. 20; *New York Dramatic News,* March 16, 1912, p. 13; *New York Globe,* March 6, 1912.

Commentary

A runway from the back of the Winter Garden to the stage cutting across the center of the auditorium was constructed for *A Night with the Pierrots*, in obvious imitation of one used two months earlier in Max Reinhardt's celebrated production of *Sumurun*. The runway, replaced in later Jolson shows by a platform extending out over the orchestra pit, became a unique trademark of Jolson's, permitting him an intimacy with his audiences enjoyed by both the star and his public. This was the first time Jolson appeared as "Gus," the blackface stage persona that would remain with him through *Big Boy* (1925)(see S25). Jolson had appeared in blackface in his two previous musical shows, but "Gus" became his permanent theatrical mask for the golden years of his stage career. As this character evolved in Jolson's stage vehicles, it was clear that unknowingly he had created a contemporary American version of a character type that was as old as the theatre itself. From the traditions of ancient Greek and Roman comedy (in the plays of the Athenian comic dramatist Aristophanes and Roman comic authors Plautus and Terence, respectively), medieval mimes and jesters, commedia dell'arte, and later forms growing out of these eras, Jolson had stumbled onto the outrageous comic servant, who bested his masters, united star-crossed lovers, and took to the forefront in a stage world in which the oppressed could create anarchy and rule the world. It is likely that Jolson never heard of his theatrical forebears, but it is clear that he instinctively allied himself with their style and he owned the stage of his time as they had in theirs. His "Gus" was resourceful, mischievious, good-hearted, friend and protector of children and the weak, and deflater of the pompous and powerful.

S20   THE HONEYMOON EXPRESS

Opened: February 6, 1913 (Winter Garden, New York) 156 performances

Tryout performances: February 3-4, 1913 (Hyperion, New Haven, Connecticut). Toured: September 18, 1913 (Nixon's Apollo, Atlantic City, New Jersey) through May 30, 1914 (Metropolitan, Minneapolis, Minnesota).

Credits

A Spectacular Farce with Music in two acts and six scenes. Staging: Ned Wayburn. Producers: The Shuberts. Book and lyrics: Joseph W. Herbert, Harold Atteridge. Music: Jean Schwartz.

Cast

(in order of appearance) Ernest Glendinning (Henri Dubonet), Harry Fox (Pierre, his friend), Harry Pilcer (Baudry, a lawyer), Lou Anger (Gardonne, hotel keeper in Arignon), Al Jolson (Gus, butler at Dubonet's), Melville Ellis (Doctor D'Zuvray), Frank Holmes (Achille), Robert Hastings (Eduard), Gerald McDonald (Gautier), Jack Carleton (Constant), Henry Dyer (Paul), Clint Russell (Guillaume), Harry Wardell (Felix, a gateman), Harland Dixon (Alfonse), James Doyle (Gaston), F. Owen Baxter (Maurice, a poster painter), Gaby Deslys (Yvonne, wife of Henri), Ada Lewis (Mme. De Bressie, Yvonne's aunt), Yansci Dolly (Marguerite, Gardonne's daughter), Fanny Brice (Marcelle, a domestic), Gilbert Wilson (Marcus, a waiter), Marjorie Lane (Noelie, a maid). Charles King and Ina Claire, among others, join the cast during the run.

Synopsis

This briskly paced farce set in the present time in the New York suburbs, with music featured Jolson, again as Gus, in a lightly plotted romance involving a divorce proceeding halted by the news that the husband would inherit four million francs from his uncle if he was married. Gus's machinations to reunite the young couple, played by Ernest Glendinning and Gaby Deslys, was the centerpiece of the fun. As would become a tradition in Jolson shows, the plot was casually discarded for impromptu clowning and interpolated songs.

Songs

"That is the Life for Me," "When the Honeymoon Stops Shining," "Syncopatia Land," "You'll Call the Next Love the First," "I Want the Strolling Good," "The Ragtime Express," "My Cocoa-Cola Belle," "You Are the Someone," "I Want a Toy Soldier Man," "Our Little Cabaret Up Home," "Bring Back Your Love," "My Raggyadore," "When Gaby Did the Gaby Glide." Jolson's songs at various times included: "That Gal of Mine," "Give Me the Hudson Shore," "My Yellow Jacket Girl," "The Spaniard That Blighted My Life," "You Made Me Love You," "Good-Bye, Boys," "I Love Her (Oh! Oh! Oh!)," "Down Where the Tennessee Flows," "He'd Have to Get Under -- Get Out and Get Under," "I'm on My Way to Mandalay," "Who Paid the Rent for Mrs. Rip Van Winkle?," "While They Were Dancing Around."

Reviews

"Al Jolson is the real star. There wasn't half enough for him to do. In fact, until just before the close of the performance he had been funnier by far in some moving pictures in which he figured than in anything he did in the flesh. But just at the end he had a Spanish song which aroused shrieks of laughter. The audience simply would not let him go; even Gaby [Deslys] herself had to take a back seat on the piano stool -- which she did with charming grace, by the way -- while the audience made Jolson sing song after song. It's really a pleasure in these apathetic theatrical days to see an artist get such an ovation. And every bit of it was deserved."(Acton Davies, *New York Evening Sun*, February 7, 1913)

"Mr. Jolson, as usual, did valiant service."(*New York Times*, February 7, 1913, p. 11)

"Even the best humor is visual; for example, Al Jolson's ridiculous parody of the dance bacchanale at the beginning of the second act."(*New York Dramatic Mirror*, February 12, 1913, Vol. LXIX, No. 1782, p. 6)

"After eleven o'clock Jolson started with *My Yellow Jacket Girl* (sounding like *Sumurun* re-written). He had to follow with four other songs, all new to the Garden and unprogrammed. Jolson completely stopped the show. He was obliged to return to sing another selection, even after Gaby [Deslys] and Harry Pilcer walked upon the stage. Gaby was pleased at being made a lay figure through applause for someone else."(Sime., *Variety*, February 14, 1913, p. 18)

"In Mr. Al Jolson it has the blackest and most amusing of minstrels."(*Theatre*, March 1913, Vol. XVII, No. 145, p. 67)

"Anyone who misses seeing the Honeymoon Express, which opened a half week's engagement at the Davidson theatre Sunday night, is loosing[sic] an opportunity to see and hear an unusually amusing comedian. His name is Al Jolson. He is a black-face comedian, and the way he establishes an intimacy with the audience, and holds it, is an example of what, for lack of a better name, has been called *personality plus*."("The Stage." *Milwaukee Journal*, March 17, 1913)

"Al Jolson is still the prime delight of the show. There isn't a funnier comedian anywhere within the reach of Broadway or a richer song than his *The Spaniard That Blighted My Life*."(*New York Dramatic Mirror*, April 30, 1913, p. 6)

"The show ended at 11:30 and Al Jolson closed it again without losing a single customer. He sang four songs making everyone a clean bull's eye. His fourth number was new. Jolson got it so far over he repeated the chorus in a lighter vein. [. . .] Then Jolson started after the audience and got 'em good. He used his two dance steps in six different ways. For faking dancing Al has something even on Billy Rock."(Review of Sunday night concert at the Winter Garden during the run of *The Honeymoon Express*: Sime., *Variety*, May 2, 1913, p. 9)

"Al Jolson, a spoiled but wonderful genius, is the star and his brilliant comedy, great voice, splendour of temperament and delightful originality place him where no entertainer has ever climbed, on the top rung, of that ladder which twenty-five years ago Nat Goodwin held undisputed till he slid down into Shylock's gabardine and oblivion. [. . .] It does not in the least matter who on this globe ever tried to sing *He Had to Get Out and Under* or *You Made Me Love You* when Al Jolson tunes his beautiful (that is the word, beautiful) voice and exacts sensational applause."(Amy Leslie, "Garrick's Great Show." *Chicago Daily News*, January 5, 1914, p. 14)

"In you have to miss a dejeuner dansant or the funeral of your dearest enemy, don't fail to see Al Jolson in *The Honeymoon Express*. Comparatively few of Columbus theatregoers had the privilege of thus exercising their funnybones in an unwonted fashion last night, but there are two more chances, matinee and night. Without exaggeration, there is no comedian in the business whom we would more cheerfully and unreservedly recommend. He's a theatrical seventh wonder."("In the Theatres."

Columbus Evening Dispatch, February 26, 1914, p. 14)

"This Jolson person has a gift of comedy that draws the laughter no matter what he does or says, and in addition he has a splendid singing voice, and last night he sang us songs that we had heard before, but hadn't heard. He gave us *I'm On My Way to Mandalay* in the first act and then for an encore he sang *Dancing Around*. Later, he convulsed us with *Who Paid the Rent For Mrs. Rip Van Winkle (When Rip Van Winkle Went Away)?* and when the audience wouldn't let him go he sat down on the stage, with his feet hanging over into the orchestra pit, and gave us *Peg O' My Heart* in such a way that they say in New York only Al Jolson can. Then there was an insistent demand for more, and he asked the audience to name the next number, and someone asked for *This Is The Life*, and he sang that, and then there came a request for *The Rosary*, and he forgot his comedy for the moment and stilled us all with the beauty of the tones of Nevin's immortal song."(*Seattle Post-Intelligencer*, May 11, 1914)

> **Additional Reviews:** *Blue Book*, August 1913, pp. 656-658; *Buffalo Courier*, December 16, 1913; *Chicago Daily News*, March 9, 1914, p. 4; *Indianapolis News*, February 24, 1914, p. 13; *Life*, February 20, 1913, p. 375; *Munsey*, April 1913, p. 149; *New York Clipper*, February 15, 1913; *New York Dramatic Mirror*, February 12, 1913, Vol. LXIX, No. 1782, p. 6; *New York Dramatic Mirror*, April 2, 1913, Vol. LXIX, p. 2; *New York Dramatic News*, February 15, 1913; *New York Dramatic News*, March 1913; *New York Evening Sun*, February 7, 1913; *Ohio State Journal*, February 27, 1914, p. 7; *St. Louis Star*, February 16, 1914; *Toledo Blade*, February 28, 1914; *Variety*, reviews of Sunday night concerts at the Winter Garden during the run of *The Honeymoon Express* appeared in the following issues: February 21, 1913; March 28, 1913; April 4, 1913; April 11, 1913; April 25, 1913; May 16, 1913.

Commentary

In the show's most talked about sequence, film footage was used to depict a wild auto chase with Jolson behind the wheel of one of the vehicles. The filmed portion ended with the speeding cars driving toward the audience as the screen flew out of sight and the cast, in actual vehicles onstage, rolled toward the audience with headlights blazing. During the run of this show, Jolson adopted one of his trademark bits of business. While singing "You Made Me Love You," he dropped to one knee. One legend suggests that he did it to relieve the pain of an ingrown toenail, but it is undoubtedly the case that he had seen vaudevillian Blossom Seeley employ this emotive technique while singing "Toddlin' the Todalo" in *The Whirl of Society* (see S19). During the run of the show, Jolson appeared in most of the Shubert-produced Sunday night concerts, and even when he was not on the bill, audiences demanded a Jolson appearance. The lengthy and enthusiastic ovations that greeted his entrance and his numbers would become commonplace throughout his stage career. The lengthy national tour that followed the New York production of *The Honeymoon Express* made Jolson a well-known star throughout the country.

S21   *DANCING AROUND*

Opened: October 10, 1914 (Winter Garden, New York) 145 performances

Tryout performances: September 28-October 3, 1914 (Hyperion, New Haven, Connecticut). Toured: February 15, 1915 (Lyric, Philadelphia, Pennsylvania) through December 4, 1915 (Belasco, Washington, D.C.).

Credits

A musical spectacle in twelve scenes. Staging: J.C. Huffman. Producers: The Shuberts. Dances: Jack Mason. Book and lyrics: Harold Atteridge. Music: Sigmund Romberg, Harry Carroll.

Cast

(in order of appearance) James Doyle (Lieutenant Larry), Harland Dixon (Lieutenant Tommy), Bernard Granville (Lieutenant Hartley), Aimee Dalmores (Clarice), Eleanor Brown (Shirley), Olga Hempstone (Dora), Kitty Doner (Pinky Roberts), Frank Carter (Lieutenant Harry Graham), Lucy Weston (Annette Truesdale), Earl Fox (Lieutenant Robert), Georgie O'Ramey (Tillie, a telephone operator), Clifton Webb (Clarence), Al Jolson (Gus, a man of many parts), Mary Robson (Mlle. Mitzi, of the Frivolity), Eileen Molyneaux (Ethel), Cecil Cunningham (Beulah Elliot, prima donna), Fred Leslie (Lord Graham), Phil Branson (Fireman), Harold Robe (Train Announcer), Melville Ellis (John Elliot), Mabel Hill (Messenger Boy), Mildred Manning (Patricia), May Dealy (Lucy), Phil Branson (Butler), Effie Graham (Miss Thames), Georgie O'Ramey (Maid), Katherine Hill (Miss Gerard), Lucy Weston (Miss Social Leader), Al Jolson (Monsieur Jean). (Edith Day made her stage debut in the tour).

Synopsis

The wisp of a plot involved the search of a British army officer for a prima donna, but, as was becoming a tradition, Jolson and his antics were the whole show. Riotous scenes involved him serving as the entire staff of New York's Hotel Lavender and as a fey designer in a satiric knock-off of the play *My Lady's Dress*, which was running on Broadway concurrently with *Dancing Around*.

Songs

"Never Trust a Soldier Man," "When an Englishman Marries a Parisian," "My Rainbow Beau," "The Call of the Colors," "By the Grand Canal." Jolson's songs at various times included: "Venetia," "I Want to Be in Norfolk," "I'm Seeking for Siegfried," "The Shuffling Shivaree," "When the Grown Up Ladies Act Like Babies," "Sister Susie's Sewing Shirts for Soldiers," "Everybody Rag With Me," "When I Leave the World Behind," "Bring Along Your Dancing Shoes."

Reviews

"Mr. Jolson is in fine form and as droll as ever, whether he is a butler wearing a *gol-dum-yah* in his buttonhole, the entire staff of the Hotel Lavender, or a gondolier in distant Venice. For once, this ebony trifler washes his face and appears as a mincing man dress-maker in a brief scene which is doubtless designed as a burlesque of one of the acts in *My Lady's Dress*, the new Knoblauch[sic] play which came last evening to the Playhouse. He sings with great gusto and success, even if the songs provided do not quite match some of his earlier favorites."(*New York Times*, October 11, 1914, Section III, p. 3)

"Al Jolson as the chief funmaker was given an enthusiastic welcome after an absence of two years. He proved as irresistable as ever, and his exceptional magnetism was clearly proved by the hearty manner in which the audience greeted his songs, decidedly inferior in lyric and melody to what he has had. His boisterous spirit of gayety[sic] was captivating and refreshing save on occasions when it had to rely upon vulgar humor and mediocre songs. Then it became, indeed, irksome and monotonous."(*New York Dramatic Mirror*, October 21, 1914, Vol. LXXII, No. 1870, p. 8)

"Al Jolson seemed to fear following Trentini's tremendous success, but he needn't fear anybody. The Winter Garden may come and the Winter Garden may go, but Al Jolson will go on forever, it seems."(*Variety*, October 24, 1914, p. 19. Not a review of the show, but of a Sunday night concert at the Winter Garden at the time the show opened)

"Al Jolson, that paradoxically darkest yet brightest of stars, heads the list of a talented cast. He is funny in an artistically coarse fashion, but his songs scarcely lend great assistance to his humor."(*Theatre*, November 1914, Vol. XX, No. 165, p. 255)

"Al Jolson [. . .] puts his songs *across* in his own inimitable way, and even takes the audience into his confidence about aspirations to serious drama. Most of Jolson's jokes are new this year. Some of them are unmitigatedly vulgar. All of them brought choruses of laughter. There is no resisting Jolson. One flaw in his act is the protracted play with the song *Sister Susie's Sewing Shirts for Soldiers*. Jolson holds up the tempo of the otherwise quick-flashing scenes to appeal piteously to a *lady* or *gentleman* in the audience to sing the song. A little of this by-play is amusing. But it soon becomes tiresome, even though two men did sing last night."("On the Pittsburgh Stage." *Pittsburgh Post*, March 23, 1915)

"When Al Jolson came upon the stage at the Garrick last night the big audience which has been drawn thither, by the prospect of seeing him in *Dancing Around* applauded for so long a time that people began to look at their watches to see whether something record breaking in the way of greetings wasn't coming off. [. . .] It's hypnotism, that's what it is."(Mollie Morris. "Al Jolson Reigns Supreme at Garrick." *Chicago Daily News*, April 19, 1915, p. 6)

"Mr. Jolson always gives the impression of doing his best for his audience; and he soon has spectators in such a condition of hilarity that they will laugh at his slightest word or look. He really has only one song number in the present show, but he has plenty of talks, regular confidential talks with his audience; for, as he observes: *What's grammar, if we know each other*? His ability as a comedian was never more evident than in this production, especially considering the scanty material he has to work on."(Alice Coon Brown, "Theatres." *Ohio State Journal*, November 4, 1915, p. 7)

"Many a show also has been saved by Mr. Jolson, and this is one of them. There is a sort of depression until he gets on the stage, and when he leaves there is a near-vacuum in the atmosphere which several rather attractive young women and two or three lively young men endeavor to fill."("Attractions at Playhouses." *Columbus Evening Dispatch*, November 4, 1915, p. 20)

Additional Reviews: *Buffalo Courier*, March 30, 1915; *Indianapolis News*, October 26, 1915, p. 9; *Munsey*, December 1914, p. 558; *New York Dramatic Mirror*, November 11, 1914, p. 2; *The Strand*, October 11, 1914; *Syracuse Post-Standard*, November 16, 1915.

Commentary

In an attempt to top the car chase sequence in *The Honeymoon Express* (see S21), *Dancing Around* included a locomotive race. Another memorable sequence involved a gavotte performed in a setting inspired by the paintings of the artist Watteau. Jolson perfected a unique gimmick in his interpolated song, "Sister Susie's Sewing Shirts for Soldiers," by having an audience member sing a chorus of the song and then inviting the entire audience to join in. Jolson also performed the song, and another specialty written in imitation of it, "Brother Bennie's Baking Buns for Belgians," in Shubert Sunday night concerts during the run of *Dancing Around*, including one in which he performed for nearly three-quarters of an hour following a bill of seventeen other performers. Such was his hold on the audience that they would not leave the theatre if he was willing to continue performing -- he usually was. During the last engagement of the tour of this production, Jolson met President Woodrow Wilson, who attended the final performance of the run with his fiancée, Mrs. Edith Bolling Galt.

S22   *ROBINSON CRUSOE, JR.*

Opened: February 17, 1916 (Winter Garden, New York) 139 performances

Tryout performances: February 10-12, 1916 (Sam S. Shubert, New Haven, Connecticut). Toured: August 28, 1916 (Globe, Atlantic City, New Jersey) through November 17, 1917 (Court Square, Springfield, Massachusetts).

Credits

A Musical Extravaganza in Two Acts and Ten Scenes. Staging: J.C. Huffman. Producers: The Shuberts. Musical Numbers Staging: Allan K. Foster. Book and Lyrics: Harold Atteridge, Edgar Smith. Music: Sigmund Romberg, James F. Hanley.

Cast

(in order of appearance) Lee Phelps (Poindexter), Frank Holmes (Frank Speed), Johnny Berkes (Bob Van Astor), Frank Grace (Jack Jitney), Louise Conti (Gladys Brookville), Claude Flemming (Hiram Westbury), Lawrence D'Orsay (Captain Chichester), Wanda Lyon (Diana Westbury), Kitty Doner (Suzie Westbury), Barry Lupino (Howell Louder), Jean Forbes (Leading Lady), Eleanor Brown (Soubrette), Lois Whitney (Miss Reel), Harry Wilcox (Leading Man), Mme. Comont (Star Feature), Bert Dunlap (Camera Man), Harry Wardell (Movie Actor), Frank Carter (Dick Hunter), Al Jolson (Gus Jackson), Edward Bowers (First Constable), Alfred Crocker (Second Constable), Frank Walters (Third Constable).

Synopsis

Jolson again appears as Gus, acting in this case as chauffeur to wealthy Hiram Westbury. Westbury exhausts himself chasing a movie company off his Long Island estate, then falls asleep and dreams he is Robinson Crusoe, Jr. and Gus is his man Friday. Crusoe and Friday move at will from one geographical location to another, including a Spanish castle, a pirate ship, and a forest with trees that come to life as chorus girls. Gus/Friday gets into comic adventures with a goat and a crocodile, and at one point must masquerade as Fatima. When Westbury awakens from his dream, he decides to throw an elaborate party in the production's final sequence. The various settings provided opportunities for different types of songs, ad libs, and impromptu clowning on Jolson's part.

Songs

"Simple Life," "You'll Have to Gallop Some," "When You're Starring for the Movies," "Go Ahead and Dance a Little More," "Pretty Little Mayflower Girl," "Happy Hottentots," "Voodoo Maiden," "Don't Be a Sailor," "My Pirate Lady," "Robinson Crusoe," "Minstrel Days." Jolson's songs at various times included: "Tillie Titwillow," "Down Where the Swanee River Flows," "Now He's Got a Beautiful Girl," "Yaaka Hula Hickey Dula," "Where Did Robinson Crusoe Go With Friday on Saturday Night?," "Where the Black-Eyed Susans Grow."

Reviews

"The two most important facts connected with the new Winter Garden production are Al Jolson's return to the scene of his former triumphs and the presence of tights upon those formerly undraped parts of the anatomy which at the Fiftieth Street playhouse go to make up the famous *bridge of thighs*. The Winter Garden company is to be congratulated for both features. Of all our blackface comedians, Al Jolson is, perhaps, the most industrious and the most varied in his methods, and his appearance has always the character of a stimulant (a virtue not despised in these days of over-production of ragtime revues)."(*New York Dramatic Mirror*, February 16, 1916, Vol. LXXV, No. 1940, p. 8)

"Anyone who likes Al Jolson, and there seem to be some such, will enjoy the new show at the Winter Garden, for it is composed almost entirely of Al Jolson."(James Metcalfe, *Life*, March 2, 1916, p. 296)

"Not much can be said for the book, based on the well-known juvenile classic, save that it gives plenty of opportunity to Al Jolson, perhaps the most popular of all our black-faced comedians. [. . .] Mr. Jolson keeps the audience amused and sings several songs in his best manner."(*Theatre*, April 1916, Vol. XXIII, No. 182, p. 238)

"But Al Jolson cannot be equalled whether in low comedy or light, in sparkling travesty or operatic burlesque. He is unique and audacious, he is without peer as a deliverer of good songs, of original songs, of pretty lilts meaningless but tuneful, of delightful high jinks in melody and mischief. He does a medley which is captivating and hints at all the other things he has sung for us so beautifully other times in Winter Garden outputs, and he has never been more devouringly capable of doing all the entertaining anybody could ask for $2.00 a throw than he is in *Robinson Crusoe, Jr.*"(Amy Leslie, "Al Jolson as Friday and Other Savages." *Chicago Daily News*, January 3, 1917, p. 5)

Additional Reviews: *Buffalo Courier*, December 19, 1916; *Chicago Herald Examiner*, January 1, 1917; *Columbus Evening Dispatch*, April 10, 1917, p. 20; *Indianapolis News*, April 3, 1917, p. 17; *Los Angeles Times*, August 1,

1917; *Munsey*, May 1916, p. 700; *New York Dramatic News,* February 26, 1916, pp. 17-18; *New York Dramatic Mirror*, February 26, 1916, Vol. LXXV, No. 1940, p. 8; *New York Dramatic Mirror*, March 25, 1916, Vol. LXXV, p. 2; *The New York Evening World*, February 18, 1916; *Ohio State Journal*, April 10, 1917, p. 7; *Variety*, February 18, 1916, p. 19.

Commentary

In many respects, this was the quintessential show of Jolson's early stage career. He was attaining unparalleled recognition as a popular entertainer, and reviews of his performances were now suggesting that he was a major theatrical artist. It was also during the tour of this production that advertisements and other publicity began to refer to Jolson as "The World's Greatest Entertainer." Jolson had not had his name billed over the title of any show until *Robinson Crusoe, Jr.* -- it would remain there for the rest of his theatrical career. He continued to tour the country far and wide, perhaps more than any other star performer of his era. This policy, willingly supported by the Shuberts who made a fortune from Jolson's shows, undoubtedly contributed to the longevity of his career. Long after he ceased performing regularly on the live stage and in films, he retained a large following, much of which was undoubtedly built through the long, gruelling tours that followed each of his stage musicals.

S23 *SINBAD*

Opened: February 14, 1918 (Winter Garden, New York) 164 performances

Tryout performances: February 4-9, 1918 (Sam S. Shubert, New Haven, Connecticut). Toured: March 30, 1919 (Poli's, Washington, D.C.) through June 25, 1921 (Metropolitan, St. Paul, Minnesota).

Credits

A Spectacular Extravaganza in two acts and fourteen scenes. Staging: J.C. Huffman, J.J. Shubert. Producers: The Shuberts. Book and lyrics: Harold Atteridge. Music: Sigmund Romberg, Al Jolson.

Cast

(in order of appearance) Rebekah Cauble (Harriet), Bess Hoban (Mildred), Winona Wilkins (Marcelle), Frank Holmes (Harry), Grace Langdon (Betty), Betty Touraine (Isabel), Jack Laughlin (Mack), Harry Kearley (Tony), Hazel Cox (Patricia de Trait), Fritzi von Busing (Mrs. Van Decker), Lawrence D'Orsay (Stephen Gilwater), Ernest Hare (Professor Graves), Kitty Doner (Stubb Talmadge), Virginia Smith (Audrey Van Decker), Virginia Fox Brooks (Nan Van Decker), Franklyn A. Batie (Jack Randall), Forrest Huff (Van Rennsellar Sinbad), Irene Farber (Jeanette Verdear), Constance Farber (Tessie Verdear), Al Jolson (Gus), John Kearney (A Yogi).

Synopsis

Jolson, again in his Gus persona (also called Inbad here), plays a porter at a country club on Long Island who is transported to old Bagdad where he encounters Sinbad and a variety of characters out of the Arabian Nights. The exotic settings, such as the Grotto of the Valley of Diamonds and the Island of Eternal Youth, once again permitted Jolson the opportunity for outrageous ad libs and clowning, along with interpolations of many different songs during the run of the show.

Songs

"On Cupid's Green," "A Little Bit of Every Nationality," "Our Ancestors," "A Thousand and One Arabian Nights," "Beauty and Beast," "Bagdad," "The Rag Lad of Bagdad," "A Night in the Orient," "I Hail from Cairo," "Love Ahoy," "The Bedalumbo," "Isle of Youth," "I'll Tell the World," "It's Wonderful," "Raz-Ma-Taz." Jolson's songs at various times included: "Rock-A-Bye Your Baby With a Dixie Melody," "Why Do They All Take the Night Boat to Albany?," "I Wonder Why She Kept on Saying *Si, Si, Si, Si, Señor*," "Cleopatra," "N'Everything," "I'll Say She Does," "On the Road to Calais," "By the Honeysuckle Vine," "I Gave Her That," "Chloe," "Swanee," "Avalon," "My Mammy," "Dixie Rose."

Reviews

"Al Jolson came back to the Winter Garden last night with his singing, dancing, and talking, and a packed house received him with all of the noise that the people could make. The Winter Garden likes Jolson and Jolson seems to like the Winter Garden -- so a joyful time was had by all. [. . .] Jolson appeared in a sort of interim scene, informed the audience that he had been looking for barbed wire so he could knit the Kaiser a sweater, and the show was really started. He sang, *Rock-a-Bye You[sic] Baby with a Dixie Melody* and *Take the Night Boat to Albany*."(*New York Times*, February 15, 1918, p. 7)

"Al Jolson! What a remarkable entertainer. He literally shoulders the entire book, for he is the only comedian, and the difficult task of providing the light and shade is his alone. From his initial entrance, Jolson had the honors sewed up, and never did he have a monotonous moments."(Wynn., *Variety*, February 22, 1918, p. 14)

"The piece needs a good deal of fattening up in the way of fun, Mr. Al Jolson, with all his cleverness, not being able alone to supply enough for such a long entertainment."(Metcalfe, "Drama." *Life*, February 28, 1918, p. 343)

"Jolson has an unflagging energy. Into every song or dance that he undertakes he puts every ounce of vigor and effort. He maintains the spirit and zest of the entire entertainment at the level at which he is working. He is ever striving to please and his enterprise and industry are communicated to the principals and the chorus surrounding him. He knows his audience -- the Winter Garden audiences and becomes for their entertainment an accomplished vulgarian. And vulgarity -- good, wholesome and amusing vulgarity -- is an ever increasing rarity in the American theatre!"(*New York Dramatic Mirror*, March 2, 1918, Vol. LXVIII, No. 2015, p. 5)

"Jolson pervades the show characteristically, brilliantly and soulfully. He rollicks irresponsively, wittily, sometimes in the rough but always melodiously. He runs the gamut of riotous humor and goes out of his beaten path to prove that Al Jolson could play any kind of a part the stage might have in store for him. His voice is clear, rich sweetness untutored and unspoiled. No artist among the thousands and one who have filled the old opera home with music could resist the wholesome melody of Jolson's balladry."(Amy Leslie, "Al Jolson's Fooling Makes Wonderful Hit." *Chicago Daily News*, January 27, 1920, p. 4)

"Al Jolson was probably never funnier than as Inbad, the dusky porter in *Sinbad*, the Shubert variety of chorus girl wiggles flowering in the Winter Garden and translated in the Alvin last night. The burntcork star also likely never put more of himself into blazing away both barrels in his song shooting. In most of Jolson's intervals on the stage, the houseful had its hilarity."("On the Pittsburgh Stage." *Pittsburgh Post*, March 30, 1920)

"Jolson [. . .] sings, as ever, with every ounce of his uniquely magnetic personality."("Back to Bagdad Goes Al Jolson in Great Success Which at Last Reaches Columbus." *Columbus Dispatch*, September 28, 1920, p. 27)

"Al Jolson stands on a pinnacle of fame all his own, and no one can take his place."("Today's Amusements." *Ohio State Journal*, September 28, 1920, p. 9)

"But after all, the whole point of the matter is that Al Jolson is Al Jolson, and people would laugh at him if he came 10 times in the same show, particularly if he took as great care not to let it deteriorate as he has with 'Sinbad'."(*Ohio State Journal*, March 15, 1921, p. 7)

> **Additional Reviews:** *Buffalo Courier*, January 1, 1920; *Indianapolis News*, November 16, 1920, p. 14; *New York Dramatic News*, February 28, 1918; *New York Evening World*, February 16, 1918; *Theatre*, April 1918, p. 227; *Theatre*, May 1918, p. 316.

Commentary

Sinbad was another stand-out vehicle for Jolson, providing perfect opportunities for his interpolations, which, in this case, included three songs that became Jolson evergreens, "My Mammy," "Rock-A-Bye Your Baby With a Dixie Melody," and "Swanee." During the run of *Sinbad*, Al Goodman became musical conductor for the show, beginning a long professional relationship with Jolson, who preferred Goodman's free-wheeling popular style to the classically-trained musicians leading orchestras of most musical comedies in those times. During the run of *Sinbad*, Jolson made a legendary appearance at a World War I bond rally following opera great Enrico Caruso. After Caruso's singing of George M. Cohan's new patriotic song, "Over There," Jolson strode onstage during the sustained ovation and shouted "You ain't heard nothin' yet!" The thunderous response from the audience to Jolson's audacity lasted longer than the applause for Caruso's entire appearance. While touring with *Sinbad* following the Broadway run, Goodman's infant son became ill when the show was in Boston. Goodman planned to rush back home to New York following a performance. During the show, Jolson had a spot in which he rubbed a magic lamp and made a wish -- usually involving an ad-libbed gag line. When it came time for this bit, Jolson, who had just learned backstage that Goodman's child had died, simply said, "I'm going to make a silent wish." Jolson's demeanor made the sad news clear to Goodman, and Jolson did much to assist Goodman in paying the expenses of the baby's illness and death. On May 18, 1919, also during the Boston run of *Sinbad*, Jolson gave a sell-out one-man recital in the Boston Opera House, undoubtedly one of the first popular music performances in a recognized bastion of classical music.

Opened: October 6, 1921 (Jolson's 59th St., New York) 219 performances

Tryout performances: September 28-October 1, 1921 (Globe, Atlantic City, New Jersey). Toured: April 10, 1922 ((Globe, Atlantic City, New Jersey) through May 31, 1924 (Curran, San Francisco, California).

Credits

A Musical Extravaganza in Two Acts and Fourteen Scenes. Staging: J.C. Huffman. Producers: The Shuberts. Dances: Allan K. Foster. Book and Lyrics: Harold Atteridge. Music: Sigmund Romberg.

Cast

(in order of appearance) Harry Ray (Harry), Durya Rudac (Elsa), Franklyn A. Batie (Paul Marcus), Vera Bayles Cole (Annabelle Downing), Frank Holmes (Jenkins), Russell Mack (Bud Wilson), Mildred Keats (Hazel Downing), Forrest Huff (Jack Christopher), Gladys Caldwell (Patricia Downing), Fred Hall (Count Garibaldi), Fritzi von Busing (Mrs. Downing), Elizabeth Reynolds (Elvira), Grace Keeshon (Inez), Janet Adair (Mona Tessa), Harry Turpin (Red), The Courier (Louis), Jack Kearns (Guisseppo), Thomas Ross (Text), Theodore Hoffman (Context), Irene Hart (Twinkle), Bernice Hart (Twilight), Janette Dietrich (Lois), Frank Bernard (Alfred), Sam Critcherson (Sam Masterson), Elizabeth Reynolds (Mrs. Moore), Al Jolson (Gus), Vivienne Oakland (Rosie). Banditti: Ernest Miller, Dennis Murray, Walter White, Harry Sievers, Edward Pooley. Miss Oakland was subsequently replaced by Ann Mason in 1922.

Synopsis

Once again Jolson is Gus, and again he is thrust into an exotic extravaganza. The plot involves Gus, here an explorer's cook, who winds up in 1492 with Christopher Columbus discovering America. Gus, who also barters with the Indians to buy Manhattan, shoots craps with King Ferdinand and wins himself a dukedom. As with his earlier Winter Garden shows, this musical entertainment permitted Jolson free range in his comedy and singing, with many song interpolations during the run of the show.

Songs

"Life Is a Gamble," "Any Place Will Do With You," "In the Way Off There," "In the Very Next Girl I See," "In Old Grenada," "Jazz-da-dadoo," "No One Loves a Clown," "Rose of Spain," "I'm Glad I'm Spanish," "In a Curio Shop," "Wait Until My Ship Comes In," "My Guiding Star," "A Girl Has a Sailor in Every Port," "Bylo Bay," "Through the Mist," "Wetona." Jolson's songs at various times included: "April Showers," "That Barber in Seville," "Give Me My Mammy," "Down South," "Toot, Toot, Tootsie," "Who Cares?," "Arcady," "I'm Goin' South," "California, Here I Come."

Reviews

"He sings five songs in his fashion -- sings them from a little platform that thrusts him out over the conductor's desk and takes the place of the old runway where he used to prowl. The last of them is another Mammy song. He sang it last night with all the earnestness of a newcomer getting his first hearing on amateur night, sang it with his old-time knee-slapping, breast-beating, eye-rolling ardor, sang it with the faith that moves mountains and audiences. You should have heard them cheer."(Alexander Woollcott, *New York Times*, October 7, 1921, p. 20)

"A rousing big show, [. . .] with Al Jolson to set the pace in fun-making -- surely a combination hard to beat."(*Theatre*, December 1921, Vol. XXXIV, No. 249, p. 424)

"Take any five-star comedians of the Jolson school and no matter how great their vogue it pales before the genius of this little minstrel from the Potomac. He has the seven seals of genuine magnetism in his finger tips. He can sing a ballad with the tonal beauty and grave sympathy that Alma Gluck applies to same and can rag and jazz one of the psalms and not offend because he does it so deliciously. He is tingling with theater, with music and poetry and a sense of gentle emotions but they never romp in and spoil a joke or settle down on his nerves to ruin a good story."(Amy Leslie. "Al Jolson Delights Crowds at Apollo." *Chicago Daily News*, September 20, 1922, p. 19)

"Jolson is the life of the party, as usual, relying on his own festivities to keep the house in continuous haw-haw."("On the Pittsburgh Stage." *Pittsburgh Post*, February 6, 1923)

"Al Jolson's hold on his Chicago public is more than mere popularity; it amounts to idolatry. He rolls his eyes and snaps his fingers and we all lie down and roll over. He sings his songs and tells his stories and we stand up and beg for more."(Margaret Mann Crolius, "Al Jolson's Here in His *Bombo* Show." *Chicago Daily News*, January 7, 1924, p. 4)

"Al Jolson, prince of blackface, master of modern song, and the man who breaks records making records, packed them in, as usual, at the Hartman Theatre last night, in his newest vehicle, *Bombo*. It was Al's first appearance in Columbus in three years, and the audience was Jolson hungry. They ate up his every word, and applauded at every opportunity or at no opportunity at all. They acted, as Al said, *as though they hadn't paid $3.85 to get in*."("Theatres and Movies." *Ohio State Journal*, February 26, 1924, p. 16)

> **Additional Reviews:** *Columbus Evening Dispatch*, February 26, 1924, p. 32; *Indianapolis News*, January 9, 1923, p. 7; *Indianapolis News*, March 7, 1924, p. 7; *New York Clipper*, October 12, 1921, p. 26; *New York Dramatic Mirror*, October 15, 1921, p. 556; *New York Evening World*, October 7, 1921; *New York Globe*, October 7, 1921; *New York Times*, October 30, 1921, Section VI, p. 1; *New York Times*, May 15, 1923, p. 23; *Pittsburgh Post*, February 6, 1923; *Variety*, October 16, 1921, p. 18.

Commentary

The show premiered at a new Shubert theatre named for Jolson. He was the youngest man ever awarded such an honor. Like *Sinbad* (see S23), *Bombo* included, at various times in its Broadway run and on tour, three interpolated songs that became Jolson classics: "April Showers," "California, Here I Come" and "Toot, Toot, Tootsie." One gag in the show involved Jolson and "Columbus" buying Manhattan from the Indians for $24 worth of trinkets. Jolson then exclaimed, "And if you'll give us Brooklyn, we'll throw in a pair of rusty scissors." It is purported that Jolson took thirty-seven curtain calls on the opening night of the show, and the lengthy tour that followed the Broadway run broke box office records around the country.

S25   BIG BOY

Opened: January 7, 1925 (Winter Garden, New York) 48 performances
Reopened: August 24, 1925 (44th Street, New York) 120 performances

Tryout performances: November 24-29, 1924 (Alvin, Pittsburgh, Pennsylvania), November 30-December 6, 1924 (Hanna, Cleveland, Ohio), December 8-13, 1924 (Teck, Buffalo, New York), December 14-20, 1924 (Sam S. Shubert, Cincinnati, Ohio), December 21, 1924-January 3, 1925 (Detroit Opera House, Detroit, Michigan), August 17-22, 1925 (Nixon's Apollo, Atlantic City, New Jersey). Toured: December 7, 1925 (Sam S. Shubert, Newark, New Jersey) through December 3, 1927 (Wieting Opera House, Syracuse, New York).

Credits

A musical comedy in two acts and twelve scenes, based, in part, on Charles T. Dazey's play, *In Old Kentucky*. Staged by J.C. Huffman. Dialogue directed by Alexander Leftwich. Producers: The Shuberts. Dances by Seymour Felix and Larry Ceballos. Book by Harold Atteridge. Music by James F. Hanley and Joseph Meyer. Lyrics by B.G. De Sylva.

Cast

(in order of appearance) Maude Turner Gordon (Mrs. Ella Bradford), Edythe Baker (Phyllis Carter), Hugh Banks (Joe Warren), Flo Lewis (Tessie Forbes), Patti Harrold (Annabelle Bedford), Frank Beaston (Jack Bedford), Ralph Whitehead (Coley Reid), Leo Donnelly (Doc Wilbur), Franklyn A. Batie (Jim Redding), George Gilday (Judkins), Colin Campbell (Steve Leslie), Al Jolson (Gus), Edith Rose-Scott (Caroline Purdy), William L. Thorne (Bully John Bagby), George Spelvin (Silent Ransom), Franklyn A. Batie (Tucker), L.C. Sherman (Manager), William L. Thorne (Wainright), William Bonelli (Legrande), Irving Carter (Danny), Charles Moran (Mr. Gray), Frankie James (Dolly Graham), Charles Moran (Tout), George Andre (Dancer), Dorothy Rudac (Dancer).

Synopsis

In this musical comedy set in the present day on a horse farm in Kentucky, Jolson appeared as Gus for the last time in his stage career (reviving the character only for the film version of this show released in 1930). The plot involves the attempts of some city slickers to rig the Kentucky Derby by replacing Gus as jockey for the Bedford Stables. Gus foils their machinations and rides "Big Boy" to victory in the Derby.

Songs

"Welcome Home," "Born and Bred in Old Kentucky," "Lead 'Em On," "The Day I Rode Half Fare," "Hello 'Tucky," "True Love," "As Long As I've Got My Mammy," "Tap the Toe," "Come on and Play," "The Dance from Down Yonder," "Something for Nothing," "Lackawanna," "Who Was Chasing Paul Revere?," "Cookies and Bookies," "The Race Is Over." At various times during the run and subsequent tours, Jolson interpolated the following songs: "Keep Smiling at Trouble," "If You Knew Susie," "Miami," "Nobody But Fanny," "It All Depends on You," "One O'Clock Baby."

Reviews

"He is all of the old Jolson and something of a new Jolson as well. He sings, both seriously and comically, and included in the song group is a Mammy number, a cheer-up number, and every other kind of number: he tells stories, both in character and out of it (one anecdote having to do with Pola Negri, probably his high point for all time), and, with all of his old skill, he uses his eyes eloquently at the precise moment when the point of a line can be greatly enhanced thereby. A great man in the theatre, Mr. Jolson, and deservedly one of its most popular."(*New York Times*, January 8, 1925, p. 28)

"Jolson had the audience at the Winter Garden Thursday (second) night in the hollow of his hand before he ever stepped on the stage. It was an audience that was on hand to see Jolson and no matter what he did it was great to them. When he came on the stage they were ready for him and the reception that he received almost amounted to a riot."(Fred., *Variety*, January 14, 1925, p. 20)

"Al Jolson has what Broadway wants, and he gives it to them with a zest in this speedy race-track musical comedy. Jolson knows more than any other comedian exactly the sort of material that will go over with a bang. He is master of the sly innuendo, the knowing wink, the sophisticated wisecrack. Everything he says or does meets with almost instant approbation. There is a primitive rhythm about his songs and dances, a punch to his delivery of lines, a gay *camaraderie* about his personality which assures him personal popularity, no matter in what kind of play he appears."(*Theatre*, March 1925, Vol. XL, No. 288, p. 19)

"He was absolutely triumphant on his return; the sceptics and the followers of strange gods fell over themselves recounting his glories. Some of us never doubted at all."(Gilbert Seldes, *Dial*, March 25, 1925, pp. 253-254)

"There is not another entertainer, even among the elect, who is such a one-man power as Al Jolson. The Apollo theater is Al's home and he curtains it with royal colorings of humor and song, affectionate expectations fulfilled immense success and he practically does it alone, though his respect for his fellow players is definite and his selection of comrades in entertainment and clever, handsome, efficient, and even stellar in themselves and Jolson gives them every chance in the world."(Amy Leslie, "Jolson in *Big Boy* Whole Show as Usual." *Chicago Daily News*, December 28, 1925, p. 17)

"For gutsy, full-throated ribaldry and galvanic animation, few American comedians can approach Mr. Al Jolson."(D.W.B., "Black-Face Regnant, Jolson Triumphant -- And a Show Besides." *Boston Transcript*, September 14, 1926)

"That prince of entertainment, Mammy's own boy, Al Jolson, last night held a Hartman audience in the hollow of his hand and juggled it about until that self-same audience nearly fainted with joy. The show was continued for possibly an extra 20 minutes while Al added extra songs and called on extra performances from members of the company. *Big Boy* is the name of the show, and it means a race horse, but if it doesn't also mean Jolson, then that's a horse on us."(H.E. Cherrington, "Mammy's Favorite Boy, Jolson, Draws Capacity." *Columbus Evening Dispatch*, March 22, 1927, p. 34)

"Whistles and shouts from the gallery kept Al long after equity hours. And he stayed on by popular vote. Whenever he made an exit the audience howled to get him back and there you are."(Nelson Budd, "Theatres and Movies." *Ohio State Journal*, March 22, 1927, p. 5)

> **Additional Reviews:** *American Mercury*, March 1925, Vol. 4, pp. 375-376; *Indianapolis News*, March 25, 1927, p. 3; *New York American*, 1925; *New York Evening Post*, 1925; *New York Evening Sun*, 1925; *Prosaic News*, December 5, 1925; *World*, 1925.

Commentary

Big Boy was a major success, but was forced to close prematurely due to Jolson's chronic laryngitis. When he recovered, the show reopened briefly on Broadway, and then toured extensively. This show became the basis for Jolson's 1930 film *Big Boy* (see F7). The tour broke box office records in Chicago, and one famous story involves Jolson and Eddie Cantor both continuing to play at rival theatres in Chicago despite the fact that they were both suffering from pleurisy and bronchitis. Each of them refused to close his respective show, fearing *Variety* headlines suggesting that the other had driven him out of town. Jolson continued until Cantor finally closed his show. When Jolson finally did close his tour due to illness, rumors circulated, and were published in several newspapers, that he was dead or on the verge of death. Shortly thereafter, he appeared in the Shubert production *Artists and Models* (see S26) for a limited run, and was clearly back in top form.

S26   *ARTISTS AND MODELS*

Opened: June 24, 1925 (Winter Garden, New York) 411 performances

Jolson appeared in this popular revue as a guest star in celebration of the fifteenth anniversary of the Winter Garden from March 20-April 24, 1926.

Credits

Director: Alexander Leftwich. Producers: The Shuberts. Music: Alfred Goodman, J. Fred Coots, Maurie Rubens. Lyrics: Clifford Grey. Sketches: Harold Atteridge, Harry Wagstaff Gribble. Choreography: Jack Haskell. Scene Designer: Watson Barratt.

Cast

Phil Baker, Sid Silvers, Brennan and Rogers, Walter Woolf, The Gertrude Hoffman Girls.

Synopsis

An edition of the annual Shubert review featuring "artistic" sequences of nude chorus girls in tableau.

Songs

"Mothers of the World," "Cellini's Dream," "Pastels," "Rotisserie Number," "Maid of the Milky Way," "The Lily Pool," "The Promenade Walk," "Jazz a la Russe," "Poi Ball." While Jolson appeared in the show, he featured a selection of his standards.

Reviews

"A revue of particularly outstanding excellence came to the Winter Garden last night. It is *Artists and Models, Paris Edition.*"(*New York Times*, June 25, 1925, p. 16)

"The Bombo of Broadway indulged in his antics of yore. He stood on his little platform over the piano and chaffed the orchestra, talked tritely about himself, told a funny story, grinned coyly at the roar of amusement, gave a Bowery whistle to command silence, told another, said *You ain't heard nothin' yet!* and then became himself, singing *Hello Kentucky.*"("Al Jolson Returns." *New York Sun*, March 22, 1926.)

> **Additional Reviews:** *Boston Transcript*, March 24, 1926; *New York Times*, June 17, 1925, p. 16; *Survey*, March 1, 1926, p. 632; *Theatre*, September 1925, pp. 3, 15.

Commentary

On Jolson's first night in the production, he sang seven songs, including "Always," "Keep Smiling at Trouble," "Nobody But Fanny," "Hello 'Tucky," "I'm Sitting on Top of the World," and "Who Wants a Bad Little Boy?" He was scheduled to perform for fifteen minutes, but stayed on for nearly three quarters of an hour due to the enthusiastic response of the audience. Sid Silvers, one of the stars of the production, can be seen in the 1929 Warner Bros. film *The Show of Shows* doing an imitation of Jolson singing "Rock-a-bye Your Baby With a Dixie Melody."

S27   A NIGHT IN SPAIN

Opened: May 3, 1927 (44th Street, New York) 174 performances

Jolson appeared in this popular revue as a guest star from March 11-April 7, 1928 while the production was on tour in Chicago, Illinois at the Four Cohans Theatre.

Credits

Director: Charles Judels. Producers: Messrs. Shubert. Libretto: Harold Atteridge. Music: Jean Schwartz. Lyrics: Al Bryan. Choreography: Ralph Reader, Allan K. Foster and Gertrude Hoffman. Scene Design: Watson Barratt.

Cast

Phil Baker, Ted and Betty Healy, Grace Hayes, Norma Terris, Brennan and Rogers, Helen Kane, Cortez and Peggy, The Gertrude Hoffman Girls.

Synopsis

An annual Shubert revue, this edition of the "A Night in. . ." series emphasized

Spanish motifs.

Songs

"My Rose of Spain," "A Spanish Shawl," "Hot, Hot Honey." Jolson performed an array of his standards during his appearance with the production.

Reviews

". . .an exceedingly lively and merry revue."(*New York Times*, May 4, 1927, p. 28)

"It is a spectacular production with the scenic effects in the conventional manner of all such shows. Unfortunately, gorgeous and lavish in expenditure as these effects are, they are not shown to their best advantage, being switched on and off with a quickness that gave one no time to take in the whole scene."(*New York Times*, July 3, 1927, Section VIII, p. 1)

"Partly because he loves to sing it and partly because his audience always insists Jolson again sings *Mammy* with the well-known catch in the voice which brings a corresponding clutch to everybody's throat. The jokes are Jolson's brand and from him they never seem vulgar. Not even the one about the tattooed girl in the museum with whom Jolson was once in love and what happened to the tattooed pictures when the girl took on weight or the one about the Swiss chambermaid or any of the others."(Margaret Mann Crolius, "Jolson Revivifies *A Night in Spain*; Walks Away With Show, Making It Seem Something Written for Him." *Chicago Daily News*, March 12, 1928, p. 13)

"And there were songs, of course. One, *Golden Gate*, sounded as if written by the Japanese minister in charge of American colonization; but, then, all pro-California songs sound like that. The point here is that Mr. Jolson sang it as if he believed it; and that is why he puts through and across more songs than any other living singer. Another was named *Four Walls*, and was the sort wherewith he can simply shake his old heart to pieces; and then, as if it had been the newest ditty in all the world last night, he sang *Mammy*, and had them cheering before he took the high note at the end. Yes: he still is the best, the most effective, and the most successful entertainer on this or any earth!"(F.D., "Theater." *Chicago Daily Tribune*, March 12, 1928, p. 25)

> **Additional Reviews:** *Life*, May 26, 1928, p. 20; *New York Times*, May 22, 1927, Section VIII, p. 1; *Theatre*, July 1927, p. 20; *Vogue*, July 1, 1927, p. 63.

Commentary

According to a March 11, 1928 *New York Times* report, Jolson was paid in excess of $40,000 for a four-week run of performances in the Chicago production of *A Night in Spain*. Jolson replaced Phil Baker who had become ill and was unable to continue in the production. Jolson's appearance in this show took place following the first success of his film *The Jazz Singer* (see F2) and before shooting began on his follow-up movie, *The Singing Fool* (see F3). While in Chicago for his appearances in *A Night in Spain*, Jolson saw Ruby Keeler for the first time in a stage show, *The Sidewalks of New York*. He actually met her a few weeks later in California where he was filming *The Singing Fool*.

S28   THE WONDER BAR

Opened: March 17, 1931 (Nora Bayes, New York) 76 performances

Tryout performances: March 5-7, 1931 (Belasco, Washington, D.C.), March 9-14, 1931 (Sam S. Shubert, New Haven, Connecticut). Toured: September 28, 1931 (Sam S. Shubert, Newark, New Jersey) through April 9, 1932 (Curran, San Francisco, California).

Credits

A Continental Novelty of European Night Life in two sections. Staged by William Mollison. Producers: The Shuberts. Book by Irving Caesar, based on Aben Kandel's adaptation of the German *Vunderbar* of Geta Herczeg and Karl Farkas. Music by Robert Katscher and Rowland Leigh. Lyrics by Irving Caesar.

Cast

(in order of appearance) Gustav Rolland (Richard), Auguste Armini (Marcel), Nikolos Engalitcheff (Prince Nikolas Engalitcheff), Jean Newcombe (Mary Evans), C. Jay Williams (Elmer Evans), Antonina Fechner (Sonya), Dagmar Oakland (Billie), Andriana Dori (Rosette), Elvira Trabert (Martha), Laura Pierpont (Helen Brown), Henry Crosby (Edgar Banks), Al Jolson (Monsieur Al Wonder), Trini (Inez), Rex O'Malley (Ramon Colmano), Arthur Treacher (Lord Caldwell), Stuart Casey (François Vale), Clarence Harvey (Oscar Wayne), Wanda Lyon (Liane Duval), Vernon Steele (Pierre Duval), Roman Arnoldoff (A Gendarme), Adrian Rosley (Monsieur Simon), Patsy Kelly (Electra Pivonka), Al Siegal (Charlie), Mohammed Ibrahim (A Rajah), Michael Daimatoff (Count Rugtoffsky), Medea Columbara (Signora Medea Columbara), Hugo Brucken (Benno Bondy), Bertha Walden (Mrs. Solomon), Leo Hoyt (Sam Solomon), Armand Crotez (Pascal), Marie Hunt (Baroness Rosseau).

Synopsis

Jolson appeared without blackface as Monsieur Al, proprietor of a modern Parisian night club, The Wonder Bar. Monsieur Al performs in the nightclub while attempting to keep backstage scandals, and particularly the conniving of the male half of a dance team, from spilling onto the stage.

Songs

"Good Evening, Friends," "Oh, Donna Clara," "I'm Falling in Love," "Ma Mere," "Lenox Avenue," "Elizabeth, My Queen," "Something Seems to Tell Me," "A Chazend'l Ohf Shabbes."

Reviews

"Naturally Jolson dominates the whole performance. A new Al Jolson has come to town -- not the same Al Jolson that starred in *Sinbad the Sailor*, not Al Jolson, the mammy singer -- save that he does put over a French and Russian version of the old heart-throbbers. It is an Al Jolson now, removed from the films, who stands out as a combination actor and concert singer, and blending into a legitimate portrait. [. . .] with Al Jolson at the height of his powers."(Daly, *Variety*, March 11, 1931, p. 62)

"But Mr. Jolson remains king of the singing fools. It is five years, the public accountants say, since he last appeared on the legitimate stage. Along toward 9:15, he comes bounding down the aisle and leaps to the stage, and presently he is singing *Good Evening, Friends* will all the joyous abandon of the old *Artists and Models* days. Everyone knows the Jolson formula; most of the musical hall minstrels like to imitate it, and imitate it well. But it is Jolson's personal formula, and what warms the audience is the beam and excitement of his personality."(J. Brooks Atkinson, *New York Times*, March 18, 1931)

"He is as good at all this as ever."(Richard Lockridge, *New York Sun*, March 18, 1931)

"And I must say that Monsieur Al est tout, the whole show. Monsieur Al and the atmosphere."(Gilbert W. Gabriel, *New York American*, March 19, 1931)

"Al Jolson is everywhere: as host he can no more forget to flatter and make merry, than he can forget what his customers are really like.   He and the other entertainers are, incidentally, very good review artists."(Francis Fergusson, "A Month of the Theatre." *Bookman*, June 1931, p. 409)

"Last night he had a new repose without surrendering any of that old spellbinding magnetism. He was on the stage more minutes than in any of his revues in my memory, yet not once did he mop his brow. He rushed out into the auditorium at the start of the evening to shake hands with newcomers, a la Raymond Hitchcock; he talked incessantly, and very comically, too, at times, but he was somehow less hectic than of yore. His two descents into the old maudlinity came at the end of the evening and then only at the insistence of an extremely Sonny Boy-ish audience. His admirers wanted *Mammy* and the dead baby song, so he gave both to them, finger in mouth, sobs and all. But he succumbed with the reluctance of a reformed tipster lured by friends into a recognized vice, and thereby begot the compassion rather than scorn of the *Sonny Boy* haters."(Lloyd Lewis, "*The Wonder Bar* Is All Jolson; New Play Is Brought to Apollo." *Chicago Daily News*, December 26, 1931, p. 7)

"He chatters in the good old Jolsonian style, letting the laughs come where they may -- and they are almost incessant. He puts on his show, which contains some highly diverting variety acts. He sings, of course, early and often; and about 10:45 he breaks loose with a typical Jolson rapid-fire concert of popular anthems. He keeps everything moving fluently, including the plot, which deals with the perils of playing with gigolos, when a lady is young, lovely and suspicious of her husband."(Charles Collins, "The Stage." *Chicago Daily Tribune*, December 26, 1931, p. 13)

Additional Reviews: *Boston Daily Telegram*, October 6, 1931; *Drama*, May 1931, p. 6; *Indianapolis News*, February 12, 1932, p. 8; *Life*, April 17, 1931, p. 20; *New York Daily Telegraph*, March 19, 1931; *New York Herald Tribune*, March 19, 1931; *New York Herald Tribune*, May 11, 1931; *New York Times*, March 8, 1931, Section VIII, p. 3; *New York Times*, March 22, 1931, Section VIII, p. 1; *New York Times*, June 2, 1931, p. 35; *Theatre Arts*, May 1931, pp. 366-367; *Vanity Fair*, June 1931, p. 52; *Variety*, March 25, 1931, p. 62.

Commentary

This production was presented on an open stage creating the illusion of an actual nightclub, thanks to the willingness of the Shuberts to convert New York's Nora Bayes Theatre for this purpose. One anecdote involves a well-known member of Jolson's supporting cast. In one scene, Jolson was supposed to fire a shot gun at comedienne Patsy Kelly, a close friend of Jolson's wife Ruby Keeler, in her "Dance of the Dying Flamingo." One night, Jolson put real buckshot in the gun -- he later apologized to Kelly and sent her a gift. On tour, a misunderstanding led to Kelly being fired -- when she had asked someone backstage for a cigarette, she was handed a marijuana cigarette instead. When she went onstage disoriented, Jolson furiously fired her. Later, following explanations and an appeal from Actors Equity, Kelly rejoined the cast. A few years later, Kelly would play a small comic role in Jolson's and Keeler's 1935 film, *Go Into Your Dance* (see F11). Thirty-five years later, Kelly would appear with Keeler in the hugely successful Broadway revival of *No, No, Nanette* (1970). For her hilarious comic performance, Kelly won the 1971 Tony Award as Best Supporting Actress in a Musical.

S29 *HOLD ON TO YOUR HATS*

Opened: September 11, 1940 (Sam S. Shubert, New York) 158 performances

Tryout performances: June 30-July 13, 1940 (Cass, Detroit, Michigan), July 15-August 24, 1940 (Grand Opera House, Chicago, Illinois), August 27-September 7, 1940 (Forrest, Philadelphia, Pennsylvania). Toured: August 27, 1941 (Garden Pier, Atlantic City, New Jersey) through November 8, 1941 (Hartman, Columbus, Ohio).

Credits

A musical comedy in two acts and thirteen scenes. Staged by Edgar J. MacGregor. Producers: George Hale and Al Jolson. Book by Guy Bolton, Matt Brooks, and Eddie Davis. Music by Burton Lane. Lyrics by E.Y. "Yip" Harburg. Sets: Raoul Pene du Bois. Dances by Catherine Littlefield.

Cast

(in order of appearance) Margaret Irving (Sierra), Gil Lamb (Slim), George Church (Lon), Jack Whiting (Pete), Martha Raye (Mamie), Jinx Falkenburg (First Dudette), Joyce Matthews (Second Dudette), Thea Pinto (Third Dudette), Lew Eccles (Sheriff), Arnold Moss (Fernando), Al Jolson (The Lone Rider), John Randolph (Radio Announcer), Joe Stoner (Shep Martin), Marty Drake (Old Man Hawkins), Bert Gordon (Concho), George Maran (Sound Effects), Russ Brown (Dinky), Ruby Keeler (Shirley), Sid Cassel (Luis), Will Kuluva (Pedro), Jinx Falkenburg (Rita). Tanner Sisters: Betty Tanner, Martha Tanner, Mickie Tanner. Radio Aces: Marty Drake, Joe Stoner, Lou Stoner. Ranchettes: Margie Greene, Anita Jakobi, Iris Wayne, Janie Williams. Ruby Keeler left the cast before the Broadway opening and was replaced by Eunice Healy on July 29, 1940.

Synopsis

Jolson plays a timid radio singing cowboy, The Lone Rider, who is convinced by his scriptwriter to head west to a Sunshine Valley ranch and to attempt to capture a notorious Mexican bandit, Fernando. The Western and Mexican settings provided ample opportunity for song, dance and clowning, and through a series of elaborate and outrageous coincidences, the Lone Rider actually manages to capture the bandit before the curtain falls.

Songs

"Way Out West Where the East Begins," "Hold On to Your Hats," "Walkin' Along, Mindin' My Business," "The World is in My Arms," "Would You Be So Kindly?," Life Was Pie for the Pioneer," "Don't Let it Get You Down," "There's a Great Day Coming Manana," "Then You Were Never in Love," "Down on the Old Dude Ranch," "She Came, She Saw, She Can-Canned," "Old Timer." In a broadcast scene late in the show Jolson interpolated some of his greatest numbers.

Reviews

"Instead of holding on to my hat I want to take it off and make a deep salaam in the direction of Al Jolson. For he has made Chicago's summer brighter in this troubled year, not only by bringing his own tonic presence back to our stage but also in surrounding himself with a brilliant, entertaining, and superbly mounted show. [. . .] Altho[sic] he admitted, to good-natured jeers of derision from the audience, that he is now at least 41, Al Jolson is still one of the greatest entertainers of the American stage. His instantaneous gift for making friends with his entire audience puts every one in a receptive mood from the first and thruout[sic] the evening he holds the audience in the hollow of his hand. His acting, to be sure, bears the marks of the seasoned old-time vaudevillian, and his singing is not without a dash of bathos. But how perfectly these old-timers learned their craft!"(Cecil Smith, "Jolson Brings His Show to Liven Up City." *Chicago Daily Tribune*, July 16, 1940, p. 13)

"Two things stopped the show last evening. One was a slip of the tongue. In the frenzy of the moment Miss Raye found herself complimenting Al for *saving the Jews* instead of *the jewels*, which was the word the book called for, and the confusion that resulted turned into comic hysteria. The other was *Down on the Dude Ranch* as sung by Al, Miss Raye and Bert Gordon. A burlesque ballad with some wonderful satiric lines, it is sung with great relish by an inspired trio of comedians, and might have gone on for a half hour if the verses had held out."(Brooks Atkinson, *New York Times*, September 12, 1940, p. 30)

"Hollywood seems not to have changed Al Jolson. Certainly he has not become slothful or lazy. His feet travel as rapidly and lightly as ever. He still throws his entire frame into every song he sings, shaking the words out of him in paroxysms of energy as in the old days, and he still projects his personality to the top row of the galleries."(Sidney B. Whipple, "*Hold On To Your Hats* Has Old-Time Jolson Flavor." *New York World-Telegram*, September 12, 1940)

"Jolson remains one of our peerless entertainers; his impromptu finale, a honey any way you look at it, conclusively proves that, and in *Hold On to Your Hats* he has a bright and gay and witty musical play, far better than the *Wonder Bar* on which he bowed out back when the decade was young. His reception last night was an amazing tribute to a sentimental jester and Al responded with everything he had, which was far more than adequate and then some."(Karl Krug, *Pittsburgh Sun-Telegraph*, October 7, 1941)

". . .but for the most part, the role he plays is the role of Al Jolson, singer and entertainer. And nobody would have it any other way. Talents like his are too rare, if not altogether non-existent, to be strapped to the limitations of a character. And so his Lone Rider is just a prefunctory non de plume[sic] for the world's greatest entertainer who continues to look in the eye any song you can name and make it say uncle -- or in this case mammy."(Harold V. Cohen, *Pittsburgh Post-Gazette*, October 7, 1941)

"All that mattered all evening was that Jolson was back. If the demon that Gilbert Seldes said possessed him seemed to be driving him less hard than it once did, if the Jolson voice was less clarion than it was not so long ago, Al still was back putting on as fine a one-man show as ever he did, selling songs as no one else has been able to do in his generation, in short doing all the things for which he is famous as only he can do them and adding a rowdy female impersonation to the lot."(Samuel T. Wilson, "Al Jolson Is Back and In Top Form." *Columbus Dispatch*, November 7, 1941, p. 18)

> **Additional Reviews:** *Billboard*, October 1941; *Boston Post*, September 1, 1941; *Catholic World*, November 1940, pp. 218-219; *Life*, July 29, 1940, pp. 60-62; *Nation*, September 28, 1940, pp. 281-282; *New York Daily Mirror*, September 12, 1940; *New York Daily News*, September 12, 1940; *New York Herald Tribune*, September 12, 1940; *New York Journal-American*, September 12, 1940; *New York Post*, September 12, 1940; *New York Sun*, September 12, 1940; *New York Times*, July 17, 1940, p. 25; *New York Times*, July 21, 1940, Section IX, p. 1; *New York Times*, September 29, 1940, Section IX, p. 1; *New York Times*, October 20, 1940, Section IX, p. 3; *Newsweek*, September 26, 1940; *Ohio State Journal*, November 7, 1941, p. 10; *Stage*, December 1940, p. 12; *Theatre Arts*, November 1940, pp. 770-773; *Time*, September 23, 1940, p. 41; *Variety*, September 18, 1940, p. 42.

Commentary

One chorine who auditioned for this show was Pearl Goldberg (later Sieben), Jolson's first biographer. She was rejected on the first round of selections. A chorine who did make it into the cast was Jinx Falkenburg, a model who would date Jolson during the production. Audiences were plentiful and enthusiastic, and even the most hardened critics responded with the fervor of life-long Jolson fans. Jolson's unhappy years in Hollywood during the late 1930's may have been washed away by this triumphant return to the stage. On opening night in New York, Jolson stopped the show repeatedly in a scene in which he interpolated a series of his musical standards, including "Swanee," "April Showers," "You Made Me Love You," "Sonny Boy," and "My Mammy." Despite a solid score, these interpolations, and Jolson's heartfelt performance of them, were the highlights of *Hold On to Your Hats*. But the cold weather in New York held little appeal for Jolson, and despite large audiences, Jolson closed the show for a prolonged rest before taking the show out on a short tour which ended in November 1941 in Columbus, Ohio -- an inauspicious ending to Jolson's stage career.

Eugenie Besserer, Al Jolson, and Warner Oland in *The Jazz Singer* (1927). Permission of Turner Entertainment.

4

Film

The following films include performances by Al Jolson or recordings of his voice. The first group includes only feature films, with Jolson's short films listed in a separate group at the end.

Feature Films

F1   *BLACK MAGIC* (Other titles: *Black and White, Mammy's Boy*)

1923. D. W. Griffith. B&W (unfinished)

__Commentary__
The plot of this film involves a young white lawyer who disguises himself as a black man to solve a murder case. Jolson began this film under the direction of the great D.W. Griffith, but after being shown some of the early footage, he became so dissatisfied that he withdrew and sailed for Europe. Griffith sued Jolson unsuccesfully. None of the footage is thought to survive. Several years later Griffith made the film without Jolson.

F2   *THE JAZZ SINGER*

1927. Warner Bros.-Vitaphone Corporation. B&W (partial sound). 89 mins.

__Credits__
Director: Alan Crosland. Producer: Jack L. Warner. Scenario: Alfred A. Cohn, based on the play by Samson Raphaelson, from Raphaelson's short story, *The Day of Atonement*. Title Design: Jack Jarmuth. Photography: Hal Mohr. Editing: Harold McCord. Assistant Director: Gordon Hollingshead. Technicians: Fred Jackman, Lewis Geib, Esdras Hartley, F.N. Murphy, "Alpharetta," Victor Vance. Orchestra conducted by Louis Silvers.

__Cast__
Al Jolson (Jakie Rabinowitz, later Jack Robin), May McAvoy (Mary Dale), Warner Oland (Cantor Rabinowitz), Eugenie Besserer (Sara Rabinowitz), Otto Lederer (Moshe Yudelson), Cantor Rosenblatt (Cantor Josef Rosenblatt), Bobby Gordon (Jakie Rabinowitz, 13 years old), Richard

Tucker (Harry Lee), Nat Carr (Levi), William Demarest (Buster Billings), Anders Randolf (Randolph Dillings), Will Walling (Doctor), Myrna Loy (First Chorus Girl), Audrey Ferris (Second Chorus Girl), Jane Arden, Violet Bird, Ernest Clauson, Marie Stapleton, Edna Gregory, Margaret Oliver (Extras in Coffee Dan's sequence), Joseph Diskay dubbed vocals for Warner Oland. Bert Fiske played the piano for Al Jolson.

Synopsis

Jolson plays Jakie Rabinowitz, the son of a Lower East Side New York cantor (well-played by Oland, the screen's "Charlie Chan") who disapproves of his son's wish to become a "jazz singer." Jakie runs away from home and becomes a performer singing in nightclubs, cabarets and musical shows. His heartbroken parents carry on their orthodox lives acting as though they have no son. When Jakie returns home as Jack Robin, a budding star on the brink of Broadway success, his father is unable to accept him, to the great distress of Jack's long-suffering mother (Besserer). Cantor Rabinowitz becomes seriously ill, forcing Jack to decide between his big chance in a Broadway opening and winning the girl he loves (McAvoy) or pleasing his dying father by singing "Kol Nidre" on Yom Kippur. An overwrought Jack opts to sing for his father on the Day of Atonement. After some time passes, Jack returns to the stage and achieves stardom as his girl and his widowed mother look on approvingly.

Songs

"My Gal Sal," "Waiting for the Robert E. Lee," "Dirty Hands! Dirty Face!," "Toot, Toot, Tootsie," "Yahrzeit," "Blue Skies," "Mother of Mine, I Still Have You," "Kol Nidre," "My Mammy."

Reviews

"Mr. Jolson's persuasive vocal efforts were received with rousing applause. In fact, not since the first presentation of Vitaphone features, more than a year ago at the same playhouse, has anything like the ovation been heard in a picture theatre. And when the film came to an end Mr. Jolson himself expressed his sincere appreciation of the Vitaphoned film, declaring that he was so happy that he could not stop the tears."(Mordaunt Hall, *New York Times*, October 7, 1927, p. 24)

"Jolson in *The Jazz Singer* is surefire for Broadway. With his songs that holds good for any town or street. Exclude Vitaphone and there crops up the problem that it amounts to a Jewish mother-son-religious story with Jolson not yet enough the screen actor to carry it."(Sid., *Variety*, October 12, 1927, p. 16)

"There is, of course, but one Jolson and he made the Jakie Rabinowitz who ran away from his orthodox father's house and became a cabaret singer, a very real young man, the choice between duty and a career a difficult matter. The Vitaphone did a great deal to help, producing the songs and some of the other sounds in the course of the action. Aside from the wonderful Jolson there are other fine actors in the cast."(Carl Sandburg, "The Jazz Singer." *Chicago Daily News*, November 30, 1927)

"Al Jolson with Vitaphone noises. Jolson is no movie actor. Without his Broadway reputation, he wouldn't rate as a minor player. The only interest in the picture is his six songs. The story is a fairly good tear-jerker about a Jewish boy who prefers jazz to the songs of his race. In the end, he returns to the fold and sings *Kol Nidre* on the Day of Atonement. It's the best scene in the film."(*Photoplay*, December 1927)

"Jolson is every bit the actor in this colorful narrative, so much so that one smiles at the recollection of his having run off to Europe when shown some of the photography in an earlier picture he never finished. His Jack Robin (Jakie Rabinowitz on the East Side) is sufficiently emotional to fit the part, and when he sings, via Vitaphone, the audiences applaud as heartily as though he was there in person."("Jolson At Best in *Jazz Singer*." *Detroit Free Press*, December 28, 1927)

"*The Jazz Singer* definitely establishes the fact that talking pictures are imminent. Everyone in Hollywood can rise up and declare that they are not, and it will not alter the fact. If I were an actor with a squeaky voice I would worry. There is one scene in *The Jazz Singer* that conclusively sounds the knell of the silent picture: that showing Jolson at the piano, playing idly and talking to his mother. It is one of the most beautiful scenes I have ever seen on a screen."(Welford Beaton, *Film Spectator*, February 4, 1928, Vol. 4, No. 12, p. 7)

> **Additional Reviews:** *Boston Transcript*, October 1927; *Close-Up*, February 1929, pp. 37-38; *Cosmopolitan*, August 1946, p. 51; *Film Daily*, October 23, 1927, p. 6; *Life*, October 27, 1927, Vol. 90; *London Times*, September 28, 1928; *Motion Picture*, January 1928, p. 55; *Moving Picture World*, October 22, 1927, p. 514; *New York Herald Tribune*, October 7, 1927; *New York Times*, August 28, 1927, Section VII, p. 4; *New York Times*, October 16, 1927, Section IX, p. 7; *New York Times*, September 28, 1928, p. 8; *New York Times*, March 8, 1936, Section IX, p. 5; *New York World*, October 7, 1927; *Photoplay*, March 1928; *Picture Play*, January 1928; *Time*, October 17, 1927, p. 27; *Times* (London), September 28, 1928; *Variety*, October 12, 1927, p. 16; *Variety*, April 1, 1931, p. 12.

Commentary

The Jazz Singer has been referred to as "the first talking picture" for so long that it is probably futile to point out that it was by no means the first. Various experiments with sound had been made since the virtual beginning of films in the 1890's, although few experiments inspired much enthusiasm from filmmakers or audiences. Jolson himself had even appeared in a sound short, *April Showers* (or *Al Jolson in a Plantation Act*) (see F27), a year before *The Jazz Singer* was made. Other sound shorts from the early 1920's survive. Also, in 1926, Warner Bros., in partnership with the Vitaphone Corporation, had released *Don Juan*, starring John Barrymore, which featured a synchronized musical score and sound effects, but included no spoken dialogue. Although it was not "the first talking picture," *The Jazz Singer* was clearly the first sound film to capture the general public's imagination, largely due to Jolson's participation, and movie-making would never be the same. *The Jazz Singer* was based on a short story, "The Day of Atonement," by Samson Raphaelson. As a stage play, Jolson's pal George Jessel had scored a major success in it and was still touring with it at the time of the film's premiere. Many versions of how Jolson got the role instead of Jessel abound, and Jessel remained bitter about it until the end of his life. However, it is clear that Jessel turned down Warner Bros. offer to do the film (as did Eddie Cantor), and the role went to Jolson who had been willing to accept Warner Bros. stock in lieu of some of his salary (at the time, Jolson's salary was reported at $75,000, plus stock). *The Jazz Singer* was given a special award at the first Academy Awards ceremony on May 16, 1929 at the Hollywood Roosevelt Hotel. Jolson accepted the statuette. The film also received two nominations: Writing (Adaptation) and Engineering Effects. In 1972 the Performing Arts Council of the University of Southern California asked a panel of film producers and critics to name the most significant American films in history. *The Jazz Singer* was listed in twelfth place. A sound promotional trailer survives showing silent footage of the New York premiere along with some excerpts from the film. So far, there have been two remakes of *The Jazz Singer*, both retaining the title. The first, and best, of the remakes appeared in 1953. It featured Danny Thomas in Jolson's role, with Eduard Franz and Mildred Dunnock as his parents, and Peggy Lee as his girlfriend. A very poor third version in 1980, starred Neil Diamond in Jolson's part, Laurence Olivier as his father, and Lucie Arnaz as his wife (replacing the mother role). Neither remake equals the original, despite the primitive techniques used in 1927.

F3   THE SINGING FOOL

1928. Warner Bros.-Vitaphone Corporation. B&W (partial sound). 105 mins.

Credits
Director: Lloyd Bacon. Scenario: Joseph Jackson, C. Graham Baker, from a story by Leslie S. Barrows. Assistant Director: Frank Shaw. Photography: Byron Haskin. Editors: Ralph Dawson, Harold McCord. Technicians: Lewis Geib, Esdras Hartley, F.N. Murphy, Victor Vance.

Cast
Al Jolson (Al Stone), Betty Bronson (Grace Farrell), Josephine Dunn (Molly Winton), Davey Lee (Sonny Boy), Reed Howes (John Perry), Edward Martindel (Marcus), Arthur Houseman (Blackie Joe), Robert Emmett O'Connor (Billy Cline), Helen Lynch (Maid), Agnes Franey (Chorus Girl).

Synopsis
The plot involves a singing waiter, Al Stone (Jolson), in love with a two-timing nightclub singer, Molly Winton (Dunn). When she sees that he is her ticket to fame and fortune, Molly consents to marry Al. He becomes a successful songwriter and performer and she a Broadway star, and they have a child, Sonny Boy (Lee, in a memorable performance). But the faithless Molly leaves Stone, taking his beloved Sonny Boy with her, and Al goes into a tailspin, quickly hitting rock bottom. The fast-moving first half of the film gives way to the sentimentalized second half tracing Stone's return to stage success with the support of Grace (Bronson), who has always loved him. Tragedy strikes unexpectedly when Al learns that Sonny Boy is seriously ill. He rushes to the hospital and comforts his son by singing "Sonny Boy" as the child dies quietly in his arms. In a daze, he returns to the theatre where he is forced to perform the very same song before an audience. He struggles pitifully until he sees a vision of Sonny Boy encouraging him. Al manages to finish the song, collapsing in grief in Grace's arms as the film ends.

Songs

"It All Depends on You," "I'm Sitting on Top of the World," "The Spaniard That Blighted My Life," "There's a Rainbow 'Round My Shoulder," "Golden Gate," "Sonny Boy," "Keep Smiling at Trouble."

Reviews

"Mr. Jolson's first rendition is called *It All Depends on You*, and after his shadow delivered this song one not only heard the applause from the screen, but virtually every pair of hands in the packed house was doing yeoman work. Then one heard this Al Stone sing *I'm Sitting on Top of the World*, which pleased the gathering equally well."(Mordaunt Hall, *New York Times*, September 20, 1928, p. 21)

"To say that here are Al Jolson and his songs on the screen, is to say that *The Singing Fool* will do what Jolson's *Jazz Singer* did -- make gold."(*Variety*, September 26, 1928, p. 14)

"Al Jolson surpasses himself. This is a better picture than *The Jazz Singer*, and it is guaranteed to pull your heart strings when you *hear* Jolson singing *Sonny Boy*."(*Photoplay*, October 1928)

"The secret of it, of course, is not the material but the amazing vitality of the actor, which can not only permeate such well-thumbed stuff but can make it emotionally effective. Through the screen and the Vitaphone he [Jolson] makes himself felt almost as he does from the stage."("The Mammies' Master-Singer." *Boston Evening Transcript*, October 22, 1928)

> **Additional Reviews:** *Film Daily*, September 23, 1928, p. 6; *Film Daily*, July 7, 1929, p. 8; *Life*, October 5, 1928, p. 28; *Los Angeles Evening Express*, October 13, 1928; *New York Times*, September 23, 1928, Section IX, p. 5; *Outlook*, October 3, 1928, p. 904; *Providence News*, January 14, 1929; *Spectator*, December 8, 1928, p. 141.

Commentary

Although *The Jazz Singer* is considered the film that made the breakthrough for sound movies, *The Singing Fool*, Jolson's second partial talkie, was the sound era's first blockbuster. *The Singing Fool* grossed approximately $4,000,000 at the box office, a record for its era. Jolson filmed a one reel trailer announcement plugging the film which was copyrighted on September 22, 1928. The film was so popular that it spawned a series of movies attempting to duplicate its popularity by tapping into the same basic elements of story and character. Some of these imitators include: *Sonny Boy* (1929), featuring Jolson's *The Singing Fool* co-stars, Davey Lee and Betty Bronson; *My Man* (1929), Fanny Brice's first starring film; *Mother's Boy* (1929), with Morton Downey; *Honky-Tonk* (1929), Sophie Tucker's film debut; *Not Quite Decent* (1929), with Jolson's *Mammy* (see F6) co-star, Louise Dresser; *The Rainbow Man* (1929), with Frankie Darro and Jolson's *Say It With Songs* (see F4) co-star, Marian Nixon; *Lucky Boy* (1930), starring George Jessel; and Jolson's own follow-up film, *Say It With Songs* (see F4). *Sonny Boy* is often listed among Jolson's credits in film encyclopedias, but he did not act in this film. Footage is glimpsed from *The Singing Fool* (see F3), and in one scene, little Davey Lee enters a movie theatre where it is playing and imitates Jolson.

F4   SAY IT WITH SONGS

1929. Warner Bros.-Vitaphone Corporation. B&W. 95 mins.

Credits

Director: Lloyd Bacon. Screenplay: Joseph Jackson, from a story by Darryl
Zanuck and Harvey Gates. Photography: Lee Garms. Editor: Owen Marks.
Orchestra conducted by Louis Silvers.

Cast

Al Jolson (Joe Lane), Davey Lee (Little Pal), Marian Nixon (Katherine
Lane), Holmes Herbert (Dr. Robert Merrill), John Bowers (Surgeon),
Kenneth Thomson (Arthur Phillips), Fred Kohler (Joe Lane's cellmate).

Synopsis

Jolson plays Joe Lane, a genially irresponsible radio singer on the rise with a wife,
Katherine (nicely played by Nixon), and child, Little Pal (Lee). When he learns
that Arthur Phillips (Thomson), the radio station manager, has been trying to steal
his wife's affections, Lane strikes him. As he falls, Phillips strikes his head on a
concrete pillar and is fatally injured. Joe is imprisoned, and he and his little family
suffer from the separation. Katherine works as a nurse for Dr. Robert Merrill
(Herbert), who has formerly loved her and wants her back, and Little Pal is sent
away to school. When Lane finally gets out of prison, he goes to visit the child.
Little Pal attempts to follow him and is struck by a car and seriously injured. Joe
rushes the boy to Merrill, but the doctor will only agree to give the child the
necessary operation if Lane will withdraw from the lives of Katherine and Little
Pal. Joe reluctantly agrees, and Little Pal comes through the operation and
recovers everything but his voice. When he hears a record of his father singing,
however, he reacts in excitement and his voice returns. In the final scene Joe is
seen back on the radio singing as Katherine and Little Pal listen at home, awaiting
his return.

Songs

"Back in Your Own Backyard," "I'm Ka-razy for You," "Used to You," "Little Pal,"
"I'm in Seventh Heaven," "Why Can't You?," "(Mem'ries of) One Sweet Kiss." The
first two songs, recorded for the film, are not included in surviving prints.

Reviews

"With Jolson, *Say It With Songs* is a marked advancement for him as a screen
player. It far overshadows *The Jazz Singer* or *The Singing Fool* in that respect.
Perhaps it is but a matter of course that it should, as his third talker in three years.
But it's not the advancement in the mechanism that helps Jolson the most here --
it's Jolson himself. He plays more naturally and looks the human Al Jolson on the
screen, even in the betterment of his makeup, than previously."(Sime, *Variety*,
August 14, 1929)

"When humor is so scarce and so precious and when such a relatively small number
of actors can supply it, why does Al Jolson so studiously eschew it? Any one of
half a hundred hams could do the Joe Lane type of slop as well as Al Jolson does
it. Only a very few could be as funny as he can be."(A.M. Sherwood, Jr., "The
Movies." *Outlook*, August 28, 1929, p. 713)

"Mr. Jolson himself breaks down too many times to cause the spectators to lose control of themselves. Perhaps it might have been far more stirring had Mr. Jolson kept a straight face and refrained from so many protestations of affection concerning his Little Pal, Davey Lee."(Mordaunt Hall, "The Screen." *New York Times*, August 7, 1929, p. 29)

> **Addtional Reviews:** *Life*, August 30, 1929, p. 23; *New York Times*, July 28, 1929, Section VIII, p. 5; *New York Times*, August 11, 1929, Section VIII, p. 3.

Commentary

Say It With Songs was shot in a mere twenty-eight days. It is the movie that best demonstrates the miscalculations Jolson and Warner Bros. were making in regard to the audience's expectations. Borrowing elements from Jolson's two previous films (including Jolson's diminutive *The Singing Fool* co-star, Davey Lee), *Say It With Songs* featured much sentimentality. As Jolson's first all-talkie, it emphasizes his weaknesses as an actor. Thanks to a poorly written script, uninspired score, and colorless direction and production values, the movie is Jolson's least interesting performance and the least successful of all his Warner Bros. pictures. It also was a box office failure at a time when Jolson's popularity was at its height. But this was not the Jolson the audience wanted, and Warner Bros. would never seem to find a way to truly showcase Jolson. Although he would make other films, his star had lost its luster in Hollywood.

F5   *SHOW GIRL IN HOLLYWOOD* (Title in Great Britain: *The Showgirl in Hollywood.*)

1930. First National-Warner Bros. B&W (with color sequences). 80 mins.

Credits

Director: Mervyn LeRoy. Producer: Robert North. Screenplay: Harvey Thew, James A. Starr, based on the novel *Hollywood Girl* by J.P. McEvoy. Photography: Sol Polito. Editor: Peter Fritch. Musical Direction: Leo F. Forbstein. Art Direction: Jack Okey. Choreography: Jack Haskell.

Cast

Alice White (Dixie Dugan), Jack Mulhall (Jimmy Doyle), Blanche Sweet (Donna Harris), Ford Sterling (Sam Otis, Film Producer), John Miljan (Frank Buelow, Film Director), Virginia Sale (Otis' Secretary), Lee Shumway (Kramer), Herman Bing (Bing), Walter Pidgeon (Guest Star), Spec O'Donnell.

Synopsis

The plot involves a young New York girl visiting Hollywood. The film makes liberal use of filmclips and newsreels of Hollywood stars and events of the day in satirizing Tinsel Town.

Songs

The songs by Bud Green, Sam H. Stept, B. G. De Sylva, Lew Brown, and Ray Henderson include "There's a Tear For Every Smile in Hollywood," "Hang On to the Rainbow," "My Sin," and "I've Got My Eye On You."

Reviews

"Flashes of fun and several interesting glimpses of work on a set and behind the cameras in a film studio are the main assets of *Show Girl in Hollywood*."(Mordaunt Hall, *New York Times*, May 5, 1930, p. 27)

"Moderately amusing programmer with much studio atmosphere."(Land., *Variety*, May 14, 1930)

Additional Reviews: *New York Times*, May 11, 1930, Section IX, p. 5.

Commentary

Jolson and Ruby Keeler are among the stars seen in silent newsreel footage attending a Hollywood film premiere.

F6   *MAMMY*

1930. Warner Bros.-Vitaphone Corporation. B&W (with color sequence) 83 mins.

Credits

Director: Michael Curtiz. Producer: Walter Morosco. Screenplay: L. Gordon Rigby, Joseph Jackson, from a story by Irving Berlin. Photography: Barney McGill. Editor: Owen Marks. Songs: Irving Berlin, with some music by Giuseppe Verdi. Orchestra conducted by Louis Silvers.

Cast

Al Jolson (Al Fuller), Lois Moran (Nora Meadows), Louise Dresser (Al's mother), Lowell Sherman (Westy), Noah Beery (Tonopah Red), Hobart Bosworth (Mr. Meadows), Tully Marshall (Slats), Mitchell Lewis (Tambo), Lee Moran (Flat Feet), Jack Curtis (Sheriff), Stanley Fields (Pig Eyes), Ray Cooke (Props).

Synopsis

Jolson plays Al Fuller, the brightest "end man" in the run-down theatrical company, Meadows' Merry Minstrels, which is touring small towns one step ahead of creditors and local authorities. Fuller loves Nora (Moran), daughter of Meadows (Bosworth) from afar, but she is in love with Westy (wryly acted by Sherman), the troupe's interlocutor. Westy's philandering leads Al to express his feelings for Nora in an attempt to make Westy jealous. The scheme backfires, however, and Nora vents her frustration on Al. He, in turn, gets drunk and is cheated in a card game by Tambo (Lewis), the troupe's other "end man" who is tired of performing in Fuller's shadow. Westy discovers the deception and confronts Tambo, forcing him to return the money he has bilked from Al and the other performers. Tambo plots his revenge by putting real bullets in place of blanks in a prop gun that Al fires at Westy onstage. Westy is seriously wounded and he and the rest of the troupe believe Al has shot him in jealousy over Nora. Al is arrested, but escapes enroute to prison. He goes to see his mother (sentimentally, but effectively played by Dresser), pretending that he is about to leave on a European tour. She is not fooled and convinces Al to return to face the music. When he does return, Al discovers that Tambo has confessed, Westy has recovered and Nora is in love with him. The film concludes with Al at the head of the now prosperous Meadows' Merry Minstrels, joyously reprising "Let Me Sing and I'm Happy."

Songs

"Knights of the Road," "Let Me Sing and I'm Happy," "Who Paid the Rent for Mrs. Rip Van Winkle?," "When You and I Were Young, Maggie," "Yes, We Have No Bananas," "My Mammy," "Looking at You," "Here We Are," "Oh, Dem Golden Slippers," "In the Morning," "The Call of the South," "Why Do They All Take the Night Boat to Albany?," "To My Mammy."

Reviews

"Mr. Jolson wastes no time in gaining an excuse for a song and his efforts were roundly applauded. His first rendition is *Let Me Sing and I'm Happy*, which comes forth with this performer's characteristic fervor."(Mordaunt Hall, *New York Times*, March 27, 1930, p. 24)

"As for Mr. Jolson's *Mammy*, little can be said of the story as a whole, but it is evident that he has endeavored to struggle away from the old vale of tears, for the first part of this film is redeemed not only by Mr. Berlin's musical compositions but also by some good touches of humor."(Mordaunt Hall, *New York Times*, March 30, 1930, Section VIII, p. 5)

"A lively picture playing fast, with Al Jolson singing new and old songs, including among the Irving Berlin new numbers a couple of melodious hits, beside a minstrel show background, will throw this *Mammy* film into the good money class in the regular picture house."(Sime, *Variety*, April 2, 1930, p. 19)

"*Mammy* differs from the other Jolson films in that it has no talkie tot toddling about in its nightie -- and that none of its tears can be taken seriously, even by the most confirmed Jolson addict."(Creighton Peet, *Outlook and Independent*, April 9, 1930, p. 594)

"Mr. Jolson is a gifted enough artist to try to get away from a formula beginning to pall."(Alexander Bakshy, *Nation*, April 16, 1930, p. 465)

"There is no denying Mr. Jolson's value as an entertainer, but it would have been a physical impossibility for Jolson or anybody else to create anything more interesting than a mediocre talkie out of the nondescript story and music which Irving Berlin has written for *Mammy*."(Harry Evans, *Life*, April 25, 1930, p. 18)

"Again Al Jolson, one of the world's greatest entertainers, rises above his story to make an entertaining movie, singing good Irving Berlin songs. *Mammy* is a minstrel piece, with good performances by Lois Moran, Lowell Sherman and Louise Dresser backing up the star. Louise is the mammy. A good spot of Technicolor, and some tunes that leave the theater with you. Good Jolson!"(*Photoplay*, June 1930)

Additional Reviews: *Chicago Daily News*, June 6, 1930; *Commonweal*, April 23, 1930, p. 715; *Exhibitor's Herald-World*, April 5, 1930, p. 37; *Film Daily*,

March 30, 1930, p. 8; *Film Spectator*, May 24, 1930, pp. 22-23; *Judge*, April 12, 1930, p. 21; *Motion Picture Classic*, June 1930; *New Yorker*, April 5, 1930, p. 91; *Time*, April 7, 1930, p. 69.

Commentary

Mammy was based on a stage play, *Mister Bones*, which Jolson had considered appearing in the previous year. Jolson's wife, Ruby Keeler, was considered for the role of Nora Meadows, but the part eventually went to Lois Moran, on loan from Fox Studios. A technicolor minstrel segment was filmed for the black-and-white film, but only all black-and-white prints survive. *Mammy* is one of the best of Jolson's Warner Bros. movies, due in large part to Irving Berlin's "Let Me Sing and I'm Happy," which later served as the thematic emblem of Jolson's screen biography, *The Jolson Story* (see F18). Interpolations of some older songs, "Why Do They All Take the Night Boat to Albany" and "Who Paid the Rent For Mrs. Rip Van Winkle," also add atmosphere to this interesting little film. The fine supporting cast features Lowell Sherman, later a noted movie director, as Westy. A one reel trailer, copyrighted May 3, 1930, was made to promote *Mammy* featuring Jolson in a dressing room being interviewed by a reporter. Jolson plugs the film and some brief clips from it are shown.

F7   BIG BOY

1930. Warner Bros.-Vitaphone Corporation. B&W. 68 mins.

Credits

Director: Alan Crosland. Screenplay: William K. Wells, Perry Vekroff, Rex Taylor, based on the musical comedy by Harold Atteridge. Photography: Hal Mohr. Editor: Ralph Dawson. Costumes: Earl Luick. General Musical Director: Erno Rapee. Orchestra conducted by Louis Silvers.

Cast

Al Jolson (Gus), Claudia Dell (Annabelle Bedford), Louise Closser Hale (Mrs. Bedford), Lloyd Hughes (Jack Bedford), Eddie Phillips (Coley Reed), Lew Harvey (Doc Wilbur), George Harris (Steve Leslie), Franklyn A. Batie (Jim Redding), John Harron (Joe Warren), Tom Wilson (Tucker), Noah Beery (Bully John Bagby), The Monroe Family Singers.

Synopsis

The movie's slight plot, based on Jolson's stage success of the same name, revolves around the fortunes of Mrs. Bedford (Hale), a Southern matriarch who owns a horse farm. She has pinned her financial hopes on her thoroughbred, Big Boy, to win the Kentucky Derby. Jolson's Gus has raised and lovingly cared for the horse since its birth and is expected to ride Big Boy at the Kentucky Derby. However, Mrs. Bedford's wayward son, Jack (Hughes), has fallen into the control of a big city hustler, Coley Reed (Phillips), and his henchman (Harvey) who want to put their own jockey, Steve Leslie (Harris), on Big Boy, the odds-on favorite, so that they can throw the race. Gus gets wind of the scheme, but not before the hustlers get him fired from the Bedford stable. Gus ends up working as a singing waiter in a Louisville hotel on the eve of the big race. With the help of Joe Warren (Harron), a friend of the Bedfords, Gus unravels the hustler's scheme, gets Jack out of trouble, and rides Big Boy to victory. There is also an extended flashback in the middle of the film wherein Mrs. Bedford recounts how Gus' grandfather (also played by Jolson) had saved Mrs. Bedford's mother from the unwanted advances of a local villain, Bully John Bagby (broadly played by Beery).

Songs

"Liza Lee," "Little Sunshine," "Dixie's Land," "All God's Children Got Shoes," "Go Down, Moses," "Tomorrow is Another Day," "Hooray for Baby and Me."

Reviews

"Here's Al Jolson's stage thriller about race-track intrigue, done into high comedy talkie. Al is blackface throughout except for a short afterpiece, cracks some old gags and some fast new ones, and sings about eight numbers, than[sic] which could any Jolson fan beg more? It's all done in a grand air of rollicking levity that adds to the fun. Go, and get a nightful of laughs."(*Photoplay*, September 1930)

"*Big Boy* on the screen as on the stage is just a setting for Al Jolson. It isn't another *Sonny Boy* coup, but it is effective popular entertainment. The wealth of comedy should insure that. It isn't any special artistic triumph for Jolson, but it will please the Jolson following."(Rush, *Variety*, September 17, 1930, p. 21)

"Jolson in the plot is innocuous, often preposterous, unhampered by the story: singing, quipping, dancing, rolling his eyes and giving the Jolson public oldtime Jolson nonsense from the day before he got mixed up with Sonny Boy."(*Time*, September 22, 1930, p. 30)

"Next we come to a big Al Jolson special called *Big Boy* -- and frankly if the Warners give Jolson a few more like this he'll soon be pushing about with dark glasses and a tin cup full of pencils."(Creighton Peet, *Outlook and Independent*, September 24, 1930, p. 150)

"However, with each new Jolson picture now we are beginning to wonder about his showmanship. Al's ability to bring tears to the eyes of most of us in *The Jazz Singer* and *The Singing Fool* has evidently given him a pathos complex that is proving a decided handicap to his natural talents for comedy."(Harry Evans, *Life*, October 17, 1930, p. 20)

> **Additional Reviews:** *Exhibitor's Herald World*, September 20, 1930, p. 40; *Film Daily*, September 14, 1930, p. 12; *New Movie Magazine*, December 1930; *New York Times*, September 13, 1930, p. 9; *New York Times*, September 21, 1930, Section IX, p. 5; *Talking Screen*, October 1930.

Commentary

This is Jolson's most unusual film in that he plays his blackfaced stage character, "Gus," throughout the entire movie (except for a brief finale). As a record of the qualities typical of his stage shows (see S25), it is an interesting document. The film is largely faithful to the plot outlines of the stage show, although the original score has been completely jettisoned. It is unfortunate that none of Jolson's musical standards was interpolated into this film, for aside from the oft-repeated "Tomorrow Is Another Day," the movie's score is bland. On stage, Jolson would have been able to interpolate a song grouping that would have raised the production to a height it cannot possibly attain with its simplistic plot and cardboard characters. The film's cast includes noted stage actress and writer Louise Closser Hale, who would play character roles in a number of movies in the early 1930's, including the classic *Dinner at Eight* (1933). Also among the supporting cast is Noah Beery (brother of actor Wallace Beery and father of television actor Noah Beery, Jr.) as Bully John Bagby.

F8   NEW YORK NIGHTS

1930. United Artists. B&W.

Credits
Director: Lewis Milestone. Producer: Joseph M. Schenck. Screenplay: Jules Furthman (adapted from Hugh Stanislaus Stange's play, *Tin Pan Alley*).

Cast
Norma Talmadge, Gilbert Roland, John Wray, Lilyan Tashman, Mary Doran, Roscoe Karns.

Synopsis
This film, mixing elements of musical comedy and gangster films, involves a musical star (Talmadge) married to an alcoholic composer (Roland). She becomes entangled with a gangster (Wray) who turns threatening when she attempts to end their relationship. Fortunately, the gangster is arrested following a shootout with police, and the star and composer are reconciled with his promise to reform.

Reviews
"*New York Nights*, as many another picture, deals with the emotional affairs of a song writer."(*New York Times*, February 1, 1930, p. 15)

Additional Reviews: *Exhibitors Herald-World*, February 8, 1930, p. 33; *Film Daily*, February 2, 1930, p. 11; *Judge*, March 1, 1930, Vol. 98, p. 32; *Rob Wagner's Script*, March 22, 1930, Vol. 3, p. 10; *Variety*, February 5, 1930, p. 24.

Commentary
This film, Talmadge's unsuccessful debut in talkies, is purported to include footage of Jolson, probably from one of his previously released films. He also collaborated on a song used in the film, "A Year from To-Day," written with Ballard MacDonald and Dave Dreyer. The director of *New York Nights*, Lewis Milestone, would direct Jolson's next (and most interesting) movie, *Hallelujah, I'm a Bum* (see F9), and Norma Talmadge would be married for a time to Jolson's sometime friend, sometime rival, George Jessel.

F9   HALLELUJAH, I'M A BUM (Title in Great Britain: *Hallelujah, I'm a Tramp*. Other titles: *New York, The Heart of New York, Happy Go Lucky, The Optimist, Lazy Bones*.)

1933. United Artists. B&W. 82 mins.

Credits

Director: Lewis Milestone. Producer: Joseph M. Schenck. Screenplay: S.N. Behrman, from a story by Ben Hecht. Music: Richard Rodgers. Lyrics: Lorenz Hart. Assistant Director: Nate Watt. Photography: Lucien Adriot. Editor: W. Duncan Mansfield. Art Direction: Richard Day. Costumes: Milo Anderson. Technical Director: V.L. McFadden. Sound: Oscar Lagerstrom. Orchestra conducted by Alfred Newman.

Cast

Al Jolson (Bumper), Madge Evans (June Marcher), Frank Morgan (Mayor Hastings), Harry Langdon (Egghead), Chester Conklin (Sunday), Edgar Connor (Acorn), Tyler Brooke (Mayor's Secretary), Tammany Young (Orlando), Bert Roach (John), Victor Potel (The General), Dorothea Wolbert (Apple Mary), Louise Carver (Ma Sunday), Lorenz Hart (Bank Teller), Richard Rodgers (Assistant Photographer).

Synopsis

Bumper (Jolson) and his pal Acorn (Connor) run into New York's Mayor, Hastings (Morgan), duck hunting in the Florida everglades. Bumper and Acorn return to New York, where Bumper reins as "Mayor of Central Park" where many fellow hobos reside, including their socialist friend Egghead (Langdon). Hastings offers to get Bumper a good job in a bank, but Bumper prefers the freedom of his life in the park. Hastings is deeply in love with the beautiful June Marcher (Evans), but he is extremely jealous despite her devotion. When they quarrel, June, in despair, attempts suicide by jumping off a bridge in Central Park. Bumper saves her from drowning, but when she revives she has lost her memory. Bumper, not realizing she is Hastings's girlfriend, is smitten with her and becomes her protector. He tells Hastings he is in love with a girl he calls "Angel" and would like to take the bank job after all. He and Acorn become bankers, and Bumper takes care of "Angel" in good style. Meanwhile, Hastings searches frantically for June, realizing the foolishness of his jealousy, while Bumper is put "on trial' by the other hobos for taking a job. When Bumper learns that "Angel" is actually Hastings's missing girlfriend, he reluctantly brings the two together. She regains her memory when she sees Hastings, and they are reconciled as Bumper sadly returns to his life as a hobo.

Songs

"I Gotta Get Back to New York," "My Pal Bumper," "Hallelujah, I'm a Bum" (first version), "Laying the Cornerstone," "Sleeping Beauty" (cut from the released film), "Dear June," "Bumper Found a Grand," "What Do You Want With Money?," "Hallelujah, I'm a Bum" (second version), "Kangaroo Court," "I'd Do It Again," "You Are Too Beautiful."

Reviews

"The picture, some persons may be glad to hear, has no *Mammy* song. It is Mr. Jolson's best film and well it might be, for that clever director, Lewis Milestone, guided its destiny, and the supporting cast includes Frank Morgan, the beautiful Madge Evans, the pathetically comic Harry Langdon and that veteran of Keystone days, Chester Conklin. It is a combination of fun, melody and romance, with a dash of satire, all of which make for an ingratiating entertainment."(Mordaunt Hall, *New York Times*, February 9, 1933, p. 15)

"*Hallelujah, I'm a Bum* must necessarily rise or fall by Al Jolson's draw. As a picture it's no wow but not half bad either, commanding attention because of its provocative nature and general treatment. Any pro and con discussion over the *rhythmic dialog* may stand it in good stead, although as a general thing the bare exposition of the premise that a bunch of bums are made to converse in lyric metre may be enough to convict, regardless. It won't bore, once in, but it's not a mass play picture unless the box office selling offsets the several shortcomings."(Abel Green, *Variety*, February 14, 1933)

"Al Jolson's performance is notable for a great air of confidence, which is generally unjustified, and for the fact that he still wobbles his lower lip as though every other word in all his songs was Mammy."("The New Pictures," *Time*, February 20, 1933, p. 22)

"Neither Mr. Milestone, the director, nor Mr. Hecht and Mr. Behrman, the authors of this picture, hitherto have interested themselves in music. Mr. Jolson is too old at his musical trade to change his tricks and subordinate himself in a show. Thus, the music, the story, and the star were constantly warring with one another."(Pare Lorentz, *Vanity Fair*, April 1933, Vol. 40, p. 43)

"A film to welcome back, especially for what it tries to do for the progress of the American musical film in the direction that Gluck began for opera."(Penelope Gilliatt, *New Yorker*, June 23, 1973)

> **Additional Reviews:** *Film Daily*, January 27, 1933, p. 5; *Hollywood Reporter*, December 20, 1932, p. 3; *Motion Picture Herald*, February 18, 1933, p. 30; *Motion Picture Herald*, March 4, 1933, pp. 11-12; *New York Herald Tribune*, February 9, 1933; *New York Post*, February 9, 1933; *New York Sun*, February 9, 1933; *New York World-Telegram*, February 9, 1933; *New Yorker*, February 18, 1933, p. 55; *New Zealand's Picture Screen*, May 1933, p. 6; *Silver Screen*, April 1933.

Commentary

The film was apparently shot in its entirety under the direction of Chester Erskine (who replaced Harry D'Arrast after one day) from July to September 1932. In this version, the songs were by Irving Caesar with Roland Young cast in the role of Hastings. This version, which apparently disappointed most of the involved parties, was completely scrapped (some stills survive), and the project was started over. Hecht's story for the film was suggested by Floyd Dell's 1926 short story, "Hallelujah, I'm a Bum!" Although the released film was not well-received in 1933, film critics now consider it the finest and most interesting of Jolson's movies. Jolson comes off well as an actor in this effort, and it is fascinating to see him both without his blackface persona and without a backstage plot in which he is playing a variation on himself. His singing of the fine score by Richard Rodgers and Lorenz Hart is strong. Rodgers and Hart wrote scores for several musical films in the early thirties, many of them experimenting with the musical form, but most of their work was done for stage musicals, culminating in another interesting experiment, *Pal Joey* (1940). Jolson delivers the title song and "You Are Too Beautiful" with particular flair, and he works well with the lovely Madge Evans and character actor, Frank Morgan, who would become a screen legend as the title character in *The Wizard of Oz* (1939). A trailer including scenes from the film survives.

F10 *WONDER BAR*

1934. First National-Warner Bros. B&W. 84 mins.

Credits

Director: Lloyd Bacon. Producer: Robert Lord. Choreography: Busby Berkeley. Screenplay: Earl Baldwin, from the continental musical by Herczeg and Farkas. Photography: Sol Polito. Editor: George Amy. Art Direction: Jack Okey. Gowns: Orry-Kelly. Music: Harry Warren. Lyrics: Al Dubin. Orchestra conducted by Leo F. Forbstein.

Cast

Al Jolson (Al Wonder), Kay Francis (Liane Renaud), Dolores Del Rio (Inez), Ricardo Cortez (Harry), Dick Powell (Tommy), Guy Kibbee (Mr. Simpson), Ruth Donnelly (Mrs. Simpson), Hugh Herbert (Mr. Pratt), Louise Fazenda (Mrs. Pratt), Hal LeRoy (Himself), Fifi D'Orsay (Mitzi), Merna Kennedy (Claire), Robert Barrat (Captain Van Ferring), Henry Kolker (Mr. Renaud), Henry O'Neill (Richards), Kathryn Sergava (Ilka), Gordon De Main (1st Detective), Harry Woods (2nd Detective), Marie Moreau (Maid), George Irving (Broker), Emile Chautard (Concierge), Pauline Garon (Operator), Mahlon Norvell (Artist), Alphonse Martel (Doorman), Mia Ichioka (Gee-Gee), William Granger (Bartender), Rolfe Sedan (Waiter), Eddie Kane (Frank), Edward Keane (Captain), Jane Darwell (Baroness), Demetrius Alexis (1st Young Man), John Marlow (2nd Young Man), Billy Anderson (Call Boy), Bud Jamison (Bartender), Hobart Cavanaugh (Drunk), Dave O'Brien (Chorus Boy), Dennis O'Keefe (Extra at Bar), Gino Corrado (Waiter), Grace Hayle (Fat Dowager), Gordon "Bill" Elliott (Norman), Paul Power (Chester), Dick Good (Page Boy), Michael Dalmatoff (Count), Renee Whitney (1st Chorus Girl), Amo Ingraham (2nd Chorus Girl), Rosalie Roy (3rd Chorus Girl), Lottie Williams (Wardrobe Woman), Clay Clement (1st Businessman), William Stack (2nd Businessman), Spencer Charters (Pete), Gene Perry (Gendarme), Louis Ardizoni (Cook), Robert Graves (Police Officer), Alfred P. James (Night Watchman), Hal LeRoy (himself).

Synopsis

Wonder Bar is a musical *Grand Hotel*, set in the Parisian nightclub owned by Al Wonder (Jolson). Wonder entertains and banters with his international clientele, including two garish American couples (played hilariously by Warners Brothers wonderful character actors Kibbee, Donnelly, Herbert, and Fazenda), and he tries to keep the passions of his floor show performers from spilling off the stage. Inez (Del Rio), the exotic star dancer of the Wonder Bar, and her partner, Harry (Cortez), are romantically involved, but Harry is also philandering with Liane (Francis), bored wife of a rich banker, Renaud (Kolker). Wonder loves Inez, as does Tommy (Powell), the Bar's bandleader, but Inez irrationally clings to the unscrupulous Harry, who has stolen a valuable necklace belonging to Liane, and is about to skip town. In a fit of passion, Inez stabs Harry at the conclusion of one of their numbers. Harry pretends not to be seriously injured and staggers to his dressing room where he dies. Wonder keeps this news from the hysterical Inez and invents a complex cover-up which involves placing Harry's body in the back of a car belonging to Captain Van Ferring (Barrat), a despondent German aristocrat who is bankrupt and plans to commit suicide by driving over a cliff. Having accomplished all this, Wonder sadly realizes that Inez belongs with Tommy. He quietly steps aside, and, as the nightclub closes its doors for the night, Wonder goes home alone.

Songs

All songs, except "Dark Eyes," by Warren and Dubin: "Vive La France," "Don't Say Goodnight," "Dark Eyes" (folk song), "Why Do I Dream Those Dreams?," "Wonder Bar," "Goin' to Heaven on a Mule."

Reviews

"*Wonder Bar* has got about everything. Romance, flash, dash, class, color, songs, star-studded talent and almost every known requisite to assure sturdy attention and attendance. [. . .] It's Jolson's comeback picture in every respect. With 10% of the gross due him, he's in for some fancy gravy besides."(Abel, *Variety*, March 6, 1934)

"If you like Al Jolson, and pretty girls in graceful movements, *Wonder Bar* is good enough entertainment."(Cy Caldwell, "To See or Not to See," *New Outlook*, April 1934, p. 45)

"Those who like Jolson should see *Wonder Bar* for it is mainly Jolson; singing the old reliables; cracking jokes which would have impressed Noah as depressingly ancient; and moving about with characteristic energy."(S.M.B. "At the University." *Harvard Crimson*, May 21, 1934)

> **Additional Reviews:** *Literary Digest*, March 17, 1934, p. 37; *New York Times*, March 1, 1934, p. 23; *New York Times*, March 11, 1934, Section X, p. 5; *Newsweek*, March 3, 1934, pp. 32-33; *Photoplay*, February 1934; *Saturday Review of Literature*, April 28, 1934; *Screen Play*, February 1934; *Vanity Fair*, April 1934; *Variety*, April 8, 1934.

Commentary

This "all-star" musical is clearly the most lavish of all Jolson's Warner Bros. movies. He is in top form, demonstrating a stronger acting ability than evident in most of his other film roles of the era. He seems to particularly enjoy is interacting with an assortment of memorable character actors, particularly Louise Fazenda, Hugh Herbert, Guy Kibbee, and Ruth Donnelly, all playing gauche wealthy Americans on the town in Paris. Jolson also has an amusing moment with Jane Darwell, who appears in a bit role a few years before her performance as Ma Joad in *The Grapes of Wrath* (1939) would make her one of Hollywood's most familiar character actors. Among the star cast, Dick Powell does well as a songwriter/conductor, Ricardo Cortez is suitably unpleasant as a gigolo, and Henry Kolker is solid as a wealthy banker. But Kay Francis as a spoiled and restless banker's wife and the beautiful Dolores Del Rio as the object of most male attention in the film give uninspired performances. *Wonder Bar*, of course, was inspired by Jolson's 1931 stage musical, *The Wonder Bar* (see S28), but, despite his strong acting, he is provided with few musical opportunities.   Director/choreographer Busby Berkeley staged the elaborate "Goin' to Heaven on a Mule" number as Jolson's featured spot in the film, but the grotesque racial stereotypes present in the blackface number undermine the film's effectiveness today. Similarly, the picture features more than a few vulgar jokes at the expense of homosexuals. These moments were undoubtedly risqué when the film was released, but are tiresome for the viewer today. *Wonder Bar* was one of the top money-making films of 1934. A trailer including numerous scenes from the film survives.

F11   *GO INTO YOUR DANCE* (Titles in Great Britain: *Casino de Paree, Casino de Paris*)

1935. Warner Bros.-First National. B&W. 92 mins.

Credits

Director: Archie Mayo. Producer: Sam Bischoff. Choreography: Bobby Connolly. Screenplay: Earl Baldwin, from a novel by Bradford Ropes. Photography: Tony Gaudio, Sol Polito. Editor: Harold McLernon. Art Director: John Hughes. Gowns: Orry-Kelly. Music: Harry Warren. Lyrics: Al Dubin. Orchestral Arrangements: Ray Heindorf. Orchestra conducted by Leo F. Forbstein.

Cast

Al Jolson (Al Howard), Ruby Keeler (Dorothy Wayne), Glenda Farrell (Molly Howard), Helen Morgan (Luana Wells), Barton MacLane (The Duke), Patsy Kelly (Irma), Sharon Lynne (Nellie, the blonde), Ward Bond (Nellie's husband), Akim Tamiroff (Mexican), Benny Rubin (Customer at bar), Phil Regan (Eddie Rio), Gordon Westcott (Fred), William Davidson (McGee), Joyce Compton (Show Girl), Joseph Cregan (Jackson), Arthur Treacher (Englishman), Fred Toones (Snowflake), Harry Warren (Harry), Al Dubin (Al), Martin Fried (Rehearsal pianist).

Synopsis

Jolson appears as Al Howard, a Broadway star with a penchant for running out on hit shows to go on benders or play the horses. A committee of angry producers bans him from Broadway, leading Al's protective sister, Molly (Farrell, in a diamond-hard "tough cookie" performance), to track him down in Caliente in an attempt to get him straightened out. She hatches a plan to get Al together with her old chorus chum, Dorothy Wayne (Keeler), a nice girl she hopes will set a good example for Howard. Molly also arranges for Al, in partnership with Dorothy, to perform at a Chicago nightclub where she brings a shady character, The Duke (MacLane), and his wife, Luana (Morgan), an ex-singer who would like to make a comeback in show business. She persuades The Duke to put up money for Al to produce his own Broadway revue with her as a featured singer. Meanwhile, Dorothy has fallen in love with Al, but her unrequited feelings lead her to the painful decision to withdraw from the act. Molly steps in and persuades Dorothy to stick it out until the show opens. Al gets the show pulled together, but is barely able to keep Luana at arms length. He is finally forced to tell her that he will have nothing to do with her romantically, and she ominously vows revenge. The worst crisis comes when Molly is falsely accused of murder and Al puts up most of his bankroll from The Duke to get her out of jail on bail in order to find a witness and prove her innocence. Molly disappears and opening night arrives with Al unable to post equity bond for his cast. He is in the process of calling off the opening only minutes before the curtain when word comes that Molly has proven her innocence. Her bail has been released, allowing the equity bond to be posted so that the show can go on. In the meantime, however, Luana has told The Duke that Al has squandered the money, so The Duke sends two gunmen to even the score. When Al an Dorothy step into the theatre's alley following the first act, Dorothy spots the gunmen taking aim at Al and jumps protectively in front of him taking the bullet herself. In a fast-paced climax, Al carries Dorothy back to his dressing room to await the doctor, realizing in his shock that he has been in love with her all the time. Preferring to stay with Dorothy, he refuses to continue with the show until she persuades him to carry on. When Al rushes offstage after stopping the show, the doctor informs him that Dorothy will recover. Al runs back onstage, and the film ends as he exuberantly performs an encore.

Songs

"Celito Lindo," "A Good Old Fashioned Cocktail," "Mammy, I'll Sing About You," "About a Quarter to Nine," "The Little Things You Used to Do," "Casino de Paree," "She's a Latin from Manhattan," "Go Into Your Dance."

Reviews

"*Go Into Your Dance* (Warner) is a good-humored backstage musicomedy of which the two most notable ingredients are Ruby Keeler's legs and Al Jolson's mother complex. Since neither constitutes a novelty to U.S. cinema audiences, *Go Into Your Dance* is not likely to add to Warner Brothers' stature as the boldest experimenters in Hollywood."("The New Pictures," *Time*, April 29, 1935, p. 56)

"It is his [Jolson's] enthusiastic presence that pulls the picture into the safety zone of musical entertainment. When he is absent from the screen one's attention is likely to stray, even in the face of Miss Keeler's nimble dancing. But when he opens up with *A Latin From Manhattan* and *About a Quarter to Nine*, which are among the seven songs written for the piece by Harry Warren and Al Dubin, one must give way to the pleasurable realization that Mr. Jolson's in his minstrel heaven and all's right with the world."(Andre Sennwald, *New York Times*, May 4, 1935, p. 17)

"*Go Into Your Dance* will get the coin generally, for it has much to recommend it as a lavishly produced, vigorously directed and agreeably entertaining musical picture. Besides everything else it has Al Jolson in top form, plus a nifty set of songs, and with Jolson to sing 'em. Along with Jolson this time, and for the first time his screen partner is the missus, Ruby Keeler -- a romantic touch that should mean considerable at the gate."(Bige., *Variety*, May 8, 1935, p. 16)

"The song numbers are tuneful and smart, with the exception of the turgid mammy song which Jolson springs so near the beginning that one suspects that the producers felt it ought to be over and done with before the real business of the picture started."(John Gammie, "What -- And What Not -- To See." *Film Weekly*, August 23, 1935)

Additional Reviews: *Esquire*, June 1935, Vol. 3, p. 144; *Film Daily*, March 19, 1935, p. 4; *Hollywood Reporter*, March 13, 1935, p. 3; *Hollywood Reporter*, May 14, 1935, p. 6; *Motion Picture Herald*, March 23, 1935, p. 42; *New*

Movie, April 1935; *Photoplay*, June 1935; *Robert Wagner's Script*, May 25, 1935, Vol. 3, p. 6; *Time*, April 29, 1935, p. 56.

Commentary

Go Into Your Dance features one of Jolson's breeziest performances, due in large part to a serviceable script, a standout score (particularly the title song, "About a Quarter to Nine," "She's a Latin From Manhattan," and "Mammy, I'll Sing About You"), and the undeniable chemistry between Jolson and his then-wife, Ruby Keeler as his co-star. Although they are fine in production numbers built around "About a Quarter to Nine" and "She's a Latin From Manhattan," the Jolsons are most effective in a scene in which she attempts to impress him with the variety of dance styles she is capable of performing. While he plays the piano and banters with her, she rolls back the rug and struts her stuff. Most of the dialogue scenes are charming, and although the dialogue is occasionally mawkish (Al: "I love ya." Ruby: "To think I had to get shot to hear you say that."), it is clear that Jolson and Keeler might have evolved into Warner Bros. answer to RKO's popular Fred Astaire and Ginger Rogers. But aside from a brief cameo in the 1937 short *A Day at Santa Anita* (see F34), the Jolsons would never work together again on film, although they made several radio appearances together during the 1930's. *Go Into Your Dance* is also aided by a solid supporting cast from the Warner Bros. stable, particularly Glenda Farrell, in top form as Jolson's sister; Patsy Kelly, as a broken down vaudevillian hoping to team up with Jolson; Helen Morgan in the slight role of a trouble-making wife of a gangster; and, Arthur Treacher in a bit role as a starchy Englishman. Bobby Connolly was nominated for an Academy Award for his dance direction of the "She's a Latin from Manhattan" number. This was the only feature film in which Jolson co-starred with his third wife, Ruby Keeler. At least two trailers for this film survive. One was made at the time of the film's release, and includes takes not used in the released print. The other was made when the film was re-released in the late 1940's when *The Jolson Story* (see F18) revived Jolson's popularity.

F12   THE SINGING KID

1936. Warner Bros.-First National. B&W. 83 mins.

Credits

Director: William Keighley. Producer: Robert Lord. Choreography: Bobby Connolly. Screenplay: Warren Duff, Pat C. Flick, from a story by Robert Lord. Photography: George Barnes. Editor: Thomas Richards. Art Direction: Carl Wey. Gowns: Orry-Kelly. Music: Harold Arlen. Lyrics: E.Y. Harburg. Orchestral arrangements: Ray Heindorf. Orchestra conducted by Leo F. Forbstein.

Cast

Al Jolson (Al Jackson), Beverly Roberts (Ruth Haines), Sybil Jason (Sybil Haines), Edward Everett Horton (Davenport Rogers), Allen Jenkins (Joe Eddy), Lyle Talbot (Bob Carey), Frank Mitchell (Dope), William Davidson (Barney Hammond), Edward Keane (Potter), Wini Shaw (Singer), Jack Durant (Babe), Joseph King (Dr. May), Joseph Cregan (Fulton), Claire Dodd (Dana Lawrence), Kay Hughes (Mary Lou), John Hale (Dr. Brown),

Hattie McDaniel (Maid), The Four Yacht Club Boys, Cab Calloway and His Band.

Synopsis

Jolson plays Al Jackson, a Broadway star who is generous and well-liked, supporting a group of hangers-on led by his factotums Davenport Rogers (Horton) and Joe Eddy (Jenkins), as well as a chiseling fiance, Dana Lawrence (Dodd), who is in cahoots with Al's crooked lawyer, Bob Carey (Talbot). When they disappear with Al's bank account and leave him with an unpaid tax bill, Al's spirit is broken and he loses his voice. To recover, he heads for a vacation in the country with Davenport and Joe, renting a lakeside house belonging to an attractive woman, Ruth Haines (Roberts), who is struggling to support herself and her young niece, Sybil (Jason). Al becomes fond of Ruth and little Sybil and immediately sets about to help them by trying to sell a play Ruth has written. Unfortunately, Jackson's producer friends regard the play as amateurish, so to spare her feelings Al sends Ruth a check for $500, pretending it is an advance on her play from a Broadway producer. However, Ruth finds out about the deception and is deeply hurt. She confronts Al and asks him to go away. Sadly, he returns to New York and prepares to open in a new musical. Unable to concentrate on his work, Al tries to reach Ruth and Sybil by phone, but fails to get through to them. On opening night of his new show, he learns that Ruth and Sybil have entrained for parts unknown and he leaves the theatre shortly before the opening night curtain in hopes of catching them at Grand Central Station. He jumps into a cab in front of the theatre only to discover Ruth and Sybil there. They have come to New York to see him and make amends. Al and Ruth are reconciled and he bursts into the theatre from the back of the auditorium, followed by Ruth and Sybil, in the nick of time to make his entrance.

Songs

Jolson medley: "My Mammy," "Swanee," "Rock-A-Bye Your Baby With a Dixie Melody," "California, Here I Come," "April Showers," "About a Quarter to Nine," "Sonny Boy"; "I Love to Sing-A," "Keep That Hi-De-Ho in Your Soul," "Who's the Swingin'est Man in Town?," "Save Me, Sister," "Here's Looking at You," "My, How This Country's Changed," "You're the Cure for What Ails Me."

Reviews

"Jolson, plus burnt cork and eight bars of music, is an evening's entertainment to many movie-goers. They will like *The Singing Kid*. It is the best of the last three Jolson pictures."("On the Current Screen," *Literary Digest*, March 28, 1936, p. 19)

". . .the new picture is one of the least entertaining of the Jolson series."(F.S.N., *New York Times*, April 4, 1936, p. 11)

"Spotty entertainment and one of Al Jolson's minor efforts for Warner Bros. The star should attract enough attention on his own for fair money, but *The Singing Kid* on its merits won't rate the customary Jolson musical grosses."(Bige., *Variety*, April 8, 1936)

"As entertainment, it boils down to a simple question of taste: Is Jolson's hoarse, good-humored style of putting over a song as acceptable to cinemaddicts now as it was eight years ago when he used it to launch an era of entertainment in the first talkie ever made, *The Jazz Singer?*"("The New Pictures," *Time*, April 13, 1936, p. 34)

Additional Reviews: *Canadian Magazine*, May 1936, p. 60; *Esquire*, June 1936, Vol. 5, pp. 110, 200; *Film Daily*, March 13, 1936, p. 6; *Hollywood Reporter*, March 10, 1936, p. 3; *Hollywood Spectator*, March 28, 1936, p. 8; *Photoplay*, March 1936; *Rob Wagner's Script*, April 11, 1936, pp. 10-11; *Screenland*, June 1936; *World Film News*, September 1936, p. 25.

Commentary

The Singing Kid was Jolson's last starring vehicle for Warner Bros. He gives a generally bright performance in this undistinguished picture, hampered only by weak musical material and the tired plotting and stock roles. Jolson's standout musical moments are all at the beginning of the film, in a montage of Jolson standards at the movie's outset, and "I Love to Sing-A," which immediately follows the montage, and partners Jolson most effectively with the great Cab Calloway. The supporting cast is generally helpful: Beverly Roberts is a bit stiff as Jolson's love interest, but little Sybil Jason and Jolson establish a delightful rapport, particularly in their duet, "You're the Cure for What Ails Me." Edward Everett Horton and Allen Jenkins as Jolson's cronies, and Lyle Talbot as Jolson's crooked lawyer, add some brio. But a talent of Jolson's caliber deserved better material than this, and apparently Jolson himself had arrived at that conclusion. He terminated his contract with Warner Bros., and he never again worked as the solo star of a major motion picture. Sybil Jason recalls that Busby Berkeley worked on the film, although he is not credited. She has home movie footage on the set made by her family confirming her recollection. Berkeley, whose career was in eclipse due to his conviction for vehicular manslaughter shortly before, was probably permitted by the Warners to work incognito. A trailer for the film survives.

F13   ROSE OF WASHINGTON SQUARE

1939. Twentieth Century-Fox. B&W. 86 mins.

Credits

Director: Gregory Ratoff. Producer: Darryl Zanuck. Dances: Seymour Felix. Associate Producer: Nunnally Johnson. Screenplay: Nunnally Johnson, a story by John Larkin, Jerry Horwin. Photography: Karl Freund. Editor: Louis Loeffler. Art Direction: Richard Day, Rudolph Sternad. Set Design: Thomas Little. Costumes: Royer. Sound: Eugene Grossman, Roger Heman. Orchestra conducted by Louis Silvers.

Cast

Tyrone Power (Bart Clinton), Alice Faye (Rose Sargent), Al Jolson (Ted Cotter), William Frawley (Harry Long), Joyce Compton (Peggy), Hobart Cavanaugh (Whitey Boone), Moroni Olsen (Buck Russell), E.E. Clive (Barouche Driver), Louis Prima (Bandleader), Charles Wilson (Mike Cavanaugh), Hal Dawson (Chump), Paul Burns (Chump), Ben Welden (Tony), Horace MacMahon (Irving), Paul Stanton (District Attorney), Winifred Harris (Mrs. Russell), John Hamilton (Judge), Adrian Morris (Jim), Charles Lane (Sam Kress), Harry Hayden (Dexter), Maurice Cass (Mr. Mork), Bert Roach (Mr. Paunch), Irene Wilson (Miss Lust), Leonard

Kilbrick (Newsboy), James Flavin (Guard), John Hamilton (Judge), Igor and Tanya (Specialty Performers).

Synopsis

This film is obviously taken from the circumstances surrounding the marriage of Ziegfeld star Fanny Brice and gambler Nicky Arnstein. A young singer, Rose Sargent (Faye), has been struggling for a break in show business with the aid of her sometime partner, Ted Cotter (Jolson). To briefly escape her frustration, she heads for a country resort where she meets Bart Clinton (Power), who turns out to be a small-time con man. They are attracted to each other, but before their relationship can bloom, Bart departs after a brush with the law over a missing necklace. Rose gets a job singing in a speakeasy, while Ted makes it to the big time. Bart comes back into Rose's life. and despite Ted's attempts to talk her out of it, Rose marries Bart. They have a happy honeymoon which ends when Rose is offered the starring spot in the Ziegfeld Follies. Bart continues to play fast and loose with the law as debts mount up and he attempts to keep Rose unaware of his financial strains. Finally, Bart is arrested for his participation in a robbery and Ted puts up the bail for Bart's release until trial. The idea of a jail term is repugnant to Bart, and he takes it on the lam. Rose is humiliated at the forfiture of the bail money Ted has posted, but he laughs it off and continues to lend her support. Rose has introduced "My Man" into the Follies, and Bart, who misses her, secretly attends a performance and is moved by her obvious declaration of her love for him in the song. He turns himself in, and, as the film ends, departs by train for five years in prison, with Rose tearfully declaring that she will wait for him.

Songs

"Pretty Baby," "I'm Sorry I Made You Cry," "Ja-Da," "The Vamp," "Rock-A-Bye Your Baby With a Dixie Melody," "Toot, Toot, Tootsie," "I'm Just Wild About Harry," "The Curse of the Aching Heart," "California, Here I Come," "I Never Knew Heaven Could Speak," "April Showers" (not in the released print of the film), "Avalon" (not in the released print of the film), "Rose of Washington Square," "My Mammy," "My Man."

Reviews

"Mr. Jolson's singing of *Mammy, California, Here I Come* and others is something for the memory book."(Frank S. Nugent, *New York Times*, May 6, 1939, p. 21)

"Of the three co-stars this is Jolson's picture. But it's not much of a filmusical, at least not to the extent that Darryl Zanuck intended it. [. . .] There's no denying the memory-lane appeal of this song cavalcade, because it's a pretty good catalog in anybody's hit parade. Jolson's real-life association with the cream of the crop lends its extra values."(Abel., *Variety*, May 10, 1939, p. 14)

Additional Reviews: *Boston Herald*, 1939; *Cinema News and Property Gazette*, May 31, 1939; *Commonweal*, May 19, 1939, p. 106; *Family Circle*, June 9, 1939; *Film Daily*, May 8, 1939, p. 8; *Film Weekly. The National Guide to Films*, July 22, 1939; *Hollywood Reporter*, May 4, 1939, p. 3; *Hollywood Spectator*, May 13, 1939, Vol. 14, pp. 11-12; *Motion Picture Herald*, May 13, 1939, p. 37; *Movie Story*, April 1939; *New York Daily Mirror*, May 6, 1939; *New York Daily News*, May 1939; *New York Herald Tribune*, May 6, 1939; *New York Times*, May 7, 1939, p. 6; *New Yorker*, May 13, 1939, p. 77;

Newsweek, May 15, 1939, p. 33; *Photoplay*, July 1939, p. 62; *Picturegoer*, September 2, 1939; *Rob Wagner's Script*, May 20, 1939, Vol. 21, pp. 17-18; *St. Nicholas*, April 1939, Vol. 66, p. 37; *Time*, May 15, 1939, p. 58.

Commentary

Fanny Brice sued Twentieth Century-Fox for invading her privacy with this film, which bore a striking resemblance to the story of her marriage to the gambler Nicky Arnstein (later presented in the Broadway musical and its subsequent film version, *Funny Girl*). Miss Brice asked for $750,000 damages; the suit was settled out of court for a reported $75,000. Brice's ex-husband Arnstein also sued, and settled out of court, in a similar case. Despite the litigation, *Rose of Washington Square* is a charming musical film of its era, enhanced by Jolson's renditions of several of his greatest songs, and Faye's smooth appeal. Tyrone Power gives a good performance as Faye's love interest, but without a musical contribution, he comes in third in spite of his billing. Jolson's singing of "Pretty Baby," "Rock-A-Bye Your Baby With a Dixie Melody," "Toot, Toot, Tootsie," "California, Here I Come," and "My Mammy," make this film an important document for Jolson admirers. He is clearly showing his age, but his vitality is all there even though he loses some spontaneity in working with a pre-recorded soundtrack. Little is asked of him on the acting side, but he exchanges some amusing "on-stage' wisecracks with Hobart Cavanaugh as a drunken heckler. William Frawley, as Jolson's manager, and Joyce Compton, as Faye's best friend, give solid support. A trailer for the film survives.

F14 *HOLLYWOOD CAVALCADE*

1939. Twentieth Century-Fox. Color. 96 mins.

Credits

Director: Irving Cummings. Silent Sequences Director: Malcolm St. Clair, supervised by Mr. Mack Sennett. Producer: Darryl Zanuck. Associate Producer: Harry Joe Brown. Screenplay: Irving Pascal, from a story by Hilary Lynn and Brown Holmes based on an idea by Lou Breslow. Photography: Allen M. Davey, Ernest Palmer. Editor: Walter Thompson. Art Direction: Richard Day, Wiard B. Ihnen. Set Decoration: Thomas Little. Costumes: Herschel. Technical Direction: Natalie Kalmus, Henry Jaffa. Sound: Eugene Grossman, Roger Heman. Musical Direction: Louis Silvers. Music by David Raksin, David Buttolph, Cyril Mockridge.

Cast

Alice Faye (Molly Adair), Don Ameche (Michael Linnett Connors), J. Edward Bromberg (Dave Springold), Alan Curtis (Nicky Hayden), Stuart Irwin (Pete Tinney), Jed Prouty (Chief of Police), Buster Keaton (Himself), Donald Meek (Lyle P. Stout), George Givot (Englishman), Eddie Collins (Keystone Kop), Hank Mann (Keystone Kop), Heinie Conklin (Keystone Kop), James Finlayson (Keystone Kop), Chick Chandler (Assistant Director), Robert Lowery (Henry Potter), Russell Hicks (Roberts), Ben Walden (Agent), Willie Fung (Valet), Paul Stanton (Wilson), Ben Turpin (Bartender), Chester Conklin (Sheriff), Mack Sennett (Himself), Marjorie Beebe (Telephone Operator), Frederick Burton (Thomas), Lee Duncan (Himself), Rin Tin Tin, Jr. (Rin Tin Tin), Al Jolson (Himself).

Synopsis

Michael Linnett Connors (Ameche), an early silent film director based on a combination of D.W. Griffith and Mack Sennett, discovers a talented unknown stage actress, Molly Adair (Faye), and he signs her to a personal contract. Against the background of early Hollywood, Connors builds a movie empire with Molly as his greatest star. Connors, however, is too preoccupied with work to realize his love for Molly, or to notice her feelings for him. Rebuffed by Connors, she marries an actor in Connors' stable, Nicky Hayden (Curtis). Connors is angry and hurt, and fires both of them. The young couple continue in films and become a successful team while Connors' professional and personal life nosedives. To salvage his career, Molly demands that Connors direct her next film. Halfway through production, Molly and Nicky are in a car accident, and Nicky dies. Molly is hospitalized and Connors refuses to finish the film without her as the sound era arrives with the success of *The Jazz Singer*. With time, Molly recovers and she and Connors are reconciled.

Song

"Kol Nidre" (sung by Jolson in Aramaic).

Reviews

"There is a brief sequence also from *The Jazz Singer*, in which Jolson sings *Kol Nidre*. Obviously, this was made especially for the film."(Flin., *Variety*, October 4, 1939, p. 12)

> **Additional Reviews:** *Commonweal*, October 27, 1939, Vol. 30, p. 14; *Film Daily*, October 4, 1939, p. 7; *Hollywood Reporter*, October 3, 1939, p. 3; *Hollywood Spectator*, October 14, 1939, Vol. 14, pp. 7-8; *Illustrated London News*, March 2/16, 1940; *Life*, October 9, 1939, pp. 63-64; *Motion Picture Herald*, October 7, 1939, p. 35; *New York Daily Mirror*, October 14, 1939; *New York Post*, October 14, 1939; *New York Times*, October 8, 1939, Section IX, p. 4; *New York Times*, October 14, 1939, p. 13; *New York Times*, October 22, 1939, Section IX, p. 5; *New Yorker*, October 21, 1939, Vol. 15, p. 74; *Newsweek*, October 16, 1939, Vol. 14, p. 43; *Photoplay*, December 1939, Vol. 53, p. 62; *Rob Wagner's Script*, October 14, 1939, Vol. 22, p. 16; *Scholastic*, October 30, 1939, Vol. 35, p. 35; *Tatler*, February 21, 1940, Vol. 155, p. 236; *Time*, October 23, 1939, p. 52.

Commentary

Hollywood Cavalcade was one of the top money-making films of 1939-1940, but the "Harvard Lampoon" listed it as one of the ten worst pictures of the year. Jolson's scene was a recreation of the "Kol Nidre" excerpt from *The Jazz Singer* (see F2). Jolson's appearance is only a cameo in a formulaic movie brightened by his presence, similar cameos from a variety of silent film greats, including Buster Keaton, Chester Conklin, Mack Sennett, several of the original Keystone Kops, and Faye's charm.

F15   SWANEE RIVER

1939. Twentieth Century-Fox. Color. 84 mins.

Credits

Director: Sidney Lanfield. Choreographers: Nick Castle, Geneva Sawyer. Producer: Darryl Zanuck. Associate Producer: Kenneth Macgowan. Screenplay: John Taintor Foote, Philip Dunne, based on the life of Stephen Foster. Photography: Bert Glennon. Editor: Louis Loeffler. Art Direction: Richard Day, Joseph C. Wright. Set Decoration: Thomas Little. Technicolor Director: Natalie Kalmus. Costumes: Royer. Sound: W.D. Flick, Roger Heman. Musical Direction: Louis Silvers.

Cast

Don Ameche (Stephen Foster), Andrea Leeds (Jane McDowell), Al Jolson (E.P. Christy), Felix Bressart (Henry Kleber), Chick Chandler (Bones), Al Herman (Tambo), Russell Hicks (Andrew McDowell), George Reed (Joe), Richard Clarke (Tom Harper), Diane Fisher (Marion Foster), George Breakstone (Ambrose), Charles Halton (Pond), Charles Trowbridge (Mr. Foster), Leona Roberts (Mrs. Foster), George Meeker (Henry Foster), Charles Tannen (Morrison Foster), Nella Walker (Mrs. McDowell), Harry Hayden (Erwin), Clara Blandick (Mrs. Griffin), Georgia Caine (Ann Rowan), Margaret McWade (Letetia Patterson), Fern Emmett (Angeline Patterson), Esther Dale (Temperance Woman), The Hall Johnson Choir.

Synopsis

This is a highly fictionalized account of the life of nineteenth century American songwriter Stephen Collins Foster (Ameche). Foster, an impractical dreamer driven to capture the sounds of his beloved antebellum South, marries Jane McDowell (Leeds) over the protestations of her father, who believes Foster will never be able to make a reliable living as a songwriter. Foster takes a song to popular minstrel man E.P. Christy (Jolson), who gives Foster a mere fifteen dollars for outright ownership of "Oh! Susanna." When the song becomes a runaway success, Foster forms a partnership with Christy. However, he shows signs of unreliability and excessive drinking. When Foster passes out from drink at his young daughter's bedside, Jane takes the child and leaves Foster, who loses all interest in his work as he falls into obscurity and poverty. Christy tries to help by bringing Jane and Foster back together, and he arranges to introduce a new Foster song into a New York stage appearance. But the resistance of the Northern audience to Foster's "Southern" songs at the outbreak of the Civil War causes resistance. Foster collapses with a heart attack before the New York debut of the new song, "Swanee River," which Christy performs for a hushed and respectful audience following news of Foster's death.

Songs

"Oh! Susanna," "Boom! (Merry Minstrel Men)," "De Camptown Races," "My Old Kentucky Home," "Old Black Joe," "Ring de Banjo," "I Dream of Jeanie With the Light Brown Hair," "Old Folks at Home (Swanee River)."

Reviews

"Picture's main attractions to retain audience interest is the liberal spotting of eight Foster songs that are both familiar and popular. Jolson sings *Oh Susannah*, *Camptown Races*, and *Swanee River* in a minstrel show setting, putting them over in showmanly presentations. His offering of *Swanee River* after telling the audience that Foster has just died and the song will live as the composer's memorial, is dramatically impressive."(*Variety*, December 21, 1939, p. 12)

"It is a rather badly Technicolored song-slide for a half-dozen of the more famous Foster tunes, supported by a dramatic continuity which is rarely better than dull and chiefly to be remembered as the film in which Al Jolson is forever appearing at the head of a minstrel troupe to sing the Foster melodies as though they were all called *Mammy*."(Frank S. Nugent, *New York Times*, December 30, 1939, p. 9)

"Further disappointment, acute and surprising too, is aroused by Al Jolson's Christy. We might expect that Mr. Jolson would find the role of E.P. Christy, the great minstrel, something friendly and suitable for his talents. Possibly the lines and the various forced and theatrical predicaments devised for him left him no leeway; anyhow, there's little spirit in the presentation."(John Mosher, *New Yorker*, January 6, 1940, p. 51)

> **Additional Reviews:** *Etude*, February 1940, Vol. 58, p. 85; *Film Daily*, December 26, 1939, p. 6; *Hollywood Reporter*, December 20, 1939, p. 3; *Hollywood Spectator*, January 6, 1940, Vol. 14, pp. 5-6; *Motion Picture Herald*, December 23, 1939, p. 40; *Rob Wagner's Script*, January 6, 1940, Vol. 23, pp. 17-18; *Time*, January 15, 1940, pp. 62-63.

Commentary

As biography, this specious account of Stephen Foster's life is ludicrous. Don Ameche seems uncomfortable in the leading role, and most of the supporting cast, including Felix Bressart and Andrea Leeds, are little more than competent. Jolson comes off best as minstrel man E.P. Christy in the "on-stage" scenes in which he performs several Foster standards. His acting is solid, and it is his only featured appearance in an all-color film. There is little else to recommend this particular film. Louis Silvers was nominated for an Academy Award for his musical direction of this film. The "Harvard Lampoon" included *Swanee River* on its list of ten worst films of the year.

F16 TAKE IT OR LEAVE IT

1944. Twentieth Century-Fox. B&W. 68 mins.

Credits

Director: Benjamin Stoloff. Producer: Bryan Foy. Screenplay: Harold Buchman, Snag Werris, Mac Benoff. Photography: Joseph LaShelle. Editor: Harry Reynolds. Art Direction: Lyle Wheeler, Leland Fuller. Special Effects: Fred Sersen. Costumes: Kay Nelson. Musical Direction: Emil Newman.

Cast

Phil Baker (himself), Phil Silvers (himself), Edward Ryan (Eddie), Marjorie Massow (Kate Collins), Stanley Prager (Herb Gordon), Roy Gordon (Dr. Edward Preston), Nan Bryant (Miss Burke), Carleton Young (Program Director), Ann Corcoran (Secretary), Nella Walker (Mrs. Preston), Renie Riano (Mrs. Bramble), Frank Jenks (Taxi Driver), B.S. Pully (Truck Driver), with film clips of Shirley Temple, the Ritz Brothers, Betty Grable, Alice

Faye, Sonja Henie, and Al Jolson, among other stars of vintage Twentieth Century-Fox films.

Synopsis

A young sailor (Ryan) goes on a quiz show to make extra money to support his pregnant wife (Massow). The quiz show questions set up a series of old film clips.

Reviews

"The manner in which a dozen clips from past Fox and Joe Schenck film productions have been intertwined is a skillful and audience-arresting device to make the film fan participate in the quiz show."(Abel., *Variety*, July 12, 1944)

"Besides these cast members the show is also patched up with clips of old pictures starring Alice Faye, Sonja Henie, Al Jolson, the Ritz and Weir Brothers, and Shirley Temple, [. . .] Moreover, even in the picture trade there likely is a certain amount of astonishment that so many feet of film can be assembled with so little expenditure -- so little expenditure both of money and of consideration for adult intelligence."(P.P.K., *New York Times*, July 23, 1944, p. 1⁴)

Additional Reviews: *Commonweal*, July 28, 1944, ɔ. 353; *New Yorker*, July 22, 1944, p. 38; *Newsweek*, July 24, 1944, p. 107; *Time*, August 21, 1944, pp. 94-95.

Commentary

Jolson's rendition of "Toot, Toot, Tootsie" from *Rose of Washington Square* (see F13) is included among the vintage film clips shown in this otherwise ordinary programmer.

F17   *RHAPSODY IN BLUE*

1945. Warner Bros. B&W. 139 mins.

Credits

Director: Irving Rapper. Producer: Jesse L. Lasky. Choreographer: LeRoy Prinz. Screenplay: Howard Koch, Elliott Paul, from a story by Sonya Levien, based on the life of George Gershwin. Director of Photography: Sol Polito. Additional Photography: Merritt Gerstad, Ernest Haller. Editor: Folmer Blangsted. Art Direction: Anton Grot, John Hughes. Set Decoration: Fred M. MacLean. Makeup: Perc Westmore. Gowns: Milo Anderson. Sound: David Forrest, Stanley Jones. Sound Recording: Nathan Levinson. Choreography: LeRoy Prinz. Montages: James Leicester. Special Effects: Ray Davidson (director), Willard Van Enger. Dialogue Director: Felix Jacobs. Orchestral arrangements: Ray Heindorf, Max Steiner. Musical Director: Leo F. Forbstein. Music by George Gershwin, lyrics by Ira Gershwin, Arthur Frances, B.G. De Sylva, Ballard MacDonald, DuBose Heyward, Gus Kahn, Irving Caesar. Musical adaption: Max Steiner. Vocal arrangements: Dudley Chambers. Orchestra conducted by Leo F. Forbstein.

Cast

Robert Alda (George Gershwin), Joan Leslie (Julie Adams), Alexis Smith

(Christine Gilbert), Charles Coburn (Max Dreyfus), Julie Blahoe (Lee Gershwin), Herbert Rudley (Ira Gershwin), Albert Basserman (Professor Franck), Morris Carnovsky (Mr. Gershwin), Rosemary DeCamp (Mrs. Gershwin), Eddie Marr (Buddy DeSylva), Oscar Loraine (Ravel), Hugo Kirchhoffer (Walter Damrosch), Mickey Roth (George Gershwin as a boy), Darryl Hickman (Ira Gershwin as a boy), Charles Halton (Mr. Kast). The following individuals portrayed themselves: Oscar Levant, Paul Whiteman, Al Jolson, George White, Hazel Scott, Anne Brown, Tom Patricola, John B. Hughes, and Elsa Maxwell.

Synopsis

This highly fictionalized treatment of George Gershwin's life is bolstered considerably by many Gershwin standards. The episodic film includes a sequence in which Gershwin (Alda) plays "Swanee" for song publisher Max Dreyfus (Coburn). Dreyfus phones Al Jolson (himself), who is impressed with the song and adds it to his Winter Garden show where it scores a hit.

Songs

"Swanee," "S'Wonderful," "Somebody Loves Me," "I'll Build a Stairway to Paradise," "Lady Be Good," "Blue Monday Blues," "Rhapsody in Blue," "The Man I Love," "Clap Yo' Hands," "I Got Rhythm," "Yankee Doodle Blues," "Embraceable You," "An American in Paris," "Cuban Overture," "Mine," "Delicious," "Summertime," "Concerto in F," "Love Walked In," "Rhapsody in Blue."

Reviews

"The musical highlights, of course, are authentic, and in real-life hands. Thus Al Jolson plays himself, introducing *Swanee*, Gershwin's first hit which he wrote with Irving Caesar (who, incidentally, is not impersonated, whereas the now ailing Buddy de Sylva, another lyricist collaborator, is shown briefly, played by Eddie Marr). Jolson at the Winter Garden, first shown blacking-up when music publisher Max Dreyfus (Charlie Coburn) phones him, is a thrill. Still among the world's greatest entertainers, Jolson in blackface is out of the memory-books and once again celluloided for posterity."(Abel., *Variety*, June 27, 1945, p. 16)

"Throughout, the brilliant music of Mr. Gershwin is spotted abundantly, and that is the best -- in fact, the only -- intrinsically right thing in the film. Even though a frog-voiced Al Jolson weakly simulates to sing *Swanee* the way he originally sang it at the Winter Garden some twenty-five years ago, the captivating life in that old rhythm is strong and exciting today."(Bosley Crowther, *New York Times*, June 28, 1945, p. 28)

". . .the brazen love call of the Winter Garden smash *Swanee*, groaned in all its original agony by blackfaced Al Jolson."("The New Pictures," *Time*, July 2, 1945, p. 85)

". . .(there's a wonderful scene in which Al Jolson sings *Swanee* for the first time)."(Philip T. Hartung, " Fascinating Rhythms," *Commonweal*, July 6, 1945, pp. 286-287)

Additional Reviews: *Film Digest*, 1945; *Life*, July 16, 1945, pp. 89-92; *Nation*, July 21, 1945, Volume 161, No. 3, p. 67; *New Republic*, July 23, 1945, p. 103;

New Statesman, November 3, 1945, p. 298; *New York Times*, April 16, 1944, Section II, p. 4; *New York Times*, July 8, 1945, Section II, p. 1; *New York Times Magazine*, June 3, 1945, pp. 24-25; *New Yorker*, July 7, 1945, pp. 34-35; *Newsweek*, July 9, 1945, p. 102; *Photoplay*, September 1945, p. 22; *Photoplay*, February 1947, p. 44; *Scholastic*, September 24, 1945, pp. 20-21; *Theatre Arts*, November 1945, p. 645.

Commentary

Jolson contributes a bright cameo appearance in this long and highly fictional screen biography of composer George Gershwin (Robert Alda). Jolson is seen backstage at the Winter Garden Theatre blacking up (undoubtedly he is seen only in blackface as an attempt to hide his age, since he is playing himself at the height of his early stage career) when he receives a call from music publisher Max Dreyfus, played by Charles Coburn. Jolson overhears Gershwin playing "Swanee" and agrees to introduce it into his stage show, *Sinbad* (see S23). Following the phone seen, Jolson is viewed backstage about to make his entrance. In a lavish plantation stage setting, Jolson runs on and gives a characteristic performance of "Swanee," garnering an ovation from the theatre audience. Backstage, he congratulates Gershwin and encourages him to write more hits. Jolson's advancing age is evident, but it is still thrilling to see him even in an obviously trumped up "recreation" of his impact on a theatre audience. This film marked Jolson's final billed screen appearance. Ray Heindorf and Max Steiner were nominated for Academy Awards for their musical direction, and Nathan Levinson was nominated for his sound recording of the film. *Rhapsody in Blue* was one of the top money-making films of 1945. A trailer for the film survives.

F18   THE JOLSON STORY

1946. Columbia Pictures. Color. 128 mins.

Credits

Director: Alfred E. Green. Assistant Director: William McGaugh. Producer: Sidney Skolsky. Associate Producer: Gordon S. Griffith. Screenplay: Stephen Longstreet (Sidney Buchman contributed, but was uncredited). Adaptation: Harry Chandlee, Andrew Solt. Editor: William Lyon. Art Directors: Stephen Gooson, Walter Holscher. Set Decorations: William Kiernan, Louis Diag. Gowns by Jean Louis. Make-up: Clay Campbell, S.M.A. Hairstyles: Helen Hunt. Director of Photography: Joseph Walker, A.S.C. Technicolor Director: Natalie Kalmus. Associate: Morgan Padelford. Sound Recording: Hugh McDowell. Music Recording: Edwin Wetzel. Re-recording: Richard Olson. Music Director: Morris W. Stoloff. Vocal Arrangements: Saul Chaplin. Orchestral Arrangements: Martin Fried. Production numbers directed by Joseph H. Lewis. Assistant Director: Wilbur McGaugh. Montage Director: Lawrence W. Butler. Choreographer: Jack Cole. Orchestra conducted by Morris Stoloff.

Cast

Larry Parks (Al Jolson), Evelyn Keyes (Julie Berson), William Demarest (Steve Martin), Bill Goodwin (Tom Baron), Ludwig Donath (Cantor Yoelson), Tamara Shayne (Mama Yoelson), John Alexander (Lew

Dockstader), Jo-Carroll Dennison (Ann Murray), William Forrest (Dick Glenn), Ernest Cossart (Father McGee), Scotty Beckett (Al Jolson as a boy), Ann E. Todd (Ann Murray as a girl), Edwin Maxwell (Oscar Hammerstein I), Emmett Vogan (Jonesy), Eric Wilton (Henry), Will Wright (Movie Patron), Eddie Kane (Florenz Ziegfeld), Jimmy Lloyd (Roy Anderson), Coulter Irwin (Young Priest), Adele Roberts (Ingenue), Bob Stevens (Henry), Harry Shannon (Riley the policeman), Bud Gorman (Call Boy), Charles Jordan (Assistant Stage Manager), Pierre Watkin (Architect), Lillian Bond (Woman), Eugene Borden (Headwaiter), Eddie Rio (M.C.), Arthur Loft (Stage Manager), Edward Keane (Director), Eddie Fetherston (Assistant Stage Manager), Bill Brandt (Orchestra Leader), Pat Lane (Cameraman), Mike Lally (Lab Manager), George Magrill (Gaffer), Helen O'Hara (Dancer-Actress), Jessie Arnold (Wardrobe Woman), Donna Dax (Girl Publicist), Fred Sears (Cutter), Franklyn Farnum (Man in Audience), Major Sam Harris (Nightclubber). The Robert Mitchell "Boychoir." **Rudy Wissler** dubbed the songs for Scotty Beckett. Jo Ann Greer dubbed the songs for Evelyn Keyes. Al Jolson dubbed the songs for Larry Parks.

Synopsis

This highly fictionalized film biography of Jolson begins with a depiction of his youth in turn-of-the-century Washington, D.C. Young Asa Yoelson (Beckett) attends a local burlesque theatre and spontaneously joins in singing with headliner Steve Martin (Demarest). Martin is impressed with Asa's voice and goes to the Yoelson home to propose a stage partnership between himself and Asa. But Cantor Yoelson (Donath), Asa's orthodox father refuses. Asa runs away to Baltimore, hoping to join Martin there. He is intercepted by police who turn him over to St. Mary's School for Boys. When his parents and Martin arrive, Mrs. Yoelson (Shayne), realizing that Asa will only run away again, agrees to let Asa go onstage with Martin. The partnership is successful until Asa's voice changes, causing him to unhappily switch to whistling. As he grows older, Asa, now calling himself Al Jolson (Parks), agitates with the reluctant Martin to switch back to singing. When Tom Baron (Goodwin) is unable to perform his blackface act in a Louisville vaudeville theatre, Al blacks up and goes on in Baron's place, scoring a hit. He joins Lew Dockstader's Minstrels, without Martin, and works his way up in the company, attempting to push Dockstader into allowing him to try new songs instead of the traditional minstrel fare. When the troupe plays New Orleans, Al hears some improvising jazz musicians and he is captivated. So much so that he forgets about his performance and arrives too late to go on. Dockstader fires him, and Al is at loose ends for a time hoping for a chance to perform his new, jazz-based songs. His chance comes when Martin intercedes with Baron, now manager of New York's new Winter Garden Theatre. On opening night, however, the show runs too long and the stage manager cuts Al's number. Refusing to miss his chance, Al impetuously rushes onstage and performs "My Mammy" to an enthusiastic response. His career rises meteorically as Martin's sinks in decline. Not forgetting Martin's help, Al asks him to be his manager as he dominates Broadway, recordings and sheet music. Martin worries about Al's workaholic ways and lack of a personal life. Al hopes to marry his childhood sweetheart (Dennison), but discovers too late that she is to marry another. He throws himself even more deeply into his work, adding Sunday night concerts to his demanding schedule, thus permitting his fellow performers an opportunity to see him. At one such performance, as he is about to depart for Hollywood to make the first talking picture, Al encounters Julie Benson (Keyes), Florenz Ziegfeld's latest protege. He is smitten with her, but he must leave for California and she is about to open on Broadway in Ziegfeld's *Show Girl*. Impulsively, on Julie's opening night, Al flies to New York. When she falters from nerves during the song "Liza," Al rises from his seat in the audience and sings the song to her, renewing her confidence. Al and Julie marry, but continue to be separated by work as *The Jazz Singer*, Al's sound film, triumphs and he signs to make more films. When *Show Girl* ends its run, Julie comes to California with the expectation of an imminent retirement for both Jolsons to a quiet life in the country. Al remains driven to perform, however, and Julie reluctantly signs on to make films, becoming a screen star herself. After a gruelling series of films, including *Go Into Your Dance*, in which both Al and Julie star, Julie demands that she and Al must either quit work or end their marriage. Al agrees and moves into a restless retirement. When his parents visit for their wedding anniversary, Al is coaxed by his father to sing. Baron arrives for a visit, inspiring a trip to a nightclub where Al is recognized by the audience. When the crowd enthusiastically demands that he sing, Al gets caught up in his performance. Julie realizes the he must sing to live, and while he blissfully performs she slips quietly away and out of his life.

Songs

"Let Me Sing and I'm Happy," "Banks of the Wabash," "Ave Maria," "When You Were Sweet Sixteen," "After the Ball," "By the Light of the Silvery Moon," "Blue Bell," "American Patrol," "Ma Blushin' Rosie," "I Want a Girl," "My Mammy," "I'm Sitting on Top of the World," "You Made Me Love You,' "Swanee," "Toot, Toot, Tootsie," "The Spaniard That Blighted My Life," "April Showers," "California, Here I Come," "Liza," "There's a Rainbow 'Round My Shoulder,' "Avalon," "She's a Latin from Manhattan," "About a Quarter to Nine," "Anniversary Song," "Waiting for the Robert E. Lee," "Rock-A-Bye Your Baby With a Dixie Melody."

Reviews

"But the real star of the production is that Jolson voice and that Jolson medley. It was good showmanship to cast this film with lesser people, particularly Larry Parks as the mammy kid. [. . .] As for Jolson's voice, it has never been better. Thus the magic of science has produced a composite whole to eclipse the original at his most youthful best."(Abel., *Variety*, September 18, 1946, p. 16)

"Noel Coward made the observation in one of his catty little plays that it really is quite remarkable how potent cheap music can be. That's the truth -- and, as evidence of it, see *The Jolson Story*, at the Music Hall. For here, in this gaudy fictionalization of Al Jolson's hurly-burly life, it is not the story of the trouper which attracts the indifferently disposed, not the extreme and mawkish drooling over a popular star of stage and screen, but rather the generous sound-tracking of a sack full of familiar old songs which imparts to the film an appealing nostalgic quality."(Bosley Crowther, *New York Times*, October 11, 1946, p. 28)

"The Hollywood hagiographers who put together *The Jolson Story* have made their hero as piously tedious as Little Lord Fauntleroy. According to the film, Al Jolson, who is played by Larry Parks, is not simply a cantor's son who becomes a successful song-and-dance man but the living embodiment of all the virtues enumerated in the Boy Scout oath."(John McCarten, "Good Old Al," *New Yorker*, October 19, 1946, pp. 102, 104)

"In this specious illustration of Al Jolson's glamorized life the songs that were sung by Mr. Jolson are, incongruously, the whole show. There is little more cinematic quality or dynamic imagery in the picturization of the story than there might be in a set of *stills*."(Bosley Crowther, *New York Times*, October 20, 1946, Section II, p. 1)

"Almost all of the familiar song favorites can be heard in *The Jolson Story*, some several times: *Swanee, April Showers, California Here I Come, Mammy* and so on. For some reason, *Sonny Boy* does not appear, but we bore up."(Hermine Rich Isaacs, *Theatre Arts*, November 1946, p. 670)

> **Additional Reviews:** *Commonweal*, October 25, 1946, p. 46; *Cosmopolitan*, October 1946, p. 73; *Film Daily*, September 16, 1946, p. 6; *Fortnight*, November 4, 1946, Vol. 1, No. 1, p. 42; *Hollywood Reporter*, September 16, 1946, p. 3; *Life*, March 10, 1947, p. 94; *Motion Picture Herald Product Digest*, September 21, 1946, p. 3209; *Nation*, November 9, 1946, p. 537; *New Movies*, November-December 1946, Vol. 21, No. 11-12, pp. 5-6; *New York Daily News*, October 11, 1946; *New York Herald Tribune*, October 11, 1946; *New York Times Magazine*, October 13, 1946, pp. 30-31; *New Yorker*, October 19, 1946, pp. 112-113; *Newsweek*, October 14, 1946, pp. 112-113; *Photoplay*, November 1946, p. 4; *Time*, October 7, 1946, p. 101; *Toronto Telegram*, June 16, 1969.

Commentary

Jolson appears (unbilled) as himself in one brief scene of this memorable screen biography. In a scene on the Winter Garden Theatre runway, Jolson recreates "Swanee." One story suggests that Jolson felt Larry Parks would not be able to successfully approximate his eccentric dance steps, but most biographers have believed that the irrepressible Jolson was compelled to make at least a gratuitous appearance in this celluloid monument to his theatrical greatness. Actually, Jolson's voice is the real star of the film. Larry Parks gives a charming and believeable performance, as does Evelyn Keyes, William Demarest, Ludwig Donath, and several members of the supporting cast. But with superb orchestrations and lovingly produced recordings, Jolson's deeper, mellower later-day is perfectly showcased. Even today, it is not difficult to understand why Jolson was catapulted back to the top ranks of show business with this film. Among screen biographies of entertainment luminaries, only *Yankee Doodle Dandy* (1942), the story of George M. Cohan, equals the pleasures to be found in this movie. *The Jolson Story* was nominated for several Oscars, including Best Actor (Larry Parks), Best Supporting Actor (William Demarest), Cinematography (Joseph Walker), and Film Editing (William Lyon). The film won two Oscars: Sound Recording (John P. Livadary) and Music Scoring of a Motion Picture (Morris W. Stoloff). *The Jolson Story* was the third biggest moneymaker of 1946, and Columbia's top grossing film of all-time, with a reported box office take in excess of $8,000,000. *The Jolson Story* was also selected for several "Photoplay" Magazine's Gold Medal Awards, and was listed on "Time" Magazine's Ten-Best List for 1946. A trailer for the film survives.

F19   OH, YOU BEAUTIFUL DOLL

1949. Twentieth Century-Fox. Color. 94 mins.

Credits
Director: John M. Stahl. Producer: George Jessel. Screenplay: Albert and Arthur Lewis. Musical Direction: Alfred Newman. Photography: Harry Jackson, Fred Sersen. Editor: Louis Loeffler. Art Direction: Lyle Wheeler, Maurice Ransford. Choreography: Seymour Felix.

Cast
S.Z. Sakall (Fred Fisher), Mark Stevens (Larry Kelly), June Haver (Doris Breitenbach), Charlotte Greenwood (Anna Breitenbach), Jay C. Flippen (Lippy Brannigan), Gale Robbins (Marie Carle), Andrew Tombes (Ted Held), Eduard Franz (Gottfried Steiner), Dick Rich (Burly Man), Al Klein, Don Kerr, Warren Jackson, Sam Ash (Quartet), Eula Morgan (Mme. Zubel), Nestor Palva (Lucca), Curt Bois (Zaltz), Torchy Rand (Sophie).

Synopsis
The plot of this highly fictionalized biographical film about composer Fred Fisher (Sakall) centers on his wish to compose opera, despite his success at writing popular music. Most of the film is devoted to the romance of Fisher's daughter, Doris (Haver), and a song plugger (Stevens).

Songs
The score was made up of many popular songs of Fisher's day, and featured his own compositions including: "Oh, You Beautiful Doll," "I Want You to Want Me to Want You," "Who Paid the Rent for Mrs. Rip Van Winkle?," "Daddy, You've Been More Than a Mother to Me," "When I Get You Alone Tonight," "Ireland Must Be Heaven Because My Mother Came From There," "Peg O' My Heart," "Chicago," "There's a Broken Heart For Every Light On Broadway," "Dardanella," and "Come Josephine in My Flying Machine."

Reviews
"One may pause to wonder what is going to happen to this type of film enterprise when all of the old songs, both the good and the bad, have been exhausted." (*Newsweek*, November 28, 1949, p. 72)

Additional Reviews: *Christian Century*, December 28, 1949, p. 1559; *New York Times*, November 12, 1949, p. 8; *Rotarian*, February 1950, p. 38; *Time*, December 19, 1949, p. 90; *Variety*, September 21, 1949.

Commentary
Jolson's voice is heard over a telephone in one scene.

F20 *JOLSON SINGS AGAIN*

1949. Columbia Pictures. Color. 96 mins.

Credits
Director: Henry Levin. Producer: Sidney Buchman. Associate Producer:

Francis Cugat. Screenplay: Sidney Buchman. Photography: William Snyder. Editor: William Lyon. Art Direction: Walter Holscher. Set Design: William Kiernan. Makeup: Clay Campbell. Hair Styles: Helen Hunt. Gowns: Jean Louis. Technicolor Direction: Natalie Kalmus. Recording: George Cooper (dialogue), Philip Faulkner (music). Re-recording: Richard Olson. Assistant Director: Milton Feldman. Montage Director: Lawrence W. Butler. Song Staging: Audrene Brier. Music Advisor: Saul Chaplin. Orchestrations: Larry Russell. Musical Score: George Duning. Musical Direction: Morris W. Stoloff.

Cast

Larry Parks (Al Jolson), Barbara Hale (Ellen Clark), William Demarest (Steve Martin), Ludwig Donath (Cantor Yoelson), Bill Goodwin (Tom Baron), Myron McCormick (Ralph Bryant), Tamara Shayne (Mama Yoelson), Eric Wilton (Henry), Robert Emmett Keane (Charlie), Larry Parks (himself), Frank McLure, Jock Mahoney (Men), Betty Hill (Woman), Margie Stapp (Nurse), Nelson Leigh (Theater Manager), Virginia Mullen (Mrs. Bryant), Philip Faulkner, Jr. (Sound Mixer), Morris Stoloff (Orchestra Leader), Helen Mowery (Script Girl), Michael Cisney, Ben Erway (Writers), Martin Garralaga (Mr. Estrada), Dick Cogan (Soldier), Peter Brocco (Captain of Waiters), Charles Regan, Charles Perry, Richard Gordon, David Newell, Joe Gilbert, David Horsley, Wanda Perry, Louise Illington, Gertrude Astor, Steve Benton, Eleanor Marvak (Bits). Al Jolson dubbed the songs for Larry Parks.

Synopsis

This highly fictionalized account of the later years of Jolson's life begins where *The Jolson Story* leaves off. Discovering that his wife, Julie, has left him, Al (Parks) returns to show business in a new Broadway show. He scores a great success, but, saddened by his failed marriage, Al quits the show and seeks "the bluebird of happiness" on an extended vacation at casinos, racetracks, beaches and boxing arenas. As World War II begins, Papa Yoelson (Donath) becomes increasingly concerned about Al's frivolous lifestyle. When Mama Yoelson (Shayne) dies suddenly, Al returns to his boyhood home in Washington, D.C., where his father confronts him about wasting his life. When Martin (Demarest) arrives to talk with the War Department about sending performers to foreign outposts to entertain American troops, Al becomes intrigued. He sets out to make a great tour of army installations beginning in Alaska where his uncertainties about performing again are calmed by Colonel Bryant (McCormick), a long-time Jolson fan. Al performs vigorously in many different locations, but he finally collapses from a tropical fever. He is flown back to the states where Papa and Martin try to convince him to quit singing until he is completely recovered. They are not very successful, but Ellen Clark (Hale), an outspoken young nurse from Arkansas, tells Al directly that to perform again so soon would be unwise. Al argues with her, but is clearly charmed by her. Papa notices the attraction and invites Ellen to dinner where he tells her that Al is a man who has never learned how to live off the stage. Al leaves the hospital and embarks on a tour of Army hospitals. When he gets to Arkansas he is anxious to see Ellen again and, although he worries about the difference in their ages, he confesses his feelings for her. Later, on tour again, Al collapses from a recurrence of the fever and undergoes surgery for removal of part of a lung. Ellen arrives to offer encouragement, and when Al leaves the hospital, they are married.

Ellen insists they move into the house that once belonged to him and Julie so that he will be forced to confront his feelings about the past. When Papa arrives for an extended visit, Ellen begins pushing Al to return to work singing. Al, however, fears he no longer can, and Martin privately tells Ellen that the show business parade has long since passed Al by. Ellen persists and Al reluctantly agrees to appear on a benefit, but he is scheduled so late in the performance that much of the audience has long-since departed. Bryant, now a movie producer, and his wife are present, and impressed with Al's undiminished ability to move an audience. Bryant gets the idea of making a film of Al's life, but Al resists the idea until Ellen pushes him into making a test recording. When the recording is effectively matched by the miming of actor Larry Parks (Parks), the result impresses Al. A film of Al's life is made, with his vocal recordings, but Al becomes so sick with nerves at the preview of the movie that he misses most of it. *The Jolson Story* is a triumph and is instrumental in returning Al to the front rank of show business luminaries, as Ellen looks on approvingly.

Songs

"Is It True What They Say About Dixie?," "For Me and My Gal," "Back in Your Own Backyard," "I'm Looking Over a Four-Leaf Clover," "When the Red, Red Robin Comes Bob, Bob Bobbin' Along," "Give My Regards to Broadway," "Chinatown My Chinatown," "I'm Just Wild About Harry," "Baby Face," "After You've Gone," "I Only Have Eyes for You," "Sonny Boy," "Toot, Toot, Tootsie," "Pretty Baby," "Carolina in the Morning," "Rock-A-Bye Your Baby With a Dixie Melody." (Also includes bits of most of the numbers from *The Jolson Story*).

Reviews

"*Jolson Sings Again* bids fair to par *The Jolson Story* grosses and may even top them. In short, a smasheroo of unqualified proportions."(Abel., *Variety*, August 1949, p. 8)

"There is heart, humor, tragedy and a warm sprinkling of sentiment in Mr. Buchman's story. Much of the latter is conjured up by a succession of nostalgic songs which run all through the film and are sung in grand style by Mr. Jolson himself. The vitality of the Jolson voice is suitably matched in the physical representation provided by Larry Parks, who by now comes close to perfection in aping the vigorous expression with which Jolson tackles a song."(T.M.P., *New York Times*, August 18, 1949, p. 16)

"As in its predecessor, *The Jolson Story*, Larry Parks is on hand to impersonate Mr. Al Jolson, and once again he subjects his entire person to the authentic duplication of Jolson's every gesture. Parks' eyes roll, his face is contorted, his body sways, his Adams's apple does time and a half, he crouches and rises like some large, flapping bird; in short, he superbly imitates the genuine article. Accompanying these physical exertions, and beautifully synchronized with them (i.e., dubbed in), is the voice of Jolson, still a formidable, awesome, and gradiosely captivating instrument."(Philip Hamburger, "Bob, Bob, Bobbin' Along," *New Yorker*, August 27, 1949, pp. 37-38)

Additional Reviews: *Commonweal*, August 26, 1949, p. 490; *Film Daily*, August 12, 1949, p. 6; *Hollywood Reporter*, August 12, 1949, p. 3; *Life*, September 12, 1949, pp. 93-94; *Motion Picture Herald Product Digest*, May

7, 1949, p. 4597; *New York Herald Tribune*, August 17, 1949; *New York Times*, August 21, 1949, Section II, p. 1; *Newsweek*, August 29, 1949, p. 73; *Photoplay*, October 1949, p. 22; *Rotarian*, November 1949, p. 34; *Theatre Arts*, November 1949, Vol. XXXIII, No. 10, pp. 2, 8; *Time*, September 5, 1949, p. 62; *Toronto Telegram*, June 16, 1969; *Woman's Home Companion*, October 1949, p. 10.

Commentary

Jolson Sings Again is a well-made sequel to *The Jolson Story* (see F18). In some ways, it betters the original. If anything, Jolson's voice sound even better in this movie, and Larry Parks' Jolson is a warmer, more human character here. Barbara Hale gives a charming performance as Jolson's wife, and William Demarest and Ludwig Donath give strong support as in the first film. Although most of Jolson's best songs, and the major events of the first half of his life, were utilized for *The Jolson Story*, this account of Jolson's career decline and ultimate resurgence, is entertaining. The film received Academy Award nominations for Writing: Story and Screenplay (Sidney Buchman), Cinematography: Color (William Snyder), and Music: Scoring of a Musical Picture (Morris Stoloff, George Duning). *Jolson Sings Again* was one of the top money-making films of 1949, with a box office take in excess of $5,500,000. A trailer for the film survives. In 1948, Columbia Pictures filmed Jolson in front of a curtain performing to several pre-recorded vocals "Is It True What They Say About Dixie?" (two takes, both full figure shots), "For Me and My Gal" (two takes, both full figure shots), "Baby Face" (two takes, one medium shot and one full figure shot), and "It All Depends on You" (one take, full figure shot). It is not clear why this film was made, but this footage is apparently either a screen test made to determine if Jolson could play himself in *Jolson Sings Again* or a practice film for Larry Parks (or both). Jolson does an impromptu burlesque "bump" at the end of one take of "Is It True What They Say About Dixie?" At the conclusion of several takes, Jolson appears dissatisfied about his performance.

F21   THE GOLDEN TWENTIES

1950. The March of Time. B&W. 68 mins.

Synopsis

This collection of scenes from vintage "March of Time" newsreels includes footage of Al Jolson, Babe Ruth, Calvin Coolidge, Bill Tilden, Will Rogers, Bobby Jones, Enrico Caruso, General Pershing, Helen Willis, Charles Lindbergh, Paul Whiteman, Herbert Hoover, George Gershwin, Gene Tunney, Gertrude Ederle, Johnny Weismuller, Woodrow Wilson, Jimmy Walker, Al Capone, Jack Dempsey, William Jennings Bryan, Warren G. Harding, Knute Rockne, Al Smith, Irene Castle, Henry Ford, Earl Carroll, Franklin Delano Roosevelt, Kennesaw Mountain Landis, and many other famous figures of the 1920's.

Reviews

". . .an hour-long documentary that sheds a nostalgic tear for the decade of the big binge. From the false Armistice of 1918 to Black Thursday of 1929, this well-edited paste-up of old newsreels recalls the fevers and foibles of the generation that lived on Florida booms, hip flasks, F. Scott Fitzgerald, the Charleston, and the out-of-sight spiral of a rocketing stock market."(*Time*, April 3, 1950, Vol. 55, pp. 92-93)

Additional Reviews: *Commonweal*, March 31, 1950, Vol. 51, p. 655; *Film Daily*, March 20, 1950, p. 8; *Films in Review*, May-June 1950, Vol. 1, pp. 19-21; *Hollywood Reporter*, March 17, 1950, p. 3; *Library Journal*, May 15, 1956, Vol. 75, p. 885; *Life*, April 17, 1950, p. 165; *Motion Picture Herald Product Digest*, March 18, 1950, p. 229; *New Republic*, May 1, 1950, Vol. 122, p. 22; *New York Times*, April 10, 1950, p. 15; *New Yorker*, April 8, 1951, Vol. 26, p. 98; *Saturday Review*, May 9, 1953, p. 39; *Variety*, March 22, 1950, p. 6.

F22 **PURPLE HEART DIARY** (Title in Great Britain: *No Time For Tears*)

1951. Columbia Pictures. B&W. 73 mins.

Credits

Director: Richard Quine. Producer: Sam Katzman. Screenplay: William Sackheim (based on the wartime column of Frances Langford). Photography: William Whitley. Editor: Henry Batista. Musical Direction: Ross Di Maggio. Art Direction: Paul Palmentola.

Cast

Frances Langford (herself), Ben Lessy (himself), Tony Romano (himself), Judd Holdren (Lt. Mike McCormick), Aline Towne (Lt. Cathy Dietrich), Brett King (Lt. Rocky Castro), Warren Mills (Elmo Slimmer), Larry Stewart (Cpl. Reeder), Joel Marston (Kalick), Richard Grant (Bunch), Rory Mallinson (Capt. Sprock), Selmer Jackson (Col. Tappen), Lyle Talbot (Maj. Green), Douglas F. Bank (Sgt. Innes), William Klein (Lt. Hughes), Harry Guardino (Lt. Roberts), Marshall Reed (Stark), Steve Pendleton (Sgt. Morse), George Offerman Jr. (Ross).

Synopsis

A sentimental musical film chronicle of the everyday efforts of USO performers to bring aid and comfort to the American GI during wartime. Made as propaganda for the United Service Organization.

Reviews

"A few clips are introduced for atmosphere, and aside from these, the aura is strictly lot-lensing."(Trau., *Variety*, November 7, 1951)

Commentary

This feature film includes newsreel footage of Jolson singing for American troops during World War II.

F23 **THE STORY OF WILL ROGERS**

1952. Warner Bros. Color. 109 mins.

Credits

Director: Michael Curtiz. Producer: Robert Arthur. Screenplay: Frank Davis, Stanley Roberts, John C. Moffitt, based on "Uncle Clem's Boy," a story by Betty Blake Rogers. Photography: Wilfrid M. Cline. Editor: Folmar

Blangsted. Art Direction: Edward Carrere. Costumes: Milo Anderson. Musical direction: Victor Young. Photography: Wilfrid M. Cline.

Cast

Will Rogers, Jr. (Will Rogers), Jane Wyman (Mrs. Will Rogers), James Gleason (Bert Lynn), Eddie Cantor (Himself), Carl Benton Reid (Clem Rogers), Eve Miller (Cora Marshall), Slim Pickens (Dusty Donovan), Noah Beery, Jr. (Wiley Post), Mary Wickes (Mrs. Foster), Steve Brodie (Dave Marshall), Pinky Tomlin (Orville James), Margaret Field (Sally Rogers), Virgil S. Taylor (Art Frazer), Richard Kean (Mr. Cavendish), Jay Silverheels (Joe Arrow), William Forrest (Flo Ziegfeld), Earl Lee (President Wilson), Brian Daly (Tom McSpadden), Robert Scott Correll (Younger Will, Jr.), Carol Ann Gainey (Younger Mary), Michael Gainey (Younger Jimmy/Young Will), Carol Nugent (Young Mary), Jack Burnette (Young Jimmy), Paul McWilliam (Dead-Eye Dick), Dub Taylor (Actor), Olan Soule (Secretary), Madge Journeay (Honey Girl Kate), Denver Dixon, Bob Rose (Bits), Monte Blue (Delegate).

Synopsis

A film biography and tribute to the beloved humorist. Rogers is played by his son, in a recounting of his life which begins with his humble childhood in Oklahoma and concludes with the fatal airplane crash that abruptly ended his successful career on the stage, radio, films and in public life.

Reviews

"In short, *The Story of Will Rogers* is not an important film. But it gives a tender reflection of a character that many people loved."(Bosley Crowther, *New York Times*, July 18, 1952, p. 10)

Additional Reviews: *BFI/Monthly Film Bulletin*, October 1952, Vol. 19, p. 145; *Christian Century*, September 24, 1952, pp. 1111; *Commonweal*, August 8, 1952, p. 436; *Film Daily*, July 11, 1952, p. 4; *Hollywood Reporter*, July 11, 1952, p. 3; *Motion Picture Herald Product Digest*, July 19, 1952, p. 1453; *National Parent-Teacher*, October 1952, p. 37; *New York Times*, January 25, 1952, p. 14; *New York Times*, July 18, 1952, p. 10; *Newsweek*, July 28, 1952, p. 80; *Time*, July 28, 1952, p. 72; *Times* (London), August 25, 1952, p. 6; *Variety*, July 16, 1952, p. 6.

Commentary

This fictionalized film biography of Will Rogers features Jolson singing a bit of "Swanee" originally filmed for *Rhapsody in Blue* (see F13), but this is a different take from that which is seen in the original film.

Aside from these films, some sources suggest that Jolson made unbilled cameos in the two features *Sonny Boy* (1929) and *Alexander's Ragtime Band* (1938), and that he is seen performing one song in the 1929 film *New York Nights*. A close viewing of *Alexander's Ragtime Band* does not reveal a Jolson appearance, but some film source books persist in including it among his credits (perhaps because songs associated with Jolson are used in the film). In 1944, Jolson recorded a track of the song, "Who Says That Dreams Don't Come True?" for Columbia Pictures film

The Impatient Years, directed by Irving Cummings from a screenplay by Virginia Van Upp, and starring Jean Arthur, Lee Bowman, and Charles Coburn. Jolson is listed on the sheet music of the song as a co-author, but his recording of the song, which was apparently a test pressing, was not used in the film. A number of films and television programs have included Jolson footage taken from his films or newsreels, or have included Jolson vocals on the soundtrack. Some recent films featuring Jolson material include: *You Are What You Eat* (1968), *Brother, Can You Spare a Dime?* (1974), *Twinkle, Twinkle, "Killer" Kane* (1979), *Phar Lap* (1983), *Hannah and Her Sisters* (1986), *Goodfellas* (1990), *Avalon* (1990), and *Jacob's Ladder* (1990). Jolson has been impersonated in at least two films: Norman Brooks appears as Jolson in *The Best Things in Life are Free* (1956), a fictional account of the lives of songwriters De Sylva, Brown, and Henderson, and Buddy Lewis plays Jolson in *Harlow* (1965), a fictional, and rather sensational dramatization of Jean Harlow's life. Performers imitate Jolson in many films; Donald O'Connor, for example, has Jolsonesque moments in *The Merry Monahans* (1944) and *Singin' in the Rain* (1952), and the principles in *On the Town* (1949) embellish a number with Jolson touches. Jolson imitations can also be seen in *Hollywood Revue of 1929*, *The Show of Shows* (1929), and the short *The Dogway Melody* (1929), among others.

Shorts

Al Jolson's participation in short films was remarkably diverse. In many instances, footage from newsreels or his feature films is the source, but in several cases Jolson contributed his voice or presence to a film.

F24 THE HONEYMOON EXPRESS

1913. Messrs. Shubert. B&W. 23 mins.

Cast

Al Jolson (Gus), Harry Pilcher (Baudry), Gaby Deslys (Yvonne), Ada Lewis (Mme. De Bressie).

Commentary

This film was made for the final scene of Act I of the stage musical, *The Honeymoon Express* (see S20). It depicted a chase scene involving a train and an automobile, driven by Jolson's Gus, also carrying Pilcher, Deslys, and Lewis. As the film ended, the train and automobile were discovered onstage at the conclusion of the chase. The film apparently does not survive.

F25 HUNTING THE FEROCIOUS AND EXTINCT CUCKOO

1915. California Motion Picture Corporation. B&W.

Cast

Al Jolson.

Commentary

This short subject was made specifically for showing at the California Building of the Panama-Pacific International Exposition in San Francisco, where it was screened from February 20-December 4, 1915. Jolson appeared in whiteface mocking silent film acting. The film itself is lost, although a series of still photographs survive.

F26   *UNTITLED*

1918. Vitagraph. B&W.

Cast

Al Jolson, others (including thirty-five New York policemen).

Commentary

This short film was made to benefit the New York Patrolman's Benevolent Association fund created to assist the children of policemen killed in the line of duty. One scene (filmed May 6, 1918) involved a chase scene including Jolson and thirty-five motorcycle police. In another scene, Jolson (in blackface) is sentenced to one day in jail for speeding and lectured by a judge. Jolson sobs and insists that the judge sentence him instead to a year. The film was shown at a special performance for police of Jolson's stage show, *Sinbad* (see S23). When Jolson learned that Vitagraph was keeping sixty percent of the film's profits, breaking their agreement with him that the PBA receive all profits from the film, he ordered that all prints be confiscated and, presumably, destroyed. No copies of the film are known to survive.

F27   *APRIL SHOWERS (or Al Jolson in a Plantation Act)*

1926. Warner Bros.-Vitaphone Corporation. B&W.

Credits

Director: Philip Roscoe. Producer: Robert Green. Orchestra conducted by Al Goodman.

Cast

Al Jolson.

Synopsis

Al Jolson in blackface enters a stage plantation scene and sings three songs: "April Showers," "Rock-A-Bye Your Baby With a Dixie Melody," and "When the Red, Red Robin Comes Bob, Bob, Bobbin' Along." Jolson also recorded "My Mammy" for this film, but it was apparently not used.

Reviews

"Al Jolson is seen, and of course heard, in three songs: *The Red, Red, Robin, April Showers* and *Rock-a-Bye Baby*, a Dixie Melody. This Vitaphone assuredly destroys the old silent tradition of the screen. This time it was the audience that was silent, so keen was everybody to catch every word and note of the popular entertainer, and when each number was ended it was obvious that there was not a still pair of hands in the house."(Mordaunt Hall, "The Vitaphone." *New York Times*, October 8, 1926, p. 23)

Additional Review: *Motion Picture World*, October 9, 1926.

Commentary

This short, certainly the most sought-after "lost" Jolson film, undoubtedly contains a unique document of the stage Jolson, as indicated by critical response singling it out of a collection of similar shorts including footage of George Jessel, Elsie Janis, and others, shown at the same time. Recently, the film footage of this short surfaced at the Library of Congress in a mislabeled can. Effort is being made by The Vitaphone Project, dedicated to the preservation and restoration of Vitaphone films, to locate the still missing Vitaphone disk in hopes of completely restoring this historic short.

F28 THEATRE OPENING

1928. Warner Bros. B&W. 15 mins.

Commentary

Jolson hosts this short designed to promote Warner Bros. Vitaphone sound process. It includes Jolson singing "Sonny Boy" and introducing several Warner Bros. stars who speak about Vitaphone. The film, which may never have been released, is lost, although it's sound disk survives.

F29 SCREEN SNAPSHOTS

1929. Columbia Pictures. B&W. 7 mins.

Commentary

Among an array of celebrities shown, Jolson and Ruby Keeler are seen arriving in Hollywood.

F30 SCREEN SNAPSHOTS

1930. Columbia Pictures. B&W. 19 mins.

Commentary

Billy Bevan gives a tour of Hollywood, with remarks by a variety of celebrities including Jolson.

F31 SEE AMERICA FIRST

1935. Warner Bros. B&W.

Commentary

According to Warner Bros. documents, a short in this series included footage of Jolson in *The Jazz Singer* (see F2).

F32   KINGS OF THE TURF

1935. Vitaphone Corporation. B&W. 9 mins.

Commentary

Jolson is seen among celebrities, including Ruby Keeler, in this short which chronicles the training of a colt from birth to racetrack.

F33   BROADWAY HIGHLIGHTS

1935. Paramount Pictures. B&W.

Credits

Producer: Adolph Zukor. Narrated by Ted Husing. Edited by Fred Waller, Milton Hocky.

Commentary

This short surveys the Broadway scene circa 1935. Scenes include a testimonial dinner at Dempsey's Restaurant for Paul Whiteman, featuring remarks by Whiteman, Rudy Vallee, Jack Benny, and Jack Dempsey; footage of Earl Carroll selecting chorus girls for a new edition of his *Vanities*; Sophie Tucker's performance at the Hollywood Restaurant, with Tucker seen singing her trademark song, "Some of These Days," and introducing Beatrice Lillie and Fanny Brice in the audience; scenes of the opening night of *Ceiling Zero* at the Music Box Theatre, with stars Osgood Perkins and Margaret Perry backstage, and first-nighters including the play's producer Brock Pemberton, critic Bernard Sobel, producer Sam Harris, William Allen White, Otis Skinner, Gary Cooper, and Walter Winchell glimpsed leaving the theatre; and footage of Victor Young rehearsing his orchestra, Jolson rehearsing a comedy sketch with fighter Max Baer, and Jolson, with Young conducting, rehearsing "Mammy, I'll Sing About You" from *Go Into Your Dance* (see F11) for an April 1935 *Shell Chateau* radio broadcast.

F34   A DAY AT SANTA ANITA

1937. Warner Bros.-Vitaphone Corporation. B&W. 18 mins.

Credits

Director: Bobby Connolly. Original Screenplay: Crane Wilbur. Photography in Technicolor: Ray Rennahan. Film Editor: Harold McLernon. Art Director: Ted Smith. Music and Lyrics: M.K. Jerome and Jack Scholl. Technicolor Director: Natalie Kalmus. Gowns: Milo Anderson.

Cast

Sybil Jason, Marcia Ralson, and cameos by a cast of Hollywood stars: Al Jolson, Ruby Keeler, Bette Davis (and her husband, Harmon Nelson),

Edward G. Robinson, Olivia de Havilland, Frank McHugh, Allen Jenkins, Mary Treen and Hugh Herbert.

Synopsis

A little girl, Peaches (Jason), and her father live in a small apartment near Santa Anita Racetrack where they own a horse, Wonder Boy. They have high hopes for clearing their many debts with a victory at the upcoming $100,000 handicap. Peaches has a particularly soothing effect on Wonder Boy, and is able to encourage the horse to run at record times. Unfortunately, before the race, Peaches' father is killed in an accident. Under the watchful eye of Biff, Wonder Boy's trainer, Peaches stays on at the track focused on the forthcoming handicap. However, Tess and Bud Creighton, two small-time racetrack crooks, plot to get Peaches away from the track, and the watchful eye of a wealthy benevolent horsewoman Mrs. Van Gordon (Ralston) as the race is about to begin. After Peaches performs at a Hunt Club luncheon shortly before the race, the Creighton's inform the local child protection agency that Peaches is without parental supervision. Child protection agent Bogard comes to take Peaches into custody moments before the race, as the grandstand fills with celebrities. However, Mrs. Van Gordon tricks the agent and she and Peaches arrive in time to encourage Wonder Boy to a great victory. As the film ends, Mrs. Van Gordon embraces Peaches who she plans to adopt.

Songs

"Where Would Cinderella Be?"(sung by Jason).

Commentary

The director of this short, Bobby Connolly, was the choreographer of Jolson's films *Go Into Your Dance* (see F11) and *The Singing Kid* (see F12). The plot of this short bears a striking resemblance to the basic plot of Jolson's early film, *Big Boy* (see F7), here re-tailored to the talents of young Sybil Jason.

F35 MINSTREL DAYS

1941. Warner Bros. B&W. 20 mins.

Credits

Director: Bobby Connolly. Original Screenplay: Owen Crump. Narration: Knox Manning. Conductor: Leo F. Forbstein.

Cast

Al Jolson, Eddie Cantor, Stepin Fetchit.

Commentary

This film includes an edited version of the medley of Jolson hits ("Swanee," "California, Here I Come," "April Showers," and "Sonny Boy") from the beginning of *The Singing Kid* (see F12).

F36 CAVALCADE OF THE ACADEMY AWARDS

1941. Vitaphone Corporation. B&W.

Commentary

The content of this short is unknown, but probably includes newsreel footage of Jolson from an Academy Awards banquet.

F37 *THE VOICE THAT THRILLED THE WORLD*

1943. Warner Bros. B&W. 17 mins.

Credits

Director: Jean Negulesco. Photography: Sidney Hickox. Narration Writer: James Bloodworth. Film Editor: Thomas Pratt. Narration: Art Gilmore. Art Director: Roland Hill.

Commentary

This short celebrates the history of sound on film, from the earliest experiments up to Warner Bros. *Yankee Doodle Dandy*, which won an Academy Award for Sound in 1942. Footage of Jolson in *The Jazz Singer* (see F2) is included.

F38 *SHOW BUSINESS AT WAR*

1943. The March of Time. B&W. 18 mins.

Reviews

"On a sun-parched desert in North Africa they remembered precious things past while Al Jolson shouted his heart out about his ageless mammy in Alabammy."(*Life*, June 21, 1943, Vol. 14, p. 71)

Commentary

Jolson, accompanied by an unseen Harry Akst, is seen in military uniform singing "My Mammy" to American forces in North Africa during World War II in this short film highlighting the various contributions of film and stage workers to the war effort.

F39 *SCREEN SNAPSHOTS: PHOTOPLAY MAGAZINE'S GOLD MEDAL AWARDS*

1947. Columbia Pictures. B&W. 9 mins.

Credits

Produced and Directed by Ralph Staub. Edited by Edmund Kinsler. Musical Score by Mischa Bakaleinikoff. Narrated by Art Baker.

Commentary

This short includes silent coverage of the banquet at which the *Photoplay* Magazine Gold Medal Awards were presented. *The Jolson Story* (see F18) won many awards, including one to Jolson himself, who is seen arriving at the banquet and performing for the audience. Other award winners and guests include Ingrid Bergman, Humphrey Bogart, Lauren Bacall, and George Jessel.

F40   SCREEN SNAPSHOTS: HOLLYWOOD'S FAMOUS FEET

1949. Columbia Pictures. B&W. 9 mins.

Credits
Produced and Directed by Ralph Staub. Edited by Edmund Kinsler. Musical Score by Mischa Bakaleinikoff. Narrated by Al Jolson.

Commentary
Jolson narrates this look at the long-time tradition of film stars putting their feet in cement squares in the forecourt of Hollywood's Grauman's Chinese Theatre. The short includes footage of Tom Mix, the Marx Brothers, the Ritz Brothers, Edgar Bergen and Charlie McCarthy, John Wayne, Gene Autry and his horse Champion, and Jolson himself immortalizing themselves in the wet cement.

F41   SCREEN SNAPSHOTS: MEMORIAL TO AL JOLSON

1951. Columbia Pictures. B&W. 8 mins.

Credits
Directed by Ralph Staub. Edited by Edmund Kinsler. Musical Score by Mischa Bakaleinikoff. Narrated by Jack Benny.

Commentary
Featuring newsreel footage of Jolson from the 1920's until his death, and including scenes from his funeral, this respectful tribute is narrated by Jack Benny. No scenes from Jolson films are included.

F42   SCREEN SNAPSHOTS: THE GREAT AL JOLSON

1955. Columbia Pictures. B&W. 11 mins.

Credits
Directed by Ralph Staub. Edited by Harold White. Musical Score by Mischa Bakaleinikoff.

Commentary
ASCAP board member L. Wolfe Gilbert who introduces and briefly interviews a number of composers and lyricists whose songs were performed by Jolson. These include Sidney Claire, M.K. Jerome, Sammy Fain, Harry Ruby, Jean Schwartz, Benny Davis, Isham Jones, and Jimmy McHugh. Also includes a bit of footage from the "Screen Snapshots" short *Hollywood's Famous Feet* (1949), narrated by Jolson.

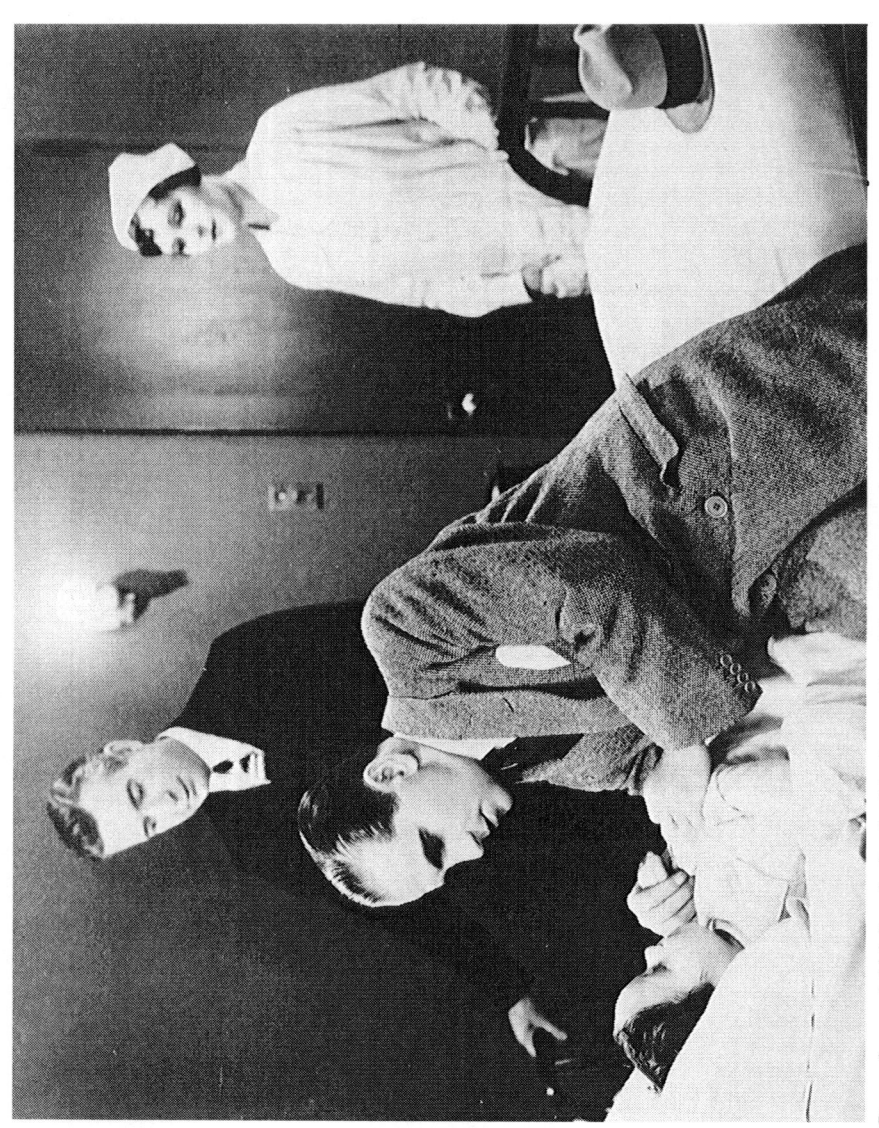

Davey Lee and Al Jolson in the deathbed scene from *The Singing Fool* (1928). Permission of Turner Entertainment.

5

Discography

Few performers have recorded as much over as long a period of time as Al Jolson. His first recording session for Edison Records was in 1910, his last, for Decca Records, was in 1950. His studio recordings appear on innumerable collections on records and, these days, on compact discs (surely no singer of popular music of his vintage can be found on as many compact discs as Jolson). Instead of listing these many collections, which include not only Jolson's studio recordings but many collections of his performances on radio and movie soundtracks, this listing covers only Jolson's many visits to the recording studio, listed chronologically, and the original label and data for each recording he made (including those not issued). More detailed data on collections and reissues can be found in several published Jolson discographies (see B8, B9, B13).

EDISON RECORDS

D1)   February 9, 1910. New York, New York. With Edison Orchestra.

"Come Along My Mandy"	Unissued
(Jack Norworth-Nora Bayes)	
"That Mesmerizing Mendelssohn Tune"	Unissued
(Irving Berlin)	

VICTOR RECORDS

D2)   December 22, 1911. Camden, New Jersey. With Victor Orchestra under the direction of Walter B. Rogers.

B-11409	*"That Haunting Melody"*	17037 (2)
	(George M. Cohan)	
	(On *Billboard* chart for 11 weeks, was #1 for 2 weeks)	
B-11410	*"Rum Tum Tiddle"*	17037 (3)
	(Jean Schwartz-Edward Madden)	
B-11411	*"Asleep in the Deep"* [parody]	17915 (1)
	(Arthur Lamb-H.W. Petrie)	

D3)   March 15, 1912. Camden, New Jersey. With Victor Orchestra under the direction of Walter B. Rogers.

B-11730	*"The Villain Still Pursued Her"*	Unissued
	(Harry Von Tilzer-William Jerome)	
B-11731	*"My Sumurun Girl"*	Unissued
	(Louis A. Hirsch-Al Jolson)	
B-11732	*"Snap Your Fingers"*	17075
	(Harry Von Tilzer-William Jerome)	
	(On *Billboard* chart for 2 weeks, was #6)	
B-11733	*"Brass Band Ephraham Jones"*	17068
	(George W. Meyer-Joe Goodwin)	

D4)   April 17, 1912. Camden, New Jersey. With Victor Orchestra under the direction of Walter B. Rogers.

B-11883	*"Ragging the Baby to Sleep"*	17081
	(Lewis F. Muir-L. Wolfe Gilbert)	
	(On *Billboard* chart for 12 weeks, was #1 for 5 weeks)	
B-11884	*"That Lovin' Traumerei"*	17119 (2)
	(Aubrey Stauffer, adapted from Robert Schumann)	
B-11885	*"Movin' Man, Don't Take My Baby Grand"*	17081
	(Ted Snyder-Bert Kalmar)	
B-11886	*"Uncle Sammy"*	Unissued
	(Abe Holzman-F. Henri Klickman)	

D5)   March 7, 1913. Camden, New Jersey. With Victor Orchestra under the direction of Walter B. Rogers.

B-12971	*"My Yellow Jacket Girl"*	17318 (1)
	(Jean Schwartz-Harold Atteridge)	
B-12972	*"The Spaniard That Blighted My Life"*	17318 (1)
	(Billy Merson)	
	(On *Billboard* chart for 9 weeks, was #1 for 5 weeks)	

COLUMBIA RECORDS

D6)   June 4, 1913. New York, New York. With Columbia Orchestra under the direction of Charles A. Prince.

38901	*"Pullman Porters on Parade"*	A1374 (1)
	(Irving Berlin-Maurice Abrahams)	
	(On *Billboard* chart for 4 weeks, was #5)	
38902	*"You Made Me Love You"*	A1374 (1)
	(Joseph McCarthy-James V. Monaco)	
	(On *Billboard* chart for 13 weeks, was #1 for 7 weeks)	
38903	*"That Little German Band"*	A1356 (2)
	(Fred Fisher-Joe Goodwin-Joseph McCarthy)	
	(On *Billboard* chart for 4 weeks, was #5)	
38904	*"Everybody Snap Your Fingers With Me"*	A1356 (1)

(Harry Puck-Bert Kalmar)

D7) September 19, 1914. New York, New York. With Columbia Orchestra under the direction of Charles A. Prince.

39567   *"Back to the Carolina You Love"*   A1621 (1,8)
        (Jean Schwartz-Grant Clarke)
        (On *Billboard* chart for 8 weeks, was #2 for 3 weeks)
39568   *"Revival Day"*   A1621 (1,5)
        (Irving Berlin)

D8) December 3, 1914. New York, New York. With Columbia Orchestra under the direction of Charles A. Prince.

39664   *"Sister Susie's Sewing Shirts for Soldiers"*   A1671
        (Hermann Darewski-R.P. Weston)
        (On *Billboard* chart for 2 weeks, was #6)(1,5,6,8)
39665   *"When the Grown Up Ladies Act Like Babies*
        (I've Gotta Love 'Em, That's All)   A1671 (1,2)
        (Maurice Abrahams-Edgar Leslie-Joe Young)

D9) January 14, 1916. New York, New York. With Columbia Orchestra under the direction of Charles A. Prince.

46335   *"There's a Broken Heart for Every*
        Light on Broadway"   Unissued
        (Fred Fisher-Howard Johnson)
46336   *"Eeny Meany Miney Moe"*   Unissued
46337   *"Yaaka Hula Hickey Dula"*   A-1956 (1)
        (Peter Wendling-E. Ray Goetz-Joe Young)
        (On *Billboard* chart for 7 weeks, was #2 for 5 weeks)

D10) February 28, 1916. New York, New York. With Columbia Orchestra under the direction of Charles A. Prince.

46459   *"Where Did Robinson Crusoe Go With Friday on Saturday*
        Night?"   A-1976 (1)
        (George W. Meyer-Sam M. Lewis-Joe Young)
        (On *Billboard* chart for 2 weeks, was #6)
46460   *"Down Where the Swanee River Flows"*   A-2007 (1)
        (Albert Von Tilzer-Charles S. Alberte-Charles McCarron)
        (On *Billboard* chart for 5 weeks, was #3)
46463   *"Now He's Got a Beautiful Girl"*   A-2080 (1)
        (Ted Snyder-Edgar Leslie-Grant Clarke)

D11) May 17, 1916. New York, New York. With Columbia Orchestra under the direction of Charles A. Prince.

46786   *"I Sent My Wife to the Thousand Isles"*   A-2021 (1)
        (Harry Von Tilzer-Ed P. Moran-Andrew B. Sterling)
        (On *Billboard* chart for 7 weeks, was #1 for 3 weeks)

| | 46787 | *"You're a Dangerous Girl"* | A-2041 (2) |

46787   *"You're a Dangerous Girl"*   A-2041 (2)
         (James V. Monaco-Grant Clarke)
         (On *Billboard* chart for 6 weeks, was #2 for 2 weeks)

D12)   June 9, 1916. New York, New York. With Columbia Orchestra under the direction of Charles A. Prince.

46820   *"I'm Saving Up the Means to Get to New Orleans"*   A-2064
         (Harry DeCosta-Howard Johnson)
         (On *Billboard* chart for 4 weeks, was #3)

D13)   September 19, 1916. New York, New York. With Columbia Orchestra under the direction of Charles A. Prince.

47029   *"Someone Else May Be There While I'm Gone"*   A-2124 (1)
         (Irving Berlin)
         (On *Billboard* chart for 4 weeks, was #2 for 1 week)
47030   *"I'm Down in Honolulu Looking Them Over"*   Unissued
         (Irving Berlin)
47031   *"Don't Write Me Letters"*   A-2106 (1)
         (Bert Grant)

D14)   November 26, 1916. New York, New York. With Columbia Orchestra under the direction of Charles A. Prince.

47191   *"A Broken Doll"*   A-2154 (1)
         (Clifford Harris-Joseph W. Tate)
47192   *"Ev'ry Little While"*   A-2181 (2)
         (Ernie Golden-Joseph W. Tate)
         (On *Billboard* chart for 2 weeks, was #5)

D15)   December 11, 1916. New York, New York. With Columbia Orchestra under the direction of Charles A. Prince.

47217   *"Pray for Sunshine"*   A-2169 (3)
         (Maurice Abrahams-Sam M. Lewis-Joe Young)
         (On *Billboard* chart for 4 weeks, was #4)
47218   *"From Here to Shanghai"*   A-2224 (3)
         (Irving Berlin)
         (On *Billboard* chart for 4 weeks, was #4)

D16)   May 29, 1917. New York, New York. With Columbia Orchestra under the direction of Charles A. Prince.

77079   *"Tillie Titwillow"*   A-2296 (1,2,3)
         (Phil Schwartz-Harold Atteridge)

D17)   December 13, 1917. New York, New York. With Columbia Orchestra under the direction of Charles A. Prince.

77571   *"Wedding Bells"*   A-2512 (4,6)

(Jean Schwartz-Sam M. Lewis-Joe Young)
(On *Billboard* chart for 1 week, was #8)

77572 *"I'm All Bound 'Round with the Mason-Dixon Line"*   A-2478 (1,2)
(Jean Schwartz-Sam M. Lewis-Joe Young)
(On *Billboard* chart for 9 weeks, was #1 for 3 weeks)

D18) December 27, 1917. New York, New York. With Columbia Orchestra under the direction of Charles A. Prince.

77602 *"'N'Everything"*   A-2519 (1,2,3)
(Al Jolson-B.G. De Sylva-Gus Kahn)
(On *Billboard* chart for 5 weeks, was #2 for 2 weeks)

77603 *"There's a Lump of Sugar Down in Dixie"*   A-2491 (1,2)
(Albert Gamble-Jack Yellen-Alfred Bryan)

D19) March 13, 1918. New York, New York. With Columbia Orchestra under the direction of Charles A. Prince.

77720 *"Rock-A-Bye Your Baby With a Dixie Melody"*   A-2560 (2)
(Jean Schwartz-Sam M. Lewis-Joe Young)
(On *Billboard* chart for 14 weeks, was #1 for 8 weeks)

D20) April 3, 1918. New York, New York. With Columbia Orchestra under the direction of Charles A. Prince.

77753 *"Hello Central, Give Me No Man's Land"*   A-2542 (1,2)
(Jean Schwartz-Sam M. Lewis-Joe Young)
(On *Billboard* chart for 8 weeks, was #1 for 3 weeks)

D21) September 10, 1918. New York, New York. With Columbia Orchestra under the direction of Charles A. Prince.

78046 *"Tell That to the Marines"*   A-2657 (1,2)
(Jean Schwartz-Al Jolson-Harold Atteridge)
(On *Billboard* chart for 5 weeks, was #2 for 1 week)

78047 *"I Wonder Why She Kept Saying Si, Si, Si, Si, Señor"*   A-2671 (1)
(Ted Snyder-Sam M. Lewis-Joe Young)

D22) October 24, 1918. New York, New York. With Columbia Orchestra under the direction of Charles A. Prince.

78153 *"I'll Say She Does"*   A-2746 (3)
(Al Jolson-Gus Kahn-B.G. De Sylva)
(On *Billboard* chart for 9 weeks, was #1 for 6 weeks)

D23) December 6, 1918. New York, New York. With Columbia Orchestra under the direction of Charles A. Prince.

78193 *"On the Road to Calais"*   A-2690 (1)

(Jean Schwartz-Al Jolson-Alfred Bryan)
(On *Billboard* chart for 3 weeks, was #5)

D24)   December 13, 1918. New York, New York. With Columbia Orchestra under the direction of Charles A. Prince.

78201   *"Don't Forget the Boys"*   Unissued
(Fred E. Ahlert-Al Jolson-Harold Atteridge)

D25)   July 23, 1919. New York, New York. With Columbia Orchestra under the direction of Charles A. Prince.

78593   *"Some Beautiful Morning"*   A-2940 (1,4)
(Al Jolson-Cliff Friend)
78594   *"Who Played Poker with Pocahontas?"*   A-2787 (1)
(Fred E. Ahlert-Sam M. Lewis-Joe Young)

D26)   July 25, 1919. New York, New York. With Columbia Orchestra under the direction of Charles A. Prince.

78600   *"Her Danny"*   Unissued
(Chris Schonberg-Hale N. Byers)

D27)   September 14, 1919. New York, New York. With Columbia Orchestra under the direction of Charles A. Prince.

78652   *"I've Got My Captain Working for Me Now"* A-2794 (2,5)
(Irving Berlin)
(On *Billboard* chart for 7 weeks, was #1 for 2 weeks)

D28)   September 21, 1919. New York, New York. With Columbia Orchestra under the direction of Charles A. Prince.

78684   *"You Ain't Heard Nothing Yet"*   A-2836 (1,2)
(Al Jolson-Gus Kahn-B.G. De Sylva)
(On *Billboard* chart for 5 weeks, was #3)
78685   *"I Gave Her That"*   A-2835 (1,2)
(Al Jolson-B.G. De Sylva)
(On *Billboard* chart for 2 weeks, was #6)

D29)   October 3, 1919. New York, New York. With Columbia Orchestra under the direction of Charles A. Prince.

78722   *"Tell Me (Why Nights Are Lonely)"*   A-2821 (1,2,3)
(Max Kortlander-J. Will Callahan)
(On *Billboard* chart for 5 weeks, was #3)

D30)   October 19, 1919. New York, New York. With Columbia Orchestra under the direction of Charles A. Prince.

78743   *"Chloe"*   A-2861 (2)

(Al Jolson-B.G. De Sylva)
(On *Billboard* chart for 4 weeks, was #5)

D31) January 8, 1920. New York, New York. With Columbia Orchestra under the direction of Charles A. Prince.

78916   *"That Wonderful Kid from Madrid"*   A-2898 (2,3)
     (Nat Osborne-Ballard MacDonald)
     (On *Billboard* chart for 3 weeks, was #5)
78917   *"Swanee"*   A-2884 (2)
     (George Gershwin-Irving Caesar)
     (On *Billboard* chart for 18 weeks, was #1 for 9 weeks)

D32) April 30, 1920. New York, New York. With Columbia Orchestra under the direction of Charles A. Prince.

79152   *"In Sweet September"*   A-2946 (2,3)
     (Pete Wendling-James V. Monaco-Edgar Leslie)
     (On *Billboard* chart for 3 weeks, was #5)

D33) August 16, 1920. New York, New York. With Columbia Orchestra under the direction of Charles A. Prince.

79371   *"Avalon"*   A-2995
     (Vincent Rose-Al Jolson-B.G. De Sylva)
     (On *Billboard* chart for 9 weeks, was #2 for 2 weeks)

D34) December 12, 1920. New York, New York. With Columbia Orchestra under the direction of Charles A. Prince.

79568   *"O-HI-O"*   A-3361 (1,2)
     (Abe Olman-Jack Yellen)
     (On *Billboard* chart for 7 weeks, was #1 for 4 weeks)

D35) January 4, 1921. New York, New York. With Columbia Orchestra under the direction of Charles A. Prince.

79624   *"Ding-A-Ring A-Ring"*   A-3375 (3)
     (Ira Schuster-Irving Bibo-Al Wilson)

D36) February 14, 1921. New York, New York. With Columbia Orchestra under the direction of Charles A. Prince.

79726   *"Scandinavia"*   A-3382
     (Ray Perkins)
     (On *Billboard* chart for 3 weeks, was #5)

D37) July 19, 1921. New York, New York. With Columbia Orchestra under the direction of Charles A. Prince.

79953   *"She Knows It"*   Unissued

(Clarence J. Marks-Jack Stern)

D38)   October 21, 1921. New York, New York. With Columbia Orchestra under the direction of Charles A. Prince.

    80041   *"April Showers"*   A-3500 (2)
                (Louis Silvers-B.G. De Sylva)
                (On *Billboard* chart for 17 weeks, was #1 for 11 weeks)
    80042   *"Give Me My Mammy"*   A-3540 (2)
                (Walter Donaldson-B.G. De Sylva)
                (On *Billboard* chart for 8 weeks, was #2 for 4 weeks)

D39)   November 7, 1921. New York, New York. With Columbia Orchestra under the direction of Charles A. Prince.

    80052   *"Yoo Hoo"*   A-3513 (1)
                (Al Jolson-B.G. De Sylva)
                (On *Billboard* chart for 5 weeks, was #4)

D40)   January 17, 1922. New York, New York. With Columbia Orchestra under the direction of Charles A. Prince.

    80140   *"Angel Child"*   A-3568 (3)
                (Abner Silver-Georgie Price-Benny Davis)
                (On *Billboard* chart for 8 weeks, was #1 for 5 weeks)

D41)   March 10, 1922. New York, New York. With Columbia Orchestra under the direction of Charles A. Prince.

    80232   *"Oogie Oogie Wa Wa"*   A-3588 (2,10)
                (Archie Gottler-Edgar Leslie-Grant Clarke)

D42)   April 24, 1922. New York, New York. With Columbia Orchestra under the direction of Charles A. Prince.

    80317   *"Coo-Coo"*   A-3626 (2)
                (Al Jolson-B.G. De Sylva)
                (On *Billboard* chart for 2 weeks, was #7)

D43)   August 4, 1922. New York, New York. With Columbia Orchestra under the direction of Charles A. Prince.

    80500   *"I'll Stand Beneath Your Window Tonight*
              and Whistle"   A-3694 (2,3)
                (Jimmy McHugh-Georgie Price-Jerry Benson)

D44)   September 9, 1922. New York, New York. With Columbia Orchestra under the direction of Charles A. Prince.

    80532   *"Toot, Toot, Tootsie!" (Goo'Bye)*   A-3705 (3)
                (Gus Kahn-Ernie Erdman-Dan Russo)

(On *Billboard* chart for 10 weeks, was #1 for 4 weeks)

80533   *"Do I? (Do I? Do I Love Her?)"*   Unissued
(Harry Akst-Sam M. Lewis-Joe Young)

D45)   October 10, 1922. Chicago, Illinois. With Frank Westphal Orchestra.

80593   *"Lost: A Wonderful Girl"*   A-3744 (1)
(James F. Hanley-Benny Davis)
(On *Billboard* chart for 3 weeks, was #4)

D46)   November 10, 1922. Chicago, Illinois. With Frank Westphal Orchestra.

80609   *"Some of These Days"*   Unissued
(Shelton Brooks)

D47)   November 13, 1922. Chicago, Illinois. With Paul Biese and his Edgewater Beach Hotel Orchestra.

80631   *"Who Cares?"*   Rejected
(Milton Ager-Jack Yellen)

D48)   December 5, 1922. Chicago, Illinois. With Paul Biese and his Edgewater Beach Hotel Orchestra.

80631   *"Who Cares?"*   A-3779 (8)
(Milton Ager-Jack Yellen)
(On *Billboard* chart for 4 weeks, was #4)

D49)   January 4, 1923. Chicago, Illinois. With Frank Westphal Orchestra.

80761   *"Coal Black Mammy"*   A-3854 (2)
(Ivy St. Helier-Laddie Cliff)
(On *Billboard* chart for 3 weeks, was #4)
80762   *"Wanita"*   A-3812 (1)
(Sam Coslow-Al Sherman)

D50)   March 31, 1923. New York, New York. With Columbia Orchestra.

80929   *"Morning Will Come"*   Rejected
(Con Conrad-Al Jolson-B.G. De Sylva)

D51)   April 15, 1923. New York, New York. With Columbia Orchestra.

80929   *"Morning Will Come"*   A-3880 (6)
(Con Conrad-Al Jolson-B.G. De Sylva)
(On *Billboard* chart for 5 weeks, was #5)

D52)   May 15, 1923. New York, New York. With Columbia Orchestra.

81016   *"Stella"*   A-3913 (1)
(Harry Akst-Al Jolson-Benny Davis)

(On *Billboard* chart for 5 weeks, was #4)

D53) June 12, 1923. New York, New York. With Columbia Orchestra.

81072   *"Waitin' for the Evenin' Mail"*   A-3933 (2,3)
(Billy Baskette)

D54) July 27, 1923. New York, New York. With Columbia Orchestra.

81152   *"That Big Blond Mama"*   A-3968 (1)
(James V. Monaco-Billy Rose)

D55) September 7, 1923. New York, New York. With Columbia Orchestra.

81201   *"You've Simply Got Me Cuckoo"*   A-3984 (1)
(Jesse Greer-Walter Hirsch)
(On *Billboard* chart for 2 weeks, was #7)

D56) October 13, 1923. New York, New York. With Columbia Orchestra.

81281   *"Mama Loves Papa"*   Unissued
(Abel Baer-Cliff Friend)

D57) November 23, 1923. New York, New York. With Columbia Orchestra.

81368   *"Arcady"*   43-D (1)
(Al Jolson-B.G. De Sylva)
(On *Billboard* chart for 2 weeks, was #6)

D58) December 18, 1923. New York, New York. With Columbia Orchestra.

81423   *"I'm Goin' South"*   61-D (1)
(Harry Woods-Abner Silver)

D59) December 20, 1923. New York, New York. With Columbia Orchestra.

81429   *"Twelve O'Clock at Night"*   79-D (3)
(Lou Handman-Roy Turk)

BRUNSWICK RECORDS

D60) January 17, 1924. Chicago, Illinois. With Isham Jones and his Orchestra.

C-20-22   *"I'm Goin' South"*   2569-A
(Harry Woods-Abner Silver)
(On *Billboard* chart for 7 weeks, was #2 for 2 weeks)
C-23-25   *"Never Again"*   2611-A
(Isham Jones-Gus Kahn)
C-26-27   *"California, Here I Come"*   2569-B
(Joseph Meyer-Al Jolson-B.G. De Sylva)

(On *Billboard* chart for 12 weeks, was #1 for 6 weeks)

C-28-29   *"The One I Love Belongs to Somebody Else"*   2567-A
(Isham Jones-Gus Kahn)
(On *Billboard* chart for 7 weeks, was #2 for 2 weeks)

D61)   January 18, 1924. Chicago, Illinois. With Isham Jones and his Orchestra.

C-41-42   *"Steppin' Out"*   2567-B
(Con Conrad-Richard Howard)
(On *Billboard* chart for 6 weeks, was #4)

C-43-44   *"Feeling the Way I Do"*   2611-A
(Walter Donaldson-B.G. De Sylva)

D62)   February 24, 1924. Chicago, Illinois. With Isham Jones and his Orchestra.

C-81-82   *"Mr. Radio Man"*   Unissued
(Ira Schuster-William Wilfred-Cliff Friend)

C-83-84   *"Home in Pasadena"*   Unissued
(Harry Warren-Grant Clarke-Edgar Leslie)

D63)   March 13, 1924. Chicago, Illinois. With Gene Rodemich and his Orchestra.

C-95-98   *"My Papa Doesn't Two Time No Time"*   2595-B
(Walter Donaldson)
(On *Billboard* chart for 1 week, was #11)

C-99-102   *"Lazy"*   2595-A
(Irving Berlin)
(On *Billboard* chart for 5 weeks, was #4)

D64)   March 14, 1924. Chicago, Illinois. With Isham Jones and his Orchestra.

C-106-107   *"Mr. Radio Man"*   2582-A
(Ira Schuster-William Wilfred-Cliff Friend)
(On *Billboard* chart for 4 weeks, was #4)

C-108-110   *"Home in Pasadena"*   2582-B
(Harry Warren-Grant Clarke-Edgar Leslie)

D65)   July 2, 1924. New York, New York. With Abe Lyman's California Orchestra.

13472-13474   *"Mandalay"*   2650-A
(Abe Lyman-Gus Arnheim-Earl Burtnett)
(On *Billboard* chart for 5 weeks, was #3)

D66)   July 3, 1924. New York, New York. With Brunswick Orchestra.

13475-13477   *"Il Barbiere di Siviglia"*   Unissued
(G. Rossini)

13478-13480   *"I, Pagliacci"*   Unissued
(R. Leoncavallo)

D67)   July 18, 1924. New York, New York. With Abe Lyman's California Orchestra.

13566-13569	*"Who Wants a Bad Little Boy?"*	Rejected
	(Fred Fisher-Joe Burke)	

D68)   July 25, 1924. New York, New York. With Abe Lyman's California Orchestra.

13617-13618	*"Who Wants a Bad Little Boy?"*	2650-B
	(Fred Fisher-Joe Burke)	

D69)   August 6, 1924. New York, New York. With Carl Fenton and his Orchestra.

13686-13688	*"Follow the Swallow"*	2671-A
	(Ray Henderson-Billy Rose-Mort Dixon)	
	(On *Billboard* chart for 6 weeks, was #3)	
13689-13691	*"I Wonder What's Become of Sally"*	2671-B
	(Milton Ager-Jack Yellen)	
	(On *Billboard* chart for 12 weeks, was #1 for 3 weeks)	

D70)   October 2, 1924. New York, New York. With Ray Miller and his Orchestra.

13864-13867	*"All Alone"*	2743-A
	(Irving Berlin)	
	(On *Billboard* chart for 9 weeks, was #1 for 5 weeks)	

D71)   October 15, 1924. New York, New York. With Ray Miller and his Orchestra.

13954-13956	*"I'm Gonna Tramp! Tramp! Tramp!"*	2743-B
	(Harry Woods-B.G. De Sylva)	

D72)   November 14, 1924. New York, New York. With Carl Fenton and his Orchestra.

14206-14207	*"Hello, 'Tucky!"*	Rejected
	(James F. Hanley-Joseph Meyer-B.G. De Sylva)	
14208-14210	*"Keep Smiling at Trouble"*	Rejected
	(Lewis Gensler-Al Jolson-B.G. De Sylva)	

D73)   November 19, 1924. New York, New York. With Carl Fenton and his Orchestra.

14264-14265	*"Keep Smiling at Trouble"*	2763-A
	(Lewis Gensler-Al Jolson-B.G. De Sylva)	
14266-14268	*"Hello, 'Tucky!"*	2763-B
	(James F. Hanley-Joseph Meyer-B.G. De Sylva)	
	(On *Billboard* chart for 3 weeks, was #5)	

D74)   October 22, 1925. New York, New York. With orchestra under the direction of Alfred Newman.

E16744-E16745 *"Nobody But Fanny"*   Unissued
          (Con Conrad-Al Jolson-B.G. De Sylva)
E16746-E16747 *"Miami"*   Unissued
          (Con Conrad-Al Jolson-B.G. De Sylva)

D75)   October 30, 1925. New York, New York. With Orchestra under the direction of Alfred Newman.

E16807-E16808 *"Miami"*   Unissued
          (Con Conrad-Al Jolson-B.G. De Sylva)
E16809-E16810 *"Nobody But Fanny"*   Unissued
          (Con Conrad-Al Jolson-B.G. De Sylva)

D76)   December 21, 1925. New York, New York. With Carl Fenton and his Orchestra.

E17172-E17173 *"I'm Sitting on Top of the World"*   3014-A
          (Ray Henderson-Sam M. Lewis-Joe Young)
          (On *Billboard* chart for 11 weeks, was #1 for 2 weeks)
E17174-E17175 *"You Forgot to Remember"*   3013-B
          (Irving Berlin)
E17176-E17177 *"You Flew Away from the Nest"*   3014-B
          (Harry Ruby-Bert Kalmar)
E17178-E17179 *"Miami"*   3013-A
          (Con Conrad-Al Jolson-B.G. De Sylva)
          (On *Billboard* chart for 3 weeks, was #6)

D77)   April 23, 1926. New York, New York. With Carl Fenton and his Orchestra.

E18852-E18854 *"I Wish I Had My Old Gal Back Again"*   3183-A
          (Milton Ager-Lew Pollack-Jack Yellen)
          (On *Billboard* chart for 3 weeks, was #5)
E18855-E18857 *"(I'd Climb the Highest Mountain) If I Knew
          I'd Find You"*   3183-B
          (Sidney Clare-Lew Brown)
          (On *Billboard* chart for 2 weeks, was #7)

D78)   May 3, 1926. New York, New York. With Carl Fenton and his Orchestra.

E18982-E18983 *"At Peace with the World"*   3196-A
          (Irving Berlin)
          (On *Billboard* chart for 5 weeks, was #3)
E18984-E18986 *"Tonight's My Night with Baby"*   3196-B
          (Joseph Meyer-Bobby Buttenuth-Irving Caesar)

D79)   June 1, 1926. New York, New York. With Carl Fenton and his Orchestra.

E19418-E19420 *"When the Red, Red Robin Comes Bob, Bob,*
          Bobbin' Along"   3222-A
        (Harry Woods)
        (On *Billboard* chart for 8 weeks, was #1 for 2 weeks)
E19421-E19423 *"Here I Am"*   3222-B
        (B.G. De Sylva-Lew Brown-Ray Henderson)

D80)   November 11, 1927. New York, New York. With William F. Wirges and his Orchestra.

E25183-E25185 *"Mother of Mine, I Still Have You"*   3719-A
        (Louis Silvers-Al Jolson-Grant Clarke)
        (On *Billboard* chart for 8 weeks, was #2 for 3 weeks)
E25186-E25189 *"Blue River"*   3719-B
        (Joseph Meyer-Alfred Bryan)
        (On *Billboard* chart for 1 week, was #16)

D81)   January 13, 1928. New York, New York. With William F. Wirges and his Orchestra.

E26010-E26011 *"Four Walls"*   3775-B
        (Dave Dreyer-Al Jolson-Billy Rose)
E26012-E26014 *"Golden Gate"*   3775-A
        (Dave Dreyer-Joseph Meyer-Al Jolson-Billy Rose)
        (On *Billboard* chart for 4 weeks, was #9)

D82)   March 8, 1928. New York, New York. With William F. Wirges and his Orchestra.

E26879-E26881 *"Ol' Man River"*   3867-A
        (Jerome Kern-Oscar Hammerstein II
        (On *Billboard* chart for 5 weeks, was #4)
E26882-E26884 *"Back in Your Own Back Yard"*   3867-B
        (Dave Dreyer-Al Jolson-Billy Rose)

D83)   March 31, 1928. New York, New York. With Abe Lyman's California Orchestra.

C-1832   *"Dirty Hands, Dirty Face"*   3912 (A)(B)(C)
        (James V. Monaco-Al Jolson-Grant Clarke-Edgar Leslie)
        (On *Billboard* chart for 4 weeks, was #8)
C-1833   *"My Mammy"*   3912 (A)(B)(C)
        (Walter Donaldson-Sam M. Lewis-Joe Young)
        (On *Billboard* chart for 4 weeks, was #2 for 2 weeks)

D84)   August 20, 1928. Los Angeles, California. With Vitaphone Orchestra under direction of Louis Silvers.

LAE-249   *"There's a Rainbow 'Round My Shoulder"*   4033 (A)(B)(C)
        (Dave Dreyer-Al Jolson-Billy Rose)
        (On *Billboard* chart for 13 weeks, was #1 for 2 weeks)

LAE-250   *"Sonny Boy"*   4033 (A)(B)
          (Al Jolson-B.G. De Sylva-Lew Brown-Ray Henderson)
          (On *Billboard* chart for 19 weeks, was #1 for 12 weeks)

D85)   April 7, 1929. Los Angeles, California. With Vitaphone Orchestra under
the direction of Louis Silvers.

LAE-446   *"I'm in Seventh Heaven"*   4400 (A) (B)
          (Al Jolson-B.G. De Sylva-Lew Brown-Ray Henderson)
          (On *Billboard* chart for 6 weeks, was #2 for 2 weeks)
LAE-447   *"Little Pal"*   4400 (A)(B)(C)
          (Al Jolson-B.G. De Sylva-Lew Brown-Ray Henderson)
          (On Billboard chart for 10 weeks, was #1 for 5 weeks)
LAE-448   *"Used to You"*   4401 (A)(B)
          (Al Jolson-B.G. De Sylva-Lew Brown-Ray Henderson)
          (On *Billboard* chart for 1 weeks, was #18)
LAE-449   *"Why Can't You?"*   4401 (A)(B)
          (Al Jolson-B.G. De Sylva-Lew Brown-Ray Henderson)
          (On *Billboard* chart for 6 weeks, was #4)
LAE-450   *"(Mem'ries of) One Sweet Kiss"*   4402 (A)(B)
          (Dave Dreyer-Al Jolson)

D86)   July 25, 1929. New York, New York. With Brunswick Orchestra under the
direction of Robert Haring.

E-30576   *"Liza"*   4402 (A)(B)
          (George Gershwin-Ira Gershwin-Gus Kahn)
          (On *Billboard* chart for 4 weeks, was #9)

D87)   January 10, 1930. Los Angeles, California. With Vitaphone Orchestra
under the direction of Louis Silvers.

LAE-685   *"Let Me Sing and I'm Happy"*   4721 (A)(B)
          (Irving Berlin)
          (On *Billboard* chart for 10 weeks, was #2 for 2 weeks)
LAE-686   *"To My Mammy"*   4722 (A)(B)
          (Irving Berlin)
          (On *Billboard* chart for 7 weeks, was #7)
LAE-687   *"Looking at You"*   4721 (A)(B)
          (Irving Berlin)
LAE-688   *"When the Little Red Roses Get the*
          Blues for You"   4722 (A)(B)
          (Joe Burke-Al Dubin)
          (On *Billboard* chart for 7 weeks, was #6)

D88)   December 20, 1932. New York, New York. With Brunswick Orchestra
under the direction of Victor Young.

B-12760   *"A Chazend'l Ohf Shabbes"*   6501
          (arranged by A.W. Binder)
B-12761   *"Hallelujah, I'm a Bum"*   6500

                        (Richard Rodgers-Lorenz Hart)
                        (On *Billboard* chart for 1 weeks, was #19)
        B-12762   *"You Are Too Beautiful"*   6500
                        (Richard Rodgers-Lorenz Hart)

D89)   December 20, 1932. New York, New York. With Guy Lombardo and his
            Royal Canadians.

        B-12763   *"April Showers"*   6502
                        (Louis Silvers-B.G. De Sylva)
        B-12764   *"Rock-A-Bye Your Baby With a Dixie Melody"*   6502
                        (Jean Schwartz-Sam M. Lewis-Joe Young)

DECCA RECORDS

D90)   August 10, 1945. Los Angeles, California. With Orchestra under the
            direction of Carmen Dragon.

        L-3912   *"Swanee"*   23470-A
                        (George Gershwin-Irving Caesar)
        L-3913   *"April Showers"*   23470-B
                        (Louis Silvers-B.G. De Sylva)
                        (On *Billboard* chart for 3 weeks, was #15)

D91)   March 20, 1946. Los Angeles, California. With Orchestra under the
            direction of Morris W. Stoloff.

        L-4126   *"Ma Blushin' Rosie"*   23613-B
                        (John Stromberg-Edgar Smith)
        L-4127   *"My Mammy"*   23614-B
                        (Walter Donaldson-Sam M. Lewis-Joe Young)
                        (On *Billboard* chart for 4 weeks, was #18)
        L-4128   *"You Made Me Love You"*   23613-A
                        (James V. Monaco-Joseph McCarthy)

D92)   March 27, 1946. Los Angeles, California. With Orchestra under the
            direction of Morris W. Stoloff.

        L-4140   *"Rock-A-Bye Your Baby With a Dixie Melody"*   23612-B
                        (Jean Schwartz-Sam M. Lewis-Joe Young)
        L-4141   *"California, Here I Come"*   23612-A
                        (Joseph Meyer-Al Jolson-B.G. De Sylva)
        L-4142   *"Sonny Boy"*   23614-A
                        (Al Jolson-B.G. De Sylva-Lew Brown-Ray Henderson)

D93)   August 21, 1946. Los Angeles, California. With Orchestra under the
            direction of Morris W. Stoloff.

        L-4269   *"Avalon"*   23714-A
                        (Vincent Rose-Al Jolson-B.G. De Sylva)

L-4270   *"Anniversary Song"*   23714-B
(Al Jolson-Saul Chaplin)
(On *Billboard* chart for 14 weeks, was #2 for 6 weeks)

D94)   March 25, 1947. Los Angeles, California. With Bing Crosby. With Orchestra under the direction of Morris W. Stoloff.

L-4386   *"Alexander's Ragtime Band"*   40038-A
(Irving Berlin)
(On *Billboard* chart for 2 weeks, was #20)

L-4387   *"The Spaniard That Blighted My Life"*   40038-B
(Billy Merson)

D95)   May 19, 1947. New York, New York. With Orchestra under the direction of Jay Blackton.

73916   *"All My Love"*   23953-A
(Harry Akst-Al Jolson-Saul Chaplin)

73917   *"Keep Smiling at Trouble"*   23953-B
(Lewis Gensler-Al Jolson-B.G. De Sylva)

D96)   June 9, 1947. Los Angeles, California. With Orchestra under the direction of Morris W. Stoloff.

L-4440   *"Back in Your Own Back Yard"*   24108-B
(Dave Dreyer-Al Jolson-Billy Rose)

L-4441   *"I'm Sitting on Top of the World"*   24107-B
(Ray Henderson-Sam M. Lewis-Joe Young)

L-4442   *"Where the Black-Eyed Susans Grow"*   24398-B
(Richard A. Whiting-Dave Radford)

L-4443   *"Toot, Toot, Tootsie!" (Goo' Bye)*   24108-A
(Gus Kahn-Ernie Erdman-Dan Russo)

D97)   June 11, 1947. Los Angeles, California. With Orchestra under the direction of Morris W. Stoloff.

L-4444   *"Carolina in the Morning"*   24109-A
(Walter Donaldson-Gus Kahn)

L-4445   *"Liza"*   24109-B
(George Gershwin-Ira Gershwin-Gus Kahn)

L-4446   *"For Me and My Gal"*   24399-A
(George W. Meyer-E. Ray Goetz-Edgar Leslie)

D98)   June 18, 1947. Los Angeles, California. With Orchestra under the direction of Morris W. Stoloff.

L-4456   *"About a Quarter to Nine"*   24400-B
(Harry Warren-Al Dubin)

L-4457   *"Waiting for the Robert E. Lee"*   24106-A
(Lewis F. Muir-L. Wolfe Gilbert)

L-4458   *"Golden Gate"*   24107-A

(Dave Dreyer-Joseph Meyer-Al Jolson-Billy Rose)
L-4459   *"When You Were Sweet Sixteen"*   24106-B
(James Thornton)

D99)   November 21, 1947. Los Angeles, California. With Orchestra under the
direction of Morris W. Stoloff.

L-4569   *"There's a Rainbow 'Round My Shoulder"*   24400-A
(Dave Dreyer-Al Jolson-Billy Rose)
L-4570   *"If I Only Had a Match"*   24296-A
(George W. Meyer-Arthur Johnson-Lee Morris)
(On *Billboard* chart for 1 week, was #26)
L-4571   *"Let Me Sing and I'm Happy"*   24296-B
(Irving Berlin)

D100)   November 28, 1947. Los Angeles, California. With Orchestra and Male
Quartet under the direction of Morris W. Stoloff.

L-4584   *"I Want a Girl (Just Like the Girl That*
Married Dear Old Dad)"   24397-A
(Harry Von Tilzer-William Dillon)
L-4585   *"By the Light of the Silvery Moon"*   24518-A
(Gus Edwards-Edward Madden)

D101)   December 5, 1947. Los Angeles, California. With Orchestra under the
direction of Morris W. Stoloff.

L-4620   *"I Wish I Had a Girl"*   24518-B
(Gus Kahn-Grace LeBoy)
L-4621   *"When I Leave the World Behind"*   24399-B
(Irving Berlin)
L-4622   *"Someone Else May Be There While I'm Gone"*   24398-A
(Irving Berlin)
L-44623   *"When the Red, Red Robin Comes*
Bob, Bob, Bobbin' Along"   24398-B
(Harry Woods)

D102)   December 19, 1947. Los Angeles, California. With Orchestra and Choir
under direction of Lou Bring.

L-4698   *"Kol Nidre"*   29251-A
(traditional)
L-4699   *"A Chazend'l Ohf Shabbes"*
(arranged by A.W. Binder)   29251-B

D103)   May 24, 1948. New York, New York. With Simon Rady Chorus.

74539   *"Hatikvoh"*   24456-A
(Nahtali Herz Imber)
74540   *"Israel"*   24456-B
(Al Jolson-Benee Russell)

D104)   December 8, 1948. Los Angeles, California. With The Mills Brothers.

L-4845	*"Down Among the Sheltering Palms"*	24534-A
	(Abe Olman-James Brockman)	
L-4846	*"Is It True What They Say About Dixie?"*	24534-B
	(Irving Caesar-Sammy Lerner-Gerald Marks)	

D105)   February 16, 1949. Los Angeles, California. With Orchestra under the direction of Morris W. Stoloff.

L-4899	*"I'm Crying Just for You"*	27410
	(James V. Monaco-Joseph McCarthy)	
L-4900	*"I Only Have Eyes for You"*	24601-B
	(Harry Warren-Al Dubin)	
L-4901	*"That Wonderful Girl of Mine"*	24601-A
	(Sammy Gallop-Jacob Jacobs-Alexander Olshanetsky)	
L-4902	*"In Our House"*	27410
	(Al Jolson-Benee Russell-Martin Fried)	

D106)   May 17, 1949. Los Angeles, California. With Orchestra under the direction of Morris W. Stoloff.

L-5017	*"Pretty Baby"*	24681-A
	(Egbert Van Alstyne-Tony Jackson-Gus Kahn)	
L-5018	*Medley: "I'm Looking Over a Four-Leaf Clover"*	24681-B
	(Harry Woods-Mort Dixon), *"Baby Face"* (Harry Akst-Benny Davis)	
L-5019	*"It All Depends on You"*	Rejected
	(B.G. De Sylva-Lew Brown-Ray Henderson)	

D107)   May 23, 1949. Los Angeles, California. With Matty Malneck's Orchestra and Four Hits & a Miss.

L-5020	*"Chinatown, My Chinatown"*	24683-B
	(Jean Schwartz-William Jerome)	
L-5021	*"After You've Gone"*	24683-A
	(Henry Creamer-J. Turner Layton)	

D108)   May 24, 1949. Los Angeles, California. With Orchestra under the direction of Morris W. Stoloff.

L-5019	*"It All Depends on You"*	24667-B
	(B.G. De Sylva-Lew Brown-Ray Henderson)	
L-5024	*"Give My Regards to Broadway"*	24682-A
	(George M. Cohan)	
L-5025	*"Is It True What They Say About Dixie?"*	24684-B
	(Irving Caesar-Sammy Lerner-Gerald Marks)	
L-5026	*"I'm Just Wild About Harry"*	24682-A
	(Noble Sissle-Eubie Blake)	

D109)   May 31, 1949. Los Angeles, California. With Orchestra under the direction of Victor Young.

L-5029	*"(Just One Way to Say) I Love You"*	24665-A
	(Irving Berlin)	
L-5030	*"Paris Wakes Up and Smiles"*	24665-B
	(Irving Berlin)	
L-5031	*"Some Enchanted Evening"*	24667-A
	(Richard Rodgers-Oscar Hammerstein II)	

D110) January 23, 1950. Los Angeles, California. With Orchestra and Chorus under the direction of Vic Schoen.

L-5345	*"Let's Go West Again"*	24905
	(Irving Berlin)	
L-5346	*"God's Country"*	24905
	(Haven Gillespie-Beasley Smith)	
L-5347	*"Remember Mother's Day"*	24971
	(Harry Akst-Ben Ryan-Solly Violinsky)	
L-5348	*"My Mother's Rosary"*	Unissued
	(George W. Meyer-Sam M. Lewis)	

D111) March 28, 1950. Los Angeles, California. With Orchestra and Chorus under the direction of Gordon Jenkins.

| L-5418 | *"My Mother's Rosary"* | 24971 |
| | (George W. Meyer-Sam M. Lewis) | |

D112) April 18, 1950. Los Angeles, California. With The Andrews Sisters.

L-5554	*"The Old Piano Roll Blues"*	27024
	(Cy Cohen)	
L-5555	*"Way Down Yonder in New Orleans"*	27024
	(Henry Creamer-J. Turner Layton)	

D113) April 28, 1950. Los Angeles, California. With Orchestra and Chorus under the direction of Gordon Jenkins.

L-5583	*"Are You Lonesome Tonight?"*	27043
	(Roy Turk-Lou Handman)	
L-5584	*"No Sad Songs for Me"*	27043
	(Harry Akst-Al Jolson)	

D114) July 13, 1950. Los Angeles, California. With Orchestra and Chorus under the direction of Gordon Jenkins.

L-5731	*"Old Black Joe"*	27364
	(Stephen Foster)	
L-5732	*"My Old Kentucky Home"*	27365
	(Stephen Foster)	
L-5733	*"Beautiful Dreamer"*	27363
	(Stephen Foster)	

L-5734   *"Massa's in De Cold, Cold Ground"*   27365
(Stephen Foster)

D115)   July 17, 1950. Los Angeles, California. With Orchestra and Chorus under the direction of Gordon Jenkins.

L-5741   *"Old Folks at Home"*   27363
(Stephen Foster)

L-5742   *"I Dream of Jeanie with the Light Brown Hair"*   27364
(Stephen Foster)

L-5743   *"Oh! Susanna"*   27181
(Stephen Foster)

L-5744   *"De Camptown Races"*   27181
(Stephen Foster)

A montage photo of Ruby Keeler and Al Jolson in costume for *Go Into Your Dance* (1935). Permission of Turner Entertainment.

6

Radio and Television

Al Jolson starred in six radio series between 1932 and 1949, in addition to making well over one-hundred known guest appearances on a wide range of radio programs beginning with his first in 1922. This radiography begins with his series work, listed in chronological order, followed by a listing of his guest appearances.

RADIO SERIES

R1   *PRESENTING AL JOLSON*

1932-33. NBC Red Network (Fridays). 15 broadcasts. 30 minutes each.

Premiered: November 18, 1932, 10 p.m. Sponsored by General Motors (Chevrolet). Announcer: Howard Claney. Lou Silvers' Orchestra. Jolson closed each broadcast with "April Showers."

1932

1) **(November 18)** Guest: Ken Strong. Jolson's songs: "Ma Mere," "Golden Gate," "Down South," "Rock-A-Bye Your Baby With a Dixie Melody."
2) **(November 25)** Jolson's songs: "Toot, Toot, Tootsie," "The Spaniard That Blighted My Life," "Dirty Hands! Dirty Face!," "Brother, Can You Spare a Dime?," "Oh, Donna Clara," "Life Is Just a Bowl of Cherries," "Why Can't You."
3) **(December 2)** Jolson's songs: "Yankee Doodle Blues," "Keep Smiling at Trouble," "We're Not Too Poor for That," "My Buddy," "Let Me Sing and I'm Happy," "Mother of Mine, I Still Have You."
4) **(December 9)** Jolson's songs: "I Gotta Get Back to New York," "Ma Mere," "Hallelujah, I'm a Bum," "The Cantor," "Sonny Boy."
5) **(December 16)** Jolson's songs: "If I Only Had a Five Cent Piece," "You Made Me Love You," "When I Leave the World Behind," "There Ain't No Color Line."
6) **(December 23)** Jolson's songs: "There's a Rainbow 'Round My Shoulder," "The Old Kitchen Kettle," "Fugitive from Justice," "Brother, Can You Spare a Dime," "Pickaninnies Heaven."

7) **(December 30)** Guest: Ben Bernie. Jolson's songs: "Ol' Man River," "Oh Donna Clara," "Here Lies Love," "Trav'lin All Alone."

1933

8) **(January 6)** Jolson's songs: "California, Here I Come," "Avalon," "Little Pal."
9) **(January 13)** Jolson's songs: "Oh Donna Clara," "Dark Eyes," "Buy American," "Hey! Young Fella," "Rock-A-Bye Your Baby With a Dixie Melody," "Mother of Mine, I Still Have You."
10) **(January 20)** Jolson's songs: "Toot, Toot, Tootsie," "It All Depends On You," "The Call of the South," "Sonny Boy."
11) **(January 27)** Jolson's songs: "Good Days Coming," "You Are Too Beautiful," "Dusty Shoes," "To My Mammy."
12) **(February 3)** Jolson's songs: "Chloe," "My Buddy."
13) **(February 10)** Guest: Greenwood Mitchell.
14) **(February 17)** Jolson's songs: "Swanee," "Trav'lin All Alone," "Young Healthy," "The Cantor," "Dirty Hands! Dirty Face!"
15) **(February 24)** Jolson's songs: "I'm Sitting on Top of the World," "How Deep is the Ocean," "The Best Things in Life Are Free," "Ol' Man River," "Brother, Can You Spare a Dime?," "My Mammy," "Sonny Boy."

Reviews

"Colossal. And should anyone by chance question the gags, the singing is still phenomenal."(M.H.S., "Review," *The Billboard*, November 26, 1932, p. 15)

Additional Review: *Variety*, November 22, 1932, p. 58.

R2   THE KRAFT MUSIC HALL

1933-34. NBC Red Network (Thursdays). 27 broadcasts. 60 minutes each.

Premiered: August 3, 1933, 10 p.m. Sponsored by the Kraft Phoenix Cheese Corporation (Kraft Cheese). Announcer: Howard Claney. Paul Whiteman's Orchestra. Cast: Deems Taylor, Jack Fulton, Peggy Healy. Jolson performed dramatizations of plays and films on many broadcasts. (Jolson had guest-starred on the two-hour premiere of the series on June 26, 1933, singing "A Cantor for the Sabbath," "My Gal Sal," "I've Got to Sing a Torch Song," "Sonny Boy," and a dramatic scene based on Jolson's boyhood).

1933

1) **(August 3)** Jolson's songs: "By a Waterfall," "In Old Kentucky," "Brother, Can You Spare a Dime?"
2) **(August 10)** Jolson's songs: "Blue Skies," "California, Here I Come," "Always," "Ol' Man River."
3) **(August 17)** Jolson's songs: "Keep Smiling at Trouble," "That's What I Like About the South," "Night and Day," "My Buddy." Dramatic scene: "The Music Master."
4) **(August 24)** Jolson's songs: unknown.
5) **(August 31)** Jolson's songs: "By a Waterfall," "Lazy Bones," "Shanghai Lil."

6) **(September 7)** Jolson's songs: "When I Leave the World Behind," "Things Look Brighter for You and Me," "You Made Me Love You," "Dirty Hands! Dirty Face!"

7) **(September 14)** Jolson's songs: "I'm Sitting on Top of the World," "Rock-A-Bye Your Baby With a Dixie Melody," "The Road is Open Again," "My Old Kentucky Home," "Oh! Susanna," "Swanee River."

8) **(September 21)** Jolson's songs: "At Sundown," "It All Depends on You," "Yes! We Have No Bananas," "Lucky Day."

9) **(September 28)** Jolson's song: "My Mammy."

10) **(October 5)** Jolson's songs: "Easter Parade," "Not For All the Rice in China."

11) **(October 12)** Jolson's songs: unknown.

1934

12) **(February 22)** Jolson's songs: unknown. Dramatic scene: *The Man Without a Country.*

13) **(March 1)** Jolson's songs: unknown.

14) **(March 8)** Jolson's songs: unknown.

15) **(March 15)** Jolson's songs: unknown.

16) **(March 22)** Jolson's songs: unknown.

17) **(March 29)** Jolson's songs: unknown.

18) **(April 5)** Jolson's songs: unknown.

19) **(April 12)** Jolson's songs: unknown.

20) **(April 19)** Jolson's songs: unknown.

21) **(April 26)** Jolson's songs: "Water Boy." Dramatic scene: *The Emperor Jones.*

22) **(July 12)** Jolson's songs: unknown.

23) **(July 19)** Jolson's songs: unknown. Dramatic scene: *Liliom.*

24) **(July 26)** Jolson's songs: "Dames," "The Call of the South." Dramatic scene: *Run, Little Chillun.*

25) **(August 2)** Jolson's songs: unknown. Dramatic scene: *The Last Mile.*

26) **(August 9)** Jolson's songs: unknown. Dramatic scene: *The Life of Stephen Foster.*

27) **(August 16)** Jolson's songs: unknown.

Reviews

"When Al Jolson came back to the New Amsterdam Roof for a return engagement on the WEAF wave length last Monday night he had things pretty much his own way. A capacity audience was there to greet him, and the presence of such familiar faces as Ed Wynn, Jack Pearl, Bert Lahr, Burns and Allen and Jack Benny in the front rows visibly cheered the comedian. Paul Whiteman supplied the music, while Jolson kept up a steady stream of banter and in general kept things going at a lively pace for such a sultry night. The applause was clamorous and appreciative. Jolson, it seems, is still New York's idol, microphones or no microphones."(*New York Times*, July 2, 1933; review of the special two-hour opening broadcast on June 26, 1933)

R3   *SHELL CHATEAU*

1935-36. NBC Red Network (Saturdays). 39 broadcasts. 60 minutes each.

Premiered: April 6, 1935, 9:30 p.m. Sponsored by the Shell Union Oil Corporation (Shell Gasoline). Victor Young's Orchestra. Cast: Benay Venuta (until April 27), Jack Stanton and Peggy Gardiner (from May 4). From the first broadcast through the end of 1935, Jolson opened each broadcast with "Good Evening, Friends." Beginning on the January 4, 1936 broadcast, he began using "Golden Gate" with special lyrics as his opening song. He closed each broadcast of the series with "Thank You Father."

1935

1) **(April 6)** Guests: Max and Buddy Baer, Miriam Hopkins, Jack Stanton and Peggy Gardiner. Jolson's song: "Mammy, I'll Sing About You."
2) **(April 13)** Guests: James J. Braddock, Smith and Dale, Constance Bennett.
3) **(April 20)** Guests: Lefty Gomez and June O'Day, Eddie Santley, Elissa Landi, Paulist Choristers.
4) **(April 27)** Guests: Babe Ruth, Polly Moran, John Barrymore.
5) **(May 4)** Guests: Clem McCarthy, Olsen and Johnson, Lupe Velez.
6) **(May 11)** Guests: Dizzy and Daffy Dean, Sheila Barrett, Eva Le Gallienne. Jolson's songs: "Oh Suzanna, Dust Off That Old Piano."
7) **(May 18)** Guests: Amelia Earhart, Lulu McConnell, Philip Holmes.
8) **(May 25)** Guests: Willie Saunders, Doc Rockwell, Ella Logan, Walter Hampden.
9) **(June 1)** Guests: Tony Canzoneri, Bert Lahr, Gloria Grafton, Lenore Ulrich.
10) **(June 8)** Guests: Josephine Morrone, Ernest Truex, Irene Bordoni, Walte Huston.
11) **(June 15)** Guests: Sam Parks, Jr., Niela Goodelle, Eddie Dowling and Ray Dooley, Alla Nazimova. Jolson's song: "California, Here I Come."
12) **(June 22)** Guests: Chief Little Wolf Man, Alice Faye, James Cagney.
13) **(June 29)** Guests: Les Reis and Artie Dunne, Maxie Rosenbloom, Sylvia Froos, Otto Kruger and Martha Sleeper. Jolson's songs: "March Winds and April Showers," "April Showers," "Oh! Susanna," "Page Miss Glory."
14) **(July 6)** Guests: Ky Elbright and Reggie Watts, Frank Gill and Bill Dowling, Dixie Lee, Richard Barthelmess. Jolson's songs: "The Lady in Red," "Green Pastures," "Swing Low, Sweet Chariot," "Moonlight and Magnolias."
15) **(July 13)** Guests: James J. Jeffries, Lee Wiley, George Sidney and Charlie Murray, Joan Blondell. Jolson's songs: "One in a Million," "A Little Bundle From Heaven," "Page Miss Glory."
16) **(July 20)** Guests: Loretta Turnbull, Willie Howard, Irene Taylor, Henry Hull. Jolson's songs: "Coney Island," "My Gal Sal," "Banks of the Wabash," "The Rose in Her Hair."
17) **(July 27)** Guests: Foghorn McGee, Al Shaw and Sam Lee, Loyce Whiteman, Ruth Chatterton. Jolson's songs: "You Little Mischief Maker," "His Majesty the Baby," "She's a Latin from Manhattan."
18) **(August 3)** Guests: Olin Dutra, George Jessel, Estelle Taylor, Bette Davis. Jolson's songs: "The Rose in Her Hair," "Mighty Lak' a Rose," "You're All I Need."
19) **(August 10)** Guests: Sam Coslow, Irvin S. Cobb, Alice Dawn, Margaret Brayton, Irving Pichel. Jolson's songs: "Avalon," "You Little Mischief Maker," "Covered Wagon Days," "The Last Round-Up."
20) **(August 17)** Guests: Pat C. "Patsy" Flick, Carmel Myers, The Watson Sisters, Lionel Barrymore. Jolson's songs: "Hello 'Tucky," "When I Leave the World

Behind."

21) **(August 24)** Guests: Colonel Roscoe Turner, Marjorie Keeler, Roscoe Ates, Dolores Del Rio. Jolson's songs: "I Feel a Song Coming On," "Oh! Susanna," "Isn't This a Lovely Day?"

22) **(August 31)** Guests: Joyce Wethered, Maxine Lewis, Boris Karloff. Jolson's songs: "Coney Island," "Plain Old Me," "Cheek to Cheek."

23) **(September 7)** Guests: Lois Terry, Ralph Forbes and Heather Angel, Betty Bordon, Joe Penner. Jolson's songs: "The Rose in Her Hair," "I'd Love to Take Orders From You," "I'd Rather Listen to Your Eyes."

24) **(September 14)** Guests: Jackie Hughes, Alex Stone and Tisha Lee, Fanny Brice, Henry Fonda. Jolson's songs: "Yes! We Have No Bananas," "Whispering," "My Melancholy Baby," "Poor Butterfly," "Moonlight and Magnolias."

25) **(September 21)** Guests: Wilmer Allison, Allen Jenkins and Frank McHugh, June Marlow, Ricardo Cortez. Jolson's songs: "Page Miss Glory," "At Sundown," "My Blue Heaven," "Night and Day," "Isn't This a Lovely Day?"

26) **(September 28)** Guests: Edward Everett Horton, Harry Savoy, Ginger Rogers. Jolson's songs: "I'd Love to Take Orders From You," "The World is Waiting for the Sunrise," "I'll See You in My Dreams," "Smoke Gets in Your Eyes," "Sonny Boy."

1936

27) **(January 4)** Guests: Walter Hagan, The Yacht Club Boys, Midge Williams, Bette Davis.

28) **(January 11)** Guests: Charles Stevenson, Lulu McConnell, Dorothy Dale, Frances Lederer.

29) **(January 18)** Guests: Patsy Kelly, Dutch Clark, Betty Ross, Edward Everett Horton.

30) **(January 25)** Guests: Ivan Nelson, Helen Troy, Cab Calloway and His Band, Herbert Marshall. Jolson's songs: "Wah-Hoo!," "I Can't Give You Anything But Love," "Boots and Saddles."

31) **(February 1)** Guests: Bob Swanson, Jack McClellan and Sara, Mike Riley and Ed Farley, Jewel Hopkins, May Robson. Jolson's songs: "Back In Your Own Backyard."

32) **(February 8)** Guests: Charles Gay, Joe E. Lewis, Winnie Shaw, George Raft.

33) **(February 15)** Guests: Barney Oldfield, The Hall Johnson Choir, Professor Robert Wildhack, Grace Saxon.

34) **(February 22)** Guests: Clem McCarthy, Joe and Cynthia Doakes, Vi Bradley, John Barrymore.

35) **(February 29)** Guests: Joe Louis, Elissa Landi.

36) **(March 7)** Guests: Fred Niblo, Benay Venuta, Bill "Bojangles" Robinson, Walter Connolly.

37) **(March 14)** Guests: Clyde Hager, Jimmy Dykes, Vi Bradley, Lionel Barrymore.

38) **(March 21)** Guests: Jesse Willard, Joe E. Lewis, Charles Ruggles.

39) **(March 28)** Guests: Virginia Gardiner, Abe Roth, Sterling Holloway, Pat O'Brien, Barbara Kent, Irene Taylor.

Reviews

"Al Jolson's singing, and brand of comedy individual to the Mammy Singer -- current hit tunes played by Victor Young's orchestra -- comedy skits and stirring drama -- this, in the main, is what the new show offers. And each department presented entertainment fare of a high order. There are those of Jolson's listeners who are prejudiced, against; and many more are rabid fans and rooters. If you like Jolson, you'll be over-enthused about this entertainment here."(Walter Sinclair and James Connors. "Heard on the Air," *Radio Guide*, April 27, 1935, p. 12)

Additional Review: "Shell Chateau." *Metronome*, February 1936.

R4   THE AL JOLSON LIFEBUOY/RINSO SHOW

1936-39. CBS Network (Tuesdays). 99 broadcasts. 30 minutes each.

Premiered: December 22, 1936, 8:30 p.m. Sponsored by Lever Brothers (Lifebuoy soap and Rinso detergent). Rush Hughes, announcer (until January 5, 1937); Paul Rickenbacher, announcer (from January 12- March 30, 1937); Tiny Ruffner, announcer (from April 6, 1937). Victor Young's Orchestra (until June 14, 1938); Lud Gluskin's Orchestra (from June 21, 1938). Cast: Martha Raye, Sid Silvers (until February 23, 1937); Harry "Parkyakarkus" Einstein (from March 2, 1937). The program was called *Al Jolson's Cafe Trocadero* for the first two episodes.   Jolson closed each episode with the song he often used as his radio theme, "April Showers."

1936

1) **(December 22)** Guest: Ruby Keeler. Jolson's song: "Sonny Boy."
2) **(December 29)** Guest: Arthur Treacher.

1937

3) **(January 5)** Guest: unknown.
4) **(January 12)** Guest: unknown. Jolson's song: "I've Got My Love to Keep Me Warm."
5) **(January 19)** Guest: Eddie Cantor. Jolson's song: "If You Knew Susie."
6) **(January 26)** Guest: Gregory Ratoff.
7) **(February 2)** Guest: unknown.
8) **(February 9)** Guest: Lionel Stander.
9) **(February 16)** Guest: Lionel Stander. Jolson's song: "The Rosary."
10) **(February 23)** Guest: Lionel Stander.
11) **(March 2)** Guest: unknown.
12) **(March 9)** Guests: Virginia Judge, George Kelley.
13) **(March 16)** Guest: unknown.
14) **(March 23)** Guest: unknown.
15) **(March 30)** Guest: unknown.
16) **(April 6)** Guest: none. Jolson's songs: "This Year's Kisses," "My Gal Sal," "After the Ball," "Alexander's Ragtime Band," "Swanee," "California, Here I Come," "My Mammy."
17) **(April 13)** Guest: unknown.
18) **(April 20)** Guest: unknown. Jolson's songs: "Alabama Barbecue," "September in the Rain."
19) **(April 27)** Guest: unknown.
20) **(May 4)** Guest: Edgecomb Pinchon.

21) **(May 11)** Guest: none.
22) **(May 18)** Guest: unknown.
23) **(May 25)** Guest: unknown.
24) **(June 1)** Guest: unknown.
25) **(June 8)** Guest: unknown.
26) **(June 15)** Guest: unknown.
27) **(June 22)** Guest: unknown.
28) **(June 29)** Guest: unknown.
29) **(September 7)** Guest: George Jessel. Jolson's songs: "Love is on the Air Tonight," "Toot, Toot, Tootsie" (duet with Jessel), "Give My Regards to Broadway" (duet with Jessel).
30) **(September 14)** Guest: unknown.
31) **(September 21)** Guest: Ben Bernie.
32) **(September 28)** Guest: Joe Penner. Jolson's songs: "Avalon," "Keep Smiling at Trouble."
33) **(October 5)** Guest: Frank Fay.
34) **(October 12)** Guests: Edward G. Robinson, Ray Heatherton.
35) **(October 19)** Guest: George Jessel.
36) **(October 26)** Guest: Sonja Henie.
37) **(November 2)** Guests: Adolphe Menjou, Veree Teasdale.
38) **(November 9)** Guest: Anna May Wong.
39) **(November 16)** Guest: Edward Everett Horton.
40) **(November 23)** Guests: Lum 'N' Abner.
41) **(November 30)** Guest: Beatrice Lillie.
42) **(December 7)** Guests: Stoopnagle and Budd.
43) **(December 14)** Guest: Zasu Pitts.
44) **(December 21)** Guest: Leo Carrillo.
45) **(December 28)** Guests: Ruby Keeler, Paul Whiteman.

1938

46) **(January 4)** Guests: Adolphe Menjou, Verree Teasdale.
47) **(January 11)** Guest: Louise Fazenda.
48) **(January 18)** Guest: John Barrymore.
49) **(January 25)** Guest: Edward Everett Horton.
50) **(February 1)** Guest: Constance Bennett.
51) **(February 8)** Guest: Basil Rathbone.
52) **(February 15)** Guest: Patsy Kelly.
53) **(February 22)** Guest: Walter Connolly.
54) **(March 1)** Guests: Grantland Rice, Florence Rice, Lyda Roberti.
55) **(March 8)** Guest: Andy Devine.
56) **(March 15)** Guest: Edna May Oliver.
57) **(March 22)** Guest: C. Aubrey Smith.
58) **(March 29)** Guest: Ned Sparks.
59) **(April 5)** Guest: Charles Ruggles.
60) **(April 12)** Guest: Franciska Gaal.
61) **(April 19)** Guest: Douglas Fairbanks, Jr.
62) **(April 26)** Guests: "The Seven Dwarfs."
63) **(May 3)** Guests: E.E. Clive, Mrs. Martin Johnson.
64) **(May 10)** Guest: John Barrymore.
65) **(May 17)** Guest: Mary Boland.

66) **(May 24)** Guests: Eric Blore, Arthur Treacher.
67) **(May 31)** Guest: Mario Chamlee.
68) **(June 7)** Guests: Walt Disney characters.
69) **(June 14)** Guest: Lupe Velez.
70) **(June 21)** Guest: Guy Kibbee.
71) **(June 28)** Guest: Alice Brady.
72) **(July 5)** Guest: Alan Hale.
73) **(July 12)** Guest: Alan Hale, Judy Garland.
74) **(September 20)** Guest: Douglas "Wrong Way" Corrigan. Jolson's songs: "My Walking Stick," "A-Tisket A-Tasket" (duet with Martha Raye), "At Long Last Love."
75) **(September 27)** Guest: Edna May Oliver.
76) **(October 4)** Guest: Pat O'Brien.
77) **(October 11)** Guest: Bob Burns.
78) **(October 18)** Guests: Marie Wilson, Charles Butterworth. Jolson's songs: "Confidentially," "Sweet Georgia Brown" (duet with Martha Raye), "When Day is Done."
79) **(October 25)** Guests: Olsen and Johnson, Kay Thompson, Red Corcoran.
80) **(November 1)** Guests: Gail Patrick, Connee Boswell, Al Smith. Jolson's songs: "So Help Me," "Avalon."
81) **(November 8)** Guests: Beatrice Lillie, Kate Smith.
82) **(November 15)** Guests: Professor Quiz, Vera Zorina, The Merry Macs.
83) **(November 22)** Guest: Mischa Auer.
84) **(November 29)** Guest: Zasu Pitts.
85) **(December 6)** Guest: Jackie Cooper.
86) **(December 13)** Guest: Fay Bainter. Jolson's songs: "Waitin' for the Robert E. Lee," "Limehouse Blues" (duet with Martha Raye), "Thanks for Everything."
87) **(December 20)** Guest: Freddie Bartholomew. Jolson's songs: "Hello 'Tucky," "Get Outa Town."
88) **(December 27)** Guest: Peter Lorre. Jolson's songs: "You Must Have Been a Beautiful Baby," "Oh, You Beautiful Doll!," "I'm Forever Blowing Bubbles" (duet with Martha Raye), "We'll Never Know."

1939

89) **(January 3)** Guest: Mary Boland.
90) **(January 10)** Guest: Richard Greene.
91) **(January 17)** Guest: Leslie Howard. Jolson's songs: "Keep Smiling at Trouble," "Japanese Sandman," "I'm Just Wild About Harry" (duet with Martha Raye), "I Promise You."
92) **(January 24)** Guest: Grand Duchess Marie of Russia. Jolson's songs: "Jeepers Creepers," "Limehouse Blues" (duet with Martha Raye), "F.D.R. Jones."
93) **(January 31)** Guest: Gene Autry. Jolson's songs: "Got to Get Some Shut Eye," "S-h-i-n-e" (duet with Martha Raye), "Get Out of Town."
94) **(February 7)** Guests: Veree Teasdale, Adolphe Menjou.
95) **(February 14)** Guest: Fibber McGee.
96) **(February 21)** Guests: Dolores Del Rio, Marjorie Wilson, Cliff Nazarro.
97) **(February 28)** Guest: Bob Burns.
98) **(March 7)** Guests: George Burns and Gracie Allen.
99) **(March 14)** Guests: Gregory Ratoff, Dick Powell.

Reviews

"New Tuesday night half-hour for Rinso bowed in with Jolson in fine vigor. But there were a number of things that kept the first broadcast from being 100%. Sid Silvers was one of them. Script kidded about his gags and his performance being bad. But the script wasn't kidding. . . .[Martha Raye] is a dubious asset. She wasn't any funnier than Silvers. Just louder."(Land., "Review," *Variety*, December 30, 1936)

". . .the program is now routined for a comedy splash, a sample of Martha Raye, and finally the dramatic one-two to the chin put over by Jolson himself."(Land., "Review," *Variety*, March 2, 1937)

R5   THE AL JOLSON COLGATE SHOW

1942-43. CBS Network (Tuesdays). 39 broadcasts. 25 minutes each.

Premiered: October 6, 1942, 8:30 p.m. Sponsored by the Colgate Palmolive Company (Colgate Tooth Powder). Fred Uttal, announcer (until March 23, 1943); Carlton Cardell, announcer (from March 30, 1943). Ray Bloch's Orchestra (until March 23, 1943); Gordon Jenkins' Orchestra (from March 30, 1943). Cast: Harry "Parkyakarkus" Einstein (until February 2, 1943), Carol Bruce (until February 23, 1943), Jo Stafford (from March 30, 1943), Monty Woolley (January 26-May 25, 1943).

1942

1) (October 6) Guests: unknown. Jolson's song: "Yankee Doodle Blues," "My Buddy."
2) (October 13) Guests: unknown. Jolson's songs: unknown.
3) (October 20) Guests: unknown. Jolson's songs: unknown.
4) (October 27) Guests: unknown. Jolson's songs: unknown.
5) (November 3) Guests: unknown. Jolson's songs: unknown.
6) (November 10) Guests: unknown. Jolson's songs: unknown.
7) (November 17) Guests: unknown. Jolson's songs: unknown.
8) (November 24) Guests: unknown. Jolson's songs: unknown.
9) (December 1) Guest: Adolphe Menjou. Jolson's songs: unknown.
10) (December 8) Guest: Gypsy Rose Lee. Jolson's songs: unknown.
11) (December 15) Guest: Lauritz Melchior. Jolson's songs: unknown.
12) (December 22) Guest: Peter Lorre. Jolson's songs: unknown.
13) (December 29) Guest: Diana Barrymore. Jolson's songs: unknown.

1943

14) (January 5) Guest: Monty Woolley. Jolson's songs: "I'm Sitting on Top of the World," medley of Gershwin songs.
15) (January 12) Guest: Robert Benchley. Jolson's songs: "Yoo-Hoo," "Sonny Boy."
16) (January 19) Guest: Monty Woolley, Col. Leroy P. Hunt, Pvt. Dana Babcock. Jolson's songs: "My Gal Sal," "We're Gonna Make Sure There'll Never Be Another War."
17) (January 26) Guest: Robert Benchley. Jolson's songs: "Where the Black-Eyed

Susans Grow," "When I Leave the World Behind."
18) **(February 2)** Guest: unknown. Jolson's songs: "Toot, Toot, Tootsie."
19) **(February 9)** Guest: Roddy McDowell. Jolson's songs: unknown.
20) **(February 16)** Guests: Ilka Chase, Kay Francis. Jolson's songs: unknown.
21) **(February 23)** Guest: Sidney Fields. Jolson's songs: unknown.
22) **(March 2)** Guests: Helen O'Connell, Sidney Fields. Jolson's songs: unknown.
23) **(March 9)** Guests: Helen O'Connell, Judy Canova. Jolson's songs: unknown.
24) **(March 16)** Guests: Helen O'Connell. Jolson's songs: unknown.
25) **(March 23)** Guest: Helen O'Connell. Jolson's songs: unknown.
26) **(March 30)** Guest: none. Jolson's song: "American Boy."
27) **(April 6)** Guest: unknown. Jolson's songs: unknown.
28) **(April 13)** Guest: Rudy Vallee. Jolson's songs: "Swanee," "I've Heard That Song Before."
29) **(April 20)** Guests: Brenda and Cobina. Jolson's songs: unknown.
30) **(April 27)** Guests: unknown. Jolson's songs: unknown.
31) **(May 4)** Guests: unknown. Jolson's songs: unknown.
32) **(May 11)** Guests: unknown. Jolson's songs: unknown.
33) **(May 18)** Guests: unknown. Jolson's songs: unknown.
34) **(May 25)** Guest: Diana Barrymore. Jolson's songs: unknown.
35) **(June 1)** Guest: Lucille Ball. Jolson's songs: unknown.
36) **(June 8)** Guest: Carole Landis. Jolson's songs: unknown.
37) **(June 15)** Guest: Jinx Falkenburg. Jolson's songs: unknown.
38) **(June 22)** Guest: George Jessel. Jolson's songs: unknown.
39) **(June 29)** Guests: unknown. Jolson's songs: unknown.

R6 THE KRAFT MUSIC HALL

1947-49. NBC Network (Thursdays). 71 broadcasts. 30 minutes each.

Premiered: October 2, 1947, 8:30 p.m. Sponsored by Kraft Foods Company (Kraft Cheese). Ken Carpenter, announcer. Lou Bring's Orchestra. Cast: Oscar Levant, Milena Miller (until October 9, 1947). Jolson opened each broadcast with a short bit of "April Showers."

1947

1) **(October 2)** Guest: Edgar Bergen. Jolson's songs: "Toot, Toot, Tootsie," "All My Love," "Sonny Boy" (duet with Bergen), "When You Were Sweet Sixteen."
2) **(October 9)** Guest: Lauritz Melchior. Jolson's songs: "Waiting for the Robert E. Lee," "Liza," "Come to Me, Bend to Me," "Annie Laurie."
3) **(October 16)** Guest: Bing Crosby. Jolson's songs: "For Me and My Gal," "Peg O' My Heart," medley of Gershwin songs (duet with Crosby).
4) **(October 23)** Guest: Groucho Marx. Jolson's songs: "I'm Sitting on Top of the World," "If I Only Had a Match," "When I Leave the World Behind."
5) **(October 30)** Guest: William Bendix. Jolson's songs: "Almost Like Being in Love," "I Only Have Eyes for You," "Smoke Gets in Your Eyes," "Far From Cayuga's Waters" (parody duet with Bendix), "I Wonder What's Become of Sally."
6) **(November 6)** Guest: Humphrey Bogart. Jolson's songs: "Golden Gate," "All My Love," "Let Me Sing and I'm Happy," "When You Were Sweet Sixteen."

7) **(November 13)** Guest: Victor Moore. Jolson's songs: "Swanee," "Banks of the Wabash," "A Fellow Needs a Girl," "I'll Be Seeing You."

8) **(November 20)** Guest: Charles Boyer. Jolson's songs: "Hello 'Tucky," "Dark Eyes," "Anniversary Song," "Ol' Man River."

9) **(November 27)** Guest: Dorothy Lamour. Jolson's songs: "California, Here I Come," "Poor Butterfly," "Ma Blushin' Rosie," "Mimi," "Put On Your Old Grey Bonnet" (parody duet with Lamour and Oscar Levant), "My Gal Sal."

10) **(December 4)** Guest: Red Skelton. Jolson's songs: "There's a Rainbow 'Round My Shoulder," "By a Waterfall," "At Sundown," "Christmas Dreaming," "The Best Things in Life are Free."

11) **(December 11)** Guests: Yehudi Menuhin, Arnold Stang. Jolson's songs: "When the Red, Red Robin Comes Bob, Bob Bobbin' Along," "A Pretty Girl is Like a Melody," "Back in Your Own Backyard," "Come to Me, Bend to Me," "Annie Laurie."

12) **(December 18)** Guest: Jimmy Durante. Jolson's songs: "Rosalie," "White Christmas," "I Wish I Had a Girl," "Chidabee Ch Ch" (duet with Durante).

13) **(December 25)** Guests: Boris Karloff, The Kraft Choral Club. Jolson's songs: "Is It True What They Say About Dixie?," "I Can't Give You Anything But Love," "My Melancholy Baby," "Near You," "By the Light of the Silvery Moon."

1948

14) **(January 1)** Guest: Madeleine Carroll. Jolson's songs: "Avalon," "My Blue Heaven," "Summertime," "Who and Where?," "Anniversary Song."

15) **(January 8)** Guest: William Powell. Jolson's songs: "Where Did Robinson Crusoe Go With Friday on Saturday Night?," "My Wild Irish Rose," "Mother Macree," "If I Only Had a Match," "Look for the Silver Lining."

16) **(January 15)** Guest: Bing Crosby. Jolson's songs: "Toot, Toot, Tootsie," "Mighty Lak a Rose," "Carolina in the Morning" (duet with Crosby), "Beautiful Dreamer" (duet with Crosby).

17) **(January 22)** Guest: Lucille Ball. Jolson's songs: "Yaaka Hula Hickey Dula," "That Lovin' Traumerei," "It Ain't Necessarily So," "Hannah in Savannah," "What'll I Do?"

18) **(January 29)** Guest: Walter O'Keefe. Jolson's songs: "Alabamy Bound," "Mandy," "People Will Say We're in Love," "Bing Crosby Calypso: Bank of America's Joy" (duet with O'Keefe), "Nearest Thing to Heaven."

19) **(February 5)** Guest: Ed "Archie" Gardner. Jolson's songs: "I'm Just Wild About Harry," "Mary's a Grand Old Name," "Maxim's," "When Irish Eyes Are Smiling," "A Fellow Needs a Girl," "Without a Song."

20) **(February 12)** Guest: Charles Laughton. Jolson's songs: "For Me and My Gal," "Pretty Baby," "Water Boy," "The One I Love Belongs to Somebody Else," "Keep Smiling at Trouble," "Memories."

21) **(February 19)** Guest: Charles Boyer. Jolson's songs: "I'm Sitting on Top of the World," "I'll Get By," "After the Ball," "After You've Gone," "Remember."

22) **(February 26)** Guest: David Niven. Jolson's songs: "Chicago," "The Darktown Strutter's Ball," "In The Good Old Summertime," "By the Light of the Silvery Moon," "I'm Crying Just for You," "April Showers," "Among My Souvenirs."

23) **(March 4)** Guest: Cary Grant. Jolson's songs: "Yaaka Hula Hickey Dula," "Hello Ma Baby," "I'm Forever Blowing Bubbles," "Someone Else May Be There While I'm Gone," "Marcheta."

24) (**March 11**) Guest: Edward Everett Horton. Jolson's songs: "I'm Looking Over a Four Leaf Clover," "Every Little Movement," "Cuddle Up a Little Closer," "Liza," "I'm Always Chasing Rainbows."

25) (**March 18**) Guest: Edward G. Robinson. Jolson's songs: "Margie," "When Irish Eyes Are Smiling," "Ramona," "About a Quarter to Nine," "Always."

26) (**March 25**) Guests: Clifton Webb, The Kraft Choral Club. Jolson's songs: "Baby Face," "In the Shade of the Old Apple Tree," "Shine on Harvest Moon," "Easter Parade."

27) (**April 1**) Guest: Jimmy Durante. Jolson's songs: "She's a Latin from Manhattan," "Take Me Out to the Ballgame," "If I Knew I'd Find You," "Don't Let It Get You Down," "Who Will Be With You When I'm Far Away"(duet with Durante), "Without a Song."

28) (**April 8**) Guest: Vera Vague. Jolson's songs: "I'm Just Wild About Harry," "At the Candlelight Cafe," "In the Good Old Summertime," "Whispering," "Ol' Man River."

29) (**April 15**) Guest: Charles Boyer. Jolson's songs: "Chinatown My Chinatown," "All Alone," "Dirty Hands! Dirty Face!," "If I Only Had a Match," "I'll See You in My Dreams."

30) (**April 22**) Guest: Dorothy Kirsten. Jolson's songs: "Alexander's Ragtime Band," "The Things You Left in My Heart," "A Hot Time in the Old Town Tonight," "Embraceable You" (duet with Kirsten), "It All Depends on You."

31) (**April 29**) Guest: Victor Moore. Jolson's songs: "I Gotta Get Back to New York," "Nature Boy," "Give My Regards to Broadway," "I Only Have Eyes for You," "California, Here I Come" (parody trio with Moore and Oscar Levant), "That Old Gang of Mine."

32) (**May 6**) Guest: Groucho Marx. Jolson's songs: "Yaaka Hula Hickey Dula," "Poor Butterfly," "Let Me Sing and I'm Happy," "Remember Mother's Day," "Come to Me, Bend to Me," "Annie Laurie."

33) (**May 13**) Guest: Dorothy Kirsten. Jolson's songs: "Baby Face," "Nature Boy," "Somebody Loves Me" (duet with Kirsten), "Remember."

34) (**May 20**) Guest: Henry Morgan. Jolson's songs: "Toot, Toot, Tootsie," "You Made Me Love You," "When You Were Sweet Sixteen," "Someone Else May Be There While I'm Gone," "Nearest Thing to Heaven."

35) (**May 27**) Guest: Dorothy Kirsten. Jolson's songs: "California, Here I Come," "April Showers," "Swanee," "Don't Let It Get You Down," "The Darktown Strutter's Ball," "What'll I Do?" (duet with Kirsten), "It All Depends on You."

36) (**June 3**) Guest: Ezio Pinza. Jolson's songs: "When the Red, Red Robin Comes Bob, Bob Bobbin' Along," "At Sundown," "Smoke Gets in Your Eyes," "I'm Crying Just for You," "Marcheta."

37) (**June 10**) Guest: Dorothy Kirsten. Jolson's songs: "Alexander's Ragtime Band," "Career Skit," "About a Quarter to Nine," "People Will Say We're in Love" (duet with Kirsten), "Israel."

38) (**September 30**) Guest: Judy Garland. Jolson's songs: "Is It True What They Say About Dixie?," "Poor Butterfly," "All Alone," "When The Red, Red Robin Comes Bob, Bob Bobbin' Along," "Pretty Baby" (duet with Garland), "When I Lost You."

39) (**October 7**) Guest: Edward G. Robinson. Jolson's songs: "Baby Face," "A Tree in the Meadow," "Chinatown My Chinatown," "In Our House."

40) (**October 14**) Guest: Ezio Pinza. Jolson's songs: "Just One of Those Things," "After You've Gone," "You Call Everybody Darling" (duet with Pinza), "If

We Can't Be the Same Old Sweethearts."

41) **(October 21)** Guest: none. Jolson's songs: "For Me and My Gal," "More Than You Know," "About a Quarter to Nine," "Toot, Toot, Tootsie," "You Made Me Love You," "Without a Song."

42) **(October 28)** Guest: Dorothy Kirsten. Jolson's songs: "I'm Just Wild About Harry," "She's a Latin from Manhattan," "Down Among the Sheltering Palms," "Hello Ma Baby" (duet with Kirsten), "I'll Be Seeing You."

43) **(November 4)** Guests: George Burns and Gracie Allen. Jolson's songs: "Yaaka Hula Hickey Dula," "Shine on Harvest Moon," "Someone Else May Be There While I'm Gone," "Put on Your Old Grey Bonnet," "How Deep is the Ocean?"

44) **(November 11)** Guest: George Jessel. Jolson's songs: "Bright Eyes," "Mandy," "I Only Have Eyes for You," "I'll Get By" (duet with Jessel), "Roses of Picardy."

45) **(November 18)** Guest: Groucho Marx. Jolson's songs: "Little Girl," "Dirty Hands! Dirty Face!," "I Wonder What's Become of Sally," "Christmas Dreaming," "In Our House."

46) **(November 25)** Guest: Victor Mature. Jolson's songs: "That Certain Party," "Lazy," "Who and Where?," "The One I Love Belongs to Somebody Else," "Little Pal."

47) **(December 2)** Guest: Peggy Lee. Jolson's songs: "When the Red, Red Robin Comes Bob, Bob Bobbin' Along," "Rock-A-Bye Your Baby With a Dixie Melody," "Lucky in the Rain," "People Will Say We're in Love" (duet with Lee), "The Birth of the Blues" (duet with Lee), "Say It Isn't So."

48) **(December 9)** Guest: Dennis Day. Jolson's songs: "Ma (She's Making Eyes at Me)," "Smoke Gets in Your Eyes," "They Didn't Believe Me," "All By Myself," "Ol' Man River."

49) **(December 16)** Guest: Dinah Shore. Jolson's songs: "I'm Sitting on Top of the World," "Dinah," "Put Your Arms Around Me, Honey" (duet with Shore), "Down Among the Sheltering Palms," "It's Been a Long, Long Time" (duet with Shore), "When Day is Done."

50) **(December 23)** Guests: The Kraft Choral Club. Jolson's songs: "Is It True What They Say About Dixie?," "Mother Macree," "She Is Ma Daisy," "Waiting for the Robert E. Lee," "When You Were Sweet Sixteen," "White Christmas."

51) **(December 30)** Guest: Doris Day. Jolson's songs: "Smiles," "Who Cares?," "My Melancholy Baby," "My Blue Heaven" (duet with Day), "Memories."

1949

52) **(January 6)** Guest: Larry Parks. Jolson's songs: "Yaaka Hula Hickey Dula," "I Want a Girl," "Don't Let It Get You Down," "Ma Blushin' Rosie," "Anniversary Song."

53) **(January 13)** Guest: Groucho Marx. Jolson's songs: "That Certain Party," "I'm Crying Just for You," "She's a Latin from Manhattan," "When I Leave the World Behind."

54) **(January 20)** Guest: Victor Moore. Jolson's songs: "I'm Just Wild About Harry," "If You Were the Only Girl in the World." "Blue Skies," "Someone Else May Be There While I'm Gone," "Nearest Thing to Heaven."

55) **(January 27)** Guest: Arthur Treacher. Jolson's songs: "Alexander's Ragtime Band," "Carolina in the Morning," "Lucky in the Rain," "Brother, Can You Spare a Dime?" (parody in support of 1949 March of Dimes), "Sonny Boy."

56) **(February 3)** Guest: Dennis Day. Jolson's songs: "Hello 'Tucky," "Why Can't You Behave," "When Irish Eyes are Smiling," "My Wild Irish Rose" (duet with Day), "Say It Isn't So."

57) **(February 10)** Guest: Peggy Lee. Jolson's songs: "Oh, You Beautiful Doll," "Back in Your Own Backyard," "So Long Mary" (duet with Lee), "Summertime" (duet with Lee), "Marcheta."

58) **(February 17)** Guest: Joan Davis. Jolson's songs: "Hello Ma Baby," "I Only Have Eyes for You," "Banks of the Wabash," "Mighty Lak' a Rose," "I Wonder What's Become of Sally."

59) **(February 24)** Guests: The Andrews Sisters. Jolson's songs: "Bright Eyes," "'Way Down Yonder in New Orleans" (duet with The Andrews Sisters), "Am I Blue?," "Sonny Boy" (duet with The Andrews Sisters), "If We Can't Be the Same Old Sweethearts."

60) **(March 3)** Guests: Dorothy Kirsten, Phil Harris, Elliot Lewis. Jolson's songs: "Waiting for the Robert E. Lee," "Come to Me, Bend to Me," "Annie Laurie" (duet with Kirsten), "Remember."

61) **(March 10)** Guest: Jimmy Durante. Jolson's songs: "After You've Gone," "I Was Born in Virginia," "Mary's a Grand Old Name," "The Song's Gotta Come from the Heart" (duet with Durante), "Dark Eyes" (duet with Durante), "Chidabee Ch Ch," "You'll Always Be Beautiful."

62) **(March 17)** Guests: Roy Rogers and Dale Evans. Jolson's songs: "At Sundown," "When Irish Eyes are Smiling," "I'm Always Chasing Rainbows."

63) **(March 24)** Guest: George Jessel. Jolson's songs: "Chinatown My Chinatown," "Spring Skit," "A Pretty Girl is Like a Melody," "Let Me Sing and I'm Happy," "De Camptown Races" (parody duet with Jessel), "Without a Song."

64) **(March 31)** Broadcast pre-empted.

65) **(April 7)** Guest: Groucho Marx. Jolson's songs: "When the Red, Red Robin Comes Bob, Bob Bobbin' Along," "Easter Parade," "Why Can't You Behave?," "That Little German Band" (duet with Marx), "Say It Isn't So."

66) **(April 14)** Guests: Margaret Whiting, Jack Kirkwood. Jolson's songs: "Give My Regards to Broadway," "Ain't We Got Fun?" (duet with Whiting), "Embraceable You" (duet with Whiting), "What'll I Do?"

67) **(April 21)** Guest: Jimmy Durante. Jolson's songs: "Ma (She's Making Eyes at Me)," "If I Could Be With You (One Hour Tonight)," "A Real Piano Player" (duet with Durante), "I'll Be Seeing You."

68) **(April 28)** Guest: Doris Day. Jolson's songs: "Swanee," "You'll Always Be Beautiful," "That Wonderful Girl of Mine," "Put Your Arms Around Me, Honey" (duet with Day), "My Gal Sal."

69) **(May 5)** Guest: Dennis Day. Jolson's songs: "California, Here I Come," "Look for the Silver Lining," "By the Light of the Silvery Moon" (duet with Day), "Remember Mother's Day."

70) **(May 12)** Guest: Victor Moore. Jolson's songs: "My Melancholy Baby," "My Blue Heaven," "Lucky in the Rain," "That Wonderful Girl of Mine," "Pretty Baby" (duet Victor Moore), "Some Enchanted Evening."

71) **(May 19)** Guests: Dorothy Kirsten, Jack Kirkwood. Jolson's songs: "Look for the Silver Lining," "People Will Say We're in Love" (duet with Kirsten), "Bali H'ai."

72) **(May 26)** Guests: Groucho Marx, Adele Norman. Jolson's songs: "Waiting for the Robert E. Lee," "Why Can't You Behave?," "Auld Lang Syne."

Reviews

"From the *April Showers* curtain-raiser to the closing nostalgic refrain cued to recollections of Luchow's 14th Street (N.Y.) restaurant as the *Stork Club of the '90's,* Jolson breezed through the KMH stanza completely at ease, sparking the whole routine with a pacing and timing that can match the best of them. [. . .] There's been no stinting on the talent layout, with Oscar Levant also a permanent fixture, along with Milena Miller as the femme vocalist, and a guest star policy that had Charlie McCarthy and Edgar Bergen on hand for the teeoff in a three-way Levant-Jolie-McCarthy barb-throwing parlay. That's talent in spades, a surfeiting of name values that under ordinary circumstances could easily bog down the comedy flow and the overall effect. Yet thanks to the Mannheim-Issacs script contrib, the neat handling of the production controls by Ezra McIntosh and Jolson's major-domo operation, each dovetails nicely into the whole."(Rose., *Variety,* October 8, 1947, p. 25)

RADIO GUEST APPEARANCES

Al Jolson's guest appearances on radio are listed below in chronological order.

R7   *Telephone Relay from the Newark, New Jersey Plant of the Westinghouse Company.* February 5, 1922. Jolson's songs: "Yoo Hoo," "April Showers."

R8   *Lambs Gambol in Tribute to General John J. Pershing.* April 26, 1925. Jolson's songs: two, unknown.

R9   *Jack Rose Benefit at the Winter Garden Theatre.* April 18, 1926. Jolson's songs: unknown.

R10   *Mississippi Valley Flood Refugee Appeal.* April 30, 1927. Jolson's songs: "My Mammy," "April Showers," "What Does It Matter?," "It All Depends on You."

R11   *The Dodge Victory Hour.* January 4, 1928. Jolson's songs: "My Mammy," "California, Here I Come," "Golden Gate," "Back in Your Own Backyard," "Four Walls," "Toot, Toot, Tootsie." This program was the first ever coast-to-coast broadcast.

R12   *Comedy Club.* April 6, 1928. Jolson did not sing.

R13   *The Warner Brothers Vitaphone Jubilee Hour.* September 17, 1928. Jolson's songs: "You'll Never Know Sweetheart," "There's a Rainbow 'Round My Shoulder," "Sonny Boy."

R14   *The Warner Brothers Vitaphone Jubilee Hour.* March 4, 1929. Jolson's songs: unknown.

R15   *Hollywood Mid-Summer Jubilee at the Hollywood Bowl.* August 7, 1929. Jolson's songs: unknown.

R16   *The Al Jolson Show.* August 16, 1929. Jolson's songs: "Little Pal," "Why Can't You?," "Use to You," "I'm in Seventh Heaven."

R17   **The Pure Oil Band Show.** October 15, 1929. Jolson's songs: "My Mammy," "Little Pal," "Sonny Boy," "Why Can't You?"

R18   **Salvation Army Radio Benefit.** May 26, 1931. Jolson's songs: unknown.

R19   **Back from the Depression League Dinner.** May 16, 1932. Jolson did not sing.

R20   **National Recovery Act Benefit.** July-August 1933. Jolson and Ruby Keeler appeared to praise President Franklin Roosevelt's NRA. Details unknown.

R21   **The Rudy Vallee Show.** December 21, 1933. Jolson sang one line of Vallee's theme song and introduced Ruby Keeler.

R22   **Jewish Consumptive Home Appeal.** March 18, 1934. Jolson's songs: unknown.

R23   **Hollywood Hotel.** November 23, 1934. Jolson's songs: "Rock-A-Bye Your Baby With a Dixie Melody," "I Only Have Eyes for You."

R24   **The Ben Bernie Show.** January 1, 1935. Jolson's song: "Mammy, I'll Sing About You." Jolson also performed a monologue, "A Telegram to 1935."

R25   **Santa Anita Races.** February 23, 1935. Jolson's songs: "California, Here I Come" (ukelele accompaniment provided by B.G. De Sylva).

R26   **NBC Hollywood Studios Opening.** December 7, 1935. Jolson's songs: "The Cantor," a medley of "Whispering," "My Melancholy Baby," "Poor Butterfly."

R27   **The Lux Radio Theatre: "Burlesque."** June 15, 1936. Jolson's songs: "Toot, Toot, Tootsie," "Is It True What They Say About Dixie?," "A Pretty Girl is Like a Melody." Co-starring Ruby Keeler.

R28   **The Lux Radio Theatre: "The Jazz Singer."** August 10, 1936. Jolson's songs: "April Showers," others.

R29   **Sears -- Then and Now.** October 1, 1936. Jolson's songs: excerpts of "The Spaniard That Blighted by Life," "You Made Me Love You," "Rock-A-Bye Your Baby With a Dixie Melody," "Hello Central, Give Me No-Man's Land," "Swanee," "Avalon," "My Mammy," "California, Here I Come," "Toot, Toot, Tootsie," "Sonny Boy," "Save Me, Sister."

R30   **Salute to KNX and KSFO.** January 2, 1937. Jolson's songs: unknown.

R31   **Eddie Cantor's "Texaco Town."** January 3, 1937. Jolson's songs: "Margie," "Dinah" (duet with Cantor).

R32   **Red Cross Program.** February 1, 1937. Jolson's song: "My Mammy."

R33   **KFWB Hollywood Studio Opening.** February 24, 1937. Jolson's songs: unknown.

R34   **Hollywood Hotel.** June 11, 1937. Jolson's songs: "Ma Blushin' Rosie," "Give

My Regards to Broadway" (duet with George Jessel).

R35　*A Tribute to George Gershwin.* July 12, 1937. Jolson's songs: "Swanee," "I've Got Plenty of Nothin'."

R36　*George Gershwin Memorial Concert at the Hollywood Bowl.* September 8, 1937. Jolson's song: "Swanee."

R37　*The Ben Bernie Show.* September 14, 1937. Jolson's songs: unknown.

R38　*The George Burns and Gracie Allen Grape Nuts Show.* November 1,1937. Jolson's songs: unknown. Jolson and Ruby Keeler subbed for Burns and Allen.

R39　*Radio Station KNX Columbia Square Studios Opening.* April 30, 1938. Jolson's songs: "I Live the Life I Love," "I See Your Face Before Me."

R40　*Salute to Irving Berlin and "Alexander's Ragtime Band."* August 3, 1938. Jolson's songs: "Let Me Sing a Berlin Song," "This is the Life," "Mandy" (duet with Eddie Cantor and Irving Berlin), "The International Rag" (duet with Sophie Tucker), "Alexander's Ragtime Band' (sung by all-star chorus including Jolson, Ethel Merman, Sophie Tucker, Tyrone Power).

R41　*March of Dimes Appeal.* January 22, 1939. Jolson's songs: unknown.

R42　*The Inside Story.* March 14, 1939. Jolson did not sing.

R43　*Kentucky Derby.* May 6, 1939. Jolson did not sing.

R44　*Screen Actors' Guild Broadcast from the Hollywood Bowl (The Need to Preserve the Federal Theatre).* June 26, 1939. Jolson's song: "Brother, Can You Spare a Dime?"

R45　*Arrowhead Springs Hotel Opening.* December 16, 1939. Jolson's songs: "California, Here I Come," "Sonny Boy."

R46　*The Kate Smith Show.* December 29, 1939. Jolson and Don Ameche performed scenes from *Swanee River.* Jolson's songs: "De Camptown Races," "Oh, Susanna!," "Old Folks at Home," "My Old Kentucky Home."

R47　*A.S.C.A.P. on Parade.* January or February 1940. Jolson's songs: "California, Here I Come," "You Made Me Love You," "Swanee," "April Showers."

R48　*The Ben Bernie Program.* January 21, 1940. Jolson's songs: unknown.

R49　*Libertyville Horse Race.* July 16, 1940. Jolson did not sing.

R50　*Hold On to Your Hats.* August 1, 1940. Jolson's songs: unknown.

R51　*Eddie Cantor's "It's Time to Smile" Show.* June 4, 1941. Jolson's songs: "Old Folks at Home," "Ida, Sweet as Apple Cider."

R52   *Star Spangled Theatre: "Uncle Tom's Cabin."* August 10, 1941. Jolson's songs: "Oh, Susanna!," "Swing Low, Sweet Chariot."

R53   *Treasury Hour: "Millions for Defense."* August 13, 1941. Jolson's songs: "Sonny Boy," "Hello Ma Baby," "My Gal Sal," "After the Ball," "Alexander's Ragtime Band," "Swanee," "My Mammy."

R54   *A.F.R.S. "Command Performance" #15.* May 13, 1942. Jolson's songs: "Swanee," "My Mammy," "California, Here I Come."

R55   *Chase & Sanborn Hour.* August 16, 1942. Jolson's songs: unknown.

R56   *Star Spangled Vaudeville.* August 19, 1942. Jolson's songs: "California, Here I Come," "My Mammy."

R57   *Army Emergency Relief Show.* September 30, 1942. Jolson's songs: unknown.

R58   *Scrap Metal Presentation to New York Mayor Fiorello LaGuardia.* October 1, 1942. Jolson did not sing.

R59   *Stage Door Canteen.* December 24, 1942. Jolson's songs: unknown.

R60   *Tell It to the Marines.* February 2, 1943. Jolson's song: "Toot, Toot, Tootsie."

R61   *Colgate Sports Newsreel.* February 13, 1943. Jolson did not sing.

R62   *"This is the Army" Promotion.* July 1943. Jolson did not sing.

R63   *Report to the Nation.* October 5, 1943. Jolson did not sing.

R64   *Soldiers in Greasepaint.* November 25, 1943. Jolson's song: "People Will Say We're in Love."

R65   *Santa Claus Time.* December 25, 1943. Jolson's songs: "For Me and My Gal," "My Mammy."

R66   *Night Clubs for Victory.* January 20, 1944. Jolson's songs: unknown.

R67   *Contact.* January 26, 1944. Jolson did not sing.

R68   *Philco Radio Hall of Fame.* May 28, 1944. Jolson's songs: "For Me and My Gal," others.

R69   *Your All-Time Hit Parade.* July 23, 1944. Jolson's songs: "Ma Blushin' Rosie," "April Showers."

R70   *The Lux Radio Theatre: "Swanee River."* April 2, 1945. Jolson's songs: "Oh! Susanna," "De Camptown Races," "My Old Kentucky Home" (duet with Dennis Morgan), "Old Folks at Home," "April Showers."

R71   *Milton Berle's "Let Yourself Go" Show.* June 6, 1945. Jolson's songs: "Ma

Blushin' Rosie," "Swanee," "April Showers," "Avalon," "My Blue Heaven," "California, Here I Come," "Sonny Boy," "My Mammy."

R72   *Jinx Falkenburg and Tex McCrary's "Hi! Jinx" Show.* June 22, 1946. Jolson did not sing.

R73   *A Salute to Al Jolson.* October 1, 1946. Jolson did not sing.

R74   *The Louella Parsons Show.* October 20, 1946. Jolson did not sing.

R75   *The Barry Gray Show.* October 27, 1946. Jolson's songs: "Ma Blushin' Rosie," "Sonny Boy," "April Showers," "When You Were Sweet Sixteen," "California, Here I Come," "Swanee," "You Made Me Love You," "My Mammy," "Ma Blushin' Rosie."

R76   *Jinx Falkenburg and Tex McCrary's "Hi! Jinx" Show.* November 20, 1946. Jolson did not sing.

R77   *Amos 'N' Andy.* December 17, 1946. Jolson's songs: "April Showers," "My Mammy," "You Made Me Love You," "California, Here I Come."

R78   *Bing Crosby's "Philco Radio Time."* January 15, 1947. Jolson's songs: "April Showers" (duet with Crosby), "Ma Blushin' Rosie" (duet with Crosby), "Swanee," "Philco Singing Commercial" (duet with Crosby), "The One I Love Belongs to Somebody Else" (duet with Crosby).

R79   *George Burns and Gracie Allen's "Maxwell House Coffee Time."* February 20, 1947. Jolson's songs: "I'm Sitting on Top of the World," "You Made Me Love You," "April Showers" (duet with Burns).

R80   *Bing Crosby's "Philco Radio Time."* March 5, 1947. Jolson's songs: "Let Me Sing and I'm Happy," "Rock-A-Bye Your Baby With a Dixie Melody," "Who Paid the Rent for Mrs. Rip Van Winkle?," "Back in Your Own Backyard" (duet with Crosby), "You Made Me Love You" (duet with Crosby), "Waiting for the Robert E. Lee" (duet with Crosby), "Philco Singing Commercial #2" (duet with Crosby), "Anniversary Song."

R81   *The Eddie Cantor Pabst Blue Ribbon Show.* March 6, 1947. Jolson's songs: "Swanee," "Anniversary Song," "If You Knew Susie," "Ida, Sweet as Apple Cider," "Toot, Toot, Tootsie" (duet with Cantor).

R82   *Bing Crosby's "Philco Radio Time."* April 2, 1947. Jolson's songs: "Oh! Susanna" (trio with Crosby and John Charles Thomas), "In the Evening By the Moonlight" (duet with Crosby), "Banks of the Wabash," "Philco Singing Commercial #3" (trio with Crosby and John Charles Thomas), "My Mammy," "Alabamy Bound" (trio with Crosby and John Charles Thomas).

R83   *The Lux Radio Theatre: "Alexander's Ragtime Band."* April 7, 1947. Jolson's songs: "Alexander's Ragtime Band," "Lazy," "A Pretty Girl is Like a Melody," "April Showers."

R84   *The Bob Hope Pepsodent Show.* April 8, 1947. Jolson's songs: "California, Here I Come," "Alexander's Ragtime Band," "Always."

R85   *Bing Crosby's "Philco Radio Time."* May 7, 1947. Jolson's songs: "Lazy," "All By Myself" (duet with Crosby), "Alexander's Ragtime Band" (duet with Crosby), "Easter Parade" (duet with Crosby).

R86   *The Jack Benny Lucky Strike Program.* May 18, 1947. Jolson's songs: "April Showers," "You Made Me Love You."

R87   *The Lux Radio Theatre: "The Jazz Singer."* June 2, 1947. Jolson's songs: "Toot, Toot, Tootsie," "I'm Sitting on Top of the World," "Blue Skies," "Keep Smiling at Trouble," "Rock-A-Bye Your Baby With a Dixie Melody," "Kol Nidre," "All My Love."

R88   *Operation Nightmare.* June 9, 1947. Jolson did not sing.

R89   *Bing Crosby's "Philco Radio Time."* December 3, 1947. Jolson's songs: "Ma Blushin' Rosie" (duet with Crosby), "Sunbonnet Sue" (duet with Crosby), "A Pretty Girl is Like a Melody" (duet with Crosby), "The Best Things in Life Are Free" (duet with Crosby).

R90   *Here's to the Veterans.* 1948. Jolson's songs: "Rosalie," "The Best Things in Life are Free," "I Wish I Had a Girl." (These were pre-recorded vocals from the Kraft Music Hall).

R91   *1948 March of Dimes Promotion.* 1948. Jolson did not sing.

R92   *Treasury Department "Guest Star" #58.* 1948. Jolson's songs: "I'm Looking Over a Four-Leaf Clover," "Weather Skit," "Liza," "I'm Always Chasing Rainbows."

R93   *Here's to the Veterans.* 1948. Jolson's songs: "Ma (She's Making Eyes at Me)," "Smoke Gets in Your Eyes," "They Didn't Believe Me," "All By Myself."

R94   *"Give My Regards to Broadway" Promotion.* 1948. Jolson did not sing.

R95   *The Eddie Cantor Pabst Blue Ribbon Show.* January 8, 1948. Jolson's songs: "Is It True What They Say About Dixie?," "Near You."

R96   *The Jimmy Durante Rexall Show.* January 21, 1948. Jolson's songs: "If I Only Had a Match," "Ol' Man River." (Jolson filled in as host for Durante).

R97   *The Edgar Bergen and Charlie McCarthy Chase and Sanborn Show.* January 25, 1948. Jolson's song: "Near You."

R98   *The Lux Radio Theatre: "The Jolson Story."* February 16, 1948. Jolson's songs: "Ma Blushin' Rosie," "My Mammy," "Toot, Toot, Tootsie," "You Made Me Love You," "April Showers," "Liza," "Anniversary Song," "Swanee," "April Showers."

R99   *Operation Nightmare: Chapter 1.* April 3, 1948. Jolson did not sing.

R100   *Operation Nightmare: Chapter 2.* April 10, 1948. Jolson's song: "Israel."

R101   *The New Sealtest Village Store.* April 15, 1948. Jolson did not sing.

R102   *Leo Forbstein Memorial Program.* April 25, 1948. Jolson did not sing.

R103   *Guest Star.* May 2, 1948. Transcribed from the February 19 and March 11, 1948 Kraft Music Hall programs.

R104   *The Eddie Cantor Pabst Blue Ribbon Show.* June 8, 1948. Jolson's song: "Anniversary Song".

R105   *The Waking Giant.* October 4, 1948. Jolson's song: "When the Red, Red Robin Comes Bob, Bob Bobbin' Along."

R106   *This Is Your Life.* November 23, 1948. Jolson's songs: "Hello 'Tucky," "An Old Fashioned Girl in a Gingham Gown."

R107   *Elgin Two Hours of Stars.* December 25, 1948. Jolson's songs: "I'm Sitting on Top of the World," "Santa Claus is Comin' to Town" (parody duet with Jack Kirkwood), "It All Depends on You," "For Me and My Gal" (parody duet with Cass Daley).

R108   *Chicago Interview.* 1949. Jolson did not sing.

R109   *1949 March of Dimes Promotion.* 1949. Jolson's songs: "Brother, Can You Spare a Dime?" (parody), "Sonny Boy."

R110   *"Jolson Sings Again" Promotion.* 1949. Jolson did not sing.

R111   *George Fischer's "Hollywood Calling" #34.* 1949. Jolson did not sing.

R112   *Parade of Stars.* January 1, 1949. Jolson's songs: "I've Heard That Song Before," "That Lovin' Traumerai," "Ma Blushin' Rosie."

R113   *The Eddie Cantor Pabst Blue Ribbon Show.* January 7, 1949. Jolson's songs: "The One I Love Belongs to Somebody Else," "April Showers" (parody), "Mandy" (duet with Cantor).

R114   *The Colgate Sports Newsreel.* January 7, 1949. Jolson did not sing.

R115   *The Jimmy Durante Camel Show.* March 4, 1949. Jolson's songs: "I'm Crying Just for You," "April Showers," "Sonny Boy," "A Real Piano Player" (duet with Durante).

R116   *Friar's Frolic.* April 16, 1949. Jolson's songs: unknown.

R117   *Opportunity U.S.A. Savings Bond Program.* May 16, 1949. Jolson's song: "Waiting for the Robert E. Lee."

R118   Operation: Dawn. May 22, 1949. Jolson did not sing.

R119   Garroway at Large. August 1949. Jolson's songs: unknown.

R120   The Colgate Sports Newsreel. October 14, 1949. Jolson did not sing.

R121   The Steve Allen Show. October 26, 1949. Jolson's songs: "California, Here I Come," "Sonny Boy," "April Showers," "Swanee."

R122   The Jimmy Durante Camel Show. November 11, 1949. Jolson's song: "A Real Piano Player" (duet with Durante).

R123   Hollywood Calling. November 12, 1949. Jolson did not sing.

R124   The Bing Crosby Chesterfield Show. November 30, 1949. Jolson's songs: "Toot Toot Tootsie," "Back in Your Own Backyard" (duet with Crosby), "Baby Face" (duet with Crosby).

R125   The Bing Crosby Chesterfield Show. December 28, 1949. Jolson's songs: "Swanee," "When the Red, Red Robin Comes Bob, Bob Bobbin' Along" (duet with Crosby), "I Only Have Eyes for You" (duet with Crosby), "Waiting for the Robert E. Lee" (duet with Crosby).

R126   The Bing Crosby Chesterfield Show. January 4, 1950. Jolson's songs: "Is It True What They Say About Dixie?," "Carolina in the Morning" (duet with Crosby), "My Blue Heaven" (duet with Crosby), "Alabamy Bound" (duet with Crosby), "The One I Love Belongs to Somebody Else" (duet with Crosby), "All By Myself" (duet with Crosby).

R127   The Edgar Bergen and Charlie McCarthy Coca Cola Show. January 15, 1950. Jolson's songs: "Waiting for the Robert E. Lee," "Let Me Sing and I'm Happy," "April Showers."

R128   The Joan Davis "Leave It to Joan" Show. January 29, 1950. Jolson's songs: "I'm Sitting on Top of the World," "Why Can't You Behave," "Mañana" (duet with Davis).

R129   The George Burns and Gracie Allen Amident Show. February 1, 1950. Jolson's songs: "Toot, Toot, Tootsie," "Swanee" (parody), "Yes Sir, That's My Baby," "Pretty Baby," "Baby Face."

R130   The Bing Crosby Chesterfield Show. February 1, 1950. Jolson did not sing.

R131   The Bing Crosby Chesterfield Show. February 8, 1950. Jolson's songs: "California, Here I Come," "Yaaka Hula Hickey Dula" (duet with Crosby), "Whispering" (duet with Crosby), "Bye Bye Baby" (duet with Crosby), "Waiting for the Robert E. Lee" (duet with Crosby).

R132   The George Burns and Gracie Allen Amident Show. March 29, 1950. Jolson's songs: "For Me and My Gal," "Easter Parade."

R133 **The Jack Benny Lucky Strike Show.** April 2, 1950. Jolson's songs: "Remember Mother's Day," "Toot, Toot, Tootsie.'

R134 **The Bing Crosby Chesterfield Show.** May 3, 1950. Jolson's songs: "Give My Regards to Broadway," "Ma Blushin' Rosie" (duet with Crosby), "Avalon" (duet with Crosby), "Lullaby of Broadway" (duet with Crosby), "My Old Kentucky Home" (duet with Crosby).

R135 **The Lux Radio Theatre: "Jolson Sings Again."** May 22, 1950. Jolson's songs: "April Showers," "Is It True What They Say About Dixie?," "Back in Your Own Back Yard," "Chinatown My Chinatown," "I'm Just Wild About Harry," "Baby Face," "I Only Have Eyes for You," "Sonny Boy," "Toot, Toot, Tootsie," "Carolina in the Morning," "Rock-A-Bye Your Baby With a Dixie Melody."

R136 **The Jinx Falkenburg and Tex McCrary "Hi! Jinx" Show.** August 14, 1950. Jolson did not sing.

R137 **Al Jolson Performance in Japan (at Itazuke Air Force Base).** September 16, 1950. Jolson's songs: "Swanee," "Brother, Can You Spare a Dime?," "April Showers," "Anniversary Song," "My Mammy," "Sonny Boy."

R138 **The Louella Parsons Show.** September 24, 1950. Jolson's songs: "Swanee," "April Showers."

R139 **Hollywood USA Permanent Charities Committee.** October 9, 1950. Jolson did not sing.

R140 **Hollywood Calling.** October 20, 1950. Jolson did not sing.

R141 **Colgate Sports Newsreel.** October 20, 1950. This program retrospective includes recordings of previous guests, including Jolson.

Reviews

"Al Jolson did a sock job as narrator of *Operation-Dawn*, a documentary on rescue and replacement of Jewish war refugees. [. . .] Jolie gave great warmth to his appeal for funds and narration of stanza. It all came off as good listener bait." ("Followup Comment," *Variety*, May 26, 1949)

TELEVISION

Al Jolson was mulling over offers to appear on television during the final months of his life (in fact, he had signed a contract with CBS-TV for some appearances). Aside from the two known appearances listed below, Jolson never appeared on national television.

T1 **BELL TELEPHONE COMPANY DEMONSTRATION.**

June 29, 1929. (Newark, New Jersey)

Jolson is thought to have sung "Sonny Boy" in a demonstration of color television, as reported in *Billboard Magazine* on July 6, 1929.

T2   *CHICAGOLAND MUSIC FESTIVAL (Soldier's Field).*

August 20, 1949. WGN-TV, (Chicago, Illinois)

Jolson appeared to promote "Jolson Sings Again." Jolson's songs: "California, Here I Come," "After You've Gone," "April Showers," "My Mammy." Footage survives.

Many television programs over the years have included footage of Jolson, or tributes to him, including *You Asked For It*, which presented a tribute segment made up of film clips and newsreel footage; *The Joe Franklin Show*, which has often featured interviews with Jolson friends and colleagues; Clive James' Fame in the 20th Century documentary, made for the BBC-TV in conjunction with WQED/Pittsburgh, and shown in 1993 on PBS-TV stations, included footage and commentary on Jolson; and virtually any documentary or musical special paying tribute to early film musicals, American stage (Larry Kert impersonated Jolson at the 1975 Tony Awards tribute to the Winter Garden Theatre), and recordings will make some mention of Jolson's pioneering achievements in those fields. Politicians using television have event made mention of Jolson on occasion. The Rev. Jesse Jackson has equated Jolson's use of blackface with white America's view of African-Americans in several speeches, and former President Ronald Reagan was fond of using Jolson's trademark saying, "You ain't heard nothin' yet!" in his speechifying. Jolson's voice or imitations of him have appeared on several television commercials -- for example, his Decca recording of "You Made Me Love You" turned up on a recent cat food commercial, and Clive Baldwin, a celebrated Jolson imitator, contributed a Jolsonesque recording of "About a Quarter to Nine" for a Citizen's watch band commercial that was subsequently dropped when Jolson's estate challenged Baldwin's right to use the Jolson style in this way. There are also two television documentaries specifically on Jolson:

T3   *HOLLYWOOD AND THE STARS: "The Immortal Jolson."*

October 28, 1963. NBC-TV. 25 mins. (New York, New York)

Credits

A David L. Wolper production. Narrated by Joseph Cotton. Produced by Jack Haley, Jr. Written by Irwin Rosen. Produced and directed by Julian Ludwig and Irwin Rosten. Production Coordinator: Jim Schmerer. Film Editor: David Newhouse. Music Composed and Conducted by Ruby Raskin. Title Music: Elmer Bernstein. Opticals and Titles: Modern Film Effects. Based on "The Immortal Jolson" by Pearl Sieben (see B14).

Commentary

This series also included an episode called "The Fabulous Musicals," narrated by Joseph Cotten. Jolson is seen in footage from *The Jazz Singer* (see F2). A special on NBC called "Hollywood: The Golden Years" the previous year, narrated by Gene Kelly, also included footage from *The Jazz Singer* (see F2).

T4   *THE SOUTH BANK SHOW: "The Real Al Jolson Story."*

May 4, 1986. ITV. 62 mins. (London, England)

Credits

Narration: Melvyn Bragg. Executive Producer: Alan Benson. Produced and Directed by Chris Hunt. Graphics: Pat Garvin. Videotape Editor: Graham Roberts. Consultant: Michael Freedland. Film Camera: Paul Bond. Film Sound: Trevor Carless, Paul Corfield. Dubbing Mixer: David Old. Rostrum Camera: Ken Morse. Film Research: Suzanne Gray, Anne Smith. Production Assistant: Xenia Ager. Researcher: Frances Dickenson. Film Editor: Peter Lindley. The South Bank Show Production Team: Xenia Ager, *The South Bank Show* edited and presented by Melvyn Bragg.

Commentary

This popular British television series included this documentary on Jolson, featuring footage from newsreels and Jolson's films, along with interviews with Irving Caesar, Evelyn Keyes, Michael Freedland, Jack Warner, Jr., Bonnie Green, Saul Chaplin, Joni Taps, and Walter Scharf. Edited versions of the program have appeared on American television with different titles.

Al Jolson and announcer Ken Carpenter at a rehearsal for the Kraft Music Hall, late 1940s. Permission of The International Al Jolson Society.

7

Sheet Music

Few performers have graced sheet music covers with the regularity of Al Jolson. Following is an alphabetical list of known sheet music with Jolson's name or image on the cover, including the size of the sheet, its publication date, the names of the composers and lyricists, and the name of the publisher. If the size (most sheet music before World War I is 11"x14", after the war most sheets are 9"x11") or date (in many cases, a sheet was issued when Jolson first performed the song, then sheets might have been issued for *The Jolson Story* and *Jolson Sings Again*) or sheet music for a song varies, a separate listing is included for each. However, if the image or color of the cover varies (which often occurred), no separate listing is included for these variances.

SM1) **"About a Quarter to Nine"**   9"x11" (1935)
    (Harry Warren, Al Dubin)
    (M. Witmark & Sons)

SM2) **"About a Quarter to Nine"**   9"x11" (1946)
    (Harry Warren, Al Dubin)
    (Harms Inc.)

SM3) **"About a Quarter to Nine"**   9"x11" (1949)
    (Harry Warren, Al Dubin)
    (Music Publishers Holding Corporation)

SM4) **"After the Ball"**   9"x11" (1946)
    (Charles K. Harris)
    (Broadway Music Corporation)

SM5) **"Ah, But It Happens"**   9"x11" (1948)
    (Walter Kent)

SM6) **"Ain't Love Grand"**   9"x11" (1922)
    (Con Conrad, Walter Donaldson, B.G. De Sylva)
    (Harry Von Tilzer Music Co.)

SM7) **"Ain't She Sweet"**   9"x11" (1927)
    (Milton Ager, Jack Yellen)

(Ager, Yellen, & Borstein, Inc.)

SM8) **"Ain't That a Grand and Glorious Feeling"**   9"x11" (1927)
(Milton Ager, Jack Yellen)
(Ager, Yellen, & Borstein, Inc.)

SM9) **"Ain't You Coming Back to Dixieland"**   11"x14" (1917)
(Richard A. Whiting, Raymond Egan)
(Jerome H. Remick & Co.)

SM10) **"Alabamy Bound"**   9"x11" (1925)
(Ray Henderson, B.G. De Sylva, Bud Green)
(Harms Inc.)

SM11) **"All My Love"**   9"x11" (1947)
(Saul Chaplin, Harry Akst, Al Jolson)
(Harms Inc.)

SM12) **"Along the Way to Waikiki"**   11"x14" (1917)
(Richard A. Whiting, Gus Kahn)
(Jerome H. Remick & Co.)

SM13) **"Always (You Can Come Back to Me)"**   9"x11" (1921)
(H. Kroll)
(Jerome H. Remick & Co.)

SM14) **"Anniversary Song"**   9"x11" (1946)
(Al Jolson, Saul Chaplin, based on a theme by Ivanovici)
(Shapiro, Bernstein & Co.)

SM15) **"Anniversary Song"**   9"x11" (1949)
(Al Jolson, Saul Chaplin, based on a theme by Ivanovici)
(Shapiro, Bernstein & Co.)

SM16) **"Any Place Will Do With You"**   9"x11" (1921)
(Sigmund Romberg, Al Jolson, Harold Atteridge)
(Sunshine Music Co.)

SM17) **"April Showers"**   9"x11" (1921)
(Louis Silvers, B.G. De Sylva)
(Harms Inc.)

SM18) **"April Showers"**   9"x11" (1946)
(Louis Silvers, B.G. De Sylva)
(Harms Inc.)

SM19) **"April Showers"**   9"x11" (1949)
(Louis Silvers, B.G. De Sylva)
(Harms Inc.)

SM20) **"Arcady"**   9"x11" (1923)

(B.G. De Sylva, Al Jolson)
(Leo. Feist)

SM21) "Are You Happy?"   9"x11" (1927)
(Milton Ager, Jack Yellen)
(Ager, Yellen & Bornstein Inc.)

SM22) "As Long As I've Got My Mammy"   9"x11" (1924)
(Joseph Meyer, James F. Hanley, B.G. De Sylva)
(Harms Inc.)

SM23) "As Long As I've Got My Mammy"   9"x11" (1925)
(Joseph Meyer, James F. Hanley, B.G. De Sylva)
(Harms Inc.)

SM24) "At Mammy's Fireside"   11"x14" (1913)
(Harry Carroll, Ballard MacDonald)
(Shapiro, Bernstein & Co.)

SM25) "At the Yiddish Cabaret"   11"x14" (1913)
(Lewis F. Muir)

SM26) "Avalon"   9"x11" (1920)
(B.G. De Sylva, Vincent Rose, Al Jolson)
(Jerome H. Remick & Co.)

SM27) "Avalon"   9"x11" (1946)
(B.G. De Sylva, Vincent Rose, Al Jolson)
(Jerome H. Remick & Co.)

SM28) "Baby Face"   9"x11" (1949)
(Harry Akst, Benny Davis)
(Remick Music Corporation)

SM29) "Back Home in Tennessee"   11"x14" (1915)
(Walter Donaldson, William Jerome)
(Waterson-Berlin & Snyder, Co.)

SM30) "Back In Your Own Backyard"   9"x11" (1928)
(Dave Dreyer, Al Jolson, Billy Rose)
(Irving Berlin Inc.)

SM31) "Back In Your Own Backyard"   9"x11" (1949)
(Dave Dreyer, Al Jolson, Billy Rose)
(Irving Berlin Inc.)

SM32) "Bagdad"   11"x14" (1918)
(Sigmund Romberg, Harold Atteridge)
(G. Schirmer)

SM33) "Barefoot Days"   9"x11" (1923)

(James A. Brennan, Al Wilson)
(Edward B. Marks Music Co.)

SM34) **"Beatrice Fairfax Tell Me What to Do"**   11"x14" (1915)
(Grant Clarke, Joseph McCarthy, James V. Monaco)

SM35) **"Beauty and the Beast"**   11"x14" (1918)
(Sigmund Romberg, Harold Atteridge)
(G. Schirmer)

SM36)**"Bebe"**   9"x11" (1923)
(Abner Silver, Sam Coslow)
(M. Witmark & Sons)

SM37) **"Because I Love You"**   9"x11" (1926)
(Irving Berlin)
(Irving Berlin Inc.)

SM38) **"Bedalumbo"**   11"x14" (1918)
(Sigmund Romberg, Harold Atteridge)
(G. Schirmer)

SM39) **"Beloved"**   9"x11" (1928)
(Joe Sanders, Gus Kahn)
(Irving Berlin Inc.)

SM40) **"Billy, Billy, Bounce Your Baby Doll"**   11"x14" (1912)
(Fred Fisher, Joseph McCarthy, Al Bryan)
(Leo. Feist)

SM41) **"Billy Used to Give Her Something Every Night"**   11"x14" (1913)
(Billy Hueston, Arthur C. Melvin)
(A.J. Stasny Music Co.)

SM42) **"Billy's Melody"**   11"x14" (1912)
(Joe Cooper, L. Wolfe Gilbert)
(Shapiro Music Publisher)

SM43) **"Blue Bell"**   9"x11" (1946)
(Dolly Morse, Edward Madden)
(Leo. Feist)

SM44) **"Born and Bred in Old Kentucky"**   9"x11" (1924)
(Joseph Meyer, James F. Hanley, B.G. De Sylva)
(Harms Inc.)

SM45) **"Born and Bred in Old Kentucky"**   9"x11" (1925)
(Joseph Meyer, James F. Hanley, B.G. De Sylva)
(Harms Inc.)

SM46) **"Bring Along Your Dancing Shoes"**   11"x14" (1915)
    (Grace LeBoy, Gus Kahn)
    (Jerome H. Remick & Co.)

SM47) **"A Bundle of Love"**   9"x11" (1921)
    (B.G. De Sylva, Al Jolson)
    (Harms Inc.)

SM48) **"By the Honesuckle Vine"**   11"x14" (1919)
    (B.G. De Sylva, Al Jolson)
    (T.B. Harms)

SM49) **"By the Light of the Silvery Moon"**   9"x11" (1946)
    (Gus Edwards, Edward Madden)
    (Harms, Inc.)

SM50) **"California, Here I Come"**   9"x11" (1924)
    (Joseph Meyer, B.G. De Sylva, Al Jolson)
    (M. Witmark & Sons)

SM51) **"California, Here I Come"**   9"x11" (1946)
    (Joseph Meyer, B.G. De Sylva, Al Jolson)
    (M. Witmark & Sons)

SM52) **"California, Here I Come"**   9"x11" (1949)
    (Joseph Meyer, B.G. De Sylva, Al Jolson)
    (M. Witmark & Sons)

SM53) **"The Cantor"**   9"x11" (1931)
    (Traditional, arr. by A.W. Binder)
    (Harms Inc.)

SM54) **"Carolina in the Morning"**   9"x11" (1949)
    (Walter Donaldson, Gus Kahn)
    (Music Publishers Holding Corporation)

SM55) **"Carolina Mammy"**   9"x11" (1923)
    (Billy James)
    (Leo. Feist)

SM56) **"Casino de Paree"**   9"x11" (1935)
    (Harry Warren, Al Dubin)
    (M. Witmark & Sons)

SM57) **"The Chicken Reel"**   11"x14" (1911)
    (Joseph M. Daly, Joseph Mittenthal)
    (Daly Music Publishers)

SM58) **"The Chicken's Ball"**   11"x14" (1912)
    (Barney Fagan, Al Jolson)

SM59) **"Chinatown, My Chinatown"**   9"x11" (1949)
(William Jerome, Jean Schwartz)
(Remick Music Corporation)

SM60) **"Chloe"**   11"x14" (1919)
(B.G. De Sylva, Al Jolson)
(T.B. Harms)

SM61) **"Cleopatra"**   11"x14" (1917)
(Harry Tierney, Alfred Bryan)
(Jerome H. Remick & Co.)

SM62) **"Cleopatra"**   9"x11" (1919)
(Harry Tierney, Alfred Bryan)
(Jerome H. Remick & Co.)

SM63) **"Coo-Coo"**   9"x11" (1921)
(B.G. De Sylva, Al Jolson)
(Harms Inc.)

SM64) **"Cotton Blossom Lullaby"**   9"x11" (1924)
(Gus Kahn, Al Jolson)

SM65) **"The Dance From Down Yonder"**   9"x11" (1924)
(Joseph Meyer, James F. Hanley, B.G. De Sylva)
(Harms Inc.)

SM66) **"The Dance From Down Yonder"**   9"x11" (1925)
(Joseph Meyer, James F. Hanley, B.G. De Sylva)
(Harms Inc.)

SM67) **"Dancing the Blues Away"**   11"x14" (1914)
(Fred Fisher, Howard Johnson, Joseph McCarthy)
(Leo. Feist)

SM68) **"Dark Eyes"**   9"x11" (1932)
(A. Fassio, arr., Carol Raven)
(Edward B. Marks Music Corporation)

SM69) **"Dat Lovin' Touch"**   11"x14" (1911)
(Sam M. Lewis, Leo Bennett)
(Shapiro Music Publishers)

SM70) **"De Cleanin' Man**   11"x14" (1906)
(Oscar F.G. Day, Charles K. Harris)
(C.C. Pillsbury Co.)

SM71) **"Dinah Might -- Dynamite"**   9"x11" (1927)
(Puss Donahoo, Bill Hawley)
(Nat Vincent)

SM72) **"Dirty Hands, Dirty Face"**   9"x11" (1923)
(James V. Monaco, Al Jolson, Grant Clarke, Edgar Leslie)
(Clarke & Leslie Songs Music Publishers)

SM73) **"Dixie Rose"**   11"x14" (1921)
(George Gershwin, B.G. De Sylva, Irving Caesar)
(T.B. Harms)

SM74) **"Don't Be a Sailor"**   11"x14" (1916)
(Sigmund Romberg, James F. Hanley, Harold Atteridge)
(G. Schirmer)

SM75) **"Don't Cry, Swanee"**   9"x11" (1923)
(Con Conrad, B.G. De Sylva, Al Jolson)
(Harms Inc.)

SM76) **"Don't Forget the Boys"**   11"x14" (1917)
(Fred E. Ahlert, Harold Atteridge, Al Jolson)

SM77) **"Don't Get Careless, Honey Dear"**   11"x14" (1911)
(Ted Henry, Al Conklin)
(Ted Henry Co.)

SM78) **"Don't Let It Get You Down"**   9"x11" (1940)
(Burton Lane, E.Y. "Yip" Harburg)
(Chappell & Co.)

SM79) **"Don't Say Goodnight"**   9"x11" (1934)
(Harry Warren, Al Dubin)
(M. Witmark & Sons)

SM80) **"Don't Send Your Wife to the Country"**   9"x11" (1921)
(Walter Donaldson, B.G. De Sylva)
(Harms Inc.)

SM81) **"Down Among the Sheltering Palms"**   11"x14" (1915)
(Abe Olman, James Brockman)
(Leo. Feist)

SM82) **"Down in Bom-Bombay"**   11"x14" (1915)
(Harry Carroll, Ballard MacDonald)
(Shapiro, Bernstein & Co.)

SM83) **"Down in Waterloo"**   11"x14" (1914)
(Jack Wells, Albert Gumble, Alfred Bryan)
(Jerome H. Remick Co.)

SM84) **"Down Old Harmony Way"**   11"x14" (1913)
(Dave Oppenheimer, Joe Cooper)
(Shapiro Music Publishers)

SM85) "**Down South**"   9"x11" (1921)
    (Walter Donaldson, B.G. De Sylva)
    (Harms Inc.)

SM86) "**Down Where the Swanee River Flows**"   11"x14" (1916)
    (Harry Von Tilzer, Charles McCarron, Charles S. Alberte)
    (Broadway Music Corporation)

SM87) "**Down Where the Tennessee Flows**"   11"x14" (1913)
    (Bert L. Rule, Ray Sherwood)
    (A.J. Stasny Music Co.)

SM88) "**Down Yonder**"   9"x11" (1921)
    (L. Wolfe Gilbert)
    (L. Wolfe Gilbert Music Corporation)

SM89) "**Dream Kisses**"   9"x11" (1927)
    (Maurice K. Jerome, Jack Yellen)
    (Ager, Yellen & Bornstein, Inc.)

SM90) "**Du Host A Liebes Punim**"   9"x11" (1951)
    (Louis Herscher, Peter Lewin, Harry Jolson)
    (Bell Song Publishing, Co.)

SM91) "**The Edinboro Wiggle**"   11"x14" (1911)
    (Jerome Kern, Frank Tours, Edward Madden)
    (T.B. Harms)

SM92) "**The Egg and I**"   9"x11" (1947)
    (Harry Akst, Harry Ruby, Bert Kalmar, Al Jolson)
    (Miller Music Corporation)

SM93) "**Elizabeth (My Queen)**"   9"x11" (1931)
    (Robert Katscher, Irving Caesar)
    (Harms Inc.)

SM94) "**Evangeline**"   9"x11" (1929)
    (Billy Rose, Al Jolson)
    (Irving Berlin Inc.)

SM95) "**Ev'ry Day Can't Be a Sunday**"   9"x11" (1931)
    (Al Jolson)
    (Remick Music Corporation)

SM96) "**Every Morning She Makes Me Late**"   11"x14" (1918)
    (B.G. De Sylva, Gus Kahn, Al Jolson)
    (Jerome H. Remick & Co.)

SM97) "**Every Rose Must Have a Thorn**"   9"x11" (1927)
    (Al Jolson, B.G. De Sylva, Lew Brown)

SM98) **"Everybody Rag With Me"**   11"x14" (1914)
(Grace LeBoy, Gus Kahn)
(Jerome H. Remick & Co.)

SM99) **"Florida Moon"**   9"x11" (n.d.)
(Alexander C. Sullivan, Al Jolson)
(Jerome H. Remick Co.)

SM100) **"For Me and My Gal"**   9"x11" (1949)
(George W. Meyer, E. Ray Goetz, Edgar Leslie)
(Mills Music Inc.)

SM101) **"For Old Times Sake"**   11"x14" (1900)
(Charles K. Harris)
(Charles K. Harris Co.)

SM102) **"Forgive Me"**   9"x11" (1927)
(Milton Ager, Jack Yellen)
(Ager, Yellen & Bornstein Inc.)

SM103) **"Forty-Second Street"**   9"x11" (1946)
(Harry Warren, Al Dubin)
(Harms Inc.)

SM104) **"Four Walls"**   9"x11" (1927)
(Dave Dreyer, Billy Rose, Al Jolson)
(Irving Berlin Inc.)

SM105) **"Friend Highball"**   11"x14" (1915)
(William C. MacKenna)

SM106) **"The Gaby Glide"**   11"x14" (1911)
(Harry Pilcer, Louis A. Hirsch)
(Shapiro Music Publishing Co.)

SM107) **"Give Me My Mammy"**   9"x11" (1921)
(Walter Donaldson, B.G. De Sylva)
(Harms Inc.)

SM108) **"Give Me the Hudson Shore"**   11"x14" (1913)
(Al Jolson, Harold Atteridge)

SM109) **"Give My Regards to Broadway"**   9"x11" (1949)
(George M. Cohan)
(Jerry Vogel)

SM110) **"Go Ahead and Dance a Little More"**   11"x14" (1916)
(Sigmund Romberg, James F. Hanley, Harold Atteridge)
(G. Schirmer)

SM111) **"Go Into Your Dance"**   9"x11" (1935)

(Harry Warren, Al Dubin)
(M. Witmark & Sons)

SM112) "The Goblin's Glide"   11"x14" (1911)
(Jerome Kern, Frank Tours, Edward Madden)
(T.B. Harms)

SM113) "Goin' to Heaven on a Mule"   9"x11" (1934)
(Harry Warren, Al Dubin)
(M. Witmark & Sons)

SM114) "Golden Gate"   9"x11" (1928)
(Billy Rose, Joseph Meyer, Dave Dreyer, Al Jolson)
(Irving Berlin Inc.)

SM115) "Good-bye Boys"   11"x14" (1913)
(Harry Von Tilzer, Andrew B. Sterling, William Jerome)
(Harry Von Tilzer)

SM116) "Goodbye, G.I. Al"   9"x11" (1950)
(Harry Akst, Eddie Maxwell)
(Bregman, Vocco & Conn)

SM117) "Good Evening, Friends"   9"x11" (1931)
(Robert Katscher, Irving Caesar)
(Harms Inc.)

SM118) "A Good Old Fashioned Cocktail"   9"x11" (1935)
(Harry Warren, Al Dubin)
(M. Witmark & Sons)

SM119) "Grieving For You"   9"x11" (1920)
(Joe Gibson, Joe Ribaud, Joe Gold)
(Leo. Feist)

SM120) "Hallelujah, I'm a Bum"   9"x11" (1932)
(Richard Rodgers, Lorenz Hart)
(Harms Inc.)

SM121) "Happy Hottentots"   11"x14" (1916)
(Sigmund Romberg, James F. Hanley, Harold Atteridge)
(G. Schirmer)

SM122) "Harding, You're the Man For Us"   9"x11" (1920)
(Al Jolson)
(unknown publisher)

**SM123) "He'd Have to Get Under-Get Out and Get Under (To Fix
His Automobile)"**   11"x14" (1913)
(Maurice Abrahams, Edgar Leslie, Grant Clarke)
(Maurice Abrahams Music Co.)

SM124) "Hello Central! Give Me No Man's Land"   11"x14" (1918)
    (Jean Schwartz, Sam M. Lewis, Joe Young)
    (Waterson-Berlin & Snyder)

SM125) "Hello 'Tucky!"   9"x11" (1924)
    (Joseph Meyer, James F. Hanley, B.G. De Sylva)
    (Harms Inc.)

SM126) "Hello 'Tucky!"   9"x11" (1925)
    (Joseph Meyer, James F. Hanley, B.G. De Sylva)
    (Harms Inc.)

SM127) "Her Danny"   9"x11" (1919)
    (Chris Schonberg, Hale N. Byers)
    (Jerome H. Remick Co.)

SM128) "Here Comes My Daddy, Oh Pop! Oh Pop!
    Oh Pop!"   11"x14" (1912)
    (Lewis F. Muir, L. Wolfe Gilbert)

SM129) "Hi-Ho Lack-A-Day, What Have We Got to Lose"

SM130) "Hitchy Coo"   11"x14" (1912)
    (Lewis F. Muir, L. Wolfe Gilbert, Maurice Abrahams)

SM131) "Hollywood Rose"   9"x11" (1927)
    (Gus Kahn, Al Jolson)
    (Irving Berlin Inc.)

SM132) "Hooray For Baby and Me"   9"x11" (1930)
    (George W. Meyer, Archie Gottler, Sidney Mitchell)
    (M. Witmark & Sons)

SM133) "How I Love You"   9"x11" (1925)
    (Cliff Friend, Lew Brown)

SM134) "How'd 'Ya Like to Be a Kid Again?"   9"x11" (1921)
    (Billy Colligan, Bennett Sisters, Jimmy McHugh)
    (Edward B. Marks Music Co.)

SM135) "How'd You Like to Be My Daddy?"   11"x14" (1918)
    (Ted Snyder, Joe Young, Sam M. Lewis)

SM136) "Hula Hula Love"   11"x14" (1915)
    (James V. Monaco, Grant Clarke)
    (Leo. Feist)

SM137) "I Can't Stand It"   9"x11" (1927)
    (Gus Kahn, Al Jolson)

SM138) "I Gave Her That"   11"x14" (1919)

(B.G. De Sylva, Al Jolson)
(T.B. Harms)

SM139) "I Got You, Steve"   11"x14" (1912)
(Ed Morton)
(Daly Music Publishers)

SM140) "I Hail From Cairo"   11"x14" (1918)
(Sigmund Romberg, Harold Atteridge)
(G. Schirmer)

SM141) "I Love Her. Oh! Oh! Oh!"   11"x14" (1913)
(James V. Monaco, Joseph McCarthy, E.P. Moran)
(Broadway Music Corporation)

**SM142) "I Love My Steady, But I'm Crazy For My
Once-In-A-While"**   11"x14" (1910)
(Irving Hinckley, Allan W.S. MacDuff)
(Daly Music Publishers)

SM143) "I Love the Heart of Dixie"   11"x14" (1918)
(Jean Schwartz, Alfred Bryan, Al Jolson)
(Jerome H. Remick & Co.)

SM144) "I Love to Sing-A"   9"x11" (1936)
(Harold Arlen, E.Y. "Yip" Harburg)
(Remick Music Corporation)

SM145) "I Never Knew Heaven Could Speak"   9"x11" (1939)
(Harry Revel, Mack Gordon)
(Robbins Music Corporation)

SM146) "I Only Have Eyes for You"   9"x11" (1949)
(Harry Warren, Al Dubin)
(Music Publishers Holding Corporation)

SM147) "I Sent a Letter to Santa Claus"   9"x11" (1942)
(Al Jolson)
(Bregman, Vocco & Conn, Inc.)

SM148) "I Sent My Wife to the Thousand Isles" 11"x14" (1916)
(Harry Von Tilzer, E.P. Moran, Andrew Sterling)
(Harry Von Tilzer)

SM149) "I Still Love You"   9"x11" (1928)
(Milton Ager, Jack Yellen)
(Ager, Yellen & Bornstein, Inc.)

SM150) "I Want a Girl"   9"x11" (1946)
(Harry Von Tilzer, William Dillon)
(Harry Von Tilzer)

SM151) "I Want to Go Home"   9"x11" (1938)
 (Cole Porter)

SM152) "I Wish I Could Sing Like Jolson" 9"x11" (1953)
 (Alf Portway, Kay Clayton)
 (Lawrence Wright)

SM153) "I Wonder What's Become of Sally" 9"x11" (1924)
 (Milton Ager, Jack Yellen)
 (Ager, Yellen & Bornstein Inc.)

SM154) "I Wonder Why She Kept on Saying
  Si-Si-Si-Si-Senor?"   11"x14" (1918)
 (Ted Snyder, Sam M. Lewis, Joe Young)
 (Waterson-Berlin & Snyder Co.)

SM155) "If I Only Had a Match" 9"x11" (1947)
 (George W. Meyer, Lee Morris, Arthur Johnson)
 (Edwin H. Morris Co.)

SM156) "If You Knew Susie"   9"x11" (1925)
 (B.G. De Sylva)
 (Shapiro, Bernstein & Co.)

SM157) "I'll Do It Again"   9"x11" (1932)
 (Richard Rodgers, Lorenz Hart)
 (Harms Inc.)

SM158) "I'll Say She Does"   11"x14" (1918)
 (B.G. De Sylva, Gus Kahn, Al Jolson)
 (Jerome H. Remick & Co.)

SM159) "I'll Say She Does"   9"x11" (1928)
 (B.G. De Sylva, Gus Kahn, Al Jolson)
 (Jerome H. Remick & Co.)

SM160) "I'll Sing You a Song About Dear
  Old Dixie Land"   9"x11" (1918)
 (Turner Layton, Harry Creamer)
 (Jerome H. Remick Co.)

SM161) "I'll Tell the World"   11"x14" (1918)
 (Sigmund Romberg, Harold Atteridge)
 (G. Schirmer)

SM162) "I'm a Fugitive From a Chain Letter Gang" 9"x11" (1949)
 (Irving Caesar, Sammy Lerner, Gerald Marks)
 (Mills Music Publishers)

SM163) "I'm Always Chasing Rainbows" 9"x11" (1939)
 (Harry Carroll, Joseph McCarthy)

(Robbins Music Corporation)

SM164) "I'm Crying Just for You"   9"x11" (n.d.)
(James V. Monaco, Joseph McCarthy)

SM165) "I'm Glad My Wife's in Europe"   11"x14" (1914)
(Archie Gottler, Howard Johnson, Coleman Goetz)
(Leo. Feist)

SM166) "I'm Goin' Back to Old Nebraska"   11"x14" (1914)
(Bert L. Rule, Ray Sherwood)
(A.J. Stasny Music Co.)

SM167) "I'm Goin' South"   9"x11" (1923)
(Abner Silver, Harry Woods)
(M. Witmark & Sons)

SM168) "I'm in Seventh Heaven"   9"x11" (1929)
(Ray Henderson, Lew Brown, B.G. De Sylva, Al Jolson)
(De Sylva, Brown & Henderson Inc.)

SM169) "I'm Just Wild About Harry"   9"x11" (1949)
(Noble Sissle, Eubie Blake)
(Music Publishers Holding Corporation)

SM170) "I'm Ka-Razy For You"   9"x11" (1929)
(Dave Dreyer, Billy Rose, Al Jolson)
(Irving Berlin Inc.)

SM171) "I'm Looking Over a Four-Leaf Clover"   9"x11" (1949)
(Harry Woods, Mort Dixon)
(Remick Music Corporation)

SM172) "I'm Sitting on Top of the World"   9"x11" (1946)
(Ray Henderson, Sam M. Lewis, Joe Young)
(Leo Feist Inc.)

SM173) "I'm Sorry I Made You Cry"   9"x11" (1939)
(N.J. Clesi)
(Leo Feist Inc.)

SM174) "I'm Tellin' the Birds"   9"x11" (1926)
(Lew Brown, Cliff Friend)
(Irving Berlin Inc.)

SM175) "I'm the Human Brush"   11"x14" (1911)
(Jerome Kern, Frank Tours, Edward Madden)
(T.B. Harms)

SM176) "In Ev'ry Nook and Corner You Are Missing"   9"x11" (1933)
(Sammy Fain, Irving Kahal)

(M. Witmark & Sons)

SM177) "In Old Grenada"	9"x11" (1921)
(Sigmund Romberg, Al Jolson, Harold Atteridge)	
(Harms Inc.)	

SM178) "In Our House"   9"x11" (1950)
(Martin Fried, Benee Russell, Al Jolson)
(Jewel Music Publishing Co.)

SM179) "In the Way Over There"   9"x11" (1921)
(Sigmund Romberg, Al Jolson, Harold Atteridge)
(Harms Inc.)

SM180) "Indian River Trail"   9"x11" (1927)
(Irving Caesar, Al Jolson)

SM181) "The Irish Tango"   11"x14" (1914)
(James Walsh, Ernest Breuer)
(Irving Berlin Inc.)

SM182) "Is It True What They Say About Dixie?"   9"x11" (1936)
(Irving Caesar, Sammy Lerner, Gerald Marks)
(Irving Caesar Inc.)

SM183) "Is It True What They Say About Dixie?"   9"x11" (1949)
(Irving Caesar, Sammy Lerner, Gerald Marks)
(Irving Caesar Inc.)

SM184) "Is She My Girl Friend"   9"x11" (1927)
(Milton Ager, Jack Yellen)
(Ager, Yellen & Bornstein Inc.)

SM185) "Israel"   9"x11" (1947)
(Benee Russell, Al Jolson, based on traditional melody)
(ABC Music Corporation)

SM186) "It All Depends on You"   9"x11" (1926)
(B.G. De Sylva, Lew Brown, Ray Henderson)
(De Sylva, Brown & Henderson Inc.)

SM187) "It's Wonderful"   11"x14" (1918)
(Sigmund Romberg, Harold Atteridge)
(G. Schirmer)

SM188) "It's You"   9"x11" (1921)
(Con Conrad, Benny Davis)
(Harms Inc.)

SM189) "Jazzadaroo"   9"x11" (1921)
(Sigmund Romberg, Al Jolson, Harold Atteridge)

(Harms Inc.)

SM190) "Keep Smiling at Trouble"   9"x11" (1924)
(Lewis Gensler, Al Jolson, B.G. De Sylva)
(Harms Inc.)

SM191) "Keep Smiling at Trouble"   9"x11" (1925)
(Lewis Gensler, Al Jolson, B.G. De Sylva)
(Harms Inc.)

SM192) "Koo-Kee-Koo"   9"x11" (1921)
(Nacio Herb Brown, King Zaney)
(Leo. Feist)

SM193) "Lackawanna"   9"x11" (1924)
(Joseph Meyer, James F. Hanley, B.G. De Sylva)
(Harms Inc.)

SM194) "Lackawanna"   9"x11" (1925)
(Joseph Meyer, James F. Hanley, B.G. De Sylva)
(Harms Inc.)

SM195) "Last Night on the Back Porch"   9"x11" (1923)
(Carl Schraubstader, Lew Brown)
(Shapiro, Bernstein & Co.)

SM196) "Learn to Croon"   9"x11" (1949)
(Harold Arlen, Jack Yellen)
(Famous Music Corporation)

SM197) "Lenox Avenue"   9"x11" (1931)
(Joseph Meyer, Irving Caesar, Al Jolson)
(Harms Inc.)

SM198) "Let the Little Joy Bell Ring"   9"x11" (1921)
(Cliff Friend)
(Waterson-Berlin & Snyder, Inc.)

SM199) "Let Me Sing and I'm Happy"   9"x11" (1929)
(Irving Berlin)
(Irving Berlin Inc.)

SM200) "Let Me Sing and I'm Happy"   9"x11" (1946)
(Irving Berlin)
(Irving Berlin Inc.)

SM201) "Let Me Sing and I'm Happy"   9"x11" (1949)
(Irving Berlin)
(Irving Berlin Inc.)

SM202) "A Little Bit Bad"   9"x11" (1925)

(Al Eldridge, Larry Conley, Benny Davis)
(Conley-Silverman)

SM203) "Little Pal" 9"x11" (1929)
(Al Jolson, B.G. De Sylva, Lew Brown, Ray Henderson)
(De Sylva, Brown & Henderson Inc.)

SM204) "Little Sunshine" 9"x11" (1930)
(George W. Meyer, Archie Gottler, Sidney Mitchell)
(M. Witmark & Sons)

SM205) "The Little Things You Used to Do" 9"x11" (1935)
(Harry Warren, Al Dubin)
(M. Witmark & Sons)

SM206) "Liza" 9"x11" (1946)
(George Gershwin, Ira Gershwin, Gus Kahn)
(Music Holding Corporation)

SM207) "Liza Lee" 9"x11" (1930)
(Sam H. Stept, Bud Green)
(M. Witmark & Sons)

SM208) "Lonely Mothers on Parade" 9"x11" (1930)
(George W. Meyer, Irving Caesar, Al Jolson)

SM209) "Longing" 9"x11" (1922)
(Eddie Lewis, Erwin R. Schmidt)
(Dixon Lane Music Publishing Co.)

SM210) "Look Me Over, Dearie" 11"x14" (1911)
(Jerome Kern, Frank Tours, Edward Madden)
(T.B. Harms)

SM211) "Looking at You" 9"x11" (1929)
(Irving Berlin)
(Irving Berlin Inc.)

SM212) "Love Is Just Like a Punch in the Nose"

SM213) "Lullaby of Broadway" 9"x11" (1946)
(Harry Warren, Al Dubin)
(M. Witmark & Sons)

SM214) "Ma Blushin' Rosie" 9"x11" (1946)
(John Stromberg, Edgar Smith)
(Music Holding Corporation)

SM215) "Ma Blushin' Rosie" 9"x11" (1949)
(John Stromberg, Edgar Smith)
(M. Witmark & Sons)

SM216) "Ma Mere"   9"x11" (1931)
    (Harry Warren, Irving Caesar, Al Jolson)
    (Harms Inc.)

SM217) "Mammy, I'll Sing About You"   9"x11" (1935)
    (Harry Warren, Al Dubin)
    (M. Witmark & Sons)

SM218) "Mammy's Little Coal Black Rose"   11"x14" (1916)
    (Richard A. Whiting, Raymond Egan)
    (Jerome H. Remick & Co.)

SM219) "Me and My Shadow"   9"x11" (1927)
    (Dave Dreyer, Billy Rose, Al Jolson)
    (Irving Berlin Inc.)

SM220) "Mem'ries of One Sweet Kiss"   9"x11" (1929)
    (Dave Dreyer, Al Jolson)
    (Irving Berlin Inc.)

SM221) "Miami"   9"x11" (1924)
    (Joseph Meyer, James F. Hanley, B.G. De Sylva)
    (Harms Inc.)

SM222) "Miami"   9"x11" (1925)
    (Joseph Meyer, James F. Hanley, B.G. De Sylva)
    (Harms Inc.)

SM223) "Minstrel Days"   11"x14" (1916)
    (Sigmund Romberg, James F. Hanley, Harold Atteridge)
    (G. Schirmer)

SM224) "Molly Dear, It's You I'm After"   11"x14" (1915)
    (Henry E. Pether)

SM225) "Morning Will Come"   9"x11" (1923)
    (Con Conrad, B.G. De Sylva, Al Jolson)
    (Harms Inc.)

SM226) "Mother of Mine, I Still Have You"   9"x11" (1927)
    (Louis Silvers, Grant Clarke, Al Jolson)
    (Irving Berlin Inc.)

SM227) "Mother's Sitting Knitting Little Mittens
    for the Navy"   11"x14" (1915)
    (Hermann E. Darewski, R.P. Weston)

SM228) "My Buddy"   9"x11" (1922)
    (Walter Donaldson, Gus Kahn)
    (Jerome H. Remick Co.)

SM229) "My Dixie"   9"x11" (1922)
(Maceo Pinkard, Al Jolson, Sidney Mitchell)

SM230) "My Kid"   9"x11" (1924)
(Al Dubin, Jimmy McHugh, Irwin Dash)
(Jack Mills Inc.)

SM231) "My Mammy"   9"x11" (1921)
(Walter Donaldson, Joe Young, Sam M. Lewis)
(Irving Berlin Inc.)

SM232) "My Mammy"   9"x11" (1946)
(Walter Donaldson, Joe Young, Sam M. Lewis)
(Bourne Inc.)

SM233) "My Mammy"   9"x11" (1949)
(Walter Donaldson, Joe Young, Sam M. Lewis)
(Bourne Inc.)

SM234) "My Man"   9"x11" (1939)
(Maurice Yvain, Channing Pollock)
(Leo. Feist)

SM235) "My Mother's Rosary"   9"x11" (1949)
(George W. Meyer, Sam M. Lewis)
(Mills Music Publishers)

SM236) "My Pirate Lady"   11"x14" (1916)
(Sigmund Romberg, James F. Hanley, Harold Atteridge)
(G. Schirmer)

SM237) "My Sumurun Girl"   11"x14" (1912)
(Louis A. Hirsch, Al Jolson)
(Shapiro Music Publishers)

SM238) "My Sweet Moana"   11"x14" (1915)
(Neil Moret)
(Charles N. Daniels)

SM239) "My Tom Tom Man"   11"x14" (1915)
(Egbert Van Alstyne, Gus Kahn)
(Jerome H. Remick Co.)

SM240) "My Yellow Jacket Girl"   11"x14" (1913)
(Jean Schwartz, Harold Atteridge)
(Jean Schwartz)

SM241) "'N' Everything"   11"x14" (1918)
(B.G. De Sylva, Gus Kahn, Al Jolson)
(Jerome H. Remick & Co.)

SM242) "'N' Everything"   9"x11" (1919)
 (B.G. De Sylva, Gus Kahn, Al Jolson)
 (Jerome H. Remick & Co.)

SM243) "Nearest Thing to Heaven"   9"x11" (n.d.)
 (Benee Russell, Al Jolson)
 (Bourne Inc.)

SM244) "Nightingale"   9"x11" (1920)
 (Billy Rose)
 (Jerome H. Remick Co.)

SM245) "No More Worryin'"   9"x11" (1926)
 (Walter Donaldson, Jay Mills, Gus Kahn)
 (Irving Berlin Inc.)

SM246) "No Sad Songs for Me"   9"x11" (1950)
 (Harry Akst, Al Jolson)
 (Bourne Inc.)

SM247) "Nobody But Fanny"   9"x11" (1924)
 (Con Conrad, Al Jolson, B.G. De Sylva)
 (Harms Inc.)

SM248) "Nobody But Fanny"   9"x11" (1925)
 (Con Conrad, Al Jolson, B.G. De Sylva)
 (Harms Inc.)

SM249) "Now He's Got a Beautiful Girl"   11"x14" (1916)
 (Grant Clarke, Edgar Leslie, Ted Snyder)

SM250) "Oh! Donna Clara"   9"x11" (1931)
 (J. Petersburshi, Irving Caesar, Beda)
 (Harms Inc.)

SM251) "O-hi-o"   9"x11" (1918)
 (Abe Olman, Jack Yellen)
 (Forster Music Publishers Co.)

SM252) "O-hi-o"   9"x11" (1920)
 (Includes "President Harding's Inaugural Version"
 written by Al Jolson)
 (Abe Olman, Jack Yellen)
 (Forster Music Publishers Co.)

SM253) "Oh! How I Wish I Could Sleep Until My
 Daddy Comes Home"   9"x11" (1918)
 (Pete Wendling, Sam M. Lewis, Joe Young)
 (Waterson-Berlin & Snyder Co.)

SM254) "Oh! Oh! Columbus"   9"x11" (1921)

(Sigmund Romberg, Al Jolson, Harold Atteridge)
(Harms Inc.)

SM255) "Oh! Shush"   11"x14" (1912)
(Lewis F. Muir, L. Wolfe Gilbert, Maurice Abrahams)
(R.A. Mills)

SM256) "Oh! What a Night"   11"x14" (1918)
(Lewis F. Muir, Maurice Abrahams)
(Maurice Abrahams Music Co.)

SM257) "Oh! You Girls"   11"x14" (1911)
(Jerome Kern, Frank Tours, Edward Madden)
(T.B. Harms)

SM258) "Old Fashioned Girl"   9"x11" (1922)
(Al Jolson)
(Richmond-Robbins Music Publishers)

SM259) "The Old Kitchen Kettle Keeps
Singing a Song"   9"x11" (1932)
(Harry Woods, Jimmy Campbell, Reginald Connelly)
(Robbins Music Corporation)

SM260) "On the Banks of the Wabash"   9"x11" (1946)
(Paul Dresser)
(Paull-Pioneer Music Corporation)

SM261) "On the Mississippi"   11"x14" (1912)
(Harry Carroll, Ballard MacDonald, Arthur Fields)
(Shapiro Music Publishers)

SM262) "On the Road to Calais"   9"x11" (1918)
(Jean Schwartz, Alfred Bryan, Al Jolson)
(Jerome H. Remick & Co.)

SM263) "On the Z.R.3."   9"x11" (1925)
(Harms Inc.)

SM264) "One O'Clock Baby"   9"x11" (1927)
(Lew Brown, B.G. De Sylva, Al Jolson)
(De Sylva, Brown & Henderson Inc.)

SM265) "Our Ancestors"   11"x14" (1918)
(Sigmund Romberg, Harold Atteridge)
(G. Schirmer)

SM266) "Outdoor Life"   9"x11" (1925)
(Joseph Meyer, B.G. De Sylva, Al Jolson)
(Harms Inc.)

SM267) "Paris Is a Paradise for Coons"   11"x14" (1911)
  (Jerome Kern, Frank Tours, Edward Madden)
  (T.B. Harms)

SM268) "Pretty Baby"   9"x11" (1949)
  (Egbert Van Alstyne, Gus Kahn, Tony Jackson)
  (Music Publishers Holding Corporation)

SM269) "The Pretty Little Leader of the Band"   11"x14" (1911)
  (Jerome Kern, Frank Tours, Edward Madden)
  (T.B. Harms)

SM270) "Pretty Little Mayflower Girl"   11"x14" (1916)
  (Sigmund Romberg, James F. Hanley, Harold Atteridge)
  (G. Schirmer)

SM271) "Pretty Little Milliners"   11"x14" (1911)
  (Jerome Kern, Frank Tours, Edward Madden)
  (T.B. Harms)

SM272) "The Rag Lad of Bagdad"   11"x14" (1918)
  (Sigmund Romberg, Harold Atteridge)
  (G. Schirmer)

SM273) "Raggin' the Baby to Sleep"   11"x14" (1912)
  (L. Wolfe Gilbert, Lewis F. Muir)
  (R.A. Mills)

SM274) "Raz-Ma-Taz"   11"x14" (1918)
  (Sigmund Romberg, Harold Atteridge)
  (G. Schirmer)

SM275) "Robinson Crusoe"   11"x14" (1916)
  (Sigmund Romberg, James F. Hanley, Harold Atteridge)
  (G. Schirmer)

SM276) "Rock-A-Bye Your Baby With a Dixie Melody"   9"x11" (1918)
  (Jean Schwartz, Joe Young, Sam M. Lewis)
  (Waterson-Berlin & Snyder Co.)

SM277) "Rock-A-Bye Your Baby With a Dixie Melody"   9"x11" (1946)
  (Jean Schwartz, Joe Young, Sam M. Lewis)
  (Mills Music Inc.)

SM278) "Rock-A-Bye Your Baby With a Dixie Melody"   9"x11" (1949)
  (Jean Schwartz, Joe Young, Sam M. Lewis)
  (Mills Music Inc.)

SM279) "Rose of Washington Square"   9"x11" (1939)
  (James F. Hanley, Ballard MacDonald)
  (Robbins Music Corporation)

SM280) "Row, Row, Row"   11"x14" (1912)
    (James V. Monaco, William Jerome)
    (Harry Von Tilzer)

SM281) "Rum Tum Tiddle"   11"x14" (1911)
    (Jean Schwartz, Edward Madden)
    (Jerome & Schwartz Publishing Co.)

SM282) "Save Me Sister"   9"x11" (1936)
    (Harold Arlen, E.Y. "Yip" Harburg)
    (Remick Music Corporation)

SM283) "Say No More"   9"x11" (1947)
    (Harry Akst, Benny Davis, Al Jolson)
    (Advanced Music Corporation)

SM284) "She Don't Wanna"   9"x11" (1927)
    (Milton Ager, Jack Yellen)
    (Ager, Yellen & Bornstein, Inc.)

SM285) "She Knows It"   9"x11" (1921)
    (Clarence J. Marks, Jack Stern)
    (Shapiro, Bernstein & Co.)

SM286) "She Used to Be the Slowest Girl in Town"   11"x14" (1914)
    (Charles McCarron, Raymond Walker)
    (Broadway Music Corporation)

SM287) "She's a Latin From Manhattan"   9"x11" (1935)
    (Harry Warren, Al Dubin)
    (M. Witmark & Sons)

SM288) "She's a Latin From Manhattan"   9"x11" (1946)
    (Harry Warren, Al Dubin)
    (M. Witmark & Sons)

SM289) "Simple Life"   11"x14" (1916)
    (Sigmund Romberg, James F. Hanley, Harold Atteridge)
    (G. Schirmer)

SM290) "Sinbad Was In Bad All the Time"   11"x14" (1917)
    (Harry Carroll, Stanley Murphy)
    (Jerome H. Remick Co.)

SM291) "Sing Trovatore"   11"x14" (1911)
    (Jerome Kern, Frank Tours, Edward Madden)
    (T.B. Harms)

SM292) "Sister Susie's Sewing Shirts for Soldiers"   11"x14" (1914)
    (Hermann E. Darewski, R.P. Weston)
    (T.B. Harms)

SM293) "Sittin' in a Corner"   9"x11" (1923)
        (Joseph Meyer, Gus Kahn)

SM294) "Snap Your Fingers"   11"x14" (1911)
        (Jerome Kern, Frank Tours, Edward Madden)
        (Harry Von Tilzer)

SM295) "So Long, Mother"   11"x14" (1917)
        (Egbert Van Alstyne, Raymond Egan, Gus Kahn)
        (Jerome H. Remick & Co.)

SM296) "Some Beautiful Morning"   9"x11" (1919)
        (Cliff Friend, Al Jolson)
        (Jerome H. Remick Co.)

SM297) "Something Seems to Tell Me"   9"x11" (1931)
        (Robert Katscher, Irving Caesar)
        (Harms Inc.)

SM298) "Sonny Boy"   9"x11" (1928)
        (Al Jolson, B.G. De Sylva, Lew Brown, Ray Henderson)
        (De Sylva, Brown & Henderson Inc.)

SM299) "The Spaniard That Blighted My Life"   11"x14" (1913)
        (Billy Merson)
        (T.B. Harms)

SM300) "The Spaniard That Blighted My Life"   9"x11" (1946)
        (Billy Merson)
        (Harms Inc.)

SM301) "The Spaniard That Blighted My Life"   9"x11" (1949)
        (Billy Merson)
        (Harms Inc.)

SM302) "Stella"   9"x11" (1923)
        (Al Jolson, Benny Davis, Harry Akst)
        (Waterson-Berlin & Snyder Co.)

SM303) "Sugar"   9"x11" (1927)
        (Maceo Pinkard, Sidney Mitchell)
        (Ager, Yellen & Bornstein, Inc.)

SM304) "Swanee"   11"x14" (1919)
        (George Gershwin, Irving Caesar)
        (T.B. Harms)

SM305) "Swanee"   9"x11" (1946)
        (George Gershwin, Irving Caesar)
        (Harms Inc.)

SM306) "Swanee"   9"x11" (1949)
    (George Gershwin, Irving Caesar)
    (Harms Inc.)

SM307) "Swanee River Trail"   9"x11" (1927)
    (Al Jolson, Irving Caesar)
    (Irving Berlin Inc.)

SM308) "Swanee Rose"   9"x11" (1921)
    (George Gershwin, B.G. De Sylva, Irving Caesar)
    (T.B. Harms)

SM309) "Sweet One"   9"x11" (1923)
    (Louis Silvers, Al Jolson)
    (Jerome H. Remick Co.)

SM310) "Sweetie Mine"   9"x11" (1919)
    (Cliff Hess, Sidney Mitchell, Al Jolson)
    (Leo. Feist)

SM311) "Take Me To That Swanee Shore"   11"x14" (1912)
    (Lewis F. Muir, L. Wolfe Gilbert)
    (R.A. Mills)

SM312) "Tallahassee"   9"x11" (1921)
    (Luckieth Roberts, Alex Rogers, B.G. De Sylva)
    (Harms Inc.)

SM313) "Tell Me With Smiles"   9"x11" (1921)
    (Walter Hirsch, Cliff Friend)
    (Richmond-Robins)

SM314) "Tell That to the Marines"   11"x14" (1918)
    (Jean Schwartz, Harold Atteridge, Al Jolson)
    (Waterson-Berlin & Snyder Co.)

SM315) "Tennessee, I Hear You Calling Me"   11"x14" (1914)
    (Jeff Godfrey, Harold A. Robe)
    (Empire Music Co.)

SM316) "That Barber in Seville"   9"x11" (1921)
    (Con Conrad, Harold Atteridge)
    (Harms Inc.)

SM317) "That Devlin' Rag"   11"x14" (1911)
    (Jerome Kern, Frank Tours, Edward Madden)
    (T.B. Harms)

SM318) "That Little German Band"   11"x14" (1913)
    (Fred Fisher, Joe Goodwin, Joseph McCarthy)
    (Leo. Feist)

SM319) "That Lovin' Traumerei"   11"x14" (1910)
  (Robert Schumann, Aubrey Stauffer)
  (Aubrey Stauffer & Co.)

SM320) "That Lullaby of Long Ago"   9"x11" (1918)
  (Richard A. Whiting, B.G. De Sylva, Raymond Egan,
  Gus Kahn)
  (Jerome H. Remick Co.)

SM321) "That Wonderful Girl of Mine"   9"x11" (1947)
  (Alexander Olshanetsky, Jacob Jacobs, Sammy Gallop)
  (Supreme Music Co.)

SM322) "That's All Right For Mulligan"   11"x14" (1911)
  (Jerome Kern, Frank Tours, Edward Madden)
  (T.B. Harms)

SM323) "That's Nice"   9"x11" (1919)
  (Arnold Johnson, Benny Davis, Al Jolson)
  (Jerome H. Remick Co.)

SM324) "There's a Great Day Coming Mañana"   9"x11" (1940)
  (Burton Lane, E.Y. "Yip" Harburg)
  (Chappell & Co.)

SM325) "There's a Lump of Sugar Down in Dixie"   11"x14" (1918)
  (Albert Gumble, Alfred Bryan, Jack Yellen)
  (Jerome H. Remick & Co.)

SM326) "There's a Rainbow 'Round My Shoulder"   9"x11" (1928)
  (Al Jolson, Billy Rose, Dave Dreyer)
  (Irving Berlin Inc.)

SM327) "There's a Rainbow 'Round My Shoulder"   9"x11" (1946)
  (Al Jolson, Billy Rose, Dave Dreyer)
  (Irving Berlin Inc.)

SM328) "There's Only One Mary in Maryland"   11"x14" (1915)
  (Richard A. Whiting)

SM329) "There's Something About You"   9"x11" (1921)
  (Joe Ribaud, Joe Gibson, Al Jolson)
  (Shapiro, Bernstein & Co.)

SM330) "They Come Back to California"   9"x11" (1925)

SM331) "They Can't Fool Me"   11"x14" (1919)
  (B.G. De Sylva, Al Jolson)
  (T.B. Harms)

SM332) "This is the Life"   11"x14" (1914)

(Irving Berlin)
(Waterson-Berlin & Snyder Co.)

SM333) **"A Thousand and One Arabian Nights"**   11"x14" (1918)
(Sigmund Romberg, Harold Atteridge)
(G. Schirmer)

SM334) **"The Tie That Binds"**   11"X14"
(Charles K. Harris)
(Charles K. Harris Co.)

SM335) **"To My Mammy"**   9"x11" (1929)
(Irving Berlin)
(Irving Berlin Inc.)

SM336) **"Tomale (I'm Hot For You)"**   9"x11" (n.d.)

SM337) **"Tomorrow Is Another Day"**   9"x11" (1930)
(Sam H. Stept, Bud Green)
(M. Witmark & Sons)

SM338) **"Toot, Toot, Tootsie!"**   9"x11" (1922)
(Dan Russo, Gus Kahn, Ernie Erdman)
(Leo. Feist)

SM339) **"Toot, Toot, Tootsie!"**   9"x11" (1946)
(Dan Russo, Gus Kahn, Ernie Erdman)
(Leo Feist Inc.)

SM340) **"Toot, Toot, Tootsie!"**   9"x11" (1949)
(Dan Russo, Gus Kahn, Ernie Erdman)
(Leo Feist Inc.)

SM341) **"Toot Your Horn, Kid, You're in a Fog"**

SM342) **"Trav'lin All Alone"**   9"x11" (1931)
(Arnold Johnson)
(Harms Inc.)

SM343) **"Try a Little Tenderness"**   9"x11" (1932)
(Harry Woods, Jimmy Campbell, Reginald Connelley)

SM344) **"Under Southern Skies"**   11"x14" (1915)
(Charles A. Bayha, Joe Goodwin)
(Shapiro, Bernstein & Co.)

SM345) **"Used to You"**   9"x11" (1929)
(Al Jolson, B.G. De Sylva, Lew Brown, Ray Henderson)
(De Sylva, Brown & Henderson Inc.)

SM346) **"The Vamp"**   9"x11" (1939)

(Byron Gay)

SM347) "The Very Next Girl I See"   9"x11" (1921)
(Sigmund Romberg, Al Jolson, Harold Atteridge)
(Harms Inc.)

SM348) "The Villain Still Pursued Her"   11"x14" (1912)
(Harry Von Tilzer, William Jerome)
(Harry Von Tilzer)

SM349) "Virginia Lee"   9"x11" (1928)
(Bob Nolan, Steele)

SM350) "Vive La France"   9"x11" (1934)
(Harry Warren, Al Dubin)
(M. Witmark & Sons)

SM351) "Waiki-Ki-Ki Lou"   9"x11" (1920)
(Cliff Friend, Al Jolson)
(Jerome H. Remick Co.)

SM352) "Waiting for the Robert E. Lee"   11"x14" (1912)
(Lewis F. Muir, L.Wolfe Gilbert)
(R.A. Mills)

SM353) "Waiting for the Robert E. Lee"   9"x11" (1946)
(Lewis F. Muir, L. Wolfe Gilbert)
(LaSalle Music Publishers, Inc.)

SM354) "Waiting for the Robert E. Lee"   9"x11" (1949)
(Lewis F. Muir, L. Wolfe Gilbert)
(Alfred Music Co., Inc.)

SM355) "War Babies"   11"x14" (1916)
(James F. Hanley, Edward Madden, Ballard MacDonald)
(Shapiro, Bernstein & Co.)

SM356) "Wetona"   9"x11" (1921)
(Sigmund Romberg, Al Jolson, Harold Atteridge)
(Harms Inc.)

SM357) "What Do You Say?"   9"x11" (1928)
(Milton Ager, Jack Yellen)
(Ager, Yellen & Bornstein, Inc.)

SM358) "What Do You Want With Money?"   9"x11" (1932)
(Richard Rodgers, Lorenz Hart)
(Harms Inc.)

SM359) "What Will I Tell Her To-night?"   11"x14" (1913)
(Roberts, Whittaker, Morrissey)

(Melody Lane Publishing Co.)

SM360) **"When I Leave the World Behind"**   11"x14" (1915)
(Irving Berlin)
(Waterson-Berlin & Snyder Co.)

SM361) **"When Sunday Comes to Town"**   11"x14" (1914)
(Harry Von Tilzer, Alfred Bryan)
(Harry Von Tilzer)

SM362) **"When the Grown Up Ladies Act Like Babies"**   11"x14" (1914)
(Maurice Abrahams, Edgar Leslie, Joe Young)
(Maurice Abrahams Music Co.)

SM363) **"When the Red Red Robin Comes Bob Bob
Bobbin' Along"**   9"x11" (1949)
(Harry Woods)
(Bourne Inc.)

SM364) **"When You're Starring in the Movies"**   11"x14" (1916)
(Sigmund Romberg, James F. Hanley, Harold Atteridge)
(G. Schirmer)

SM365) **"When You Were Sweet Sixteen"**   9"x11" (1946)
(James Thornton)
(Shapiro, Bernstein & Co.)

SM366) **"Where Did Robinson Crusoe Go With Friday
on Saturday Night"**   11"x14" (1916)
(George W. Meyer, Sam M. Lewis, Joe Young)
(Waterson-Berlin & Snyder Co.)

SM367) **"Where Is My Wandering Boy Tonight?"**   11"x14" (1914)
(Gene Buck, Dave Stamper)
(Shapiro, Bernstein & Co.)

SM368) **"Where the Black-Eyed Susans Grow"**   11"x14" (1917)
(Richard A. Whiting, Dave Radford)
(Jerome H. Remick & Co.)

SM369) **"Which Switch Is the Switch, Miss,
For Ipswich?"**   11"x14" (1915)
(Hermann E. Darewski, J. Barnett, Worton David)
(T.B. Harms)

SM370) **"While They Were Dancing Around"**   11"x14" (1913)
(James V. Monaco, Joseph McCarthy)
(Broadway Music Corporation)

SM371) **"Who and Where"**   9"x11" (c. 1940's)
(Martin Fried, Benee Russell)

SM372) "Who Cares?"   9"x11" (1921)
    (Milton Ager, Jack Yellen)
    (Ager, Yellen & Bornstein, Inc.)

SM373) "Who Paid the Rent for Mrs. Rip Van Winkle"   11"x14" (1913)
    (Fred Fisher, Alfred Bryan)
    (Leo. Feist)

SM374) "Who Said Dreams Don't Come True?"   9"x11" (1944)
    (Harry Akst, Benny Davis, Al Jolson)
    (Williamson Music)

SM375) "Who Was Chasing Paul Revere?"   9"x11" (1924)
    (Joseph Meyer, James F. Hanley, B.G. De Sylva)
    (Harms Inc.)

SM376) "Who Was Chasing Paul Revere?"   9"x11" (1925)
    (Joseph Meyer, James F. Hanley, B.G. De Sylva)
    (Harms Inc.)

SM377) "Who-oo! You-oo! That's Who!"   9"x11" (1927)
    (Milton Ager, Jack Yellen)
    (Ager, Yellen & Bornstein, Inc.)

SM378) "Why Can't You?"   9"x11" (1929)
    (Al Jolson, B.G. De Sylva, Lew Brown, Ray Henderson)
    (De Sylva, Brown & Henderson, Inc.)

SM379) "Why Do I Dream Those Dreams?"   9"x11" (1934)
    (Harry Warren, Al Dubin)
    (M. Witmark & Sons)

SM380) "Why Do They All Take the Night
      Boat For Albany?"   11"x14" (1918)
    (Jean Schwartz, Joe Young, Sam M. Lewis)
    (Waterson-Berlin & Snyder Co.)

SM381) "The Winder"

SM382) "Wonder Bar"   9"x11" (1934)
    (Harry Warren, Al Dubin)
    (M. Witmark & Sons)

SM383) "Wond'rous Eyes of Araby"   11"x14" (1918)
    (Herbert Spencer, Fleta Jan Brown)
    (Jerome H. Remick & Co.)

SM384) "The World Is In My Arms"   9"x11" (1940)
    (Burton Lane, E.Y. "Yip" Harburg)
    (Chappell & Co.)

SM385) "Would You Be So Kindly"   9"x11" (1940)
      (Burton Lane, E.Y. "Yip" Harburg)
      (Chappell & Co.)

SM386) "Yaaka Hula Hickey Dula"   11"x14" (1916)
      (Pete Wendling, E. Ray Goetz, Joe Young)
      (Waterson-Berlin & Snyder Co.)

SM387) "Yankee Doodle Blues"   9"x11" (1922)
      (George Gershwin, B.G. De Sylva, Irving Caesar)
      (Irving Berlin Inc.)

SM388) "A Year From Today"   9"x11" (1929)
      (Dave Dreyer, Ballard MacDonald, Al Jolson)
      (Irving Berlin Inc.)

SM389) "Yoo-Hoo"   9"x11" (1921)
      (B.G. De Sylva, Al Jolson)
      (Maurice Richmond Inc.)

SM390) "You Ain't Heard Nothing Yet"   9"x11" (1919)
      (B.G. De Sylva, Al Jolson, Gus Kahn)
      (Jerome H. Remick Co.)

SM391) "You Ain't Talkin' to Me"   11"x14" (1910)
      (Shelton Brooks)
      (Will Rossiter)

SM392) "You Are Too Beautiful"   9"x11" (1932)
      (Richard Rodgers, Lorenz Hart)
      (Harms Inc.)

SM393) "You Go In, Mister Friend of Mine,
      I'll Stay Out Here"   11"x14" (1910)
      (Shelton Brooks)
      (Will Rossiter)

SM394) "You Made Me Love You"   11"x14" (1913)
      (James V. Monaco, Joseph McCarthy)
      (Broadway Music Corporation)

SM395) "You Made Me Love You"   9"x11" (1946)
      (James V. Monaco, Joseph McCarthy)
      (Broadway Music Corporation)

SM396) "You Made Me Love You"   9"x11" (1949)
      (James V. Monaco, Joseph McCarthy)
      (Broadway Music Corporation)

SM397) "You'd Never Know That Old Home
      Town of Mine"   11"x14" (1915)

(Walter Donaldson, Howard Johnson)
(Leo. Feist)

SM398) "You'll Always Be Beautiful"   9"x11" (c. 1948)
   (Al Jolson, Saul Chaplin)

SM399) "You'll Have to Gallop Some"   11"x14" (1916)
   (Sigmund Romberg, James F. Hanley, Harold Atteridge)
   (G. Schirmer)

SM400) "You'll Never Know"   9"x11" (1928)
   (Arthur Franklin, Billy Rose, Al Jolson)
   (De Sylva, Brown & Henderson, Inc.)

SM401) "You're a Better Man Than I Am, Gunga-Din"   11"x14" (1918)
   (Nat Osborne, Sam Ehrlich)
   (Harry Von Tilzer)

SM402) "You're the Coaxinest Man I Ever Knew"   11"x14" (n.d.)
   (J.O. Williams, Eddie Dustin)
   (Thiebes-Stierlin Music Co.)

SM403) "You're the Cure For What Ails Me"   9"x11" (1936)
   (Harold Arlen, E.Y. "Yip" Harburg)
   (Remick Music Corporation)

SM404) "You're a Dangerous Girl"   11"x14" (1916)
   (James V. Monaco, Grant Clarke)
   (Leo. Feist)

SM405) "You're the Most Wonderful Girl"   11"x14" (1913)
   (Maurice Abrahams, Edgar Leslie, Grant Clarke)
   (Maurice Abrahams Music Co.)

Song Books

SM406) *Al Jolson's Favorite Collection of Comedy Song Hits.* New York: Irving Berlin, Inc., 1927.

SM407) *Al Jolson. Jazz Singer.* Foreword by Russell Wiltse. New York: Charles Hansen Music and Books, Inc., n.d.

SM408) *Jolson Songs.* New York: Bourne Company Music Publishers, Inc., 1947.

SM409) *Al Jolson's Old Time Minstrel Show.* New York: Warock Music, 1952.

8

Bibliography

BOOKS

Any bibliography of Al Jolson is by definition incomplete. Virtually any book on the history of the American popular stage, films (especially film musicals), radio and vaudeville will be likely to make some mention of his predominance in the field. This bibliography attempts to be reasonably comprehensive, but will undoubtedly not include many works that make mention of Jolson. With rare exceptions, reference works or textbooks are not included, nor are books with very brief mentions of Jolson unless the particular entry has been judged unique in character. The first section of this bibliography lists books and consists of three parts: (1) books specifically about Jolson, (2) books on Jolson's films, and (3) books with significant mention of Jolson. The second section of the bibliography covers magazines and periodicals, the third section is a bibliography of all *New York Times* references to Jolson (not including reviews, which are listed in the stage and film sections) and the fourth section is a bibliography of *Variety* references to Jolson.

Books Specifically About Jolson

B1   Abramson, Martin. *The Real Story of Al Jolson*. Forewords by Jack Benny, George Jessel, Eddie Cantor. With a postscript by Walter Winchell. Spectrolux Corporation, 1950. 48 pp.   A heavily-illustrated magazine published in Jolson's memory shortly after his death.

B2   Anderton, Barrie. *Sonny Boy! The World of Al Jolson*. London: Jupiter Books, 1975. One of the most celebratory books on Jolson; it is a heavily-illustrated biography that stresses the diversity of Jolson's work, and his phenomenal impact on show business.

B3   Freedland, Michael. *Al Jolson*. London: W.H. Allen, 1972. [Also appeared as a paperback (London: Abacus/Sphere, 1975), a U.S. hardback edition titled *Jolson* (New York: Stein and Day, 1972) followed by a paperback version (New York: Warner Brothers, 1973), and a revised version, *Jolie - The Story of Al Jolson* (London: W.H. Allen, 1985]. A general survey of Jolson's life and career based mostly on previously published accounts and following the broad outlines of the Jolson biographical films, leading to the inevitable distortions and dependence on myth.

B4   Goldman, Herbert G. *Jolson. The Legend Comes to Life*. New York: Oxford University Press, 1988. To date, this is by far the most detailed biography of Jolson, filled with dates and previously unpublished information, particularly about the earliest and least known years of Jolson's career. Goldman otherwise stresses the negative aspects of Jolson's personal life, based on interviews with survivors and a fair amount of heresay.

B5   *Jolie - The World of Jolson*. Publication of The International Al Jolson Society. First issue published in 1979. This publication by one of the two Jolson societies, published irregularly, features reprints of articles, reviews and photographs from magazines and newspapers.

B6   Jolson, Harry. *Mistah Jolson*. As told to Alban Emley. Hollywood: House-Warven, 1951. This memoir, published after Jolson's death by his brother Harry, provides the one of the few substantial resources about Jolson's early life and first years in show business.

B7   *Jolson Journal*. Publication of The International Al Jolson Society. First issue published in 1950. This publication of one of the two Jolson societies features a variety of reprints of articles, reviews and photographs from magazines and newspapers, along with newly generated articles on aspects of Jolson's life and career, along with material on artists who worked with or knew Jolson and data on club members.

B8   Kiner, Larry F. *The Al Jolson Discography*. Westport, Connecticut: Greenwood Press, 1983. Kiner had previously put out a nine-page mimeographed listing of Jolson discs, but this was the first substantial published discography on Jolson. It features a number of illustrations of Jolson and various album covers.

B9   Kiner, Larry F. and Philip R. Evans. *Al Jolson. A Bio-Discography*. Metuchen, New Jersey and London: Scarecrow Press, Inc., 1992. Over 800 pages of highly detailed information, mostly on Jolson's recordings (those made in the studio and those drawn from radio performances and soundtracks). It generally follows the format of Kiner's 1983 discography, adding brief bibliographies and lists, along with numerous illustrations, and spreading tidbits of biographical information here and there between the chronological entries. The detail in the discography entries is admirable, but other aspects of Jolson's career are given scant attention.

B10   *The Legend of Al Jolson*. England: Truman Book Company, 1951. A well-illustrated magazine published in tribute to Jolson at the time of his death.

B11   McClelland, Doug. *Blackface to Blacklist: Al Jolson, Larry Parks and The Jolson Story*. Metuchen, New Jersey: Scarecrow Press, 1987. This interesting study focuses on the making of the Jolson biographical films, with considerable information on both Jolson and Parks. McClelland interviewed virtually all of the surviving participants in the making of *The Jolson Story* and *Jolson Sings Again.*

B12 Oberfirst, Robert. *Al Jolson - You Ain't Heard Nothin' Yet.* Los Angeles: A.S. Barnes, 1980. A biography of Jolson in which the author has provided little or no scholarly base. Conversations that could not have been recorded in any way are offered in an attempt to personalize (fictionalize?) the general highs and lows of Jolson's life.

B13 Plath, Warren K. *Jolson on Wax.* With an introduction by Tom Linnell. Cover design by Maurice Brenner. Privately published. An early discography of Jolson recordings.

B14 Sieben, Pearl. *The Immortal Jolson. His Life and Times.* New York: Frederick Fell, 1962. The first full-fledged biography of Jolson by a woman who knew him later in his life. A generally interesting accounting by an admiring fan, but lacking in much specific detail or reference to sources.

B15 Tatchell, Peter, ed. *The Al Jolson Career Guide.* Privately published in Australia. A small publication usefully including lists of Jolson's career achievements on stage, screen, record, etc.

B16 Wigransky, David Pace "Jay." *Jolsonography.* England: Barrie Anderton, 1970. Second edition published in 1974. In this privately published work, Wigransky offers a potpourri of Jolson information. Filled with fascinating tidbits, Wigransky's eccentric style and structure make it difficult to use the work effectively as a resource. However, it offers a staggering amount of information (with a few distortions, numerous editorial remarks, and some inaccuracies) and will provide considerable pleasure for any Jolson fan.

Books On the Jolson Films

B17 *Al Jolson in "The Singing Fool."* Warner Bros., 1928. An illustrated magazine published in conjunction with the release of the film including stills from the production.

B18 Carringer, Robert L. ed. *The Jazz Singer.* Madison, Wisconsin: The University of Wisconsin Press, 1979. The shooting script of *The Jazz Singer,* with an engrossing introduction and considerable annotation. Including stills and several detailed appendices, such as Samson Raphaelson's "The Day of Atonement," and a few articles on the making of the film and the development of the Vitaphone process from vintage film magazines.

B19 Dail, Hubert. *The Singing Fool -- and the Story of Sonny Boy.* New York: Grosset and Dunlap, 1928. (Also published by The Readers Digest Library Publishing Company, 1929). A novelization of the film with a few stills of scenes included.

B20 DeHaas, Arlene. *The Jazz Singer -- A Story of Pathos and Laughter.* New York: Grossett and Dunlap, 1927. A novelization of the film with a few stills of scenes included.

B21   DeHaas, Arlene. *Say It With Songs*. New York: Grossett and Dunlap, 1929. A novelization of the film with a few stills included.

B22   *Go Into Your Dance*. Saalfield Publishing Company, 1935.   A novelization of the film with a few stills of scenes included.

B23   *Jolson Sings Again*. Cinema Souvenirs, Inc., 1949.   An illustrated magazine published in conjunction with the release of *Jolson Sings Again*.

B24   Macall, Martin. *Rhapsody in Blue*. London: Hollywood Publications, Ltd., 1946. An illustrated magazine published in conjunction with the release of *Rhapsody in Blue*.

B25   *The Singing Kid*. Saalfield Publishing Company, 1936. A novelization of the film with a few stills included.

B26   Tucker, Alan. *The Jolson Story*. Glasgow: McKenzie Vincent and Company, 1946. An illustrated magazine published in conjunction with the release of *The Jolson Story*.

Books With Significant Mention of Jolson

B27   Adams, Joey. *Here's to the Friars. The Heart of Show Business*. New York: Crown Publishers, Inc., 1976. This anecdotal history of the Friar's Club includes numerous mentions of Jolson, along with a photo showing Jolson at a Friar's Roast with George Burns and Gracie Allen, Eddie Cantor, and others.

B28   Adler, Irene. *I Remember Jimmy*. New York: Arlington House, 1980. Adler's illustrated biography of the life and times of Jimmy Durante includes references to his friendship with Jolson.

B29   Agate, James. *Around Cinemas I* London: Home and Van Thal, 1946. This collection of the critic's reviews includes a piece touching on the rise of sound in in the early Vitaphone shorts made by Warner Bros. and *The Jazz Singer*.

B30   Agee, James. *Agee on Film*. Vol. I. New York: McDowell, Obolensky, 1958. Includes a brief critique of *The Jolson Story* in an essay on the films of 1946. Agee admits to admiring Jolson's singing and the actors in the film, but finds the movie otherwise lacking.

B31   Allen, Fred. *Much Ado About Me*. New York: Little, Brown and Co., 1956. This autobiography of the stage and radio comedian includes a 1921 letter from Jolson in response to Allen's letter suggesting that Jolson had stolen one of Allen's jokes. Jolson denies this, but Allen recounts that years later Jolson admitted to him that he frequently helped himself to Allen's jokes.

B32   Alpert, Hollis. *Broadway. 125 Years of Musical Theatre*. New York: Museum of the City of New York, 1991. A lavishly illustrated history of Broadway musicals featuring comment on Jolson's shows.

B33   Altman, Rick. *The American Film Musical*. Bloomington and Indianapolis, Indiana: Indiana University Press, 1987. In examining the history of the musical film, Altman makes numerous references to Jolson's films.

B34   Appelbaum, Stanley, and James Camner. *Stars of the American Musical Theatre in Historic Photographs. 361 Portraits from the 1860s to 1950*. New York: Dover Publications, Inc., 1981. Photos of Jolson in his stage roles are included.

B35   Armitage, Merle. *George Gershwin. Man and Legend*. With a note on the author by John Charles Thomas. New York: Duell, Sloan and Pearce, 1958. Jolson's relationship with Gershwin is touched on in this biography of the composer.

B36   Arnaz, Desi. *A Book*. New York: William Morrow & Company, Inc., 1976. Arnaz recalls running afoul of Bob Hope while leading the orchestra for Hope's radio show. Jolson was to appear as guest star and Hope feared the ovation on Jolson's entrance would be of such length that he would have to cut some of his jokes. Hope insisted that Arnaz start the music for Jolson's first song immediately upon Jolson's appearance, however Jolson sensed this and asked Arnaz to wait for his signal. The expected ovation occurred and Hope expressed his anger to Arnaz after the performance.

B37   Astaire, Fred. *Steps in Time*. New York: Harper and Brothers, 1959. Astaire makes brief mention of appearing with his sister, Adele, at a Sunday night concert at the Winter Garden with Jolson.

B38   Atkinson, Brooks. *Broadway*. New York: Macmillan Publishing Co., Inc., 1970. This history of the golden age of Broadway, from just before World War I until the early 1960's, written by the *New York Times's* long-time theatre critic, touches on Jolson's success on the musical stage.

B39   Balio, Tino, ed. *The American Film Industry*. Madison, Wisconsin, 1985. In one of the collected essays, "The Coming of the Talkies: Invention, Innovation, and Diffusion," J. Douglas Gomery examines the development of Vitaphone, and its first truly successful use in *The Jazz Singer*. A still of Jolson and Eugenie Besserer from the film, as well as a photo of crowds outside the Warners' Theatre for a showing of *The Jazz Singer*, are included.

B40   Barraclough, David. *Movie Record Breakers*. Secaucus, New Jersey: Chartwell Books, Inc., 1992. A heavily illustrated survey of top film moneymakers of their time (including *The Singing Fool*, *The Jolson Story* and *Jolson Sings Again*), awards, and leading box-office stars. A brief account of the importance of *The Jazz Singer* as the first talking picture is included.

B41   Beardsley, Charles. *Hollywood's Master Showman. The Legendary Sid Grauman*. Cranbury, New Jersey: Cornwall Books, 1983. This biography of Grauman with a history of his Chinese Theatre in Hollywood, includes numerous references to Jolson.

B42   Behlmer, Rudy. *Inside Warner Bros. (1935-1951)*. New York The Viking Press, 1985. This history of the inside workings of Warner Bros. includes commentary on Jolson's involvement in the studio.

B43   ---------- and Tony Thomas. *Hollywood's Hollywood*. Secaucus, New Jersey: The Citadel Press, 1975. Behlmer and Thomas include *The Jolson Story*, *Jolson Sings Again* and *Hollywood Cavalcade* among those films that depict Hollywood, and also describe the scene involving Jolson (played by Norman Brooks) in *The Best Things in Life Are Free*.

B44   Benny, Mary Livingstone and Hilliard Marks, with Marcia Borie. *Jack Benny*. Garden City, New York: Doubleday & Co., Inc., 1978. Includes the complete text of Benny's speech when dedicating the Jolson monument in 1951, along with a reminiscence by Marks of watching from the wings with Benny when Jolson performed in blackface at a charity benefit.

B45   Bergan, Ronald. *Glamorous Musicals. Fifty Years of Hollywood's Ultimate Fantasy*. Foreword by Ginger Rogers. London: Octopus Books (Cathay Books), 1984. Includes a brief special piece on Jolson's career in films and his relationship with Ruby Keeler, with a studio portrait, photo from *The Jazz Singer*, and a few mentions of his films throughout text.

B46   ----------. *The United Artists Story*. New York: Crown Publishers, Inc., 1986. This heavily illustrated, year-by-year history of the films made by United Artists includes a still and brief analysis of Jolson's film, *Hallelujah, I'm a Bum*.

B47   Bergreen, Laurence. *As Thousands Cheer. The Life of Irving Berlin*. New York: Viking Press, 1990. Bergreen's copious biography of Berlin includes numerous references to his work and friendship with Jolson.

B48   Berle, Milton. *An Autobiography*. With Haskel Frankel. New York: Delacorte Press, 1974. Berle recalls several encounters with Jolson, including the time as a juvenile performer that his mother literally pushed him onstage with Jolson at a Sunday night Winter Garden concert. Jolson allowed Berle to do his Jolson impression, but apparently was not pleased by the intrusion. Many years later, Berle was dating Joyce Matthews (who later became Mrs. Berle), a chorine in *Hold On to Your Hats*. Berle recounts the night that he pulled Matthews off-stage when Jolson was performing innumerable encores.

B49   ----------. *B.S. I Love You. Sixty Years With the Famous and the Infamous*. New York: McGraw-Hill Book Company, 1988. This Berle memoir includes a few light-hearted references to Jolson.

B50   Blesh, Rudi and Harriet Janis. *They All Played Ragtime*. New York: Knopf, 1950. Includes only a passing reference to Jolson and the song "Yaaka Hula Hickey Dula."

B51   Bloom, Ken. *Broadway. An Encyclopedic Guide to the History, People and Places of Times Square*. New York: Facts On Files, Inc., 1991. This reference work on the glory days of Broadway includes an entry on Jolson.

B52 Blum, Daniel. *Great Stars of the American Stage. A Pictorial Record*. New York: Greenburg, 1952. Includes a two-page spread on Jolson.

B53 ----------. *A Pictorial History of the American Theatre. 1860-1970*. Third Edition. New York: Crown Publishers, Inc., 1969, 1971. Includes numerous photos of Jolson in his many stage shows.

B54 Bogle, Donald. *Toms, Coons, Mulattoes, Mammies, and Bucks: An Interpretive History of Blacks in American Films*. New York, 1973. A superb survey of racial stereotyping in Hollywood films. Bogle criticizes Jolson's blackface performances in several films, noting that Jolson's popularity contributed to the widespread acceptance of stereotypical images.

B55 Bordman, Gerald. *American Musical Comedy. From Adonis to Dreamgirls*. New York and Oxford: Oxford University Press, 1982. This survey history of musical comedy touches on the Jolson shows.

B56 ----------. *American Musical Theatre*. New York/Oxford: Oxford University Press, 1978. Bordman's useful chronicle of Broadway musicals from the beginning through 1977 offers brief commentary on all of Jolson's stage appearances.

B57 ----------. *Jerome Kern. His Life and Music*. New York and Oxford: Oxford University Press, 1980. Jolson's relationship with Kern is touched on in this fine biography of the composer.

B58 Boskin, Joseph. *Sambo: The Rise and Demise of an American Jester*. New York, 1986. A critical study of the minstrel tradition in America from its beginnings in the nineteenth century. *The Jolson Story* and *Jolson Sings Again* are depicted as marking the end of the minstrel era in an interesting study, although Boskin makes a few errors in fact, including stating that Jolson appeared in a 1933 film called *Hi Lo Broadway* (he may be thinking of *Hallelujah, I'm a Bum*).

B59 Bowers, Dwight Blocker. *American Musical Theater. Shows, Songs, and Stars*. Washington, D.C.: Smithsonian Collection of Recordings, 1989. Guide for a collection of great songs and performances from Broadway musicals.

B60 Breslin, Jimmy. *Damon Runyon. A Life*. New York: Ticknor & Fields, 1991. Only a passing reference to Jolson, but some interesting comments on Ruby Keeler, during the time she was the girlfriend of mobster Johnny "Irish" Costello, and later as Mrs. Jolson.

B61 *Broadway Portraits*. Samuel Marx, 1929. Includes a profile of Jolson.

B62 Brown, Peter H. and Jim Pinkston. *Oscar Dearest. Six Decades of Scandal, Politics and Greed Behind Hollywood's Academy Awards 1927-1986*. New York: Harper and Row, 1987. Backstage gossip about the Academy Awards includes a few anecdotes involving Jolson.

B63   Brownlow, Kevin. *Behind the Mask of Innocence. Sex, Violence, Prejudice, Crime: Films of Social Conscience in the Silent Era*. Berkeley, California: University of California Press, 1992.   In his examination of prejudice, Brownlow touches on Jolson and *The Jazz Singer*. Includes a still of Jolson in the "Kol Nidre" sequence and a portrait of Cantor Josef Rosenblatt.

B64   ----------. *The Parade's Gone By*. New York: Alfred A. Knopf, Inc., 1968. Examines Jolson's film career, with particular reference to *The Jazz Singer*.

B65   Brundidge, Harry T. *Twinkle, Twinkle, Movie Star*. With an introduction by Jesse L. Lasky. New York: E.P. Dutton & Co., 1930.   A collection of interviews of film stars, including one on Jolson.

B66   Burns, George. *All My Best Friends*. Written with David Fisher. New York: Putnam, 1989.   A memoir in which Burns recounts stories of his long-time show business friends, including George Jessel, Eddie Cantor, Jack Benny, Jimmy Durante, Ed Wynn, Fred Allen, Fanny Brice, Milton Berle, Groucho Marx, and Jolson, among others.   Burns includes many anecdotes involving Jolson.

B67   ----------. *Dear George. Advice and Answers From America's Leading Expert on Everything From A to B*. New York: Putnam, 1985.   In one chapter, Burns reminisces about the legends of show business, including Jolson.

B68   ----------. *Gracie. A Love Story*. New York: G.P. Putnam's Sons, 1988.   Jolson is mentioned in this charming memoir of Burns' marriage to Gracie Allen, including a Hollywood party when Jolson asked to perform. Burns said yes, but that Jolson could only do one song. At which point, Jolson stormed out of the party, insulted, followed by Burns singing.

B69   ----------. *I Love Her, That's Why*. London: Simon and Schuster, 1955.   In this comic memoir of his life with Gracie Allen, Burns makes several mentions of their friendship with Jolson, particularly during his marriage to Ruby Keeler.

B70   ----------. *Living It Up*. New York: G.P. Putnam's Sons, 1976.   In this memoir of his career, Burns makes numerous references to Jolson and their long friendship.

B71   Burton, Jack. *The Blue Book of Hollywood Musicals*. Watkin's Glen, New York, 1953.   A resource book on the musical theatre, with short introductory essays by decade and entries on composers and lyricists. Jolson is covered in the era of 1910-20, particularly in connection with the shows for which Sigmund Romberg wrote the score.

B72   Buxton, Frank and Bill Owen. *The Big Broadcast 1920-1950*. New York: The Viking Press.   Includes entries on Jolson's various radio series.

B73   Cagney, James and Doug Warren. *Cagney. The Authorized Biography*. New York: St. Martin's Press, 1983.   This memoir by Cagney includes his recollection of Jolson seeing *Penny Arcade*, a show starring Cagney and Joan

Blondell. Jolson bought the play for Warner Bros. and insisted they sign Cagney and Blondell to contracts.

B74 ----------. *Cagney by Cagney*. Garden City, New York: Doubleday, 1976. Cagney's biography makes mention of his appearance in the play *Penny Arcade*, which was seen by Jolson, who bought the play and sold it to Warner Bros. with the proviso that they hire Cagney and his co-star, Joan Blondell.

B75 Cahn, Sammy. *I Should Care*. New York: Arbor House, 1974. The renowned lyricists recalls that "Jolson was really not the nicest man in the world, though unquestionably a great entertainer. When singing *This Is My Lucky Day*, no man sounded so lucky. Or singing of heartbreak, so heartbreaking."(p. 83)

B76 Cahn, William. *A Pictorial History of the Great Comedians*. New York: Grosset and Dunlap, Inc., 1957, 1970. This heavily illustrated history of American comedians includes several pages devoted to Jolson, stressing the comedic aspects of his work.

B77 Cameron, Evan William, ed. *Sound and the Cinema: The Coming of Sound to American Film*. Pleasantville, New York, 1980. Inevitably, this study of the arrival of sound films touches on Jolson and *The Jazz Singer*.

B78 Cantor, Eddie. *As I Remember Them*. New York: Duell, Sloan and Pearce, 1963. Includes a chapter on Jolson, along with illustrations of Jolson with Cantor and Burns and Allen.

B79 ----------. *My Life is in Your Hands*. As told to David Freedman. New York: Harper and Brothers, 1928.

B80 ----------. *Take My Life*. With Jane Kesner Ardmore. Garden City, New York: Doubleday, 1957. Includes an anecdote-filled chapter on Jolson, "the greatest minstrel of them all"(p. 95) and a 1947 photograph of Jolson and Cantor in rehearsal for a radio broadcast.

B81 ----------. *The Way I See It*. Edited by Phyllis Rosenteur. Englewood Cliffs, New Jersey: Prentice-Hall, 1959. In this memoir, Cantor includes several anecdotes about Jolson and recalls recalls that "Show Business dubbed him *The King* and for 40 years he reigned supreme. He was the only entertainer who could dismiss the cast at eleven o'clock -- hold the audience for an hour and have them shouting for more. On such occasions, he had to pay the stage hands overtime. When asked about this, he said, *It was worth it -- they loved me out there*."(p. 110)

B82 Carroll, Carroll. *None of Your Business, or My Life With J. Walter Thompson: Confessions of a Renegade Radio Writer*. Cowles Book Company, 1970. Carroll, a successful writer for various radio and television shows, touches on his relationship with Jolson in radio.

B83 Cawkwell, Tim and John M. Smith, eds. *The World Encyclopedia of the Film*.

New York: World, 1972. Includes an entry on Jolson.

B84   Chaplin, Charles. *My Autobiography*. New York: Simon and Schuster, 1964. This memoir by Chaplin includes his assessment of many of his contemporaries, including Jolson.

B85   *The Chronicle Of The Movies*. Foreword by Leonard Maltin. New York: Crescent Books, 1991. A year-by-year chronicle of the highlights of the history of films (mostly American and English), beginning with *The Jazz Singer*. Includes coverage of Jolson's films *The Jazz Singer*, *The Singing Fool*, *Say It With Songs*, *The Jolson Story*, and *Jolson Sings Again*.

B86   Churchill, Allen. *Remember When*. A Ridge Press Book/Golden Press, 1967. Includes color illustrations of Jolson sheet music.

B87   Clark, Ronald, ed. *The Penguin Encyclopedia of Popular Music*. New York: Viking Press, 1989. This encyclopedia includes an entry on Jolson.

B88   Clymer, Floyd. *Cars of the Stars*. Floyd Clymer Publications, 1955. Includes several photos of Jolson with various cars he owned.

B89   Coffey, Frank. *Always Home. 50 Years of the USO. The Official Photographic History*. McLean, Virginia: Brassey's, 1991. This richly illustrated history of the USO discusses Jolson's performance tours during World War II and Korea, and includes a photo of Jolson singing in uniform during the Korean War.

B90   Cohen, Sarah Blacher, ed. *The Jewish-American Stage and Screen*. Bloomington, Indiana: Indiana University Press, 1983. A study of great Jewish performers and works for the stage and screen created by Jews in America, including Jolson.

B91   Cohn, Art. *The Joker is Wild. The All But Incredible True Story of Joe E. Lewis*. New York: Random House, 1955. Jolson's acquaintance with Lewis is chronicled in this biography of the comedian.

B92   Cohn, Art. *The Nine Lives of Michael Todd*. New York: Pocket Books, 1959. Touches on producer Todd's relationship with Jolson.

B93   *The Colonel: An Affectionate Remembrance of Jack L. Warner*. Los Angeles, California: Friends of USC Libraries, 1980. A tribute to the long-time head of Warner Bros. touches on his long professional and personal connection with Jolson.

B94   Corio, Ann. *This Was Burlesque*. With Joseph Di Mona. New York: Madison Square Press, 1968. Includes several backstage photographs of Jolson during the years of his stage career.

B95   Coslow, Sam. *Cocktails for Two*. New York: Arlington House, 1977. In this memoir the well-known songwriter makes many references to Jolson and *The Jolson Story*.

B96 Crosby, Bing. *Call Me Lucky*. As Told to Pete Martin. New York: Simon and Schuster, 1953. Crosby makes a number of references to Jolson, particularly involving the success of their appearances together on radio in the late 1940's.

B97 Crowther, Bosley. *The Lion's Share. The Story of an American Empire*. New York: E.P. Dutton & Co., 1957. This history of MGM includes some commentary on *The Jazz Singer*, Jolson and the rise of sound films.

B98 Croy, Homer. *Our Will Rogers*. New York: Duell, Sloan and Pearce, 1953. Includes some discussion of the Al Jolson estate.

B99 Custen, George F. *Bio/Pics. How Hollywood Constructed Public History*. New Brunswick, New Jersey: Rutgers University Press, 1992. Custen's survey of movies on historical subjects makes reference to Jolson and the two biographical films based on his life.

B100 Denton, Clive, and others. *The Hollywood Professionals--Volume 2: Henry King, Lewis Milestone, Sam Wood*. New York, 1974. This examination of the work of the three directors touches on Milestone's direction of Jolson in *Hallelujah, I'm a Bum*.

B101 Dick, Bernard. *The Merchant Prince of Poverty Row*. Harry Cohn of *Columbia Pictures*. Lexington, Kentucky: University of Kentucky Press, 1993. This study of Cohn includes references to his relationship with Jolson and the making of *The Jolson Story*.

B102 Dick, Bernard F. *The Star-Spangled Screen*. Lexington, Kentucky: University of Kentucky Press, 1985. References to Jolson films are included in this history of patriotic films.

B103 Dimeglio, John E. *Vaudeville, U.S.A.* Bowling Green, Ohio: Bowling Green University Popular Press, 1973. This survey history makes mention of Jolson's early years in vaudeville.

B104 Diner, Hasia R. *In the Almost Promised Land: American Jews and Blacks 1915-1935*. Westport, Connecticut: Greenwood Press, 1977. Jolson is cited among prominent American Jews.

B105 Douglas, George H. *The Early Days of Radio Broadcasting*. Jefferson, North Carolina: McFarland, 1987. Jolson's rocky success in radio is chronicled in this history of radio's salad days.

B106 Dunn, Don. *The Making of* No, No, Nanette. Secaucus, New Jersey: The Citadel Press, 1972. The saga of the remarkably successful 1971 revival of the 1925 musical, *No, No, Nanette*, which brought Ruby Keeler out of a long retirement. Predictably, the book includes much background material on Keeler, including her professional and personal relationship with Jolson.

B107 Durante, Jimmy and J.C. Kofoed. *Night Clubs*. New York: Alfred A. Knopf, 1931. This anecdotal history of night clubs includes a few comments on

Jolson.

B108 Eastman, Max. *Enjoyment of Laughter*. New York: Simon & Schuster, 1936. Jolson is included in an analytical discussion of the styles of various comedians.

B109 Eels, George. *Hedda and Louella*. New York: G.P. Putnam's Sons, 1972. Jolson and the coming of sound to films in *The Jazz Singer* is discussed.

B110 Elliott, Arnold. *Deep in My Heart. A Story Based on the Life of Sigmund Romberg*. New York: Duell, Sloan & Pierce, 1949. Romberg's work on Jolson's early musicals is examined in this biography of the composer.

B111 Ellis, Jack C. *A History of Film*. Englewood Cliffs, New Jersey, 1979. This survey history touches on Jolson's film work, particularly *The Jazz Singer*.

B112 Endres, Stacy and Robert Cushman. *Hollywood at Your Feet*. With a Foreword by Ginger Rogers. Los Angeles, California: Pomegranate Press, 1992. A well-illustrated history of Graumann's Chinese Theatre includes coverage of each Hollywood star whose footprints have been immortalized in the forecourt of the Theatre, including Jolson. A photo is included of Jolson putting his knee prints in cement in 1936.

B113 Engel, Lehman. *The American Musical Theater*. Introduction by Brooks Atkinson. New York: Collier Books, 1975. Engel's well-respected survey of Broadway musicals touches on the Jolson shows.

B114 Epstein, Jerry. *Remembering Charlie. A Pictorial History*. New York: Doubleday, 1989. Includes a brief Chaplin assessment of Jolson's genius.

B115 Erenberg, Lewis. *Steppin' Out: New York Nightlife and the Transformation of American Culture, 1890-1930*. Chicago, 1981. The involvement of Jolson and Ruby Keeler in nightclubs and Broadway is chronicled in this cultural history of New York's popular entertainments.

B116 Erens, Patricia. *The Jew in American Cinema*. Bloomington, Indiana: Indiana University Press, 1984. A detailed, well-documented study with references to Jolson as a Jew, and the ways his Jewishness was depicted in *The Jazz Singer* and *The Jolson Story*.

B117 Everson, William K. *American Silent Film*. New York, 1978. This history of silent films deals with the transition to sound via *The Jazz Singer*.

B118 ----------. *Love in the Film. Screen Romance from the Silent Days to the Present*. Secaucus, New Jersey: The Citadel Press, 1979. Includes commentary and stills from Jolson's film *Hallelujah, I'm a Bum*.

B119 Ewen, David. *All The Years of American Popular Music*. New York: Prentice-Hall, 1977. A detailed survey history of American popular music including much familiar material on Jolson's stage and film work, with an emphasis on particular songs and Jolson's influence on other singers.

B120 ----------. *American Popular Songs. From the Revolutionary War to the Present.* New York: Random House, 1966. This history touches on Jolson's impact on popular music as both a performer and a songwriter.

B121 ----------. *Complete Book of the American Musical Theatre.* New York: Holt, Rinehart and Winston 1958, 1959, 1970. This encyclopedic work includes entries on many of the Jolson shows.

B122 ----------. *George Gershwin. His Journey to Greatness.* New York: The Ungar Publishing Company, 1970, 1986. Jolson's relationship with Gershwin is touched on in this biography of the composer.

B123 ----------. *A Journey to Greatness. Biography of George Gershwin.* New York: Henry Holt & Co., 1957. Ewen refers to Jolson several times in this important biography of Gershwin, particularly in regard to Jolson's introduction of "Swanee," and its subsequent success.

B124 ----------. *Panorama of American Popular Music.* New York: Prentice-Hall, 1957. Ewen's survey includes references to Jolson's impact on American popular music.

B125 ----------. *Richard Rodgers.* New York: Henry Holt & Co., 1957. This biography of the composer touches on Rodgers' music for Jolson's film, *Hallelujah, I'm a Bum.*

B126 ----------. *The Story of George Gershwin.* New York: Henry Holt & Co., 1945. Jolson's relationship with Gershwin is chronicled in this biography of the composer.

B127 ----------. *The Story of Irving Berlin.* New York: Henry Holt & Co., 1950. Jolson's long relationship with Berlin is surveyed in this biography of the composer-lyricist.

B128 Faith, William Robert. *Bob Hope. A Life in Comedy.* New York: G.P. Putnam's Sons, 1982. Jolson is often referred to as a leading show business figure in this largely celebratory biography of Hope.

B129 Falkenburg, Jinx. *Jinx.* New York: Duell, Sloane and Pearce 1951. This anecdotal biography of Falkenburg touches on her relationship with Jolson and her appearance in *Hold On to Your Hats.*

B130 Feather, Leonard. *The New Edition of the Encyclopedia of Jazz.* New York: Horizon Press, 1960. This encyclopedic work includes an entry on Jolson.

B131 Fein, Irving. *Jack Benny.* New York: Putnam, 1976. Fein, Benny's long-time manager, recalls several anecdotes about Jolson and his relationship with Benny.

B132 Fennell, John P. *"You Ain't Heard Nothin' Yet!"* Secaucus, New Jersey: The Citadel Press, 1989. This collection of over five-hundred famous one-liners from well-known films includes as its title Jolson's renowned declaration that was first heard on film in *The Jazz Singer*. A still from that film is included on the back cover of the book.

B133   Fetrow, Alan G. *Sound Films, 1927-1939*. A United States Filmography. Jefferson, North Carolina: McFarland, 1992. A compendium of the early years of sound films, including those in which Jolson appeared.

B134   Feuer, Jane. *The Hollywood Musical*. Bloomington, Indiana: Indiana University Press, 1982. Feuer offers some analysis and background on several of Jolson's musical films.

B135   *The Film Buff's Checklist of Motion Pictures (1912-1979)*. Hollywood, California: Hollywood Film Archives, 1979. This checklist includes most of the Jolson films.

B136   Fisher, John. *Call Them Irreplaceable. How and Why the Great Ones Soared*. New York: Stein and Day, 1976. A celebration of the greatest entertainers of the twentieth century, including chapters on Judy Garland, Bob Hope, Frank Sinatra, Danny Kaye, Jimmy Durante, Maurice Chevalier, Marlene Dietrich, and Jolson.

B137   Flannery, Thomas D. *1939 - The Year in Movies: A Comprehensive Filmography*. Jefferson, North Carolina: McFarland, 1990. Information on Jolson's three film appearances of 1939, *Swanee River*, *Rose of Washington Square* and *Hollywood Cavalcade*, is included.

B138   Fletcher, Tom. *100 Years of the Negro in Show Business*. New York: Da Capo Press, 1984. Jolson is discussed as a white performer who succeeded in the blackface minstrel tradition.

B139   Fordin, Hugh. *Getting to Know Him. A Biography of Oscar Hammerstein*. With an Introduction by Stephen Sondheim. New York: Random House, 1977. Jolson's acquaintance with Hammerstein is touched on in this important biography of the lyricist-librettist.

B140   Fowler, Gene. *Schnozzola*. New York: Viking Press, 1951. Jolson's long friendship and professional association with Jimmy Durante is examined in this biography of the comedian.

B141   Francisco, Charles. *The Radio City Music Hall*. New York: Dutton, 1979. This history of the famous New York theatre touches on Jolson films shown there (including *The Jolson Story*).

B142   Frank, Rusty E. *Tap! The Greatest Tap Dance Stars and Their Stories, 1900-1955*. New York: William Morrow and Company, 1990. Includes a brief chapter on Ruby Keeler, who describes herself as "a hoofer. A real Buck and Wing dancer,"(p. 30) with several mentions of Jolson, as well as two photographs from *Go Into Your Dance*. In another chapter, Jeni LeGon, an African-American dancer, recalls Jolson and her days in film.

B143   Freedland, Michael. *Irving Berlin*. New York: Stein and Day, 1974. Jolson's long friendship and professional connection with the great composer-lyricist is examined in this biography.

B144 ----------. *Jerome Kern. A* Biography. New York: Stein and Day, 1978. Jolson's relationship with Kern is chronicled in this standard biography of the composer.

B145 ----------. *So Let's Hear the Applause.* London, 1984. This anecdotal history of popular entertainment makes numerous references to Jolson.

B146 ----------. *The Warner Bros.* New York: St. Martin's Press, 1983. Freedland's survey history of Warner Brothers includes numerous anecdotes involving Jolson's involvement with the company.

B147 Freeman, Larry. *The Melodies Linger On.* New York: Century House, 1951. This history of Tin Pan Alley includes references to Jolson's significance as a performer.

B148 Friedman, Lester D. *Hollywood's Image of the Jew.* New York, 1982. This heavily illustrated history of the depiction of Jews in American films includes an examination of *The Jazz Singer,* with several superbly reproduced stills from the film.

B149 ----------. *The Jewish Image in American Film.* Secaucus, New Jersey: The Citadel Press, 1987. This lavishly illustrated history includes discussion of Jolson, *The Jazz Singer,* and the two Jolson biographical films, with reference to the depiction of Jews inherent in Jolson performances and the films themselves.

B150 Friedrich, Otto. *City of Nets: A Portrait of Hollywood in the 1940's.* New York, 1986. This anecdotal history touches on Jolson and the biographical films of his life.

B151 Friedwald, Will. *Jazz Singing. America's Great Voices from Bessie Smith to Bebop and Beyond.* New York: Charles Scribner's Sons, 1990. Jolson is mentioned in this history of the performers of popular music from the early twentieth century to rock-and-roll.

B152 ---------- and Jerry Beck. *The Warner Bros. Cartoons.* Metuchen, New Jersey: Scarecrow Press, 1981. This chronicle of Warner Bros. cartoons includes references to those satirizing Jolson, Jolson's songs and his performance style.

B153 Fuld, James M. *American Popular Music Redbook, 1875-1950.* Musical Americana, 1955. This encyclopedic work touches on Jolson and his songs.

B154 Gabler, Neal. *An Empire of Their Own: How the Jews Invented Hollywood.* New York, 1988. Includes an account of the making of *The Jazz Singer* and its impact on the arrival of sound films.

B155 Gammond, Peter. *The Oxford Companion to Popular Music.* Oxford and New

York: Oxford University Press, 1991. This encyclopedic work includes an entry on Jolson.

B156 Gardiner, J. *Gaby Deslys. A Fatal Attraction*. London: Sidgwick & Jackson, 1986. Deslys's personal and professional assessment of Jolson is recounted in this biography of Jolson's co-star in his earliest musicals.

B157 Gaver, Jack. *There's Laughter In The Air*. New York: Greenburg, 1945. This anecdotal account of radio comedy features references to Jolson.

B158 Geduld, Harry M. *The Birth of the Talkies. From Edison to Jolson*. Bloomington, Indiana and London: Indiana University Press, 1975. The dawn of the sound age in film includes a considerable account of Jolson's involvement in *The Jazz Singer*.

B159 Gehman, Richard. *Sinatra and His Rat Pack*. Belmont Books, 1961. Jolson is mentioned in this anecdotal history of Sinatra's nightclub predominance.

B160 Gernsback, Sidney. *1927 Radio Encyclopedia*. New York: Vintage Radio Publishers (Museum of Broadcasting), 1927. This encyclopedia includes references to Jolson on radio.

B161 Giddins, Gary. *Riding on a Blue Note: Jazz and American Pop*. New York, 1981. Includes a number of reference to Jolson in comparison to early jazz singers, from Ethel Waters to Bing Crosby to Elvis Presley. Giddins notes that "In Jolson, theatrical show-biz schmaltz was mated with an irresisitable vitality -- maudlin sentiment was the flip side of snappy eye-rolling rhythms."(p. 33)

B162 Gilbert, Douglas. *American Vaudeville. Its Life and Times*. New York: Dover Publications, Inc., 1940, 1968. This survey of vaudeville history makes several references to Jolson.

B163 Gilbert, L. Wolfe. *Without Rhyme or Reason*. New York: Vantage Press, 1956. A memoir by the Tin Pan Alley songwriter who contributed to Jolson's repertoire with such songs as "Waiting for the Robert E. Lee."

B164 Goldberg, Isaac. *Tin Pan Alley. A Chronicle of the American Popular Music Racket*. The John Day Co., 1930. Jolson's significance as a singer of popular songs is discussed in this history of popular music.

B165 ----------. *George Gershwin. A Study of American Music*. New York: Frederick Ungar Publishing Co., 1958. Goldberg's biography of Gershwin touches on the composer's relationship with Jolson.

B166 ---------- and Isidore Witmark. *From Ragtime to Swingtime. The Story of the House of Witmark*. Lee Furman, 1939. This history of the music publishing firm makes reference to Jolson's importance in popular music.

B167 Goldman, Herbert G. *Fanny Brice. The Original Funny Girl*. New York: Oxford University Press, 1992. Includes references to Jolson's personal and professional relationship with Brice, from their early Shubert shows to the end of Jolson's life.

B168 Goodman, Ezra. *The Fifty Year Decline and Fall of Hollywood.* New York: Simon and Schuster, 1961. This survey history of Hollywood makes reference to Jolson and his films.

B169 Gottfried, Martin. *Broadway Musicals.* New York: Harry N. Abrams, 1979. Gottfried's lavishly illustrated survey of musical comedies includes reference to Jolson and his shows, as well as some photos.

B170 ----------. *In Person. The Great Entertainers.* New York: Harry N. Abrams, 1985. This opulent chronicle of popular entertainers includes photos and references to Jolson.

B171 ----------. *Jed Harris. The Curse of Genius.* New York: Little, Brown and Co., 1984. Jolson's interaction with producer Harris is chronicled in this biography.

B172 Green, Abel and Joe Laurie, Jr. *Show Biz. From Vaude to Video.* New York: Henry Holt & Co., 1951. This panoramic history of show business contains a multitude of references to Jolson's achievements in various entertainment media.

B173 Green, Fitzhugh. *The Film Finds Its Tongue.* New York: G.P. Putnam's Sons, 1929. A fascinating behind-the-scenes examination of the making of early talkies. Includes photos of Jolson on and off-screen, and an account of the making of *The Singing Fool.*

B174 Green, Stanley. *Encyclopedia of the Musical Film.* New York/Oxford: Oxford University Press, 1981. References to Jolson's films are included.

B175 ----------. *Encyclopedia of the Musical Theatre.* New York: DaCapo Press, Inc., 1976. Some of Jolson's musical shows are given individual entries.

B176 ----------. *Hollywood Musicals. Year By Year.* Milwaukee, Wisconsin: Hal Leonard Publishing Corporation, 1990. Green includes references to several Jolson films.

B177 ----------. *Ring Bells! Sing Songs! Broadway Musicals of the 1930's.* Introduction by Brooks Atkinson. New Rochelle, New York: Arlington House, 1971. *The Wonder Bar* and *Hold On to Your Hats* are referred to in this heavily illustrated survey of 1930's musical comedies.

B178 ----------. *Rodgers and Hammerstein Fact Book. A Record of Their Works Together and With Other Collaborators.* New York: Drama Book Specialists, 1980. Includes references to Jolson's film *Hallelujah, I'm a Bum.*

B179 ---------- . *The Rodgers and Hammerstein Story.* New York: DaCapo Press, 1963. Rodgers' work on *Hallelujah, I'm a Bum* is referred to, along with Jolson's involvement in the film.

B180 ----------. *The World of Musical Comedy*. South Brunswick and New York: A.S. Barnes and Company, 1960, 1968, 1974. Green's survey history of Broadway musicals includes numerous references to Jolson's shows.

B181 Greenfield, Thomas Allen. *Radio. A Reference Guide*. Westport, Connecticut: Greenwood Press. Jolson's radio shows are referred to in this encyclopedic work.

B182 Gregg, E.S. *The Shadow of Sound*. New York: Vantage Press, 1967. This history of the rise of sound films touches on Jolson and *The Jazz Singer*.

B183 Griffith, Richard. *The Talkies: Articles and Illustrations From a Great Fan Magazine, 1928-1940*. New York: Dover Publications, 1971. A collection of articles from *Photoplay* magazine, includes material on Jolson.

B184 Grossman, Barbara W. *Funny Woman. The Life and Times of Fanny Brice*. Bloomington and Indianapolis: Indiana University Press, 1991. In this well-researched biography of the great comic, Grossman recounts some incidents involving Jolson and Brice when they appeared in *The Whirl of Society* and *The Honeymoon Express*. One anecdote centers on Jolson's annoyance when Brice moved away from her "Yiddish songs" and added a "coon song" to her repertoire.

B185 Guild, Leo. *Zanuck: Hollywood's Last Tycoon*. Los Angeles, California: Holloway House, 1970. Includes an account of the making of *The Jazz Singer*.

B186 Gussow, Mel. *"Don't Say Yes Until I Finish Talking," A Biography of Darryl F. Zanuck*. Garden City, New York: Doubleday, 1971. Jolson's professional and personal relationship with Zanuck, beginning with *The Jazz Singer*, is traced in this biography of the flamboyant producer.

B187 Halliwell, Leslie. *Seat in All Parts*. New York: Scribner, 1985. Halliwell's film-going memoir includes references to Jolson's films.

B188 Hammond, Percy. *But -- Is It Art*. Garden City, New York: Doubleday, Page & Company, 1927. In this opinionated examination of various plays and performers, Hammond recounts an anecdote about playing golf with Jolson.

B189 Handy, W.C. *Father of the Blues*. New York: The Macmillan Co., 1955. Jolson's singing is referred to in this biography of Handy.

B190 Harmon, Jim. *The Great Radio Comedians*. Garden City, New York: Doubleday and Co., Inc., 1970. This history of radio comics includes discussion of Jolson's various radio shows, and an excerpt of dialogue involving Jolson and Oscar Levant from the Kraft Music Hall.

B191 Hart, Dorothy. *Thou Swell, Thou Witty. The Life and Lyrics of Lorenz Hart*. New York: Harper and Row, 1976. Hart's work on *Hallelujah, I'm a Bum* is covered, along with inclusion of some of the film's lyrics.

B192 Haskins, Jim and N.R. Mitgang. *Mr. Bojangles. The Biography of Bill Robinson*. New York: William Morrow and Company, 1988. Jolson's encounters with Robinson are referred to in this biography of the legendary dancer.

B193 Hays, Will H. *See and Hear*. Motion Picture Producers and Distributors of America, Inc., 1929. Hollywood's censorship czar surveys the history of the film medium to 1929, culminating with the coming of sound. Hays devotes a few pages to *The Jazz Singer, The Singing Fool*, and Jolson.

B194 Hecht, Ben. *A Child of the Century*. New York: Simon and Schuster, 1954. Hecht's work on *Hallelujah, I'm a Bum* is referred to in this memoir.

B195 Hemming, Roy and David Hajdu. *Discovering Great Singers of Classic Pop*. New York: Newmarket Press, 1991. Jolson's predominance as a singer of popular songs is referred to in this survey.

B196 Henderson, Mary. *Broadway Ballyhoo. The American Theater Seen in Posters, Photographs, Magazines, Caricatures, and Programs*. New York: Harry N. Abrams, 1989. Jolson's shows are touched on in this emphemeral history of Broadway.

B197 Herman, Hal C., ed. *How I Broke Into the Movies*. Hollywood, California: Published by the Author, 1928, 1930 (revised). A collection of brief illustrated autobiographies of film stars, including Jolson.

B198 Higby, Mary Jane. *Tune In Tomorrow*. Cowles, 1968. Refers to Jolson's Lifebuoy radio series and includes a photo of Jolson with Martha Raye and Sid Silvers.

B199 Higham, Charles. *The Art of the American Film*. Garden City, New York: Anchor Books, 1974. Touches on *The Jazz Singer* (including a photograph of Jolson in the Coffee Dan sequence with May McAvoy) and *Hallelujah, I'm a Bum*.

B200 Hirschhorn, Clive. *The Columbia Story*. New York: Crown Publishers, Inc., 1989. This excellent year-by-year chronicle of the films made by Columbia Pictures includes illustrations and references to *The Jolson Story* and *Jolson Sings Again*.

B201 ----------. *The Hollywood Musical*. Foreword by Gene Kelly. New York: Portland House, 1991. A superb, highly illustrated history of the musical movies, year-by-year, includes entries on all of the Jolson films, as well as *The Jolson Story* and *Jolson Sings Again*.

B202 ----------. *The Warner Bros. Story*. New York: Crown, 1979. This excellent year-by-year chronicle of the films made by Warner Bros. includes illustrations and references to all of Jolson's Warner films, from *The Jazz Singer* to *Rhapsody in Blue*.

B203 Hope, Bob with Peter Martin. *Have Tux, Will Travel*. New York: Simon and

Schuster, 1954. Hope includes several anecdotes involving Jolson in this light-hearted memoir.

B204 *How I Broke Into the Movies. Signed Stories by Sixty Screen Stars*. Hal C. Herman Publishers, 1928. An autobiographical profile of Jolson is included.

B205 Huff, Theodore. *Charlie Chaplin*. Henry Schuman, 1951. Chaplin's admiration of Jolson and the rise of sound films via *The Jazz Singer* are touched on in this biography.

B206 Huntley, John and Roger Manvell. *The Technique of Film Music*. England: Focal Press Ltd. The use of music on film touches on Jolson's significance in the rise of the film musical.

B207 *The International Dictionary of Films and Filmmakers: Vol. III. Actors and Actresses*. Chicago and London: St. James Press, 1986. This dictionary includes an entry on Jolson.

B208 Iwaschkin, Roman. *Popular Music. A Reference Guide*. New York and London: Garland Publishing, 1986. This guide includes references to Jolson's popularity as a singer of popular songs.

B209 Jablonski, Edward. *Harold Arlen. Happy With the Blues*. Garden City, New York: Doubleday and Co., 1961. Jolson's interpretations of Arlen's songs is mentioned in this biography of the composer.

B210 ---------- and Lawrence D. Stewart. *The Gershwin Years*. New York: Doubleday and Company, Inc., 1958, 1973. Jolson's relationship with Gershwin, both professional and personal, is surveyed in this fine biography.

B211 Jackson, Arthur. *The Best Musicals from "Show Boat" to "A Chorus Line."* Foreword by Clive Barnes. New York: Crown Publishers, 1977. Jolson's musicals are referred to in this chronicle of musical comedies.

B212 Jackson, Arthur and John Russell Taylor. *The Hollywood Musical*. London: Secker and Warburg, 1971. Many of Jolson's film musicals are referred to in this expansive work.

B213 Jacobs, Dick. *Who Wrote That Song?* White Hall, Virginia: Betterway, 1988. Jolson's singing and his authorship of several songs is referred to in this survey of popular music.

B214 Jacobs, Lewis. *The Rise of the American Film*. New York: Teachers College Press, 1937. This early history of American movies touches on Jolson's significance in the transition from silent films to talkies.

B215 Jessel, George. *Elegy in Manhattan*. Foreword by Ben Hecht. New York: Holt, Rinehart and Winston, 1961. A collection of poetry (!) by Jessel paying tribute to the greats of show business (and other celebrities) he had known. One poem is about Jolson, and another concerns Jolson's long-time manager, Louis "Eppie" Epstein.

B216 ----------. *So Help Me.* With a foreword by William Saroyan. The World Publishing Co., 1944. Jessel touches on his experiences with Jolson throughout this book, and in praising fellow performers he writes that among those "who, single-handed have been able to hold an audience in the palm of their hands, without benefit of manuscript are: Al Jolson, and the lengths behind, Harry Lauder, Eddie Cantor, Ed Wynn."(p. 219)

B217 ----------. *This Way, Miss.* With a foreword by William Saroyan. New York: Henry Holt & Co., 1955. Jessel includes his eulogy for Jolson along with many anecdotes about "this great, great, dynamic personality and talent" who "was a man with many idiosyncrasies."(p. 59) Jessel concludes that Jolson was "cruel most times [. . .] but God, what a great artist he was!"(p. 64)

B218 ----------. *The World I Lived In.* With John Austin. Chicago: Regnery, 1975. Jessel's anecdotal memoir includes numerous references to Jolson.

B219 Johnson, Grady. *The Five Pennies.* New York: Dell, 1959. Includes anecdotal mentions of Jolson.

B220 Josefsburg, Milt. *The Jack Benny Show.* New Rochelle, New York: Arlington House Publishers, Inc., 1977. Jolson is only mentioned in passing, but Josefsburg includes a photo of Jolson on Benny's radio show.

B221 Kane, Frank. *Juke Box King.* New York: Dell, 1959. This memoir of popular American music mentions Jolson.

B222 Kanin, Garson. *Hollywood.* New York: Viking, 1974. Kanin's novel refers to Jolson as a major figure in early Hollywood.

B223 Katkov, Norman. *The Fabulous Fanny. The Story of Fanny Brice.* New York: Alfred A. Knopf, 1953. This first biography of Brice touches on her work with Jolson, and their personal relationship.

B224 Keyes, Evelyn. *I'll Think About That Tomorrow.* New York: Dutton, 1991. In another memoir, following up on the success of her *Scarlett O'Hara's Younger Sister*, Keyes makes several mentions of *The Jolson Story*.

B225 ----------. *Scarlett O'Hara's Younger Sister.* Secaucus, New Jersey: Lyle Stuart, 1977. Keyes recalls her work in *The Jolson Story* in some detail, and remembers seeing Larry Parks' test for the role of Jolson, "mouthing to Jolson's voice. Jolson himself was in the projection room as well. He scowled and squirmed when we all praised Larry's work. I had a sneaking suspicion that Jolson wanted to play Jolson."(p. 75)

B226 Kimball, Robert, and Alfred Simon. *The Gershwins.* New York: Atheneum, 1973. This biography includes reference to the Gershwin's relationship with Jolson.

B227 Kiner, Larry F. and Harry Mackenzie. *AFRS Basic Musical Library "P" Series 1-1000.* Westport, Connecticut: Greenwood Press, 1990. Includes an accounting of Jolson's contribution to these recordings.

B228 Kinkle, Roger D. *The Complete Encyclopedia of Popular and Jazz Music.* New York: Arlington House. Includes an entry on Jolson.

B229 Knight, Arthur. *The Liveliest Art. A Panoramic History of the Movies.* Mentor, 1959. Touches on several Jolson films, particularly *The Jazz Singer* and *Hallelujah, I'm a Bum.*

B230 ----------, intro. *The New York Times Directory of the Film.* New York: Arno, 1971. Includes references to Jolson's films.

B231 Kobal, John. *Gotta Sing, Gotta Dance.* London: Hamlyn, 1970. A heavily illustrated, oversized history of the musical film, with many references to Jolson's films and stills *The Jazz Singer, The Singing Fool, Go Into Your Dance, The Singing Kid, Wonder Bar,* and *Hallelujah, I'm a Bum.*

B232 ----------. *People Will Talk.* New York: Alfred A. Knopf, 1986. This collection of interviews includes one with Joan Blondell in which she recalls seeing Jolson perform: "I think to this day that there are two great performers that hit this world: one is Jolson and one is Judy Garland. They had some kind of a magic in front of people that nobody could surpass. [. . .] what mark they hit nobody could touch. Nobody. I get chills when I think of the two of them. And I knew them both, thank God."(p. 187)

B233 Kobler, John. *Capone.* New York: G.P. Putnam's Sons, 1971. An anecdote about Jolson performing for Capote figures in this biography of the legendary mobster.

B234 Krueger, Miles, ed. *The Movie Musical From Vitaphone to 42nd Street.* New York: Dover Publications, Inc., 1975. A collection of features, reviews, and other items from "Photoplay" magazine covering the years 1927 to 1933.

B235 ----------, ed. *Souvenir Programs of Twelve Classic Movies.* New York, 1977. Includes *The Jazz Singer.*

B236 Kuhns, William. *The Moving Picture Book.* Dayton, Ohio: Pflaum, 1975. Kuhns' well-illustrated survey of the technique of filmmaking uses Jolson's film *Hallelujah, I'm a Bum* as a recurring example. Illustrations from the film and a brief analysis of it are included.

B237 Lahr, John. *The Autograph Hound.* London: Jonathan Cape, 1973. This novel about a movie fan/autograph collector drops many film and theatrical names, including Jolson's.

B238 ----------. *Notes on a Cowardly Lion.* New York: Alfred A. Knopf, 1969. Includes a mention of songs written by Jolson and various collaborators.

B239 Larkin, Rochelle. *Hail, Columbia.* New Rochelle, New York: Arlington House, 1975. This survey of the films made by Columbia Pictures includes commentary on *The Jolson Story* and *Jolson Sings Again.*

B240 Lasky, Jesse L. *I Blow My Own Horn.* As Told to Don Weldon. New York:

Doubleday, 1956. Jolson's friendship with Lasky is examined in this biography of the noted producer.

B241 Lauder, Sir Harry. *Roamin' in the Gloamin'*. London: J.P. Lippincott, 1928. Lauder's thoughts on Jolson's artistry are included in this memoir.

B242 Laufe, Abe. *Broadway's Greatest Musicals*. New York: Funk & Wagnalls, 1977. Jolson's shows are surveyed in this history of American musical comedy.

B243 Laurie, Joe, Jr. *Vaudeville: From the Honky-Tonks to the Palace*. New York: Henry Holt & Co., 1953. Jolson's rise as a performer is discussed in this engaging history of vaudeville.

B244 Leab, Daniel J. *From Sambo to Superspade. The Black Experience in Motion Pictures*. Boston: Houghton Mifflin, Co., 1975. Leab examines the image of blacks in film, beginning with the earliest appearances of white actors in blackface. He touches on Jolson's films, especially *The Jazz Singer*.

B245 Lee, Sonia. *Hollywood Follies. Tattle-Telling on the Stars*. With caricatures by Joe Grant. 1932. Includes a caricature of Jolson and some backstage gossip.

B246 Leonard, William T. *Masquerade in Black*. Scarecrow Press, 1978. This study of performers who worked in blackface includes a discussion of Jolson.

B247 ----------. *Theatre: Stage to Screen to Television*. Two Volumes. Scarecrow Press, 1981. Includes an entry on *The Jazz Singer*. An updated version of this book is currently in the works.

B248 Lerner, Alan Jay. *The Musical Theatre. A Celebration*. London: Collins, 1986. Lerner refers to Jolson's stage shows in this anecdotal and opinionated survey of musical comedy.

B249 Levant, Oscar. *The Memoirs of an Amnesiac*. New York: G.P. Putnam's Sons, 1965. Levant comments on Jolson's artistry in this memoir.

B250 ----------. *A Smattering of Ignorance*. Garden City, New York: Garden City Publishing, Inc., 1942. Includes some passing references to Jolson, published before he and Jolson worked together on the Kraft Music Hall.

B251 ----------. *The Unimportance of Being Oscar*. New York: G.P. Putnam's Sons, 1968. Discusses his work with Jolson on "The Kraft Music Hall." Includes a photograph of Jolson with Levant and Lucille Ball.

B252 Levin, Martin, ed. *Hollywood and the Great Fan Magazines*. New York: Harrison House, 1970. This collection of articles and illustrations from vintage movie magazines includes items related to Jolson and his films.

B253 Lewis, Tom. *Empire of the Air. The Men Who Made Radio*. Edward Burlingame Books. Includes some passing references to Jolson.

B254   Lowell, Juliet, ed. *Dear Hollywood*. New York: Dell, 1959.   Includes an amusing letter to Larry Parks confusing him with Jolson.

B255   Loy, Myrna and James Kotsilibas-Davis. *Myrna Loy. Being and Becoming*. New York: Alfred A. Knopf, Inc., 1987.   In her critically acclaimed autobiography, Loy recalls her work as a bit player during the making of *The Jazz Singer*.

B256   MacAdams, William. *Ben Hecht. The Man Behind the Legend*. New York: Charles Scribner's Sons, 1990.   Includes some commentary on Hecht's involvement with Jolson on the making of *Hallelujah, I'm a Bum*.

B257   Magill, Frank N., ed. *Magill's American Film Guide*. Englewood Cliffs, New Jersey: Salem, 1980. Five Volumes.   Includes entries on several of Jolson's films.

B258   Malone, Ted. *Ted Malone's Favorite Stories*. New York: Doubleday, 1950. Malone includes an anecdote about Jolson.

B259   Maltin, Leonard. *TV Movies & Video Guide*. New York: NAL Penguin, Inc., 1988.   One of the literally dozens of movie and video guides rating films published annually.   Most include brief critiques of some or all of Jolson's films.

B260   Maney, Richard. *Fanfare*. New York: Harper & Brothers, 1957.   In this memoir by a noted Broadway press agent, Jolson is mentioned as a participant in the Actors Equity strike of 1919.

B261   Marks, Edward B. and Abbott J. Liebling. *They All Sang*. New York: The Viking Press, 1934.   Refers to Jolson among other singers of popular songs in the first three decades of the twentieth century.

B262   Martin, Len D. *The Columbia Checklist. The Feature Films, Serials, Cartoons and Short Subjects of Columbia Pictures Corporation, 1922-1988*. Jefferson, North Carolina and London: McFarland and Co., Inc. Publishing, 1991. This encyclopedic survey includes information on *The Jolson Story* and *Jolson Sings Again*.

B263   Marx, Groucho. *Grouchophile*. Indianapolis/New York: Bobbs-Merrill, 1976. Includes a few anecdotes about Jolson.

B264   Mast, Gerald. *Can't Help Singin'. The American Musical on Stage and Screen*. Woodstock, New York: Overlook Press, 1987.   This survey of the musical on stage and screen includes numerous references to Jolson, *The Jazz Singer* (including a still of the final scene), *The Jolson Story*, and *Jolson Sings Again*.

B265   Mates, Julian. *America's Musical Stage. Two Hundred Years of Musical Theatre*. Westport, Connecticut: Greenwood Press, 1985.   Jolson's significance as a purveyor of the minstrel tradition and as a popular singer is discussed.

B266 Mattfeld, Julius. *Variety Music Cavalcade. 1620-1961.* New York: Prentice-Hall, 1962. Jolson's predominance as a singer is surveyed in this examination of American popular music as reported in *Variety.*

B267 McCarthy, Albert J. and Dave Corey. *Jazz Directory.* Cassel & Co., 1955. Includes an entry on Jolson suggesting that he was not truly a jazz singer.

B268 McClelland, Doug. *Forties Film Talk. Oral Histories of Hollywood, with 120 Lobby Posters.* Jefferson, North Carolina: McFarland, 1992. Includes references to Jolson, particularly in McClelland's interview with Evelyn Keyes, and remarks from William Demarest and Barbara Hale about the Jolson biographical films.

B269 McNamara, Brooks. *The Shuberts of Broadway.* Foreword by Beverly Sills. New York/Oxford: Oxford University Press, 1990. This fine, well-illustrated, scholarly account of the productions mounted by the Shuberts includes considerable information about Jolson and his stage shows produced under the Shubert banner.

B270 McNamara, Daniel I., ed. *The ASCAP Biographical Dictionary of Composers, Authors and Publishers.* New York: Thomas Y. Crowell Co., 1948, 1952, 1966, 1980. Includes a profile of Jolson.

B271 McVay, Douglas. *The Musical Film.* New York: Barnes, 1967. A survey history of movie musicals touching on several of Jolson's films.

B272 Meyer, William. *Warner Bros. Directors.* New Rochelle, New York: Arlington House, 1978. Meyer offers analysis of the work of the major Warner Bros. directors, including Alan Crosland, Archie Mayo, William Keighley, and Lloyd Bacon, with references to Jolson's films under their direction.

B273 Mezzrow, Milton and Bernard Wolfe. *Really the Blues.* New York: Signet Books, 1964. Jolson's popularity as a singer is surveyed in this account of aspects of American music.

B274 Michael, Paul, ed. *The American Movies Reference Book: The Sound Era.* New York: Prentice-Hall, 1972. Illustrated encyclopedic listing of many sound era American films, includes detailed credits. Jolson films listed include *The Jazz Singer, The Singing Fool, Wonder Bar, Rhapsody in Blue, The Jolson Story, Jolson Sings Again,* plus an entry on Jolson himself.

B275 Michael, Paul, and James Robert Parish, eds. *The American Movies Reference Book.* Englewood Cliffs, New Jersey: Prentice-Hall, 1969. Jolson and his films are referred to in this useful reference source.

B276 Milberg, Doris. *Repeat Performances. A Guide to Hollywood Movie Remakes.* Shelter Island, New York: Shelter Press, 1990. This survey of Hollywood films and their remakes includes information about and a photograph a scene from *The Jazz Singer.*

B277 Miller, Robert Milton. *Star Myths: Show-Business Biographies on Film.*

Metuchen, New Jersey and London: Scarecrow Press, 1983. A study of film biographies of show business legends, including considerable material on *The Jolson Story* and *Jolson Sings Again*. Miller also refers to *Rhapsody in Blue*, *Rose of Washington Square*, and Norman Brooks' impersonation of Jolson in *The Best Things in Life Are Free*.

B278 Millichip, Joseph. *Lewis Milestone*. Boston: Twayne, 1981. Milestone's direction of *Hallelujah, I'm a Bum* is discussed in this survey of the director's work.

B279 Mitchell, Curtis. *Cavalcade of Broadcasting*. Foreword by Bob Hope. Chicago, Illinois: Follett Publishing Company, 1970. This heavily illustrated history of radio and television includes references to Jolson's numerous radio shows and includes a photo of Jolson and Ruby Keeler.

B280 Monaco, James. *The Encyclopedia of Film*. New York: Perigee, 1991. Includes an entry on Jolson.

B281 Moore, MacDonald Smith. *Yankee Blues: Musical Culture and American Identity*. Bloomington, Indiana: Indiana University Press, 1985. Jolson figures among the significant American sings referred to in this cultural history of American popular music.

B282 Mordden, Ethan. *Better Foot Forward. The History of American Musical Theatre*. New York: Grossman Publishers, 1976. Jolson's shows and performance style are examined in this eccentric history of Broadway musical comedy.

B283 ----------. *Broadway Babies. The People Who Made the American Musical*. New York and Oxford: Oxford University Press, 1983. In his delightfully opinionated account of the great stars of musical comedy, Mordden states that "Jolson sang as if his songs could stop a war. He threw his whole person into his numbers, committed, ironic, overthrowing the vaudeville tradition of presenting songs without overt emotional involvement."(p. 31)

B284 ----------. *The Hollywood Musical*. New York: St. Martin's Press, 1981. Jolson's film musicals, particularly *The Jazz Singer*, are touched on in this survey of movie musicals.

B285 Morgereth, Timothy A. *Bing Crosby: A Discography, Radio Program List and Filmography*. Jefferson, North Carolina: McFarland, 1987. Includes information on Jolson's radio appearances and recordings with Crosby.

B286 Morris, James R., J.R. Taylor, and Dwight Blocker Bowers. *Six Decades of Songwriters and Singers*. Washington, D.C.: The Smithsonian Collection of Recordings, 1984. Guide to a collection of popular vocalists from the early twentieth century to approximately 1960.

B287 Morris, Lloyd. *Not So Long Ago*. New York: Random House, 1949. Includes a mention of Jolson and *The Jazz Singer*.

B288 Mosedale, John. *The Men Who Invented Broadway. Damon Runyon, Walter Winchell, and Their World*. New York: Richard Marek Publishers, 1981. Jolson's prominence in the golden days of Broadway is mentioned, particularly in regard to his relationship with Winchell and the musical stage.

B289 Mosley, Leonard. *Zanuck: The Rise and Fall of Hollywood's Last Tycoon*. Boston: Little, Brown, 1984. References to Jolson's professional and personal relationship with Zanuck are included.

B290 Murrells, Joseph. *Daily Mail Book of Golden Discs. The Story of Every Disc That Has Sold a Million Copies Since 1903*. England: McWhirter Twins, Ltd. Includes many references to Jolson and a photograph of *The Jazz Singer*.

B291 Nash, Jay Robert and Stanley Ralph Ross, eds. *The Motion Picture Guide*. Twelve Volumes. Chicago, Illinois: Cinebooks, 1985. This excellent encyclopedic work includes entries on most of Jolson's films.

B292 Nicholson, Frank Ernest. *The Favorite Jokes of Famous People*. Popular Book Co., 1930. A joke by Jolson is included.

B293 Nolan, Frederick. *The Sound of Their Music. The Story of Rodgers and Hammerstein*. New York: Walker and Co., 1978. Jolson's performance in *Hallelujah, I'm a Bum* is referred to in an account of Rodgers' early work in film musicals in partnership with Lorenz Hart.

B294 Oberfirst, Robert. *Rudolph Valentino. The Man Behind the Myth*. New York: The Citadel Press, 1962. Jolson's acquaintance with Valentino is mentioned.

B295 Oliviero, Jeffrey. *Motion Picture Players' Credits*. McFarland & Co., 1991. Includes an entry on Jolson.

B296 Osgood, Henry O. *So This is Jazz*. New York, 1926, 1978. Jolson's supremacy as a "jazz singer" is examined.

B297 Parish, James Robert, and Michael R. Pitts. *Great Hollywood Musicals*. Metuchen, New Jersey: Scarecrow Press, 1992. Jolson's films are referred to in this excellent account of the golden age of movie musicals.

B298 Parish, James Robert, and Leonard DeCarl. *Hollywood Players: The Forties*. New Rochelle, New York: Arlington House, 1976. Includes material on *The Jolson Story* and *Jolson Sings Again*.

B299 ---------- and Michael R. Pitts. *Hollywood Songsters*. New York: Garland Publishing, 1991. A volume containing biographies of over one hundred singing film stars from Jolson to Dolly Parton. The Jolson entry surveys his major film appearances, and includes a list of all Jolson films, stage musicals, radio series, and a discography.

B300 Parker, David and Burton Shapiro. *Close-Up: The Contract Director*. Metuchen, New Jersey: Scarecrow, 1976. Jolson's films are mentioned in regard to the work of several Hollywood directors.

B301 Parsons, Louella O. *The Gay Illiterate*. Garden City, New York: Doubleday, Doran & Co., Inc., 1944. Parsons' memoir touches on the coming of sound to films, and Jolson's involvement with it.

B302 Paskman, Dailey. *"Gentlemen, Be Seated!" A Parade of the American Minstrels*. New York: Clarkson N. Potter, Inc., 1976. Jolson is discussed as among the last great "minstrel" stars.

B303 Paul, Elliot. *That Crazy American Music*. New York: The Bobbs-Merrill Co., 1957. This anecdotal history of popular music touches on Jolson's great popularity between the two World Wars.

B304 *Personal Glimpses of Famous Folks*. Lee Shippey, 1929. Includes a profile of Jolson.

B305 Pickard, Roy. *Hollywood's Fallen Idols*. London: B.T. Batsford Ltd., 1989. Includes a photograph of Jolson with Charlie Chaplin in 1930's.

B306 Pierce, David. *Motion Picture Copyrights and Renewals 1950-1959*. Laurel, Maryland: Milestone Publishing, 1989. Data on the copyrighting of some of Jolson's films is included.

B307 Pines, Jim. *Blacks in Films: A Study of Racial Themes and Images in the American Film*. London, 1975. Jolson's contribution to blackface traditions in movies is examined.

B308 Pratt, George. *Spellbound in Darkness*. Greenwich, Connecticut: New York Graphic Society Ltd., 1966. Includes references to Jolson films.

B309 Quinlan, David. *Quinlan's Illustrated Registry of Film Stars*. New York: Henry Holt, 1991. Includes an entry on Jolson.

B310 Reader, Ralph. *It's Been Terrific*. England: Warner Ltd., 1953. Reader recounts his relationship with Jolson and his memories of seeing Jolson perform.

B311 Rice, Edward LeRoy. *Monarchs of Minstrelsy*. Kenny Publishing Co., 1911. Includes a profile of Jolson and a photograph.

B312 Richman, Harry. *A Hell of a Life*. With Richard Gehman. New York: Duell, Sloane and Pearce, 1966. Richman makes a few scattered mentions of Jolson in this memoir.

B313 Rivadue, Barry. *Alice Faye. A Bio-Bibliography*. Westport, Connecticut: Greenwood Press, 1990. In covering Faye's career, Rivadue makes reference to her radio and screen performances with Jolson, particularly *Rose of Washington Square*.

B314 Robbins, Jhan. *Inka Dinka Doo: The Life of Jimmy Durante*. New York:

Paragon House, 1991. Jolson is referred to in several contexts in this biography of the great Schnozzola. Robbins relates one of several variant accounts of Jolson's involvement with *Show Girl.*

B315 Robinson, David. *Hollywood in the Twenties.* New York: A.S. Barnes, 1968. Jolson's domination of musical films at the end of the 1920's is discussed.

B316 Roddick, Nick. *A New Deal in Entertainment: Warner Bros. in the 1930's.* London: The British Film Institute, 1983. Jolson's 1930's films are referred to in this look at the diverse Warner Bros. films of the era.

B317 Rodgers, Richard. *Musical Stages.* New York: Random House, 1975. Rodgers recalls working on *Hallelujah, I'm a Bum,* and his encounters with Jolson. He recalls that "Jolson, who I had been told might prove difficult, turned out to be a sweet man who at the time was undergoing one of his frequent estrangements from his wife, Ruby Keeler. He was completely cooperative, though it often took a little patience to corner him to get down to business."(p. 157)

B318 Rogers, Ginger. *Ginger. My Story.* New York: Harper Collins Publishers, 1991. Rogers recalls auditioning for Ziegfeld's *Show Girl,* but losing the role because Jolson persuaded Ziegfeld to hire Ruby Keeler to star opposite him. Rogers' recollections are faulty, for Jolson never appeared opposite Keeler on stage in a Ziegfeld production.

B319 Rose, Peter. *Mainstream and Margins: Jews, Blacks and Other Americans.* New Brunswick, New Jersey, 1983. Jolson figures among prominent American Jews in the entertainment field in this cultural survey.

B320 Rosenberg, Bernard and Harry Silverstein. *The Real Tinsel.* New York: Macmillan, 1970. Among the oral histories by Hollywood veterans included in this collection Edward Everett Horton, Conrad Nagel, and Hal Mohr recall Jolson and the advent of talking pictures with *The Jazz Singer.*

B321 Rosenblatt, Samuel. *Yosselle Rosenblatt.* New York: Farrar, Straus and Young, 1954. Rosenblatt's work on *The Jazz Singer,* and his interaction with Jolson, is recounted in this memoir.

B322 Roth, Philip. *When She Was Good.* New York: Bantam, 1968. Novel which quotes the lyrics to "The Anniversary Song."

B323 Rotha, Paul. *Movie Parade.* London and New York: Studio Publications, 1936. An illustrated history of international film, including a still from *The Singing Fool.*

B324 Rowland, Mabel, ed. *Bert Williams, Son of Laughter.* The English Crafters, 1923. Jolson's encounters with Williams are examined in this biography of the stage star.

B325 Runyon, Damon. *Short Takes.* New York: McGraw-Hill Book Co., 1945. Includes "Mammy Man," an essay by Runyon on Jolson.

B326   Russell, Francis. *The Shadow of Blooming Groves. Warren Harding and His Times*. New York: McGraw-Hill Book Co., 1968.   Refers to Jolson and quotes the lyrics of "Harding (You're the Man For Us)," Harding's campaign song purportedly written by Jolson, along with lyrics to an unpublished song, "Take Away the Gun From Every Mother's Son," which Jolson also "wrote" for Harding.

B327   Sampson, Henry T. *Blacks in Blackface: A Sourcebook on Early Black Musical Shows*. Metuchen, N.J., 1980.   Jolson's blackface performances are touched on in this history of black musical comedy.

B328   Sanders, Ronald. *The Downtown Jews: Portraits of an Immigrant Generation*. New York, 1987.   Jolson is one of Sanders' examples of a prominent Jew in popular entertainment and American culture in general.

B329   Sarris, Andrew. *The American Cinema. Directors and Directions. 1929-1968*. New York: Dutton, 1968.   Focuses on American film directors, including mentions of Jolson's films and their directors.

B330   Sayler, Oliver. *Our American Theatre*. Westport, Connecticut: Greenwood Press, 1970 (reprinted from Brentano's edition, 1923).   Sayler refers to Jolson and Will Rogers as the flourishing comedians on the American popular stage in the post-World War I era.

B331   Schatz, Thomas. *The Genius of the System. Hollywood Filmmaking in the Studio Era*. New York: Pantheon Books, 1988.   This scholarly history of the Hollywood studio system includes an examination of the making and importance of *The Jazz Singer*, including a still of Jolson in a scene from the film.

B332   Scheuer, Steven H. *The Movie Book*. Chicago Illinois: The Ridge Press and Playboy Press, 1974.   A heavily illustrated compendium of the golden age of Hollywood films includes references to Jolson, *The Jazz Singer*, and *The Jolson Story*.

B333   Schwartz, Charles. *Cole Porter. A Biography*. New York: The Dial Press, 1977.   Schwartz makes some references to the formulaic qualities of Jolson's films *The Jazz Singer* and *The Singing Fool*.

B334   ----------. *Gershwin. His Life and Music*. Indianapolis and New York: Bobbs-Merrill, 1973.   Jolson's friendship and professional connection with Gershwin is discussed.

B335   Seldes, Gilbert. *The Seven Lively Arts*. New York: Harper & Bros., 1924.   Includes Seldes' essay "The Daemonic in the American Theatre," an examination of the styles of Fanny Brice and Jolson.

B336   Sennett, Ted. *Hollywood Musicals*. New York: Harry N. Abrams, 1981.   Sennett's survey of movie musicals touches on Jolson's films.

B337   ----------. *Lunatics and Lovers*. New Rochelle, New York: Arlington House,

1973. This survey of screwball comedy includes a brief discussion of the transition to talkies via *The Jazz Singer*.

B338 ----------, ed. *The Old-Time Radio Book*. New York: Pyramid, 1976. Includes information on Jolson's radio work.

B339 ----------. *Warner Bros. Presents*. New Rochelle, New York: Arlington House, 1971. Jolson's films for Warner Bros. are examined in this survey of the studio's history.

B340 Settel, Irving. *A Pictorial History of Radio*. Secaucus, New Jersey: The Citadel Press, 1962. Includes a 1949 photo of Jolson with Bing Crosby on Crosby's radio show.

B341 Shaw, Arnold. *Dictionary of American Pop/Rock and Blues*. New York: Schirmer Books, 1982. Jolson is referred to in this dictionary of popular music in America.

B342 ----------. *The Jazz Age: Popular Music in the 1920's*. New York, 1987. Jolson's predominance as a singer is examined.

B343 ----------. *What is the Secret Magic of Belafonte?* New York: Pyramid Books, 1960. Jolson is cited as a popular singer influencing performers of a later era.

B344 Shipman, David. *The Great Movie Stars: The Golden Years*. London: Hamlyn, 1970. Makes reference to Jolson as a film star of the late 1920's and the early 1930's.

B345 ----------. *The Great Movie Stars: The International Years*. London: Angus and Robertson, 1972. Jolson is mentioned as a great film star of the early days of talkies.

B346 Siegel, Scott and Barbara. *Encyclopedia of Hollywood*. Facts on File, 1990. Includes an entry on Jolson.

B347 Silke, James R. *Here's Looking at You, Kid. Fifty Years of Fighting, Working and Dreaming at Warner Bros.* Boston: Little, Brown and Company, 1976. This heavily illustrated survey of the great Warner Bros. films refers to Jolson's movies, particularly *The Jazz Singer*.

B348 Skolsky, Sidney. *Don't Get Me Wrong -- I Love Hollywood*. New York: Putnam, 1975. Skolsky's involvement in the creation of *The Jolson Story* is recalled in this memoir.

B349 Slide, Anthony. *The Vaudevillians. A Dictionary of Vaudeville Performers*. New York: Arlington House, 1981. Jolson is included among the great vaudevillians of the popular stage.

B350 Slobin, Mark. *Tenement Songs. The Popular Music of the Jewish Immigrants*. Urbana, Chicago and London: University of Illinois Press, 1982. Jolson, as a major figure in American Jewish culture, and *The Jazz Singer* are discussed in some depth.

B351 Smith, Bill. *The Vaudevillians*. New York: Macmillan, 1976. Jolson is referred to in this memoir of the great vaudeville performers.

B352 Smith, Cecil and Glenn Litton. *Musical Comedy in America*. New York: Theatre Arts Books, 1950, 1981. Includes many references to Jolson and a photograph from *Robinson Crusoe, Jr.*

B353 Sollors, Werner. *Beyond Ethnicity: Consent and Descent in American Culture*. New York, 1986. Jolson's Jewish heritage and his blackface performance style is referred to in this cultural survey.

B354 Spaeth, Sigmund. *The Facts of Life in Popular Song*. New York: McGraw-Hill Book Co., 1934. Jolson's work as a singer and songwriter is touched on in this examination of popular music.

B355 ----------. *A History of Popular Music in America*. New York: Random House, 1948. Includes many references to Jolson.

B356 Springer, John. *All Talking! All Singing! All Dancing!* Secaucus, New Jersey: The Citadel Press, 1966. Includes numerous references to Jolson's films, especially *The Jazz Singer* and *The Singing Fool*, as well as *The Jolson Story*.

B357 ----------. *They Sang, They Danced, They Romanced. Hollywood Musicals From Sound Until Today*. Secaucus, New Jersey: The Citadel Press, 1966, 1991. A pictorial history of Hollywood musicals includes stills and commentary on *The Jazz Singer*, *The Singing Fool*, *The Jolson Story*, and *Jolson Sings Again.*

B358 Stagg, Jerry. *The Brothers Shubert*. New York: Random House, 1968. Includes many references to Jolson as a Shubert star, and several photographs of Jolson, on-stage and off.

B359 Stein, Charles W., ed. *American Vaudeville As Seen By Its Contemporaries*. New York: Alfred A. Knopf, 1984. Jolson is referred to in a number of performer's recollections of the vaudeville era.

B360 Sterling, Christopher H. and John M. Kittross. *Stay Tuned. A Concise History of American Broadcasting*. Second Edition. Belmont, California: Wadsworth Publishing Company. Includes references to Jolson's switch to radio from the stage.

B361 Stern, Lee Edward. *The Movie Musical*. New York, 1974. Jolson's film musicals are touched on in this survey of the genre.

B362 Stevens, Ashton. *Actorsviews*. Chicago: Convici-McGee, 1923. In this collection of Chicago theatre critic Stevens' feature interviews, "Al Jolson Acts Up for His Bride" is included. Stevens interviewed Jolson during the Chicago run of *Bombo*, and reports on the relationship of Jolson and his second wife, Ethel Delmar, and their whirlwind life.

B363 Stuart, Ian, ed. *Immortals of the Screen*. New York: Bonanza Books, 1965. This largely pictorial book contains a two-page spread on Jolson, including a portrait and stills from *The Jazz Singer, The Singing Fool, Say It With Songs, Mammy*, and *Go Into Your Dance*.

B364 Suskin, Steven. *Opening Night on Broadway*. New York: Schirmer Books, 1990. Jolsonesque aspects in the work of Eddie Fisher, Joel Grey and Sammy Davis, Jr. is referred to in this compendium of Broadway shows since 1943.

B365 Taylor, Deems. *Some Enchanted Evenings. The Story of Rodgers and Hammerstein*. New York: Harper & Bros., 1953. Includes references to Jolson's appearance in *Hallelujah, I'm a Bum*, for which Rodgers composed music with lyrics by Lorenz Hart.

B366 Terrace, Vincent. *Radio's Golden Years. The Encyclopedia of Radio Programs, 1930-1960*. San Diego and New York: A.S. Barnes Company. Includes references to Jolson's various radio series and appearances.

B367 Thomas, Bob. *Clown Prince of Hollywood. The Antic Life and Times of Jack L. Warner*. New York: McGraw Hill Publishing Company, 1990. This biography of Warner includes anecdotes about the making of *The Jazz Singer* and Warner's relationship with Jolson, including his attempt to lure Jolson away from Columbia Pictures in order to make *The Jolson Story* at Warner Bros.

B368 ----------. *King Cohn. The Life and Times of Harry Cohn*. New York: G.P. Putnam's Sons, 1967. Biography of Columbia Pictures' mogul Harry Cohn includes a chapter on the making of *The Jolson Story*, stressing Cohn's respect for Jolson and his occasional qualms about the viability of the project, which ultimately became one of Columbia's greatest financial successes.

B369 ----------. *Winchell*. Garden City, New York: Doubleday, 1971. Jolson's tempestuous relationship with Winchell is recounted in this biography of the columnist.

B370 Thomas, Nicholas, ed. *International Dictionary of Films & Filmmakers*. Detroit, Michigan/London: St. James Press, 1985, 1990, 1992. Volume 1 (Films) and Volume 3 (Actors and Actresses) of the 1990-92 version, include valuable entries *The Jazz Singer* and Jolson, respectively.

B371 Thomas, Tony. *The Films of the Forties*. Secaucus, New Jersey: The Citadel Press, 1975. This pictorial account of the great films of the 1940's includes a two-page spread on *The Jolson Story*.

B372 ----------. *Harry Warren and the Hollywood Musical*. Secaucus, New Jersey: The Citadel Press, 1975. Warren's songwriting for Jolson's films is referred to in this examination of Warren's work.

B373 ---------- and Aubrey Solomon. *The Films of 20th Century Fox*. Secaucus, New

Jersey: The Citadel Press, 1985. This lavishly illustrated survey of all of the Fox feature films includes illustrations and information about Jolson's three Fox films, *Rose of Washington Square*, *Hollywood Cavalcade*, and *Swanee River*.

B374 Thompson, Charles. *Bing*. New York: David McKay Company, 1975. This biography of the great crooner includes references to Crosby's admiration of Jolson and their joint radio appearances.

B375 Thrasher, Frederick. *Okay For Sound: How the Screen Found Its Voice*. New York, 1946. Jolson and *The Jazz Singer* figure prominently in this history of the arrival of the talkies.

B376 Toll, Robert C. *On With the Show. The First Century of Show Business in America*. New York/Oxford: Oxford University Press, 1976. Includes several references to Jolson's stage work, particularly his early years.

B377 Treadwell, Bill. *50 Years of American Comedy*. Exposition Press, 1951. Jolson's work as a comedian is included in this history of American comedy.

B378 Trotta, Vincent and Cliff Lewis. *Screen Personalities*. New York: Grosset and Dunlap, 1933. The many profiles making up this book include Jolson and Ruby Keeler.

B379 Tucker, Sophie. *Some of These Days*. Garden City, New York: Garden City Publishing Co., 1945. Jolson's interaction with Tucker is recalled in the memoirs of the "Last of the Red Hot Mommas."

B380 Tynan, Kenneth. *Curtains*. London: Longmans, 1961. *The Jolson Story* is referred to as a popular American film by the English critic.

B381 ----------. *He That Plays the King*. London: Longmans, 1950. Tynan compares Danny Kaye to Jolson.

B382 ----------. *Tynan Right and Left*. London: Longmans, 1957.

B383 Ulanov, Barry. *A History of Jazz in America*. New York: The Viking Press, 1952. Includes a number of references to Jolson and *The Jazz Singer*. Ulanov depicts Jolson as the embodiment of American jazz in the 1920's.

B384 Vallance, Tom. *The American Musical*. New York: Barnes, 1970. Jolson's significance as a musical comedy performer is examined.

B385 Vermilye, Jerry. *The Films of the Twenties*. Secaucus, New Jersey: The Citadel Press, 1985. *The Singing Fool* is included in this heavily illustrated overview of the films of the 1920's.

B386 Vinson, James, ed. *Actors and Actresses*. Chicago, 1986. Makes reference to Jolson's predominance as a musical comedy performer.

B387 Wagner, Walter. *You Must Remember This*. New York: G.P. Putnam's Sons,

1975. This collection of reminiscences about the heyday of Hollywood includes a chapter on George Jessel's involvement with *The Jazz Singer* and Jolson.

B388 Walker, Alexander. *The Shattered Silents: How the Talkies Came To Stay.* New York: William Morrow, 1979. As its title suggests, Walker's book examines the transition from silent films to sound, with some emphasis on the significance of *The Jazz Singer,* but, more importantly, *The Singing Fool,* a film of such phenomenal success that it led to most of America's film theatres being wired for sound.

B389 ----------. *Stardom.* London: Michael Joseph, 1970. This analysis of the "Hollywood phenomenon" makes mention of Jolson, noting that audiences of the 1920's "got aroused by Al Jolson or Billy Sunday or anybody else who put his heart into his job."(p. 136)

B390 Walker, Leo. *The Wonderful Era of the Great Dance Bands.* Howell-North Brooks, 1964. Includes a photograph of Jolson with President Calvin Coolidge.

B391 Walker, Stanley. *The Night Club Era.* With an Introduction by Alva Johnson. New York: Frederick A. Stokes Company, 1933. Jolson and Ruby Keeler figure among the notables of the nightclub world of the 1920's and early 1930's.

B392 *The Warner Brothers Golden Anniversary Book.* New York: Dell, 1973. Includes references to Jolson's Warner movies.

B393 Warner, Jack L. *My First Hundred Years in Hollywood.* With Dean Jennings. New York: Random House, 1964. Warner recalls his friendship with Jolson and the making of *The Jazz Singer* in this memoir.

B394 Waters, Ethel. *His Eye Is On the Sparrow.* With Charles Samuels. New York: Doubleday, 1951. Waters includes her assessment of Jolson and recalls a dinner in Chicago in 1931 at which both she and Jolson performed.

B395 Wenzel, Lynn and Carol J. Binkowski. *I Hear America Singing. A Nostalgic Tour of Popular Sheet Music.* New York: Crown Publishers, 1989. Includes reproductions of Jolson sheet music.

B396 Whitcomb, Ian. *Irving Berlin and Ragtime America.* London: Century, 1987. Refers to Jolson's importance as a singer of popular songs.

B397 Whiting, Margaret and Will Holt. *It Might As Well Be Spring.* New York: William Morrow, 1987. Whiting recalls appearing with Jolson on the Kraft Music Hall.

B398 Wilde, Larry. *The Great Comedians Talk About Comedy.* New York: The Citadel Press, 1968. A collection of interviews about comedy with a wide array of talents, from Woody Allen to Ed Wynn. Many of them make mention of Jolson's skills as a performer.

B399 Wiley, Mason and Damien Bona. *Inside Oscar. The Unofficial History of the Academy Awards.* New York: Ballantine Books, 1986. Includes several references to Jolson's involvement, particularly with the first Academy Awards banquet.

B400 Wilk, Max. *They're Playing Our Song.* New York: Atheneum, 1973. Jolson as a singer and songwriter is referred to in this survey of American popular music.

B401 *Will Rogers Weekly Articles.* Oklahoma: Oklahoma State University Press, 1982. Rogers makes references to Jolson in Vol. 3, p. 126 (January 29, 1928), Vol. 5, p. 233 (February 19, 1933), and Vol. 6, pp. 21-22 (May 21, 1933).

B402 Wilson, Earl. *The Show Business Nobody Knows.* Chicago and New York: Cowles Book Company, Inc., 1971. Columnist Wilson recalls his show business experiences, and a few brief anecdotes about Jolson.

B403 Woll, Allen L. *Songs From Hollywood Musical Comedies, 1927 to the Present: A Dictionary.* New York: Garland, 1978. Includes references to many songs sung and written by Jolson.

B404 Wright, Basil. *The Long View.* London: Martin Secker and Warburg, 1974. This history of movies analyzes the importance of *The Jazz Singer* in the transition to sound film, and Wright notes that theatre stars in early movies such as "Jolson and Eddie Cantor, found a new life not merely by adapting but by developing their existing techniques; not in fact very difficult, this, since their films were nearly all backstage musicals, and thus involved no more than an enlargement of scale."(pp. 128-129)

B405 Wylie, Max, ed. *Best Broadcasts of 1938-39.* New York and London: Whittsley House. Jolson's radio work in referred to in this look at radio programs of 1938-39.

B406 Zierold, Norman. *The Moguls.* New York: Coward-McCann, 1969. This treatise on the great movie moguls touches on Jolson's relationships with Jack L. Warner and Harry Cohn.

B407 Zinman, David. *Saturday Afternoon at the Bijou.* New Rochelle, New York: Arlington House, 1973. Jolson's films are referred to in this anecdotal look at the movies.

B408 Zolotow, Maurice. *No People Like Show People.* New York: Random House, 1951. Includes an anecdote about Jolson interrupting Jimmy Durante's act in 1929.

B409 Zwisohn, Laurence J. *Bing Crosby: A Lifetime of Music.* Los Angeles, California: Palm Tree Library, 1978. The influence of Jolson on Crosby, as well as their work together, is examined.

PERIODICALS/MAGAZINES

PM1   Ager, Cecilia. "Re. The Movies." *Park East*, October 1952.
PM2   Akst, Harry. "The Jolson Nobody Knew." As Told to Ernest Lehman. *Cosmopolitan*, February 1951, pp. 33-36, 106-117.
PM3   ----------. "Love That Fisher." *TV World*, September 1954.
PM4   "Al Jolson." *Metronome*, January 1951, p. 33.
PM5   "Al Jolson." *Music Memories*, July 1961.
PM6   "Al Jolson." *Radio Album*, Summer 1948, p. 19.
PM7   "Al Jolson." *Radio Guide*, February 27, 1937, cover story.
PM8   "Al Jolson." *Radio Stars Magazine*, May 1934.
PM9   "Al Jolson." *Theatre*, April 1918, Vol. XXVII, No. 206, p. 201.
PM10 "Al Jolson." *Time*, October 11, 1943, p. 39.
PM11 "Al Jolson." *Time*, July 12, 1948, p. 31.
PM12 "Al Jolson." *Time*, October 9, 1950, p. 43.
PM13 "Al Jolson -- Adventurer in Entertainment." *Radio Guide*, February 13, 1937, p. 22.
PM14 "Al Jolson--Beloved Minstrel." (illustrated by Fred B. Guardineer) *Juke Box Comics*, Vol. 1, No. 1, July-August 1948.
PM15 "Al Jolson Leaves Hidden Treasure in Bank Vault." *The New Musical Express*, November 14, 1958.
PM16 "Al Jolson Says *Merry Christmas* With Songs." *Screenland*, December 1929.
PM17 "The Al Jolson Show." *Radio Album*, Winter 1942.
PM18 "Al Jolson (Lifebuoy) Will Conclude His Series.' *Radio Guide*, March 18, 1939, p. 5.
PM19 "Al Jolson Writes and Acts a Scenario." *The Call*, April 18, 1914.
PM20 "Al Jolson Writes His Own Life Story." *Metronome*, September 1935, pp. 26, 72.
PM21 "Al's Golden Dollars." *Picture Play*, January 1933.
PM22 "An Open Letter to Ruby Keeler." *Screenland*, October 1933.
PM23 Anderson, Dick. "Jolson Sings Again." *Shazam*, No. 3 (fanzine), Autumn 1963.
PM24 "Assignment in Hollywood." *Good Housekeeping*, December 1946, Vol. 23, pp. 12-13.
PM25 "At Home With the Al Jolsons." *Picturegoer*, February 13, 1937, p. 19.
PM26 Aylesworth, Merlin H. "*Mammy* Man Nervous But Colossal as Per Usual." *Collier's Magazine*, November 1932.
PM27 Banner, Jack. "The Private Life of Walter Winchell." *Radio Guide*, March 2, 1935, pp. 8, 29.
PM28 ----------. "These Feuding Stars." *Radio Guide*, May 25, 1935, pp. 4-5.
PM29 Baskette, Kirtley. "Everybody's Stooging Now." *Photoplay*, February 1934, pp. 52-53, 117-119.
PM30 ----------. "The Man All Hollywood Fears." *Photoplay*, November 1933.
PM31 ----------. "Now--It's Horses." *Photoplay*, February 1936.
PM32 Beasley, Irene. "So You Want to Go On the Air." *Radio Guide*, October 27, 1934, p. 4.
PM33 Belfrage, Cedric. "Al Jolson Answers Chaplin." *Motion Picture*, August 1929, 38:28-29, 109.
PM34 ----------. "Let Jolson Sing and He's Happy." *Motion Picture*, February 1930, p. 39.
PM35 ----------. "They Still Play You, Sonny Boy!" *Motion Picture Classic*, June

1930, p. 32.

PM36 Belton, John. "The Backstage Musical." *Movie*, Spring 1977, No. 24, pp. 36-44.

PM37 Benchley, Robert. "Continued Applause." *Life*, January 29, 1925, p. 18.

PM38 Bentinck, Henry. "The Fascinating Romance of Al Jolson and Ruby Keeler." *Radio Guide*, April 19, 1934, pp. 3, 38; April 21, 1934, pp. 2-3, 29; April 28, 1934, pp. 2-3, 34; May 5, 1934, pp. 2-3, 34; May 12, 1934, pp. 3, 34; May 26, 1934, pp. 2, 38; June 2, 1934, pp. 9, 39.

PM39 Berg, Shelley. "Yours in Pain--Al." *The Passing Show*, Summer 1982, Vol. 6, No. 2, pp. 5-7.

PM40 "Biography." *Current Biography*, 1940.

PM41 Black, Bud. "The Vintage Victrola: Facts and Fancies or *Thank you, Mr. Jolson*," *Tape Squeal*, March/April 1992 (reprinted from the December 1970 issue), p. 8.

PM42 "Blackface Hall of Fame." *Theatre*, September 1923.

PM43 Bleeden, Joe. "Al Jolson: One Man's Memories." *Emmy Magazine*, Vol. 8, No. 6, November/December 1986, p. 93.

PM44 Bradford, Kay. "Happy-Go-Lucky." *Screen Romances*, January 1933.

PM45 "Burns and Allen Will Be Jolson's Guests." *Radio Guide*, March 11, 1939, p. 5.

PM46 C.J. "When Mr. and Mrs. Star Together." *Picturegoer Weekly*, July 13, 1935, p. 14.

PM47 "Call for Music." *Radio Album*, Summer 1948, p. 42.

PM48 Carlisle, John. "Ruby Beats the Jolson Jinx." *Screenland*, June 1933, pp. 14, 77-78.

PM49 Casale, Paul and Rick Hoffman. "Al Jolson Sheet Music Catalog." *Sheet Music Exchange*, Vol. VIII, Nos. 4 & 5, August/October 1990.

PM50 Champion, Fred. "Polishing Up the Stars." *Radio Guide*, August 18, 1934, p. 6.

PM51 Cheatham, Maude. "Interview." *Movie Classic*, June 1935, pp. 8-31.

PM52 Clifton, Bernice. "Al Jolson." *Motion Picture*, December 1935.

PM53 ----------. "Appreciation." *Motion Picture*, December 1927, p. 35.

PM54 Clurman, Harold. "The New York Actor: The Truth About Us Is in Our Stars." *New York*, February 11, 1974, pp. 30-39.

PM55 Conacher, Karen. "Unmasking the Minstrel Mask's Black Magic in Ntozake Shange's *spell #7*." *Theatre Journal*, Vol. 44, No. 2, May 1992, pp. 177-193.

PM56 Cook, Burr Chapman. "Manufacturing Stage Laughter." *Theatre*, June 1916, pp. 359-360, 362.

PM57 Coons, Robin. "We Adopted a Baby." *Radio and TV Mirror*, June 1948.

PM58 Cooper, John R. "The Comedians." *Hero-Hobby*, No. 6 (fanzine), Autumn 1966 (part 5), Winter 1966-1967 (part 6).

PM59 "Coronet's Celebrity Night," *Coronet*, March 1948, p. 86.

PM60 "Cover Profile of Al Jolson." *Radio Best*, June 1949.

PM61 Cowley, Robert. "The Phoney Cult of the Classic Film." *Cavalier*, July 1962.

PM62 Crocker, H. "Larry Parks Becomes Jolson's Pal in Preparation For His Part in *The Jolson Story*." *Good Housekeeping*, December 1946, p. 12.

PM63 Cruikshank, Herb. "Interview." *Motion Picture*, November 1928, p. 33.

PM64 Cruikshank, Herb. "What Did Radio Do to Al's Family Life?" *Radio Mirror*, July 1934.

PM65   "The Curtain Falls--A Tribute to Al Jolson." *Famous Stars*, Vol. I, No. 1, May-June 1951.

PM66   Dave, Paul. "You Ain't Heard Nothing Yet -- The Jazz Singer." *Idols*, January 1989.

PM67   "Death of the Jazz Singer." *Life*, November 6, 1950, pp. 115-116, 118.

PM68   Debus, Allen G. "Records of Al Jolson." *Hobbies-The Magazine for Collectors*, April, 1955, p. 25; May, 1955, pp. 27-28; June, 1955, p. 27; July, 1955, p. 27; August, 1955, p. 27.

PM69   Deere, D. "Almost Down to Earth." *Photoplay*, May 1947, pp. 30-36.

PM70   Delamater, Jerome. "Busby Berkeley: An American Surrealist." *Wide Angle*, Spring 1976, No. 1, pp. 30-37.

PM71   Downing, H. "Journey From Fear." *Photoplay*, July 1948, p. 68.

PM72   Dumont, Lou. "Historical Tape Recordings. Radio and TV. Al Jolson." *Hobbies*, V. 79, November 1974, pp. 54-55.

PM73   "Early Musicals." *Hollywood Studio Magazine*, September 1979, Vol. 13, No. 5, p. 14.

PM74   Emge, Charles. "Advent of Sound Recalled by *Jazz Singer* Musician." *Down Beat*, December 17, 1952, p. 22.

PM75   "Ex-Cop Fired for Jolson Skit Wins Court Case.' *Jet*, January 23, 1986, p. 16.

PM76   "Feels Lost When Not in Intimate Contact With His Audience." *Theatre*, July 1929, p. 43.

PM77   Fenton, Maurice. "The Birth of the Theme Song." *Photoplay*, November 1929.

PM78   Fidler, Jimmy. "Behind the Hollywood Front." *Radio Mirror*, August 1937.

PM79   Fleming, William J. "King of Cork." *Illustrated World*, January 1923, Vol. 38, pp. 663-665.

PM80   "Flicker Veteran. *Cue*, July 20, 1935.

PM81   Fontaine, Leo. "It Must Be Love." *Radio Guide*, September 2, 1933, p. 3.

PM82   French, William F. "Al Knows Better Now." *Photoplay*, November 1933, pp. 37, 108-111.

PM83   ----------. "The Bond Hollywood Can't Break." *Picture Play*, May 1936, p. 40.

PM84   ----------. "The Love Story of Al and Ruby." *Motion Picture*, March 1935, p. 36.

PM85   ----------. "Only Al Jolson Wanted to Play." *Photoplay*, March 1934, pp. 31-33, 111-112.

PM86   Friedman, Favius. "Unsinkable Al." *Radio Best*, February 1948, pp. 11-14, 19.

PM87   "From Bellevue to Broadway." *Confidential*, July 1954.

PM88   "Gard's Chosen People." *Radio Mirror*, December 1933.

PM89   Garrett, Betty. "I'm Just Wild About Larry Parks." *Photoplay*, October 1948, p. 48.

PM90   Gilmore, Francis. "Oh, Mammy. Al Jolson Sings the Celluloid Blues." *Motion Picture Classic*, November 1927, p. 25.

PM91   "Go Into Your Dance." *Popular Song Hits*, June 1935.

PM92   "Go Into Your Dance." *Screen Romances*, May 1935.

PM93   Goldman, Herbert J. "M-M-M-Mammy's Boy." *Moment*, November 1988, pp. cover, 22-29, 46-49.

PM94   Gomery, J. Douglas. "Article." *Screen*, Spring 1976.

PM95   Gordon, Franklin. "Jolson." *American Hebrew*, September 6, 1929, pp. 422,

425.

PM96   Gottschall, Morton. "The Story Behind The Jolson Story." *Alumnus* (alumni magazine of The City College of the City University of New York), October 1950, Vol. 46, No. 1, pp. 15-16.

PM97   Gould, Bob. "No Wedding Ring! No Picture, Says Ruby." *RKO Movie Parade Magazine*, June 1938.

PM98   Grant, Jack. "Jolson Says He's Leaving the Movies." *Movie Classic*, April 1934, p. 46.

PM99   "Great Jolson Recordings." *Music Memories*, July 1961.

PM100   Green, Chet. "Yours Truly Rural, Al Jolson." *Photoplay*, May 1936, p. 28-29, 84.

PM101   "Hail, Hail, The Gang's All Here." *Radio Mirror*, December 1937.

PM102   Hale, Barbara. "Jolson's Other Wife." *Screen Guide*, November 1949.

PM103   Hands, Martin. "Jolson - Was He a Man or a Myth?" *Picturegoer*, December 19, 1953.

PM104   Hanks, Stephen. "The Jolson Story." *Memories*, October 1990, pp. 46-51.

PM105   "Happy Ending." *Time*, May 26, 1947, pp. 52-53.

PM106   Harris, Radie. "And Now There is Al Jolson, Jr." *Photoplay*, July 1935, pp. 24-25, 106.

PM107   Hastings, Charles. "The True Jolson Story." *Motion Picture*, November 1947, pp. 40-41, 78-80.

PM108   Hastings, Tom. "Sonny Boy." *Photoplay*, January 1929, pp. 29, 101.

PM109   Haynes, Ernest. "Mammy." *Screen Secrets*, May 1928.

PM110   Hempel, Amy. "In the Cementery Where Al Jolson Is Buried." *Tri-Quarterly*, No. 78, Spring/Summer 1983, pp. 175-182; reprinted in No. 63, 1985, pp. 532-539; reprinted in No. 78, Spring/Summer 1990, pp. 160-167.

PM111   Hoberman, J. "Yiddish Transit." *Film Comment*, July-August 1981, Vol. 17, p. 36.

PM112   Hoffman, Jerry. "Westward the Course of Tin-Pan Alley." *Photoplay*, September 1929.

PM113   Hogarth, D. "Dancing Thru." *Silver Screen*, May 1936, pp. 6-7.

PM114   "Hollywood Cavalcade." *Photoplay*, December 1939.

PM115   "Hollywood Hobbies." *Talking Screen*, October 1930.

PM116   "Hollywood Is Domestic." *Screenland*, April 1935.

PM117   Hopper, Hedda. "Watch Larry Parks." *Modern Screen*, October 1946, pp. 44-45, 94-96.

PM118   Howard, Clive. "A Fortune in Old Wax." *Varsity*, February 1949.

PM119   Hoyt, Caroline Somers. "How Jolson Came Back." *Radio Stars*, November 1933.

PM120   ----------. "It's Ruby's Turn Now." *Modern Screen*, October 1933.

PM121   Hutchens, John. "Al Jolson and Others." *Theatre Arts Monthly,* May 1931, Vol. 15, p. 366-374.

PM122   "Interview with Al Jolson." *Downbeat*, May 15, 1943.

PM123   "Is Al Jolson Through?" *Screen Book*, May 1933.

PM124   Isaacs, Charles. "Swanee Song." *Park East*, October 1951.

PM125   "It's All Greek to the Greeks." *Radio Mirror*, November 1937.

PM126   Jacobs, Mary. "Al Jolson Can't Let Radio Lick Him!" *Radioland*, July 1934, pp. 24-25, 71.

PM127   Jay, Dave [Wigransky]. "Al Jolson. The World's Greatest Entertainer. *Radio Dial*, No. 5 (fanzine of Radio Historical Society), Winter 1968-1969.

PM128   "Jews on the Screen." *Film Comment*, July-August 1981, Vol. 17, pp. 34-48.

PM129 Johnston, Carol. "The Mammy Man." *Motion Picture Classic*, January 1929, p. 51.

PM130 Jolson, Al. "Al Jolson Answers His Fans." *Screen Secrets*, January 1930.

PM131 ----------. "Al Jolson Writes His Own Life Story." *Metronome*, September 1935.

PM132 ----------. "Archie, The Manager -- I Knew Ed Gardner When." *Radio Best*, 1940's.

PM133 ----------. "The Art of Minstrelsy." *Theatre*, May 1918, Vol. XXVII, No. 207, pp. 290, 292.

PM134 ----------. *"Dat Ol Debbil* Radio Exposed by Al Jolson." *Radio Guide*, April 7, 1934, p 11.

PM135 ----------. "From Mammy to Mike." As Told to Jerry Wald. *Radio Mirror*, December 1933, pp. 6-7, 59.

PM136 ----------. "Here's One You'll Like." *Illustrated World*, January 1923, Vol. 38, pp. 665-667, 780-781.

PM137 ----------. "If I Don't Get Laughs and Don't Get Applause -- The Mirror Will Show Me Who is to Blame." *American Magazine*, April 1919, pp. 18-19, 154-158.

PM138 ----------. "Making People Laugh." *Green Book Magazine*, Vol. 14, August 1915, p. 333.

PM139 ----------. "My First Days in Hollywood." *Moving Picture Stories*, pp. 10-11, 33.

PM140 ----------. "My First Day in Pictures." *Theater*, October 1927, Vol. XLVI, No. 319, p. 9.

PM141 ----------. "The Role I Liked Best." *Saturday Evening Post*, August 31, 1946.

PM142 ----------. "Sound Idea." *Saturday Evening Post*, 1946.

PM143 ----------. "Sure I Miss the Stage." *Theatre*, July 1929, p. 43.

PM144 ----------. "Training An Audience to Laugh." *Theatre*. October 1913, Vol. 18, pp. 134, 136, vi.

PM145 ----------. "What's Wrong With Radio." *Radio Guide*, December 7, 1935, p. 7.

PM146 Jolson, Erle Galbraith. "My Husband Al Jolson." As told to Jerry Wald. *Radio Mirror*, December 1947.

PM147 Jolson, Harry. "Under the Cork." *The Saturday Evening Post*, December 7/28, 1929.

PM148 "Jolson Estate Sues Decca on Royalties." *Billboard*, March 19, 1955, p. 14.

PM149 "Jolson Monument Planned for Coast." *Billboard*, February 17, 1951, p. 3.

PM150 "Jolson On USO Tour." *Time*, October 11, 1943

PM151 "Jolson Resurgent." *Cue*, May 3, 1947, pp. 12-13.

PM152 "Jolson Sings Again." *Life*, September 12, 1949, pp. 93-94.

PM153 "Jolson Sings Again." *Movie Story*, November 1949, p. 25.

PM154 "Jolson Sings Again." *Picturegoer*, December 31, 1949, pp. 10-11.

PM155 "Jolson Sings Again." *Screen Stories*, November 1949, pp. 47-51, 78-79.

PM156 "Jolson Still *World's Greatest Entertainer.*" *Cosmopolitan*, November 1958.

PM157 "The Jolson Story." *Look*, October 29, 1946. Illustrated review of the film.

PM158 "The Jolson Story." *Screen Romances*, November 1946, pp. 34-36, 68-74.

PM159 "Jolson Super-Salesman of Song." *Metronome*, September 1935, pp. 26, 41.

PM160 "Jolson Talks About Film Rehearsals." *Radio Guide*, February 17, 1939, p. 15.

PM161 "The Jolsons." *Radio Stars*, November 1934.

PM162 "Jolson's $7,000 Night." *Varsity Magazine*, March 30, 1921.

PM163   Jones, Carlisle. "Marriage Before a Career." *Picturegoer*, February 10, 1934.

PM164   ----------. "The Inside Story of the Keeler-Jolson Household." *Shadowplay*, December 1934, pp. 20-21, 68.

PM165   Kaczynski, Dolores. "The Jolson Epic." *Theme*, December 1953/January 1954; March 1954.

PM166   Kaczynski, Dolores. "The Jolson Legend." *Pat Schnee's International Set Magazine*, Spring 1957.

PM167   Kantor, MacKinlay. "They Loved Me in Korea." *True*, February 1951, pp. 26-28, 92-96.

PM168   Kaufman, George S. "The Other Side of Al Jolson." *Everybody's Magazine*, April 1921, Vol. 44, p. 16-17.

PM169   Keeler, Mrs. Ralph. "My Son, Al Jolson." *Radio Stars*, July 1935, pp. 33, 72.

PM170   Kelly, Fred. "Hollywood Bows to Radio." *Radio Guide*, December 21, 1935, p. 6.

PM171   Kerr, Bess. "To Break Your Heart." *Motion Picture*, February 1962.

PM172   Kiner, Larry F. "Al Jolson Discography." *Theme*, November 1954.

PM173   Kinzlev, Morris. "Jolson's Chauffeur is Al's Friend and Pal." *Screen Mirror*, November 1930.

PM174   Knight, Arthur. "Busby Berkeley." *Action*, May-June 1974, No. 9, pp. 11-16.

PM175   Kobal, John. "Al Jolson & Wonder-bar." *Film*, Summer 1970, pp. 21-23.

PM176   Kolososki, Bob. "All That Jazz." *Chuck Schaden's Nostalgia Digest*,6, October-November 1992, pp. 2-5.

PM177   Kupferberg, Audrey. "The Jazz Singer." *Take One*, January 1978, Vol. 6, pp. 28-32. (also includes "Opening Night: A Memoir From The Only Warner Who Was There" by George Morris (p. 32) and "*The Jazz Singer*: Debunking a Few Myths" by Joe Medjuck (p. 32).

PM178   Kursh, Harry. "Treasury in Old Records." *Coronet*, May 1953, pp. 34-37.

PM179   Lang, H. "Interview." *Movie Classic*, June 1936, p. 28.

PM180   Lee, Kenyon. "It's Raining Violets for Al." *Screen Guide*, December 1947, p. 72.

PM181   Lee, Sonia. "Al Jolson Gives Up Two Million Dollars." *Motion Picture*, August 1932, p. 31.

PM182   ----------. "Mrs. Jolson Enters Films. Al Not Afraid He Will Lose Her." *Movie Classic*, November 1932, p. 29.

PM183   Lester, Gene. "His Honor, Mayor Jolson: Encino, California." *Radio Guide*, September 11, 1937, pp. 24-26.

PM184   Lewis, Martin. "Along the Airrialto." *Radio Guide*, April 7, 1934, p. 9.

PM185   ----------. "Along the Airrialto." *Radio Guide*, July 14, 1934, p. 4.

PM186   ----------. "Along the Airrialto." *Radio Guide*, August 25, 1934, p. 6.

PM187   ----------. "Along the Airrialto." *Radio Guide*, May 4, 1935, p. 7.

PM188   ----------. "Inside Stuff." *Radio Guide*, October 3, 1936, p. 12.

PM189   Lindemann, Herman, Jr. "You Ain't Heard Nothing Yet. The Story of Al Jolson." *The World of Yesterday*, July 1977, No. 12, pp. 1-20.

PM190   Locke, Quentin (with Manny Weltman). "Al Jolson." *Shocking Screen*, January 1969.

PM191   MacAndrew, John. "Star-Studded Shellac." *Record Changer*, November 4, 1955, p. 18.

PM192   Maddox, B. "Larry's Phenomenal Swoop." *Silver Screen*, November 1947, p. 46.

PM193 "Mammy!" *Photoplay*, November 1927, p. 78.

PM194 "Mammy Songs And How." *Picturegoer*, January 1931.

PM195 Manners, D. "Not Quitting the Screen." *Motion Picture*, November 1933, p. 41.

PM196 "Martha Raye Set for Show at $1,000 Per Week." *Radio Guide*, December 12, 1936, p. 15.

PM197 McConnell, Sheldon. "How to Imitate the Stars." *Hi Fi Tape Recording*, September 1957.

PM198 McVeigh, Gladys. "Jolson Shares the Spotlight." *Screen Play*, April 1934, pp. 48-49, 70.

PM199 "The Melody Lingers On." *Hollywood Year Book*, 1951.

PM200 Mermey, Maurice. "The Vanishing Fiddler." *North American Review*, March 1929, pp. 301-307.

PM201 Michaels, Joan. "The Guy Who Plays Jolson." *Movieland*, May 1946, pp. 42-44, 99-100.

PM202 Miller, Don. "Films on TV." *Films in Review*, April 1962, Vol. XIII, No. 4, pp. 239-241.

PM203 Mitchell, Curtis. "The True Story of Why Jolson Quit." *Radio Stars*, June 1933.

PM204 Mitchell, Walt. "From Horn to Mike. The Al Jolson Discography. "*The World of Yesterday*, July 1977, No. 12, pp. 21-29; December 1977, No 13, pp. 21-24.

PM205 Moffitt, C.F. "Censorship for Interviews Hollywood's Latest Wild Idea." *Cinema Digest*, January 9, 1933, p. 9.

PM206 Mooring, W.H. "Brooklyn Cinderella." *Film Weekly*, April 17, 1937.

PM207 Morton, Rex. "Say, Don't You Remember? They Called Him Al and the Rest of the Name Was Jolson." *The New Musical Express*, July 30, 1954.

PM208 Mulholland, Bland. "Al Jolson Surrenders." *Radio Stars*, February 1933.

PM209 "The New Pictures." *Time*, October 7, 1946. 9

PM210 "Nominated for Stardom." *Motion Picture*, April 1933, p. 42.

PM211 Norberg, Gunnar. "Memorial of Music." *Radio Guide*, September 11, 1937, pp. 3, 16.

PM212 Nye, Carroll. "The Ad-Lib That Made Movie History." *American History Illustrated*, 1966, Vol. 1, No. 2, pp. 38-43. [An excerpt was reprinted in *Modern Maturity*, June-July 1984].

PM213 Obituaries: *Billboard*, November 4, 1950, 62:55; *Current Biography*, December 1950, p. 25; *Current Biography Yearbook*, 1951, p. 281; *Newsweek*, October 30, 1950, p. 28; *Newsweek*, November 6, 1950, p. 87. Written by John Lardner; *Scholastic*, November 1, 1950, p. 16; *Screen World*, 1951, p. 234; *Senior Scholastic*, November 1, 1950; *Time*, October 30, 1950, p. 89; *Time*, November 6, 1950, p. 43.

PM214 O'Gee, Jay. "Princeton Goes Talkie." *Photoplay*, July 1929.

PM215 "The Original Jazz Singer -- Al Jolson." (illustrated by Charles Wessell. *Super Magician Comics*, Vol. II, No. 2, June 1943.

PM216 O'Sullivan, Joseph. "When the Music Tells the Story." *Motion Picture Herald*, March 4, 1933.

PM217 "Pals Rush to Defend Jolson From Detractors." *Billboard*, February 24, 1951, p. 2.

PM218 Parks, Larry. "Happy Am I." *Photoplay*, February 1949, pp. 40-41, 92.

PM219 Parks, Larry. "I Believe." *Photoplay*, February 1948, p. 44.

PM220 Parks, Larry. "Isn't It Wonderful?" *Photoplay*, February 1950, p. 44.

PM221 Parsons, Frank. "His Light Dimmed by Big Names." *Radio Guide*, September 3, 1933, p. 3.

PM222 Parsons, Louella O. *"Cosmopolitan's* Movie Citations of the Month." *Cosmopolitan*, October 1946, pp. 74.

PM223 ----------. "The Larry Parks Puzzle." *Photoplay*, October 1947, p. 30.

PM224 ----------. "Memorial Column." *Movie Screen*, January 1951.

PM225 Pérez, M. "Le musical avant Busby Berkeley." *Positif*, November-December 1972, No. 144-145, pp. 48-53.

PM226 Perlmutter, Ruth. "The Melting Pot and the Humoring of America: Hollywood and the Jew." *Film Reader*, 1982, Vol. 5, pp. 247-256.

PM227 "Photoplay Award for The Jolson Story." *Photoplay*, March 1948.

PM228 "Photoplay's Gold Medal Party." *Photoplay*, May 1948.

PM229 Plummer, Evans. "Hollywood Showdown." *Radio Guide*, February 4, 1939, p. 12.

PM230 ----------. "Plums and Prunes." *Radio Guide*, April 27, 1935, p. 6.

PM231 Porter, M. "Reviewing Radio." *Radio Guide*, August 20, 1933, p. 20.

PM232 ----------. "Reviewing Radio." *Radio Guide*, August 27, 1933, p. 20.

PM233 ----------. "Reviewing Radio." *Radio Guide*, December 15, 1934, p. 7.

PM234 "A Preview of First Scenes From *Wonder Bar*." *Hollywood*, April 1934.

PM235 Proctor, Kay. "Scared Into Stardom." *Motion Picture*, 1946.

PM236 "Producer Tells of Last Jolson Visit to Studio." *Down Beat*, December 1, 1950, p. 7.

PM237 Raphaelson, Samson. "Article" *American Hebrew*, October 14, 1927, p. 812.

PM238 "The Re-Creation of Al Jolson." *Making Films*, October 1973, p. 22.

PM239 Redd, Robert. "Babes in the Hollywood." *Radio Guide*, March 2, 1935, p. 9.

PM240 Reeves, Mary Watkins. "How Ruby Keeler Holds Her Man." *Film Pictorial*, September 29, 1934.

PM241 "The Return of the Native." *The Playbill* (for *Hold On to Your Hats*), December 30, 1940, pp. 2-3, 6, 34.

PM242 "Return of the Old Jolson." *Parade*, May 30, 1948, pp. 10-11.

PM243 Revell, Nellie. "Behind the Dial." *Radio Tower Magazine*, November 1934.

PM244 Reynolds, Thomas. "Goodbye, Mammy, Hello Drama." *Radio Tower Magazine*, November 1934.

PM245 *"Rhapsody in Blue* Prizewinner for 1946." *Photoplay*, February 1947.

PM246 Robinson, Clarke. "America's Master Minstrel." *World Digest*, December 1940, p. 65.

PM247 Robinson, Hester. "The Fairy Princess of the Films." *The New Movie Magazine*, January 1934.

PM248 Rogin, Michael. "Blackface, White Noise: The Jewish Jazz Singer Finds His Voice." *Critical Inquiry*, Spring 1992, Vol. 18, No. 3, pp. 417-453.

PM249 "Rose of Washington Square." *Movie Mirror*, June 1939.

PM250 Roth, Mark. "Some Warners Musicals and the Spirit of the New Deal." *The Velvet Light Trap*, Winter 1977, No. 17, pp. 1-7.

PM251 "Ruby and Al At Home." *Screenland*, July 1936.

PM252 "Ruby Keeler/Al Jolson." *Movie Mirror*, September 1935.

PM253 "Ruby Keeler (Mrs. Al Jolson) Is Ziegfeld's *Show Girl*." *Theatre*, July 1929, p. 13.

PM254 "Ruby Keeler Tells Intimate Details of Life with Al Jolson." *True Confession*, 1934.

PM255 St. John, Adela Rogers. "Al Jolson." *The New Movie Magazine*. April

1930.

PM256 ----------. "Give This Little Girl a Hand." *Photoplay*, April 1935, pp. 26-27, 106-107.

PM257 Sarris, Andrew. "The Cultural Guilt of Musical Movies. *The Jazz Singer*, Fifty Years After." *Film Comment*, September/October 1977, No. 13, pp. 39-41.

PM258 "Say It With Songs." *Screen Book*, November 1929.

PM259 Schallert, Edwin. "Vitaphone Activity in Hollywood." *Motion Picture News*, July 8, 1927, pp. 35-36.

PM260 Scher, S.N. "The American Film Musical: Golden Age, Neglected Art." *Audience*, April-May 1975, No. 7.

PM261 Scott, Diane. "Larry Parks Sings Again." *Photoplay*, February 1950, p. 44 (also October 1950, p. 46).

PM262 Segal, Alfred. "Al Jolson's Talith." *The American Hebrew*, November 10, 1950.

PM263 Seldes, Gilbert. "Bunk and Hokum on the Stage." *Theatre*, May 1924, Vol. 39, No. 5, pp. 10, 68.

PM264 ----------. "The Daemonic in the American Theatre." *Dial*, September 1923, pp. 303-308.

PM265 "Selling Shell Chateau." *Shell Progress*, January 1936, p. 4.

PM266 Sharpe, Howard. "The Ten Best Gags of Al Jolson." *Liberty*, October 1941, pp. 32-33.

PM267 Shipp, Cameron. "Al Jolson. America's Minstrel Man." *Coronet*, May 1948, pp. 100-104.

PM268 Shteir, Rachel B. "The Vaudeville Mirror. The Best and Worst in the American Character Were Reflected on Vaudeville's Stages." *American Theatre*, September 1992, pp. 12-17.

PM269 Simmons, Matty. "Who Are You Bill Eckstine and Why Are You Saying Those Silly Things About Al Jolson." *Liberty*, Winter 1972, p. 13.

PM270 Simon, George. "The Jolson Story." *Metronome The Review of Modern Music*. July 1947, pp. 11, 44.

PM271 "The Singing Fool." *Screen Book*, December 1928.

PM272 "The Singing Kid." *Picture Play*, June 1936.

PM273 "The Singing Kid." *Screen Romances*, May 1936.

PM274 "Sketch." *Harper's Bazaar*. October 1923, p. 178.

PM275 "Sketch." *National*, January 1925, pp. 269.

PM276 "Sketch." *National*, March 1928, pp. 314.

PM277 "Sketch." *Strand*. March 1915, pp. 278.

PM278 Skinner, Richard Dana. "Al Jolson Again." *Commonweal*, April 23, 1930, pp. 715.

PM279 Skolsky, Sidney. "The Parks Story." *Photoplay*, February 1947, pp. 66-69, 93.

PM280 "*Sounding* a Song." *Photoplay*, January 1929.

PM281 Staunton, D. "Test for Lovers, Hollywood Style." *Silver Screen*, May 1935, p. 27.

PM282 Stewart, Robert. "Al Jolson and the Talkies." *Nostalgia Illustrated*, April 1975.

PM283 Sullivan, Ed. "The Jolson-Crosby Story." *Modern Screen*, August 1947, pp. 85-86.

PM284 Sutton, Sally. "Mammy! Meet Radio-Stage-Screen Star, Al Jolson." *Popular Songs*, December 1935, pp. 24, 32.

PM285 "Swanee River." *Screen Romances*, January 1940.
PM286 Swindell, Larry. "The Day the Silents Stopped." *American Film*, October 1977, Vol. 3, pp. 24-31.
PM287 "The Switcheroo." *Time*, October 6, 1947, p. 78.
PM288 Tankel, Jonathan D. "The Impact of *The Jazz Singer* on the Conversion to Sound." *Journal of the University Film Association*, Winter 1978, Vol. 30, pp. 21-25.
PM289 Teizlin, Ida. "Jazz Singer vs. Hollywood." *Screenland*, November 1933.
PM290 "Television Step Ahead." *Boardwalk Magazine*, July 6, 1929.
PM291 "$10 Mil to Disk Trade Via Jolson-Decca Case." *Billboard*, April 23, 1955, p. 28.
PM292 Testoni, G. "Gli autori dei temi." *Music Jazz*, December 1959, p. 37.
PM293 Tibbett, Lawrence. "Debunking Classical Music." *Radio Guide*, October 20, 1934, p. 2.
PM294 "Time is Money." *Picture Play*, January 1933.
PM295 Townsend, Leo. "Winning the Hollywood Handicap!" *Radio Stars*, March 1937, pp. 24-25, 56.
PM296 Treasure, John H. "Jolson Sings Again." *Big Reel* (fanzine), August 15, 1991, pp. 104-105.
PM297 "Tribute to Al Jolson." *Silver Screen*, May 1946.
PM298 "Tributes To *The Greatest of Them All*." *Billboard*, November 5, 1950, p. 55.
PM299 "The True Jolson Story." *Movie Stars Parade*, 1947.
PM300 "27,000 Judgement in Jolson Suit." *Billboard*, September 24, 1955.
PM301 "Unsinkable Al." *Radio Best*, February 1948.
PM302 Vallee, William L. "Straight From the Cold Shoulder." *Radio Stars*, May 1938.
PM303 Van Beek, Greg. "Bing and Al. The World's Greatest Entertainers." *Bingang* (a fanzine of Club Crosby), December 1991, Vol. LVI, No. 2, pp. 6-10.
PM304 "Vaudeville," *This Was Show Business*, 1956, p. 21.
PM305 Walker, B. "Sketch." *Movie Classic*, April 1933, p. 17.
PM306 Walker, Elizabeth. "Cradle Snatching." *Radio Guide*, March 21, 1936, pp. 20-21.
PM307 Walsh, J. "Favorite Pioneer Recording Artists. Thomas A. Edison's Colorful Correspondence." *Hobbies*, March 1982, 87:64-7.
PM308 ----------. "Pioneer Recording Artists: Parodies on Bygone Popular Songs (Parody of *Asleep in the Deep*)." *Hobbies*, March 1984, pp. 64-67.
PM309 ----------. "Theo Karle." *Hobbies*, September 1972, pp. 37-8.
PM310 Warner, Jack L., with Dean Jennings. "My First Hundred Years in Hollywood." *McCall's*, September 1964, pp. 72-73, 142-148; October 1964, pp. 128-129, 167-169; November 1964, pp. 100-101, 194, 196-199.
PM311 Warwick, Irvin R. "Jolson Notes." *Lachute Watchman*, beginning October 21, 1954 (reprinting of items from Jolson fan publication, *The Jolson Journal*).
PM312 Weissman, Howard. "Me, I Just Sing." *Salute*, August 1947.
PM313 "What Al Jolson Thinks of Ruby Keeler." *Picturegoer Weekly*, June 20, 1936, p. 17.
PM314 "What Al Jolson Thinks of Ruby Keeler." *Screen and Radio Weekly*, 1935.
PM315 "What's Wrong With Our Radio Entertainment?" *Movie-Radio Guide*, October 19-25, 1940, p. 1.

PM316 Wheeler, Dan. "Their Friendship Brought Them Stardom. The Amazing Story of Al Jolson and Al Goodman." *Radio Mirror*, February 1938, pp. 44-45, 67.

PM317 "When a Broadway Comedian Went to a Ball Game." *Stage Pictorial*, 1912, p. 29.

PM318 White, Stanley W. "The Burnt Cork Illusion of the 1920's in America: A Study in Nostalgia." *Journal of Popular Culture*, November 3, 1971, Volume 5, No. 3, pp. 530-542.

PM319 Whitfield, Steve. "Jazz Singers." *Moment*, March-April 1981, p. 19-25.

PM320 Wilcox, Howard. "Call the Song Doctor." *Radio Guide*, May 18, 1935, pp. 7, 29.

PM321 ----------. "Great Lovers of Radio." *Radio Guide*, November 10, 1934, pp. 5, 23.

PM322 Wild, Roland. "Jolson Comes of Age." *Illustrated*, October 1, 1949.

PM323 Wilkinson, Harry. "Looking Hollywood Way: Al Jolson," *Good Old Days*, January 1989, pp. 57-60.

PM324 Wilson, E. "The Stepping Star." *Silver Screen*, April 1933, p. 20.

PM325 Witwer, Allan. "Thanks for the Memory." *Liberty*, October 5, 1946.

PM326 Wolfe, Charles. "Vitaphone Shorts and *The Jazz Singer*." *Wide Angle*, July 1990, Vol. 12, No. 3, pp. 58-78.

PM327 "Wonder Bar." *Photoplay*, February 1934.

PM328 "Wonder Bar." *Screen Romances*, April 1934.

PM329 "Wonder Bar", *Silver Screen*, April 1934.

PM330 "The World's Greatest Entertainer." *Cosmopolitan*, November 1958.

PM331 Zeitlin, Ida. "The Jazz Singer vs. Hollywood." *Screenland*, November 1933.

PM332 Zolotow, Maurice. "Ageless Al." *Reader's Digest*, January 1949, pp. 73-76.

PM333 Zolotow, Maurice. "That Young Al Jolson." *Esquire*, January 1949, pp. 39, 134-135.

NEW YORK TIMES

NYT1 "Actors Eat Cakes With the Coolidges." *New York Times*, October 18, 1924, p. 1.

NYT2 "Aid For Blind in Israel." *New York Times*, May 4, 1951, p. 29.

NYT3 "Al Jolson Aids War Bond Drive." *New York Times*, May 7, 1942, p. 21.

NYT4 "Al Jolson Appointed a Deputy Sheriff." *New York Times*, March 15, 1925, p. 18.

NYT5 "Al Jolson Arrives in Tokyo." *New York Times*, September 14, 1950, p. 4.

NYT6 "Al Jolson Back in *Big Boy*." *New York Times*, February 10, 1925, p. 20.

NYT7 "Al Jolson Back on Stage." *New York Times*, March 6, 1931, p. 26.

NYT8 "Al Jolson Bequeaths a Million To Widow." *New York Times*, December 19, 1950, p. 40.

NYT9 "Al Jolson Explains Why He Abandoned Comedy on Air." *New York Times*, July 29, 1934, Section VIII, p. 15.

NYT10 "Al Jolson Gets Ovation." *New York Times*, August 25, 1925, p. 12.

NYT11 "Al Jolson Has Bad Cold." *New York Times*, January 10, 1925, p. 9.

NYT12 "Al Jolson Has Bronchitis." *New York Times*, May 14, 1931, p. 27.

NYT13 "Al Jolson Has Influenza." *New York Times*, February 9, 1932, p. 31.

NYT14 "Al Jolson Has Pneumonia." *New York Times*, October 9, 1943, p. 11.

NYT15 "Al Jolson Heads Harding League." *New York Times*, August 11, 1920, p.

6.

NYT16   "Al Jolson Honored." *New York Times*, April 9, 1931, p. 30.

NYT17   "Al Jolson Ill; Matinee Omitted." *New York Times*, January 21, 1925, p. 19.

NYT18   "Al Jolson, Ill, Recovering." *New York Times*, December 27, 1932, p. 10.

NYT19   "Al Jolson in Curacao." *New York Times*, July 31, 1942, p. 10.

NYT20   "Al Jolson in North Africa." *New York Times*, September 3, 1943, p. 15.

NYT21   "Al Jolson Is Back; Visited 3 Fronts." *New York Times*, October 1, 1943, p. 14.

NYT22   "Al Jolson Is Ill Again." *New York Times*, May 31, 1931, p. 20.

NYT23   "Al Jolson Is In Hospital." *New York Times*, November 22, 1939, p. 16.

NYT24   "Al Jolson Leases Home." *New York Times*, June 30, 1935, Sections XII & XIII, p. 1.

NYT25   "Al Jolson Made a Director." *New York Times*, August 2, 1929, p. 27.

NYT26   "Al Jolson Married Again." *New York Times*, August 19, 1922, p. 7.

NYT27   "Al Jolson Marries 21-Year-Old Actress." *New York Times*, March 25, 1945, p. 39.

NYT28   "Al Jolson Much Better." *New York Times*, January 11, 1925, p. 31.

NYT29   "Al Jolson Reappears in *Big Boy*." *New York Times*, August 18, 1925, p. 14.

NYT30   "Al Jolson Resigns from Country Club." *New York Times*, May 21, 1926, p. 20.

NYT31   "Al Jolson Sails for Rest Abroad." *New York Times*, June 24, 1923, p. 18.

NYT32   "Al Jolson Seriously Ill." *New York Times*, December 25, 1944, p. 15.

NYT33   "Al Jolson To Reappear Tonight." *New York Times*, January 12, 1925, p. 15.

NYT34   "Al Jolson To Star in New Musical Play." *New York Times*, November 20, 1930, p. 30.

NYT35   "Al Jolson Welcomed Back." *New York Times*, May 15, 1923, p. 22.

NYT36   "Al Jolson's Silks Will Be Seen on Turf; Buys a Horse." *New York Times*, July 24, 1921, VIII, p. 2.

NYT37   "Albert Jolson, Jr. in Hospital." *New York Times*, May 20, 1935, p. 20.

NYT38   "All America Used As a Radio Station." *New York Times*, January 5, 1928, p. 24.

NYT39   "Appeal Gets $200,000 From Amusement Unit." *New York Times*, July 16, 1947, p. 27.

NYT40   "Army Minstrel." *New York Times*, August 30, 1942, Section IV, p. 2.

NYT41   Atkinson, Brooks. "Low and High Comedy." *New York Times*, April 4, 1926, VIII, p. 1.

NYT42   ----------. "Singing Al Comes to Town." *New York Times*, September 29, 1940.

NYT43   "Broadway's Big Boy." *New York Times*, September 6, 1925, Section VII, p. 1.

NYT44   "Carroll Case Goes to the Jury Today." *New York Times*, May 27, 1926, p. 8.

NYT45   "Celebration for Jolson." *New York Times*, April 17, 1935, p. 21.

NYT46   "Charities Get Most of Jolson Estate." *New York Times*, October 27, 1950, p. 30.

NYT47   "City College Honors Jolson." *New York Times*, November 6, 1950, p. 25.

NYT48   Clarity, James F. and Warren Weaver, Jr. "A Two-Gloved Star." *New York Times*, April 11, 1985, p. B8.

NYT49   Daley, Arthur. "30,246 See Giants and Packers Tie." *New York Times*, November 23, 1942, p. 27.

NYT50   "Denies Jews Will Resign." *New York Times*, May 22, 1926, p. 7.

NYT51   "Dinners to Precede *Big Boy*." *New York Times*, February 10, 1925, p. 20.

NYT52   "Disputed Bequest in Al Jolson Will Goes to City College, Court Rules." *New York Times*, May 21, 1952, p. 29.

NYT53   Effrat, Louis. "Mitchell Defeats Dodds By 4 Yards in Millrose Mile." *New York Times*, February 7, 1943, Section III, p. 1.

NYT54   "4,044,147 Estate Left By Al Jolson." *New York Times*, July 26, 1952, p. 13.

NYT55   "Friars Honor Al Jolson." *New York Times*, April 1, 1918, p. 9.

NYT56   "Funeral of Jolson Set For Tomorrow." *New York Times*, October 25, 1950, p. 38.

NYT57   Gould, Jack. "The News of Radio: Canadian Drama on WNEW--Hooper Listings." *New York Times*, June 18, 1947, p. 50.

NYT58   ----------. "The News of Radio: Commentators Oppose Station Editorials--Jolson May Join Music Hall." *New York Times*, June 23, 1947, p. 36.

NYT59   ----------. "The News of Radio: Crosby and Jolson Differ Over Fall Show." *New York Times*, June 17, 1947, p. 50.

NYT60   ----------. "The Jolson Story." *New York Times*, April 13, 1947, Section II, p. 9.

NYT61   Haitch, Richard. "Freedom of Song." *New York Times*, November 20, 1983, p. 49.

NYT62   "Harry Jolson, 71, Brother of Singer." *New York Times*, April 28, 1953, p. 27.

NYT63   Holden, Stephen. "Ruby Keeler, Tap-Dancing Actress, Is Dead at 82." *New York Times*, March 1, 1993, p. B11.

NYT64   "Holding Medal Awarded Posthumously to His Father." *New York Times*, December 7, 1950, p. 44.

NYT65   "Hoover Appeals for Aid Over Radio." *New York Times*, May 1, 1927, p. 2.

NYT66   "Hope Wins Al Jolson Award." *New York Times*, July 16, 1952, p. 21.

NYT67   "Hotel Sues Jolson For Radio *Slander*." *New York Times*, June 21, 1935, p. 21.

NYT68   "Hungary Reds Call Jolson Untrue to the Negro Race." *New York Times*, December 22, 1950, p. 19.

NYT69   Hutchens, John. "Entrance for a Winter Garden Hero." *New York Times*, March 22, 1931, Section VIII, pp. 1-2.

NYT70   "Hylan on the Income Tax." *New York Times*, March 23, 1918, p. 11.

NYT71   "Jolson Arrives in Korea." *New York Times*, September 18, 1950, p. 4.

NYT72   "Jolson Asks Truman If He'll Run in 1952." *New York Times*, September 29, 1949, p. 26.

NYT73   "Jolson Back From Korea." *New York Times*, September 29, 1950, p. 32.

NYT74   "Jolson Break Is Certain." *New York Times*, October 28, 1939, p. 11.

NYT75   "Jolson Buys Home for Old Parents." *New York Times*, December 19, 1926, p. 26.

NYT76   "Jolson Canteen Opened." *New York Times*, April 15, 1951, Section V, p. 9.

NYT77   "Jolson Canteen Planned." *New York Times*, March 25, 1951, Section V, p. 8.

NYT78   "Jolson a Coolidge Leader." *New York Times*, October 12, 1924, p. 4.

NYT79   "Jolson Denies Row with Screen Star." *New York Times*, September 17, 1942, p. 20.

NYT80   "Jolson Estate Brings $112,500." *New York Times*, March 23, 1953, p. 27.

NYT81 "Jolson Estate Estimated." *New York Times*, May 30, 1951, p. 14.

NYT82 "Jolson Faces Operation." *New York Times*, December 5, 1930, p. 30.

NYT83 "Jolson *Fairly Comfortable*." *New York Times*, December 26, 1944, p. 22.

NYT84 "Jolson Gets $18,000 for Orphans." *New York Times*, November 29, 1926, p. 3.

NYT85 "Jolson Gets Rose Award." *New York Times*, May 30, 1948, p. 22.

NYT86 "Jolson Gives Dinner for Needy." *New York Times*, January 2, 1936, p. 21.

NYT87 "Jolson Has Relapse; *Big Boy* Stays Closed." *New York Times*, February 10, 1926, p. 20.

NYT88 "Jolson Ill Again; *Big Boy* Closes." *New York Times*, March 16, 1925, p. 17.

NYT89 "Jolson Ill With Influenza." *New York Times*, October 31, 1934, p. 17.

NYT90 "Jolson in Governor Smith's Box. *Two Als* Tell Winter Garden Audience of Golf Game in Albany." *New York Times*, February 21, 1925, p. 11.

NYT91 "Jolson in *Sons O' Guns*." *New York Times*, March 25, 1930, p. 35.

NYT92 "Jolson Leaves Millions." *New York Times*, October 26, 1950, p. 38.

NYT93 "Jolson Made Mayor of Encino." *New York Times*, December 29, 1935, p. 13.

NYT94 "Jolson Musical Wins Approval in Chicago." *New York Times*, July 17, 1940, p. 25.

NYT95 "Jolson Needs Rest; Closes *Big Boy*." *New York Times*, January 27, 1926, p. 16.

NYT96 "Jolson On Brunswick-Balke Board." *New York Times*, August 1, 1929, p. 19.

NYT97 "Jolson Receives Award." *New York Times*, November 20, 1949, p. 73.

NYT98 "Jolson, Ruby Keeler Parted, He Reports." *New York Times*, October 26, 1939, p. 25.

NYT99 "Jolson Secretly Weds Ruby Keeler, Actress; Captain of Olympic Barred From Officiating." *New York Times*, September 22, 1928, p. 1.

NYT100 "Jolson Shrine Unveiled." *New York Times*, September 24, 1951, p. 28.

NYT101 "Jolson Signs Film Contract." *New York Times*, April 24, 1934, p. 26.

NYT102 "Jolson Sings Again." *New York Times*, October 29, 1982, p. C8.

NYT103 "*The Jolson Story*. Biography of a Voice." *New York Times Magazine*, October 13, 1946, pp. 30-31.

NYT104 "Jolson Sued by Brother." *New York Times*, May 7, 1941, p. 24.

NYT105 "Jolson To Adopt Baby. Wishes a Child Under 3, But It May Be a Boy or a Girl." *New York Times*, January 20, 1925, p. 19.

NYT106 "Jolson To Get $40,000 Salary For Four Weeks." *New York Times*, March 11, 1928, p. 26.

NYT107 "Jolson To Make 3 More Films." *New York Times*, November 21, 1933, p. 23.

NYT108 "Jolson To Rest 2 Weeks." *New York Times*, January 26, 1925, p. 17.

NYT109 "Jolson To Retire As Screen Actor." *New York Times*, November 20, 1933, p. 23.

NYT110 "Jolson To Take Brief Rest." *New York Times*, May 15, 1931, p. 21.

NYT111 "Jolson Undergoes Operation." *New York Times*, January 17, 1945, p. 18.

NYT112 "Jolson Weighs Operetta." *New York Times*, October 7, 1933, p. 18.

NYT113 "Jolson Widow Loses." *New York Times*, March 6, 1952, p. 33.

NYT114 "Jolson Wins $25,000 Suit." *New York Times*, July 22, 1941, p. 22.

NYT115 "Jolson Would Star In Film as *De Lawd*." *New York Times*, June 1, 1931, p. 14.

NYT116 "Jolsons Adopt a Boy." *New York Times*, May 8, 1935, p. 21.

NYT117   "Jolson's Age Sought." *New York Times*, May 29, 1951, p. 27.

NYT118   "Jolson's $5,000 Fee Too Much For Vienna." *New York Times*, January 24, 1930, p. 23.

NYT119   "Jolson's Jury Discharged." *New York Times*, October 16, 1926, p. 8.

NYT120   "Jolson's Own Gag Costs NBC $15,000," *New York Times*, February 1, 1939, p. 2.

NYT121   "Jury Picked for Jolson Trial." *New York Times*, October 6, 1926, p. 39.

NYT122   "Just Before the Battle." *New York Times*, April 18, 1926, Section VIII, p. 2.

NYT123   "The Lambs Gambol to Tune of $72,000." *New York Times*, April 27, 1925, p. 15.

NYT124   Lawson, Carol. "Kert Determined: Jolson On Broadway." *New York Times*, July 25, 1979, Section III, p. 17.

NYT125   Lejeune, C.A. "Americans in London." *New York Times*, September 20, 1942, Section VIII, p. 3.

NYT126   Lewis, Lloyd. "Streamlined Jolson." *New York Times*, July 21, 1940, Section IX, p. 1.

NYT127   "Louis Epstein, 68, Managed Al Jolson." *New York Times*, May 16, 1954.

NYT128   "Many Stage People Honor the War Dead." *New York Times*, November 12, 1921, p. 13.

NYT129   "The Microphone Will Present." *New York Times*, October 13, 1929.

NYT130   "A Minstrel Passes." *New York Times*, October 25, 1950, p. 34.

NYT131   "Miss Oberon, Jolson In Britain." *New York Times*, August 25, 1942, p. 8.

NYT132   "Mme. Stern-Wheeler." *New York Times*, December 31, 1939, Section IX, p. 4.

NYT133   Morgenstern, Joseph. "Sunshine Boy At 85." *New York Times Magazine*, January 25, 1981, Section VI, p. 27.

NYT134   "Mr. Jolson Discusses Several Things." *New York Times*, January 25, 1925, Section VII, p. 1.

NYT135   "Mr. Jolson Replies." *New York Times*, October 30, 1921, Section VI, p. 1.

NYT136   "Mrs. Jolson Gets $3,333 a Month." *New York Times*, June 7, 1951, p. 35.

NYT137   "Mrs. Jolson Guardian." *New York Times*, November 10, 1950, p. 31.

NYT138   "Mrs. Jolson in Hospital." *New York Times*, July 31, 1929, p. 23.

NYT139   "Mrs. Jolson Loses Case." *New York Times*, August 16, 1951, p. 16.

NYT140   "Mrs. Jolson Loses Coat." *New York Times*, October 27, 1951, p. 34.

NYT141   "Musicians To Get Apollo Figurines." *New York Times*, July 10, 1956, p. 28.

NYT142   "News and Gossip of the Studios." *New York Times*, July 2, 1933.

NYT143   "9,000 at Al Jolson Tribute." *New York Times*, May 27, 1952, p. 30.

NYT144   "Only a Voice." *New York Times*, June 27, 1943.

NYT145   Photographs Only: *New York Times*, June 8, 1930, Section IX, p. 4; March 8, 1931, Section VIII, p. 8; March 15, 1931, Section IX, p. 1; November 13, 1932, Section VIII, p. 6; December 18, 1932; January 15, 1933, Section IX, p. 10; February 19, 1933, Section IX, p. 5; March 12, 1933, Section IX, p. 4; July 16, 1933, Section X, p. 7; October 31, 1934, p. 17; April 14, 1935, Section IX, p. 17; May 20, 1935, p. 20; August 18, 1935, Section X, p. 11; June 14, 1936, Section X, p. 10; January 10, 1937, Section X, p. 12; September 5, 1937, Section X, p. 10; September

18, 1938, Section X, p. 10; October 13, 1946, Section II, 3; October 13, 1946, Section VI, pp. 30-31; September 21, 1950, p. 3.

NYT146 "Pictures." *New York Times*, November 24, 1946, Section VI, p. 28.

NYT147 "Playwright's Suit Against Jolson Opens." *New York Times*, October 7, 1926, p. 12.

NYT148 Pryor, Thomas. "Film Will Depict Scott Fitzgerald. Wald To Base Movie on Book By Sheila Graham -- *Jazz Singer* is 30 Tomorrow." *New York Times*, October 5, 1957, p. 9.

NYT149 "Ratoff: The Last Roman." *New York Times*, May 7, 1939, Section X, p. 6.

NYT150 "Re-Enter Mr. Jolson." *New York Times*, August 30, 1925, Section VII, p. 2.

NYT151 "The Returning Mr. Jolson." *New York Times*, March 8, 1931, Section VIII, p. 3.

NYT152 Rothenberg, Randall. "High-Powered Marketing Gives *Jolson* a Comeback." *New York Times*, March 4, 1991.

NYT153 "Ruby Keeler At Film." *New York Times*, August 7, 1929, p. 28.

NYT154 "Ruby Keeler's Condition *Excellent*." *New York Times*, August 3, 1929, p. 7.

NYT155 "Ruby Keeler Divorces Al Jolson On Coast." *New York Times*, December 27, 1939, p. 16.

NYT156 "Ruby Keeler Files Suit," *New York Times*, October 31, 1939, p. 27.

NYT157 "Ruby Keeler Gets Final Divorce." *New York Times*, December 29, 1940, p. 24.

NYT158 "Ruby Keeler Jolson Improving." *New York Times*, August 4, 1929, p. 19.

NYT159 "Ruby Keeler Jolson to Leave *Show Girl*." *New York Times*, July 29, 1929, p. 23.

NYT160 "Ruby Keeler Operated On." *New York Times*, August 2, 1929, p. 17.

NYT161 "Ruby Keeler Quits Jolson Show." *New York Times*, July 30, 1940, p. 16.

NYT162 "Ruby Keeler Quits Cast." *New York Times*, September 30, 1930, p. 24.

NYT163 "Ruby Keeler Released." *New York Times*, July 28, 1940, p. 29.

NYT164 "Ruby Keeler To Resume Role." *New York Times*, July 30, 1929, p. 19.

NYT165 "Ruby Keeler Would Quit." *New York Times*, July 25, 1940, p. 14.

NYT166 "Says Film Defamed Her." *New York Times*, July 15, 1939, p. 17.

NYT167 "Says Jolson Filmed Well." *New York Times*, October 8, 1926, p. 23.

NYT168 Schriftgiesser, Karl. "Holding To Their Hats." *New York Times*, October 20, 1940, Section IX, p. 3.

NYT169 "Seeks Honor Medal for Jolson." *New York Times*, November 28, 1950, p. 38.

NYT170 "$7,500 for Ten Minutes." New York Times, October 13, 1929.

NYT171 Shepard, Richard. "Jolson Sings Again in Jamaica." *New York Times*, July 10, 1981.

NYT172 ----------. "Jolson Song Contest Here Draws a Million Smiles." *New York Times*, August 23, 1975.

NYT173 "Show Tickets End Jolson Suit." *New York Times*, October 12, 1941, p. 54.

NYT174 "Shuberts Sue Over Film." *New York Times*, October 15, 1946, p. 29.

NYT175 "*Singing Policeman* Files Suit After Ban on Blackface Role." *New York Times*, September 8, 1983, p. A15.

NYT176 "The Singing Tramp." *New York Times*, February 19, 1933, Section IX, p. 4.

NYT177   "Stander Leaves Jolson Show." *New York Times*, July 4, 1940, p. 12.
NYT178   Stanley, Fred. "Hollywood Reports: Now It's Jolson." *New York Times*, February 27, 1944, Section II, p. 3.
NYT179   "Starts Suit Over *Big Boy*." *New York Times*, February 7, 1926, p. 13.
NYT180   "The Story of Al Jolson." *New York Times*, February 24, 1918, p. 4.
NYT181   "Sues Al Jolson For Divorce." *New York Times*, June 27, 1919, p. 16.
NYT182   "Thousands Mourn Jolson On Coast." *New York Times*, October 27, 1950, p. 30.
NYT183   "Truman Honors Jolson." *New York Times*, December 6, 1950, p. 44.
NYT184   "Vaudeville For Prisoners." *New York Times*, November 29, 1911, p. 2.
NYT185   "V.F.W. Honors Eddie Cantor." *New York Times*, August 5, 1954, p. 18.
NYT186   "Who's Who In Pictures. From St. Petersburg to Broadway With Mr. Jolson -- Mae West and Mr. Summerville." *New York Times*, February 12, 1933, Section IX, p. 4.
NYT187   "*The Wonder Bar* Closes Abruptly." *New York Times*, June 2, 1931, p. 35.
NYT188   Woolf, S.J. "Army Minstrel." *New York Times Magazine*, September 27, 1942, Section VII, p. 19.

VARIETY

At the height of his fame, between the early 1910's through his death in 1950, it was rare for Jolson's name to be missing from the pages of *Variety*, the major trade paper for show business. Reviews are included in the stage, film, radio and discography sections; no listing of advertisements is included.

V1   "Ad Agency's V.P., Reber, Sits On Top of Jolson-Whiteman Hour On Roof; Good As Any Show B'way Premiere." *Variety*, August 8, 1933, p. 34.
V2   "*Ain't Heard Nothin' Yet*." *Variety*, October 20, 1948, p. 1.
V3   "Al Jolson." *Variety*, July 5, 1918, p. 11.
V4   "Al Jolson Dies." *Variety*, October 24, 1950.
V5   "Al Jolson Enshrined." *Variety*, September 24, 1951.
V6   "Al Jolson Film's 130G Song Rights." *Variety*, April 3, 1946, p. 47.
V7   "Al Jolson 1st Trouper To Korea." *Variety*, September 11, 1950.
V8   "Al Jolson Imitator in Blackface May Keep On, Sez Court." *Variety*, June 4, 1986, p. 1.
V9   "Al Jolson, Jr. Can't Live Up to His Name in U.K." *Variety*, May 8, 1968, p. 2.
V10   "Al Jolson Lies in State." *Variety*, October 26, 1950.
V11   "Al Jolson Managing Brother." *Variety*, June 7, 1918, p. 3.
V12   "Al Jolson Musical Scholarships." *Variety*, October 15, 1958, p. 55.
V13   "Al Jolson Receives $10,000 Bonus to Sign For Seven Years." *Variety*, February 28, 1913, p. 10.
V14   "Al Jolson Wants Brother Harry's Suit Thrown Out." *Variety*, July 16, 1941, p. 2.
V15   "Al Jolson Will Star In Todd's B'way Musical." *Variety*, June 13, 1945, p. 1.
V16   "Al Jolson's Air Return Following 2-Hour Hit." *Variety*, July 4, 1933, p. 37.
V17   "Allied Members File Affidavits vs. Col On Hiked *Jolson* Scale." *Variety*, December 7, 1949, p. 4.
V18   "American Legion Creates Al Jolson Post." *Variety*, January 18, 1951.
V19   "Asa's Stand-in for Jolie." *Variety*, December 6, 1950.

V20 "Balto Biz Takes Spurt; *Woman* Surprising 20G, *South* 21G, *Rue* 13G." *Variety*, February 5, 1947, p. 15.

V21 "Barry Gray Marketing That Al Jolson Show At $48.96 Per Album." *Variety*, November 20, 1946, p. 43.

V22 "Berlin's Camp Songs." *Variety*, May 17, 1918, p. 8.

V23 "Bing, Guy, Jolie Key To Decca's 16th Anni." *Variety*, June 7, 1950, pp. 1, 20.

V24 Bodec, Ben. "Radio's Top Names--1932." *Variety*, January 3, 1933, p. 59, 68.

V25 "Bogie vs. Jolie Proves You Gotta Do More Than Glad-To-Be-Here." *Variety*, November 2, 1949, p. 27.

V26 "Cantor Eulogizes Jolson in Gotham Memorial Services." *Variety*, October 30, 1950, p. 8.

V27 "Cantor, Jolson, Burns & Allen NBC Parlay An Old Palace Vaude Routine." *Variety*, July 23, 1947, p. 27.

V28 "Cantor to Dedicate *Jolson Corner* in Florida." *Variety*, February 21, 1951, p. 2.

V29 "Capital-Variety Club Pays Honor To Jolson." *Variety*, November 21, 1949.

V30 "Chev'let Lifts Check For B&K Jolson Feed." *Variety*, January 3, 1933, p. 59.

V31 "Church Group Frowns On *Jolson*, 7 Others." *Variety*, September 7, 1949, p. 4.

V32 "Coast Break-in For Jolson Before B'way." *Variety*, February 27, 1946, p. 2.

V33 "Coast Friar Benefit." *Variety*, April 20, 1949, p. 2.

V34 "Col. Terms Shuberts' *Jolson* Suit Ridic." *Variety*, March 26, 1947, p. 7.

V35 "Cold Dents Seattle B.O.; *Rue, Shadowed* 15G." *Variety*, February 5, 1947, p. 15.

V36 "Col's Early Oscar Start With *Men, Jolson Sings*." *Variety*, July 27, 1949, p. 13.

V37 "Col's Selective Dating On *Jolson* Sequel Pic." *Variety*, June 29, 1949, p. 4.

V38 "Crosby, Cantor Shows to Salute Al Jolson." Variety, October 25, 1950.

V39 "D.C. Goes All Out For Al Jolson." *Variety*, November 23, 1949, p. 6.

V40 "D.C. Variety Tags Jolie Tops In Biz." *Variety*, October 19, 1949, p. 9.

V41 "Decca Wins in Jolson Suit, Affirming Industry's Royalty Payoff." *Variety*, April 13, 1955, p. 57.

V42 "Dedicate *Jolson Corner* in Miami Tarleton at $50-A-Plate Dinner." *Variety*, March 6, 1951.

V43 "Divert Jolson's Will Request to Saranac." *Variety*, June 28, 1961, pp. 1, 70.

V44 "Dockstader Still Laying Off." *Variety*, January 1, 1910, p. 4.

V45 "Early, Important Musical Influx To B'way Seen; Jolson, Ed Wynn." *Variety*, July 17, 1940, pp. 1, 45.

V46 "Ed Wynn First Name To Go Kine; Thinks Other Comics *Fear* TV." *Variety*, July 20, 1949, pp. 1, 16.

V47 "$80,000 Jolson Shrine Dedicated in Los Angeles." *Variety*, September 26, 1951, p. 2.

V48 "Epstein Files 14G Claim Against Jolson Estate." *Variety*, September 13, 1951.

V49 "Epstein Gets $6,500 From Jolson Estate; Widow Adds $1,000,000." *Variety*, January 23, 1952, p. 10.

V50 "Fair Bids 75G For Jolie." *Variety*, November 30, 1949, p. 1.

V51 "*Father* Gets $13,000 in Chi; Jolson Opens." *Variety*, July 17, 1940, p. 43.

V52 "$50-Per-Plate Jolson Memorial Benefits NCCJ." *Variety*, March 7, 1951.

V53 "4,282,730 Jolson Estate." *Variety*, June 21, 1954.

V54 "Gala Tribute to Al Jolson Emceed By Eddie Cantor." *Variety*, December 17, 1947, p. 2.

V55 Galloway, Doug. "National Jolson Tribute Kicks Off in New York." *Variety*, May 30, 1985.

V56 ----------. "New York Remembers Al Jolson As 100th Anni Tribute Kicks Off." *Variety*, June 5, 1985, p. 78.

V57 ----------. "Weekend Tributes Commemorate the 100th Anni of Jolson's Birth." *Variety*, July 23, 1985.

V58 "Gallup Poll Caps Jolson Story In Pix, Radio, Disks." *Variety*, February 11, 1948, p. 1, 48.

V59 "Garden's $32,000 Week." *Variety*, March 29, 1918, p. 3.

V60 "Geo. Hale Argues Jolson Is Hale, Hearty And Not Too Ill To Play in Show." *Variety*, February 19, 1941, p. 3.

V61 "George Hale Would Pre-exam Al Jolson." *Variety*, July 2, 1941, p. 3.

V62 Gilbert, L.W. "60 Years a Songsmith: Some Show Biz Greats." *Variety*, January 1, 1969, p. 160.

V63 Green, Abel. "Ad Agency's V.P., Reber, Sits On Top Of Jolson-Whiteman Hour On Roof; Good As Any Show B'way Premiere." *Variety*, August 8, 1933, p. 34.

V64 ----------. "Al Jolson's Sequel *Story* May Stress *Only Millionaire Who Did A Comeback*." *Variety*, July 16, 1947, pp. 1, 47.

V65 ----------. "Iron-Man Jolson Whams NY in *Live-Trailer* Swing of Loew's Circuit." *Variety*, August 17, 1949, p. 2.

V66 ----------. "Jolson Leaves $4,000,000 to Charity After Trusts for Widow, 2 Children." *Variety*, October 25, 1950, p. 1.

V67 ----------. "Nation in Jolson Tribute." *Variety*, November 1, 1950, pp. 2, 22.

V68 "Harry Jolson's Comeback; Al's Brother Formerly Agreed To Stay Off Stage." *Variety*, September 10, 1941, p. 3.

V69 "*Highway* Speedy." *Variety*, October 12, 1949, p. 10.

V70 "Hope's Tribute To Jolson." *Variety*, November 1, 1950, pp. 2, 22.

V71 "If Jolson Radio Show Set, He'll Not Defer *Hats*." *Variety*, July 9, 1941, p. 3.

V72 "Inside Stuff-Legit." *Variety*, November 20, 1940, p. 50.

V73 "Inside Stuff-Legit." *Variety*, February 5, 1947, p. 18.

V74 "Insurance Companies Cue Stew on Jolson Policies; Would Pay On Basis of Age 70." *Variety*, May 30, 1951, p. 2.

V75 "Irving Brown Wants to Become Al Jolson, Jr." *Variety*, August 19, 1964.

V76 "Jeanne Crain *Doing A Jolson* For *Pinky*." *Variety*, September 14, 1949, p. 18.

V77 "Jessel Feels Victim of Film *Jazz Singer*." *Variety*, March 7, 1928, Vol. 90, No. 8, p. 49.

V78 Jessel, George. "Eulogy to Al Jolson." *Variety*, November 27, 1950.

V79 "Jolie's Insurance Claim." *Variety*, May 28, 1951.

V80 Jolson, Al. "Death Is Their Neighbor." *Variety*, May 14, 1947, pp. 28-29.

V81 ----------. "The Fight at Reno." *Variety*, July 9, 1910, p. 4.

V82 ----------. "A Tribute To A Hero." *Variety*, July 9, 1941, p. 13.

V83 "Jolson And Jacobs Eye Palm Spr. Hotel." *Variety*, April 24, 1946, p. 2.

V84 "*Jolson* Another Story With New Stereo Added." *Variety*, August 19, 1953, p. 1.

V85 "Jolson As Opener Planned By Todd For N.Y. 2-A-Day." *Variety*, July 20, 1949, pp. 1, 16.

V86 "Jolson At $5,000." *Variety*, July 25, 1933, p. 39.

V87 "Jolson Awed by Yanks' Courage in Korea." *Variety*, September 1950.

V88 "Jolson Biog Ready to Shoot Oct. 1." *Variety*, July 5, 1944, p. 2.

V89 "Jolson Biog Tops 25th Anniversary Sked At Columbia." *Variety*, January 30, 1946, p. 9.

V90 "Jolson Calls Off Deal For Metro Biog Sequel." *Variety*, April 7, 1948, p. 3.

V91 "Jolson-Crosby Paired On Pair For Decca." *Variety*, April 16, 1947, p. 37.

V92 "Jolson Crowds In One." *Variety*, August 26, 1942, pp. 1, 25.

V93 "Jolson Details Why His Musical Too Costly For 1-Night Road Jumps." *Variety*, November 12, 1941, pp. 2, 61.

V94 "Jolson Disk Sales Soar After His Death." *Variety*, November 1, 1950, p. 22.

V95 "Jolson Does Comeback On Wax Also; He's The First 1,000,000 Album Seller." *Variety*, April 16, 1947, p. 1.

V96 "Jolson Due On Coast Soon For Film Biog." *Variety*, January 19, 1944, p. 2.

V97 "Jolson Estate Gift." *Variety*, January 29, 1958, p. 2.

V98 "Jolson Estate Sues Decca for More Royalties." *Variety*, March 16, 1955, p. 45.

V99 "Jolson Estate Worth More, Now Nearer $4,500,000." *Variety*, March 21, 1951, p. 1.

V100 "Jolson Eyes $3,500,000 As His Share From Pic." *Variety*, May 14, 1947, pp. 1, 25.

V101 "Jolson $50,000 Ahead." *Variety*, June 14, 1918, p. 3.

V102 "Jolson For 43 Minutes." *Variety*, March 24, 1926, p. 21.

V103 "Jolson For U.A. Musicals." *Variety*, November 17, 1931, p. 3.

V104 "*Jolson* Garners Nov. B.O. Honors; *Ribbon* 2d, *Forsythe Deadline* Next." *Variety*, December 7, 1949, p. 4.

V105 "Jolson Getting Fee Plus 50% Split For Wald-Krasna *Stars*." *Variety*, October 18, 1950, p. 4.

V106 "Jolson *Hatikvah, Israel* Disks For Weizmann." *Variety*, May 26, 1948, p. 1.

V107 "Jolson - *Hats* Smash 32G In Philly." *Variety*, September 11, 1940, p. 42.

V108 "Jolson - *Hats* 20 1/2G In 5th Chi Wk." *Variety*, August 21, 1940, p. 59.

V109 "Jolson Hits Plattered For Decca Disk Album." *Variety*, April 24, 1946, p. 47.

V110 "Jolson, In *Debut* As London Actor, But For U.S. Khaki." *Variety*, September 9, 1942, p. 3.

V111 "Jolson, In Fla., Orders Sun Lamp From N.Y." *Variety*, February 12, 1941, p. 1.

V112 "Jolson In Korea To Entertain Troops." *Variety*, September 13, 1950, p. 1.

V113 "Jolson in London." *Variety*, September 9, 1942, p. 3.

V114 "Jolson In Next Film, But Not As Himself." *Variety*, April 5, 1950, p. 2.

V115 "Jolson In Polaroid to Have Been Another First." *Variety*, October 25, 1950, p. 62.

V116 "Jolson Is Named As *Personality of Yr.*" *Variety*, November 9, 1949.

V117 "Jolson - Keeler - Raye 21G In Det. Windup." *Variety*, July 17, 1940, p. 43.

V118 "Jolson - Korch's No. 2 Complaint Vs. Setay." *Variety*, May 13, 1934, p. 4.

V119 "Jolson, Lily Damita and Cantor For U.A. Musicals." *Variety*, November 17, 1931, p. 3.

V120 "Jolson May Be First Entertainer in Korea." *Variety*, August 30, 1950, p. 1.

V121 "Jolson, Merle Oberon, Et Al., 1st USO Show Un To Reach AEF." *Variety*, August 26, 1942, pp. 1, 25.

V122 "Jolson, Miss Hopkins Would Again Adopt." *Variety*, September 30, 1934, p. 30.

V123 "Jolson, Murray Shows May Follow on CBS." *Variety*, October 28, 1934, p. 35.

V124 "Jolson Nixes Miami Cafe Dates; Weinger, Schulyer Battle For Names."

Variety, November 23, 1949, p. 53.

V125 "Jolson on the Road." *Variety*, March 28, 1919, p. 13.

V126 "Jolson Overseas Tours Seen Filmed By W-K; May Include Dinah, Groucho." *Variety*, October 11, 1950, p. 2.

V127 "Jolson P.A.'ing East." *Variety*, April 1, 1934, p. 3.

V128 "Jolson Pays Klein $700." *Variety*, February 21, 1913, p. 5.

V129 "Jolson Pays Off." *Variety*, October 15, 1941, p. 2.

V130 "Jolson Pic Keys To Col. Pix-Decca Tie." *Variety*, November 26, 1947, p. 47.

V131 "Jolson Planes East." *Variety*, May 10, 1944, p. 2.

V132 "Jolson Rests." *Variety*, October 28, 1934, p. 4.

V133 "Jolson Says No To Elgin, Texaco." *Variety*, February 19, 1947, p. 23.

V134 "Jolson Scoffs At 250G For 6 Teevee Shots." *Variety*, July 6, 1949, p. 1.

V135 "Jolson Services." *Variety*, October 25, 1950.

V136 "Jolson $17,000." *Variety*, April 15, 1934, p. 9.

V137 "Jolson Show Opens Season Aug. 27." *Variety*, August 21, 1940, p. 59.

V138 *"Jolson Sings Again* Will Afford The Star A Capitol Gain Deal." *Variety*, April 21, 1948, pp. 3, 18.

V139 "Jolson Sings (And Talks) Again." *Variety*, January 1, 1968, p. 38.

V140 "Jolson Sings - In Spades." *Variety*, November 17, 1948, p. 1.

V141 *"Jolson Sings* Mulls 2 Broadway Houses." *Variety*, June 8, 1949, p. 6.

V142 *"Jolson* 16M May Start Aussie War." *Variety*, September 14, 1949, p. 15.

V143 "Jolson, Skolsky Talk Remake Of *Burlesque*." *Variety*, July 3, 1946, p. 3.

V144 "Jolson Smash $53,000, Frisco." *Variety*, May 17, 1932, p. 9.

V145 "Jolson Sound in Paris." *Variety*, January 30, 1929, p. 6.

V146 "Jolson Sticks To Music Hall." *Variety*, April 7, 1948, p. 25.

V147 "Jolson Still Hot For Cole Bros. Circus Offer." *Variety*, September 21, 1949, p. 2.

V148 *"Jolson Story* Col's Top Grosser Admits V.P. Suit By Shuberts." *Variety*, March 5, 1947, pp. 3, 54.

V149 "Jolson Story Finales With World's No. 1 Single Entertainer Dead at 64." *Variety*, October 25, 1950, pp. 2, 53, 62.

V150 *"Jolson Story* Reissue A Must For Stereo." *Variety*, March 24, 1954, pp. 3, 17.

V151 "Jolson Theater May Become Roller Rink." *Variety*, August 15, 1933, p. 47.

V152 "Jolson To Get Variety D.C. Citation, Nov. 19." *Variety*, November 9, 1949, p. 18.

V153 "Jolson To Hollywood." *Variety*, February 9, 1944, p. 3.

V154 "Jolson Trailers." *Variety*, February 6, 1946, p. 3.

V155 "Jolson Tribute." *Variety*, November 3, 1950.

V156 "Jolson Trying It Alone." *Variety*, May 9, 1919, p. 3.

V157 "Jolson Upsets Skeptics With Lux Airer." *Variety*, March 3, 1947, p. 1.

V158 "The Jolson Story Video Release." *Variety*, July 30, 1986, p. 63.

V159 "Jolson West, B'way Show Cold." *Variety*, September 2, 1934, p. 3.

V160 "Jolson-Whiteman Hour." *Variety*, August 8, 1933, p. 34.

V161 "Jolson Winds Tour of Korean Front." *Variety*, September 19, 1950.

V162 "Jolson Would Like To Be Neighbor of Crosby On ABC Wax." *Variety*, June 4, 1947, p. 1.

V163 "Jolson, Wynn Closings Hard On Actors." *Variety*, November 5, 1941, pp. 1, 57.

V164 "Jolson Yens Gershwin's *Porgy* As Whiteface Pic." *Variety*, April 19, 1950, p. 1.

V165 *"Jolsonesque* Brooks Ride Carbon To Click." *Variety*, March 18, 1953, p. 1.

V166 "Jolson's Big Business." *Variety*, April 11, 1919, p. 3.

V167 "Jolson's B'way Yen." *Variety*, March 8, 1944, p. 3.

V168 "Jolson's Epstein Left $8,449 Net." *Variety*, January 26, 1955, p. 2.

V169 "Jolson's Estate Worth More, Now Nearer $4,500,000." *Variety*, March 21, 1951, pp. 1, 54.

V170 "Jolson's Fast One Gets *Wonderbar* As Own Feature." *Variety*, October 28, 1932.

V171 "Jolson's $55,000 Is The Big Noise In The Loop; *Kingdom* A Royal 23G." *Variety*, January 3, 1933, p. 9.

V172 "Jolson's Film Bid." *Variety*, August 26, 1942, pp. 1, 25.

V173 "Jolson's Final Year." *Variety*, February 15, 1918, p. 13.

V174 "Jolson's 1st Full W'k S.R.O. $29,000 In Generally OK B'way Biz; *Dinner* Spurts To $17,300, *Night*, $17,000." *Variety*, September 25, 1940, p. 59.

V175 "Jolson's 1st New Act Review in *Variety*." *Variety*, October 25, 1950.

V176 "Jolson's 4 Million." *Variety*, July 30, 1952, p. 4.

V177 "Jolson's Hospital Tour." *Variety*, May 31, 1944, p. 2.

V178 "Jolson's Hosp Tour." *Variety*, October 11, 1944, p. 2.

V179 "Jolsons In Court." *Variety*, July 5, 1919, p. 5.

V180 "Jolson's Increased Terms." *Variety*, March 1, 1918, p. 5.

V181 "Jolson's Kraft Show Up And Ready To Go." *Variety*, August 20, 1947, p. 24.

V182 "*Jolson's* Loew Record." *Variety*, March 5, 1947, pp. 3, 54.

V183 "Jolson's Malaria Has Complications." *Variety*, January 10, 1945, p. 1.

V184 "Jolson's *Music Master*." *Variety*, August 15, 1933, p. 1.

V185 "Jolson's Observation." *Variety*, May 23, 1945, p. 2.

V186 "Jolson's Screen Biog Ready To Shoot Oct. 1." *Variety*, July 5, 1944, p. 2.

V187 "Jolson's Song *Requests* Sparkplug UJA Campaign." *Variety*, May 7, 1947, p. 29.

V188 "Jolson's *Sonny Boy* Now A Nitery Singer." *Variety*, December 16, 1942, p. 1.

V189 "Jolson's Tax Plea." *Variety*, April 20, 1949, p. 2.

V190 "Jolson's Troubles." *Variety*, February 20, 1946, p. 3.

V191 "Jolson's USO Pic." *Variety*, August 2, 1950, p. 1.

V192 "Jolson's Views on the Future of TV." *Variety*, November 1, 1950, pp. 2, 22.

V193 "Jolson's When & If TV Contract With CBS." *Variety*, October 25, 1950, p. 62.

V194 "Jolson's Wonderment." *Variety*, February 9, 1944, p. 52.

V195 Kanter, Hal. "Jolson's Views on the Future of TV." *Variety*, November 1, 1950, p. 2.

V196 "*Kentuckian* Hot." *Variety*, October 12, 1949, p. 10.

V197 "The King." *Variety*, October 25, 1950, p. 2. An editorial tribute to Jolson.

V198 Kupcinet, Irv. "Just for Variety." *Variety*, October 31, 1950.

V199 Langdon With Jolson." *Variety*, May 17, 1932, p. 2.

V200 "The Liberty Loan Campaign." *Variety*, April 19, 1918, p. 9.

V201 "L'ville Keen For *Razor*, $22,000." *Variety*, February 5, 1947, p. 15.

V202 "Medal for Jolson." *Variety*, November 22, 1950.

V203 Moger, Art. Jolson Ad Libs, Talkies Are Born." *Variety*, January 4, 1978.

V204 "Moss Quits *Hats* For *Journey*; Vitale In." *Variety*, September 18, 1940, p. 41.

V205 "Mpls. Indies Expel Exhib-member For Defying *Jolson* Tabu." *Variety*, May 7, 1947, p. 11.

V206 "Mrs. Bugs Baer Sparks Jolson Memorial Plans; Favor All-Star Minstrel."

Variety, November 15, 1950, p. 1.

V207 "Mull *Jolson* Sequel." *Variety*, March 19, 1947, p. 1.

V208 "Muni As *Jazz Singer* In Warner's Remake." *Variety*, January 24, 1945, p. 1.

V209 "Music Shops Find Demand For Jolie Wax Unequalled." *Variety*, October 27, 1950, p. 7.

V210 "Nation in Jolson Tribute." *Variety*, November 1, 1950, pp. 2, 22.

V211 "National Box Office Survey." *Variety*, March 5, 1947, pp. 3, 54.

V212 "National Box Office Survey." *Variety*, November 2, 1949, p. 3.

V213 "New Acts: Al Jr. r.n. Harry Brown." *Variety*, January 26, 1966, p. 60.

V214 "New York Remembers Al Jolson As 100th Anni Tribute Kicks Off." *Variety*, June 5, 1985, p. 78.

V215 "No Military Pomp, At Widow's Request." *Variety*, October 27, 1950, p. 2.

V216 "No. 2 *Sinbad*." *Variety*, April 4, 1919, p. 13.

V217 "Obituary." *Variety*, October 25, 1950, p. 3.

V218 "Obituary." *Variety*, November 1, 1950.

V219 "Oral Testimony Ends In Shuberts' 500G *Jolson Story* Suit." *Variety*, April 2, 1947, p. 8.

V220 "*The Outlaw* Joins *GWTW*, *Jolson* As Champ Reissue." *Variety*, June 4, 1947, p. 6.

V221 "Patsy Kelly Leaves Jolson Show in Wash." *Variety*, November 24, 1931, p. 48.

V222 "Philly Prospects Bright For '40 - 41; Jolson Show Opens Season Aug. 27." *Variety*, August 21, 1940, p. 59.

V223 "Pitt Perks; *Jolson* Huge 28G." *Variety*, February 19, 1947, p. 16.

V224 "Play On Broadway." *Variety*, September 18, 1940, p. 42.

V225 "Posthumous U.S. Medal for the Late Al Jolson." *Variety*, November 22, 1950, p. 1.

V226 "Prospects Good For Jolie To Play Himself In Sequel." *Variety*, July 28, 1948, p. 2.

V227 "Radio Followup," *Variety*, August 24, 1949.

V228 "Recalls Old Toledo Feud." *Variety*, November 5, 1941, pp. 1, 57.

V229 "Reissue of '35 Jolson Pic Fizzles In Bid To Cash In On *Story* BO." *Variety*, July 23, 1947, p. 7.

V230 "Return Patsy Kelly to Show on Equity Ruling." *Variety*, December 1, 1934, p. 45.

V231 "Revival Under The *L*." *Variety*, August 28, 1934, pp. 1, 55.

V232 "The Saga of Jolson." *Variety*, September 18, 1940, p. 2.

V233 "Sat. Is *Jolson Day* In Nation's Capital." *Variety*, November 17, 1949.

V234 "See Col And Par Modifying A Bit On Terms For *Jolson* And *Samson*." *Variety*, November 2, 1949, pp. 5, 24.

V235 "Seek Replacement for Jolson in *Stars* Pic Tribute to Show Biz." *Variety*, November 1, 1950, p. 22.

V236 "Sez Harry Jolson." *Variety*, November 20, 1946, p. 62.

V237 "Show Biz Nostalgia Pays Off." *Variety*, July 23, 1947, pp. 1, 18.

V238 "Showbiz Salutes (Again) Al Jolson, B'nai B'rith's *Man of the Year*." *Variety*, December 16, 1947.

V239 "Shuberts Miss Friar's Dinner to Jolson." *Variety*, April 5, 1918, p. 11.

V240 "*Sinbad* Re-opens at 44th Street." *Variety*, June 7, 1918, p. 12.

V241 "Sock $8.80 Preem Of Jolson -- *Hats* May Signalize Flourishing B'way Season; *Tightest* Debut In Years." *Variety*, September 18, 1940, p. 41.

V242 "Song Tribute to Jolie By Bene Russell-DeRose." *Variety*, November 15,

1950, p. 1.

V243 "Sophie Tucker and Jolson Firsts (Early Recordings)." *Variety*, January 1, 1957, p. 257.

V244 "Stage-struck Jolie." *Variety*, September 14, 1949, p. 18.

V245 "Still Beating 'Em." *Variety*, June 28, 1918, p. 11.

V246 "Successful N.V.A. Benefit." *Variety*, May 17, 1918, p. 9.

V247 "Summon Eastern Doc To Jolson's Bedside." *Variety*, January 17, 1945, p. 2.

V248 "Texaco To Kunder; Bracken Cancelled." *Variety*, February 19, 1947, p. 23.

V249 "That Winchell Socko By Jolson Behind Columnist's $500,000 Suit." *Variety*, August 8, 1933, p. 1.

V250 "Theatrical Liberty Loan Division Sees Goal in Sight." *Variety*, April 26, 1918, p. 5.

V251 "TOA Argues Public Has *Natural Right* To See *Better* Pix At Fixed B.O." *Variety*, November 16, 1949, pp. 6, 29.

V252 "Too Many Cooks at Jolson Nite?; Lack of Names." *Variety*, October 31, 1951, p. 2.

V253 "Tunesmith's Cancer Cause Wins Support." *Variety*, December 17, 1947, p. 49.

V254 "27G Judgement vs. Decca for Jolson Estate." *Variety*, September 21, 1955, p. 58.

V255 "20,000 Pay Respects at Jolson Services." *Variety*, October 27, 1950, p. 1.

V256 "Uncle Sam May Foot Bill On Jolson's Radio Pitch For Army Recruiting." *Variety*, May 7, 1947, p. 1.

V257 "*Variety* Boosts *Jolson*." *Variety*, December 12, 1945, p. 2.

V258 "Vets Honor Jolson." *Variety*, October 25, 1950, p. 62.

V259 "WB Plea To Arnold Gets MD's Planed To Jolson." *Variety*, January 24, 1945, p. 1.

V260 "Well-Healed." *Variety*, November 9, 1950.

V261 "Whiteman May Join Jolson in WB Film." *Variety*, September 19, 1933, p. 31.

V262 "Who Put B.O. Freezer On?" *Variety*, November 9, 1949, p. 18.

V263 "Will Is Probated; Bulk of Fortune Goes to Charity." *Variety*, October 27, 1950, p. 6.

V264 "Winchell Laughing Off Al's Socks Says Coast Jam Publicity For Film; Framing Round Robin For Hearst." *Variety*, July 25, 1933, pp. 3, 25.

Appendix A: Stage Shows Based on Jolson's Life

There have been several musical plays based on Jolson's life and career. Some have included original music while others have depended on the vast catalogue of Jolson standards. These include:

SS1) *THE MAGIC OF JOLSON*

1975. Provincetown Playhouse, New York. 5 performances.

Credits

A musical based on the life of Al Jolson. Music and lyrics: Various composers. Additional music: Richard De Mone. Additional lyrics and book: Pearl Sieben. Conductor: Richard De Mone.

Cast

Norman Brooks (Al Jolson), Linda Gerard, John Medici.

Songs

"Toot Toot Tootsie," "Sweet Singer," "Alabamy Bound," "If You Knew Susie," "Ma, He's Makin' Eyes at Me," "Where Did Robinson Crusoe Go With Friday on Saturday Night," "You Made Me Love You," "All My Love," "Swanee," "Rock-A-Bye Your Baby With a Dixie Melody," "Faces," "You Ain't Heard Nothin' Yet," "Mammy," "I've Gotta Get Back to New York," "Hello Tucky!," "California, Here I Come," "Ma Blushin' Rosie," "April Showers," "A Goil Like Me," "I Still Love You," "Makin' Whoopee," "I Could Not Get Along Without a Song," "Avalon," "Sonny Boy," "Give My Regards to Broadway," "Anniversary Song," "I'm Sittin' On Top of the World," "God's Country."

Commentary

Brooks had played Al Jolson in the movie *The Best Things in Life Are Free*, a fictionalized film biography of De Sylva, Brown, and Henderson. Sieben authored the first major biography of Jolson. Information about this production is included in David Hummel's *The Collector's Guide to the American Musical Theatre. Volume I: The Shows*. Metuchen, New Jersey and London: The Scarecrow Press, Inc., 1984, pp. 357-358.

SS2) JOLSON

1978. Papermill Playhouse, Milburn, New Jersey. (Also performed in 1979, Royal Poinciana Playhouse, Palm Beach, Florida).

Credits

A musical play based on the life of Al Jolson. Music and lyrics: Irwin Levine, L. Russell Brown. Book: Leslie Eberhard, David Levy. Direction and Choreography: Bill Guske.

Cast

Clive Baldwin (Al Jolson), Sherry Rooney, Joseph Leon, Nina Dova, Reuben Shafer, George Bamford, Maureen Brennan, Humphrey Davis, Renee Roy, Scott Stevenson, Kaylyn Dillehay, Ron Schwinn, Hal Shane, Bob Heath, Ken Mitchell, Michael Lichtefeld, Suzanne Walker, Dennis Batutis, Barbara Hanks, Paula Lynn, Barbara Mandra, Roxanna White.

Songs

"I Got a Song in Me," "Nobody Do Me Like My Daddy Do Me," "Jolie's Back in Town," "We're Only Here for a Day," "Little Sammy," "If It Wasn't for You," "The Good Guy Always Gets the Girl," "The Question," "Who Needs Love?," "Tappin-G-Minor," "Falena," "It's a Great Idea," "Why Can't I Be Happy Too?," "Boyala," "When Ya Get Yourself Married," "Give Me a Good Old Mammy Song."

Commentary

A photograph, along with production specifics on *Jolson* can be found in *John Willis' Theatre World*, 1978-1979, Volume 35. New York: Crown Publishers, 1980, p. 200. Information is also included in David Hummel's *The Collector's Guide to the American Musical Theatre. Volume I: The Shows*. Metuchen, New Jersey and London: The Scarecrow Press, Inc., 1984, p. 301.

SS3) *JOLEY. A MUSICAL ABOUT THE LIFE AND TIMES OF AL JOLSON.*

1979. Northstage, Glen Cove, New York.

Credits

A musical in two acts about the life and times of Al Jolson from 1894 to 1950. Book and lyrics: Herbert Hartig. Music: Milton DeLugg. Director: Jay Harnick. Choreography and Musical Staging: George Bunt. Scenery: David Chapman. Costumes: Carole H. Beule. Lighting: Marc B. Weiss. Musical Director: Lisa Redfield. Orchestrations: Walt Levinsky. Dance and Vocal Arrangements: Donald Jonston. Hairstylist: Patrick D. Moreton. Assistant Choreographer: Bob Heath. Production Coordinator: David Kissell. Presented by Bob Funking and Bill Stutler by special arrangement with Jeff Britton. Press: M.J. Boyer. Stage Manager: Robert H. Barth. Conductor: Lisa Redfield.

Cast

Mitchell Greenburg (Harry Akst, Ren Shields, Camembert, Ray Henderson), Clement Fowler (Louis Epstein, Printer, Dumond), Larry Kert

(Al Jolson), Gibby Brand (George Jessel, Lee Shubert, Buddy DeSylva, Doctor), Randy Brenner (Hersch Yoelson), Jeff Yonis (Asa Yoelson, Georgie Yoelson), Jerry Jarrett (Rabbi Moses Yoelson), Merwin Goldsmith (Harry Jolson), Gloria Hodes (Naomi Yoelson, Lulu), Suzanne Walker (Rose, Suzette, Ruby), Ilene Frazer (Etta, First Nurse), Hessi (Laura Ackermann), Diana Broderick (Aggie Beeler), Mitchell Jason (Agent, Jake Shubert, Impressario, Joe Schenck), Kurt Knudson (Joe Palmer, Patapouf, H.M. Warner, Harry Cohn), Dana Moore (Mitzi), Eileen Casey (Josie, Second Nurse), Joleen Fodor (Henrietta Keller, Nun, Erle), Lisby Larson (Ethel Delmar, Texas Guinan), Albert Stephenson (Jimmy), Dorothy Stanley (Louella Parsons). Ensemble: Laura Ackermann, Diana Broderick, Eileen Casey, Ilene Frazer, Bob Heath, Timothy R. Kratoville, Dana Moore, Stephen Moore, Danny Robins, Randy Skinner, Dorothy Stanley, Albert Stephenson.

Songs

"I'm Just Wild About Harry," "Here We Are Again," "Song of the Immigrant Mothers," "Melons," "You Ain't Seen Nuthin' Yet," "Henrietta," "Darktown Strutters Ball," "Shubert Serenade," "Robert E. Lee Cakewalk," "Swanee," "Rock-A-Bye Your Baby," "Mrs. Ulysses," "A Graceful Exit," "Dullest Couple in Scarsdale," "Toot-Toot Tootsie," "Alabamy Bound," "'Ello Hengland 'Ello," "Mama," "Sonny Boy," "Ruby," "This Time," "Pardon Me Porter," "Pettin' on the Old Porch Swing," "The Kissing Rock," "Times Square," "I Gotta Perform," "World War Two Medley," "Oh! You Beautiful Doll," "Finale."

Commentary

Photographs of *Joley*, along with production details can be found in *John Willis' Theatre World*, 1978-1979, Volume 35. New York: Crown Publishers, 1980, p. 161. Information is also included in David Hummel's *The Collector's Guide to the American Musical Theatre. Volume I: The Shows.* Metuchen, New Jersey and London: The Scarecrow Press, Inc., 1984, p. 300.

SS4) *AL JOLSON, TONIGHT*

1980 (toured to numerous cities).

Credits

A new Musical about the Life and Times of Al Jolson, "The World's Greatest Entertainer." Book: Nicholas Dante. Words and Music: America's Best Loved Composers and Lyricists. Director and Choreographer: Michael Shawn. Scenic Design: Michael Bottari and Ronald Case. Costume Design: Dona Granata and Walter Pickette. Lighting Design: William Strom. Musical Direction and Vocal Arrangements: Michael David Biagi. Orchestrations: Edward Sauter. Dance Music Arrangements: Dorothea Freitag. Additional Orchestrations: Randall L. Biagi. Music Supervision: Earl Shendll.

Cast

Larry Kert (Al Jolson, song and dance man), Alan Kass (Al's Manager, Eppy), Stuart Zagnit (Al's Accompanist, Fingers), Roxann Parker (Al's First

Wife, Henrietta), Michael McCarty (Al's First Producer, Jake Shubert), Hal Maxwell (Al's Second Producer, Lee Shubert), Matthew Kwiat (Al's Brother, Harry), Elliot Levine (Al's Father, Moses Yoelson), Michon Peacock (Al's Second Wife, Ethel), Lawrence Raiken (Al's Special guest, Eddie Cantor), Maureen Moore (Al's Third Wife, Ruby). A Bevy of Al's Favorite Broadway Beauties and Buddies: Paula Grider, Richard Haskin, Nancy Hess, Brenda Holmes, Suzie Jary, Robert Kellett, Chrissy Kellogg, David Michael Lang, Kitty Laub, Paige Massman, Annette Michel, Brad Miskell, Gina Paglia, D'Arcy Phifer, Freda Soifer, Christina Stolberg, Gary Sullivan, Carla Farnsworth Webb, David Westphal, Barrie Wood. Al Jolson Understudy: Lawrence Raiken.

Songs

"Waiting For the Robert E. Lee," "The Spaniard That Blighted My Life," "Sweet Sixteen," "When the Grown-up Ladies Act Like Babies," "Hello, My Baby," "How You Gonna Keep 'Em Down On the Farm," "I Wonder Who's Kissing Her Now," "It All Depends On You," "Don't Let It Get You Down," "If I Only Had a Match," "Rock-A-Bye Your Baby," "Soft Shoe," "You Let Me Down," "Mammy," "Gee, I Wish I Had a Girl," "Margie," "Ida," "Dinah," "Rosie," "Liza," "Sittin' On Top Of The World," "My Blue Heaven," "After You've Gone," "California, Here I Come," "If You Knew Susie," "Toot, Toot Tootsie," "Crazy Rhythm," "Darn That Dream," "April Showers," "Jolson Medley," "Finale."

Appendix B: Newsreels

A considerable amount of vintage newsreel footage of Al Jolson survives in various film repositories. Some of these items include:

N1) Al Jolson
1951. Universal. Can No. 24-494. 54 ft..
Footage of the dedication of the Al Jolson Memorial at the Hillside Memorial Park.

N2) Al Jolson at Inaugural Handicap
1930. Pathé. Issue No.: NR; Library No.: 197.
Jolson and Ruby Keeler are seen talking to the winner of the race.

N3) Al Jolson -- Final Curtain
1950. Pathé. Issue No.: PSN 23 C-3. Negative No.: 34578. 160 ft..
Includes footage of Jolson from films and earlier newsreels, along with new film of his funeral service.

N4) Al Jolson in Sicily
1943. Army Pictorial Center. ADC 1007. No. 0-102.
Jolson is seen on a platform entertaining American soldiers during World War II.

N5) Al Jolson in Tokyo General Hospital
1950. Army Pictorial Center. ADC 8379-1.
Includes footage of Jolson entertaining patients and staff of Tokyo General Hospital during the Korean War.

N6) Al Jolson is Marshall of Motion Picture Divisions in NRA Parade
1933. Pathé. Issue No.: 13. Library No.: 3291.
Jolson is briefly interviewed and remarks comically about the event.

N7) Al Jolson Memorial Unveiled
1951. Pathé. Issue No.: PSN 13 C2B. Negative No.: 34956. 117 ft..
Includes footage of Jack Benny and Erle Jolson placing a wreath on the shrine dedicated to Jolson at the Hillside Memorial Park.

N8) Al Jolson Remembered. . .Washington
1951. Paramount News.
This is footage of Secretary of State George Marshall presenting Jolson's adopted son, Asa, with the Medal of Merit. Jolson's widow, Erle, is also seen.

N9) Along Broadway: "This Is the Army" Has Premiere in New York
1943. Movietone. Story No.: 49-803.
Jolson, along with Jack Warner, Albert Warner, and some military personnel, is seen speaking outside the Hollywood Theatre in New York at the film's premiere.

N10) Celebrities Salute Bob Hope
1947. Pathé. Issue No: 23. Library No.: G-9836. 116 ft..
A number of entertainers, including Jolson, are seen at a tribute to Hope.

N11) "Cover-Up" Wins Gold Cub
1947. Pathé. Issue No.: 97. Library No.: C-9385. 139 ft..
Footage includes Jolson at Hollywood Park, with a crowd of 50,000 for the $100,000 Gold Cup race.

N12) 15-To-1 Shot Wins $100,000 Horse Race
1947. Pathé. Issue No.: 55. Library No.: C-8633. 152 ft..
Jolson and his wife, Erle, are seen watching a Chilean horse, Olhaverry, win a $100,000 race at Santa Anita racetrack.

N13) 50000 Turf Fans See He Did Win Xmas H'Cap
1937. Universal. Can No. v9 r 627. Neg. 1131. 23 ft..
Jolson is seen at Santa Anita racetrack.

N14) Forward Together
1935. Vitaphone. 11 minutes.
This tribute to the great events of the twentieth century includes footage of Jolson in *The Jazz Singer*.

N15) Gigantic NRA Parade Thrills New York.
1933. Pathé. Negative No.: 5945.
Jolson is seen marching up New York's Fifth Avenue in an NRA parade.

N16) Gold Cup Race (1948) Won by "Shannon"
1948. Universal. Issue No.: 5942x5. 647 ft..
Jolson is viewed among a crowd including Betty Grable, William Powell, Diana Lynn, and Ann Rutherford at the Gold Cup Race in Los Angeles.

N17) Hollywood Gold Cup Race
1946. Hearst Metrotone Newsreel. Issue No. 294, Vol. 17.
Jolson is among the stars watching Fred Astaire's horse, "Triplicate," win the Gold Cup race by a nose.

N18) Hollywood Unveils Al Jolson Shrine
1951. Movietone News.
Footage of the ceremonies unveiling the shrine at the Jolson gravesite in Hollywood Memorial Park.

N19) Honeymooners Are Home Again. Al Jolson and His Beautiful Bride the Former Ruby Keeler Arrive in New York City
1928. International Newsreel. Vol. 10, Issue 85.
Jolson and Ruby Keeler are seen returning from their European honeymoon. The footage is silent.

N20) Japan--Al Jolson Entertains
1950. Telenews.
Footage of Jolson performing for American soldiers in Tokyo during the early days of the Korean War.

N21) Jolson at the Loew's Paradise Theater in Brooklyn, New York
1949. Hearst Metrotone Newsreel. Can 2670 Roll 7.
This is apparently unused newsreel footage of Jolson performing at Loew's Paradise Theater during his promotional tour for *Jolson Sings Again*.

N22) Jolson Sings Again
1949. News of the Day.
Footage of Jolson's arrival at Loew's Theatre on Grand Concourse during his tour of New York theatres to promote *Jolson Sings Again*. Includes footage of Jolson performing and a large crowd watching his arrival by open car.

N23) Jolson's Story Ends. . .
1950. Pathé. Issue No.: 21. Library No.: D-3321. 71 ft..
Scenes of Jolson's funeral are shown, along with footage of him entertaining American soldiers in Korea a few weeks before his death.

N24) Korea--U.N. Forces Dig in Against China Reds
1950. Universal. Can No. 23-412. Neg. 172. 182 ft..
Includes footage of Secretary of Defense George C. Marshall presenting Jolson's widow and son with the Medal of Merit recognizing Jolson's efforts in entertaining American troops in Korea.

N25) Korea--U.N. Forces Strike Back at Retreating Red Foe
1950. Hearst. Can No. 23-388. Neg. 181. 190 ft..
Includes footage of Jolson singing to American troops in Korea.

N26) Korean War, Al Jolson
1950. Army Pictorial Center. ADC 8260-2.
Footage includes Jolson with various military personnel and receiving a U.N. flag from Nancy Kimm and some officers.

N27) Korean War, Al Jolson
1950. Army Pictorial Center. ADC 8260-3.
Jolson is seen entering an arena in Pusan where he performs for American soldiers during the Korean War.

N28) Korean War, Al Jolson
1950. Army Pictorial Center. ADC 8263-3.
Jolson is greeted by Col. Noble J. Wiley, Jr. and Lt. Col. Samuel E. Spitzer in

Pusan during the Korean War.

N29) *Korean War, Al Jolson*
1950. Army Pictorial Center. ADC 8330-3.
Jolson is seen performing for the Eighth Army in Taegu during the Korean War.

N30) *Korean War, Al Jolson*
1950. Army Pictorial Center. ADC 8379-1.
Jolson and Harry Akst are seen exiting a plane and being greeted by General Paul Kelly.

N31) *Marion, Ohio*
1920. Pathé. Issue No.: Sil. 69. Negative No.: 4561. 82 ft..
Includes silent footage of Jolson singing on the lawn of Presidential candidate Warren G. Harding's Marion, Ohio home during a political rally.

N32) *Meet the Real Al Jolson: Famous Mammy Singer Tells How It Feels To Be Working in New York*
1930. Hearst Metrotone Newsreel. Issue No.: 201, Vol. 2.
Jolson is seen standing in front of a curtain talking directly to the camera. He discusses being back in New York and tells a few jokes.

N33) *Men of Destiny: Al Jolson*
1950. Pathé.
Narrated by Bob Considine, this item offers a quick overview of Jolson's career, including vintage newsreel footage, a scene from *The Jazz Singer*, and ending with footage of the Jolson funeral.

N34) *Movie Stars Entertain*
1942. Army Pictorial Center. ADC 1335.
Merle Oberon, Patricia Morrison, Frank McHugh, and Jolson are seen entertaining American soldiers in Africa during World War II.

N35) *Nags "Take" California*
1937. Pathé. Issue No.: 42. Library No.: 6776. 99 ft..
Jolson and Ruby Keeler are seen at the Santa Anita racetrack.

N36) *Nation Mourns Al Jolson*
1950. Telenews.
George Jessel's eulogy to Jolson is heard as a voice over footage of Jolson's funeral.

N37) *New Track For Movie Colony*
1938. Hearst Metrotone Newsreel. Issue No. 272, Vol. 9.
Jolson stars at preview of the opening of Hollywood Park.

N38) *News of Nation: New York Show For Army War Relief*
1942. Movietone. Story No.: 47-650, 47-651, Vol. 25/9. 100 ft..
Movie, stage, and radio personalities are seen performing for a war bond drive, including footage of Jolson singing "April Showers."

N39) Opening Inglewood, California Racetrack
1938. Pathé. Issue No.: NR. Library No.: 5240.
Jolson and Ruby Keeler are seen at the races.

N40) Paramount News
1945. Paramount. Vol. 4, No. 89. 7 mins.
Don Ameche, Joe E. Brown, and Jolson are seen at the Santa Anita race track.

N41) Paramount News
1947. Paramount. Vol. 6, No. 55. 8 mins.
Includes footage of Louis B. Mayer, Betty Grable, Don Ameche, and Jolson attending the races at Santa Anita.

N42) Paramount News
1951. Paramount. Vol. 10, No. 39. 7 mins.
Footage of Jolson singing is included marking Jolson's death as one of the significant news events of 1950.

N43) Pathé Audio Review
1928. Pathé. Cat. No. DR-2. One reel.
Footage of Jolson and golf pro Jimmy Farrell on a golf course.

N44) Play Ball!
1940. Pathé. Issue No.: 67. Library No.: 9416. 256 ft..
Jolson is seen in attendance at a baseball game.

N45) Race Track Scenes and Personalities
1946. Pathé. Issue No.: NR. Library No.: C-6923.
Footage of Jolson and his wife, Erle, at the races in Arcadia, California.

N46) Rosemont Wins Richest Race by a Whisker
1930. Pathé. Issue No.: 60. Library No.: 6090.
Jolson is seen at the races at Santa Anita.

N47) Santa Anita Opens California Racing
1936. Pathé. Issue No.: 42. Library No.: 5901. Reissue No.: 375.
Jolson and Ruby Keeler are seen at the races.

N48) Santa Anita -- Park Opens
1938. Pathé. Issue No.: NR. Negative No.: 8002.
Includes footage of Jolson at the racetrack.

N49) Sports: (A) Weight Lifting (B) Horse Race
1948. Universal. Can No. 22-209. Neg. 93-109.
Jolson and Buddy Clark are seen at Santa Anita.

N50) Stars See Hollywood Derby
1941. Hearst Metrotone Newsreel. Issue No.: 287, Vol. 12.
Jolson is seen among such stars as Jimmy Stewart, Chico Marx, Betty Grable, and George Raft at the races.

N51) "This Is the Army"
> 1943. Universal. Can No. 16-211. Neg. 85. 93 ft..

Includes footage of Jolson at the premiere of the film version of Irving Berlin's *This Is the Army*.

N52) "Thumbs Up" Wins Santa Anita
> 1945. Pathé. Issue No.: PSN 23 C-3. Negative No.: 34578. 160 ft.

Jolson is seen at the first running of California's $100,000 race.

N53) $25,000 Hollywood Derby Won by Staretor!
> 1941. Pathé. Issue No.: 82. Negative No.: C-1085. 49 ft..

Jolson and Chico Marx are seen clowning in the stands at the racetrack.

N54) 2,000,000 Dollar Race Track Opens
> 1929. Movietone. Story No.: 4-755. 1,100 ft..

Scots Grey wins the last race at a new Mexican racetrack and Jolson and Ruby Keeler are seen in the winner's circle with the horse and jockey.

N55) U.N. Offensive
> 1950. Signal Corps. Combat Bulletin No. 103. 21 mins.

Includes footage of Jolson entertaining American troops near the front during the Korean War.

N56) World Honors Adolph Zukor, Film Pioneer
> 1936. Pathé.Issue No.: 36. Library No.: 5864.

Jolson is seen among the celebrities marking Zukor's twenty-fifth year in movies.

N57) Yesterday's Newsreel
> c. 1950. TV Highlights.

A compilation of vintage newsreels on various topics. Jolson, in derby and sporting a monocle, is seen in 1924 clowning with reporters on a ship deck following his return from a trip to England.

Appendix C: Cartoons

Few performing artists have been as frequently imitated or caricatured as Al Jolson. Most cartoon shorts featuring Jolson caricatures, vocal imitations, or Jolson songs made during his lifetime were produced by Warner Bros. (with one notable exception, *The Jazz Fool*, made by Walt Disney), and these are listed below in chronological order. Each entry includes the title, year, producing company, cartoon series title, and credits, as well as brief commentary.

C1) *Bosko The Talk-Ink Kid*
> 1929. Warner Bros., Looney Tunes. B&W.
> Producers: Hugh Harman, Rudolf Ising

This pilot cartoon for the "Bosko" series includes the character performing a tap dance and playing Jolson's "Sonny Boy" from *The Singing Fool* (see F3) on the piano.

C2) *The Jazz Fool*
> 1929. Walt Disney. B&W.

Tribute is paid to Jolson and his popular films, *The Jazz Singer* (see F2) and *The Singing Fool* (see F3), in this "Mickey Mouse" cartoon from the early days of sound cartoons.

C3) *Sinkin' in the Bathtub*
> 1930. Warner Bros., Looney Tunes. B&W.
> Supervision: Hugh Harman, Rudolf Ising. Animation: Isadore Freling. Music: Frank Marsales.

In this very musical cartoon featuring "Bosko," Jolsonesque moments are seen when "Bosko" sings in the bathtub, using his feet, nose, and the shower stream as musical instruments.

C4) *Congo Jazz*
> 1930. Warner Bros., Looney Tunes. B&W.
> Supervision: Hugh Harman, Rudolf Ising. Animation: Max Maxwell, Paul Smith. Music: Frank Marsales.

The Jolsonesque "When the Little Red Roses Get the Blues for You" is performed by animals in the Congo, and featuring "Bosko."

C5) *Box Car Blues*
> 1931. Warner Bros., Looney Tunes. B&W.
> Supervision: Hugh Harman, Rudolf Ising. Animation: Rollin Hamilton, Max
> Maxwell. Music: Frank Marsales.

While careening down a mountain in a runaway box car, "Bosko" bursts into a
Jolson imitation singing, "My Mammy."

C6) *Ups 'N Downs*
> 1931. Warner Bros., Looney Tunes. B&W.
> Supervision: Rollin Hamilton, Paul Smith. Music: Frank Marsales.

"Bosko" plays a hot dog salesman who sells a wiener to a dog who recognizes it as
his long lost "Sonny Boy," and the dog and wiener dance away singing the Jolson
standard in Jolsonesque style.

C7) *Lady Play Your Mandolin*
> 1931. Warner Bros., Looney Tunes. B&W.
> Supervision: Frank Marsales. Animation: Rollin Hamilton, Norm Blackburn.
> Music: Abe Lyman and His Brunswick Recording Orchestra.

In this cartoon, "Foxy," a new character in the Looney Tunes series loosely based
on Disney's "Mickey Mouse," does Jolson impressions in an "on stage" scene.

C8) *You Don't Know What You're Doin'*
> 1931. Warner Bros., Looney Tunes. B&W.
> Supervision: Hugh Harman, Rudolf Ising. Animation: Isadore Freleng,
> Norm Blackburn. Music: Gus Arnheim's Brunswick Recording Orchestra.

"Piggy" and "Fluffy," two pigs, go to a vaudeville show. A doorman scoffs at them,
but he is turned into a blackfaced Jolson when their motorcycle backfires in his
face.

C9) *It's Got Me Again*
> 1932. Warner Bros., Merrie Melodies. B&W.
> Supervision: Hugh Harman, Rudolf Ising. Animation: Isadore Freleng,
> Thomas McKimson.

When a mouse is cornered by a cat, it bursts into the cartoon's title song ala
Jolson. This cartoon was nominated for an Academy Award.

C10) *Goin' To Heaven On A Mule*
> 1934. Warner Bros., Merrie Melodies. Color.
> Supervision: Isadore Freleng. Animation: Rollin Hamilton, Bob McKimson.
> Music: Norman Spencer.

A lazy boy in the South dreams of "Goin' to Heaven on a Mule," like Jolson in
Wonder Bar (see F10).

C11) *Into Your Dance*
> 1935. Warner Bros., Merrie Melodies. Color.
> Supervision: Isadore Freleng. Animation: Cal Dalton, Ben Clopton. Music:
> Norman Spencer.

A quartet sings "Go Into Your Dance" in Jolsonesque blackface, featuring the song
from Jolson's 1935 film of the same name (see F11), and "Alabamy Bound" is also
included.

C12) *I Love To Sing-A*
>   1936. Warner Bros., Merrie Melodies. Color.
>   Supervision: Fred Avery. Animation: Charles M. Jones, Virgil Ross. Music:
>   Norman Spencer.

A young owl ("Owl Jolson") with a penchant for jazz is the son of classical music professor Fritz Owl, who throws the youngster out of the house because he repeatedly sings the jazzy "I Love to Sing-A" from Jolson's film *The Singing Kid* (see F12). "Owl Jolson" redeems himself with the family by winning "Jack Bunny's" radio talent show.

C13) *Clean Pastures*
>   1937. Warner Bros., Merrie Melodies. Color.
>   Supervision: I Freleng. Animation: Phil Monroe, Paul Smith. Musical
>   Direction: Carl W. Stalling.

This Harlem-style jazz fest features imitations of many black jazz greats, and the score includes Jolson's song "Save Me Sister" from *The Singing Kid* (see F12).

C14) *The Woods Are Full Of Cuckoos*
>   1937. Warner Bros., Merrie Melodies. Color.
>   Supervision: Frank Tashlin. Story: Melvin Millar. Animation: Robert
>   Bentley. Musical Direction: Carl W. Stalling.

Among the show business personalities satirized in this animal cartoon are Jolson ("Al Goatson" -- the singing kid) and Ruby Keeler ("Ruby Squealer").

C15) *Porky in Wackyland*
>   1938. Warner Bros., Looney Tunes. Color.
>   Supervision: Robert Clampett. Animation: Norman McCabe, I. Ellis.
>   Musical Direction: Carl W. Stalling.

This take-off on *Alice in Wonderland* includes several caricatures of film stars, including a strange blackfaced creature that mutters "Mammy!"

C16) *Leon Schlesinger Presents Bugs Bunny*
>   1942. Warner Bros. Color.
>   Director: Robert Clampett. Animation: Virgil Ross, Bob McKimson, Rod
>   Scribner.

A special cartoon used as a trailer to sell war bonds during World War II, featuring the Irving Berlin song, "Any Bonds Today?," and starring Bugs Bunny, who does a Jolson imitation for one chorus of the song.

C17) *The Swooner Crooner*
>   1944. Warner Bros., Looney Tunes. Color.
>   Supervision: Frank Tashlin. Story: Warren Foster. Animation: George
>   Cannata. Musical Direction: Carl W. Stalling.

This Academy Award-nominated cartoon includes caricatures of the leading popular singers of the day, including Jolson singing "September in the Rain."

C18) *Curtain Razor*
>   1949. Warner Bros., Looney Tunes. Color.
>   Director: Fritz Freleng. Story: Todd Pierce. Animation: Manuel Perez, Ken
>   Chapin, Virgil Ross, Peter Burness. Layouts: Hawley Pratt. Backgrounds:
>   Paul Julian. Voice Characterization: Mel Blanc. Musical Direction: Carl W.

Stalling.

Porky Pig is a barnyard talent scout who auditions several acts, including animal versions of Jolson, Bing Crosby, and Frank Sinatra who all sing a chorus of "April Showers."

C19) *What's Up Doc?*

1950. Warner Bros., Looney Tunes. Color.

Director: Robert McKimson. Story: Warren Foster. Animation: J.C. Melendez, Charles McKimson, Phil DeLara, Wilson Burness. Layouts: Cornett Wood. Backgrounds: Richard H. Thomas. Voice Characterization: Mel Blanc. Musical Direction: Carl W. Stalling.

In one scene, an out-of-work Bugs Bunny is shown sitting on a park bench with such other stars as Jolson, Jack Benny, Eddie Cantor, and Bing Crosby. When Elmer Fudd, "the big vaudeville star," walks by Jolson says, "I hear he's looking for a partner for his act." Everyone auditions for Fudd, but he chooses Bugs Bunny as his new partner.

Appendix D: Awards

For a performer of his stature, Jolson received relatively few awards. His greatest days as a stage star pre-date many modern theatrical awards; the same is true of his film career. Most of his awards came in the last few years of his life, following his post-World War II comeback, and after his death. Among the awards he did receive were several from the United States government and the military in recognition of his efforts in entertaining American servicemen and women in World Wars I, II, and Korea.

A1) The Al Jolson Memorial Award
1950.Veterans of Foreign Wars
Hollywood, California

This award was first presented after Jolson's death. It is awarded to deserving members of the show business community for their contributions to the armed services. Among the early recipients was Jolson's old friend Eddie Cantor.

A2) Al Jolson Post of the American Legion
1951. American Legion
New York, New York

This post was established in January 1951 as a tribute to Jolson.

A3) Award of Merit
1951. County Council of the American Legion
Patriotic Hall, Los Angeles, California

This award from the Legion was presented postumously to Jolson on April 6, 1951. Jolson's widow, Erle, accepted the award from William P. Haughton, Past Post Commander.

A4) Certificate of Esteem
1954. Department of Defense
Black-Foxe Military Academy, Los Angeles, California

The certificate was presented postumously for Jolson's work entertaining American troops in Korea. It was presented to his adopted son, Asa, Jr., at the boy's school. Jolson's widow, Erle, was also present to accept the certificate presented for the Department of Defense by Senator Thomas H. Kuchel.

A5) Honorary Mayor and President of the Chamber of Commerce

1934. City of Encino, California.

Encino, California

Not long after Jolson and Ruby Keeler took up residence in Encino, Jolson was accorded this honor.

A6) Jolson Corner

1951. National Conference of Christians and Jews

Lord Tarleton Hotel, Miami Beach, Florida

In Jolson's honor, a "corner" in the Lord Tarleton would include a display from*Variety* of Jolson's career.

At a dinner with 150 guests, and Eddie Cantor as master of ceremonies, celebrities appeared including Phil Foster, Jimmy Durante, Joe E. Lewis, Kay Armen, and Danny Thomas, who spoke of Jolson's contributions to inter-racial understanding. Proceeds from the event were donated to specifically aid the National Conference of Christians and Jews in their inter-racial work.

A7) Jolson Day

1949. Washington, D.C. Board of Commissioners

Washington, D.C.

This special day in Jolson's home town was planned in tandem with the release of *Jolson Sings Again* and the naming of Jolson as "Personality of the Year" by the local Variety Club tent in November 1949. Jolson received the keys to the city from J. Russell Young, president of the District Commissioners.

A8) Man of the Year Award

1947. B'nai B'rith

Beverly Hills, California

Eddie Cantor served as emcee for a tribute to Jolson at the Biltmore Bowl with nearly 1,100 people in attendance. Among the celebrities present were Jimmy Durante, Bob Hope, Jack Benny, Danny Kaye, Lou Holtz, Abbott and Costello, Tony Martin, The Ritz Brothers, Ted Lewis, Evelyn Knight, and Shirley Ross.

A9) Medal of Merit

1950. Department of Defense

Washington, D.C.

Defense Secretary George Marshall presented the Medal of Merit to Jolson, "to whom this country owes a debt which cannot be repaid." The medal, carrying a citation noting that Jolson's "contribution to the U.N. action in Korea was made at the expense of his life," was presented to Jolson's 3-year-old adopted son, Asa, Jr. while Jolson's widow, Erle, looked on. President Harry S Truman had ordered the medal to be presented postumously to Jolson partly in response to a public outcry, led by New York Congressman Louis B. Heller, a Democrat, that Jolson be awarded the Congressional Medal of Honor following his death in October 1950.

A10) Personality of the Year Award

1949. Variety Club Tent 11

Washington, D.C.

Awarded to Jolson at the time of the release of *Jolson Sings Again* in November 1949. Stephen T. Early, Undersecretary of Defense, presented a scroll to Jolson for "his outstanding contributions to the world of entertainment."

A11) Photoplay Gold Medal Award
    1946. Photoplay Magazine
    Crystal Room, Beverly Hills Hotel, Beverly Hill, California
A special award presented to Jolson in the aftermath of the success of*The Jolson Story*. The film also won several awards, including acting awards to Larry Parks and Evelyn Keyes, a producing award to Sidney Skolsky, and the award for best film, accepted by Columbia Pictures mogul Harry Cohn. Among the celebrities present were Humphrey Bogart and Lauren Bacall, Claudette Colbert, June Allyson and Dick Powell, Ingrid Bergman, Jeanne Crain, Alan Ladd, Loretta Young, William Holden, Claude Jarman, Jr., and Jack Benny serving as master of ceremonies.

A12) Salute to Al Jolson
    1946. American Veterans Committee
    Hotel Astor, New York
At a dinner at New York's Hotel Astor on October 1, 1946, Jolson was feted and presented with a scroll by the American Veterans Committee. The celebration was broadcast on the radio, with stars appearing in New York and on hook-ups from Los Angeles and San Francisco. Former New York City Mayor James J. Walker and George Jessel were masters of ceremonies, and among those appearing or performing Jolson songs in his honor were Eddie Cantor, Hildegarde, Bob Hope, Burns and Allen, Perry Como, Martha Raye, Dinah Shore, and Frank Sinatra.

A13) Special Award
    1928. Academy of Motion Picture Arts and Sciences
    Hollywood, California
A special award presented to Warner Bros. and Jolson for their pioneering achievements in sound film with *The Jazz Singer*.

A studio portrait of Al Jolson in the later days of his career (1940s). Permission of The
International Al Jolson Society.

Appendix E: Endorsements

During his long career, Al Jolson endorsed many products. As a radio guest, he occasionally endorsed the products of the show's sponsors, most memorably in two "singing commercials" with Bing Crosby for Philco radios. When he toured the country with various musical shows between 1911 and 1940, Jolson often endorsed products and services provided by local businesses, ranging from shoe repair shops to dentists. These are far too numerous to include. The following list includes products and companies with whom Jolson had a major relationship.

E1) Brunswick Records
    1924-1932.
While Jolson recorded for Brunswick, his image and name appeared in many print ads.

E2) Chevrolet (General Motors)
    1932-33.
During his first radio series, *Presenting Al Jolson*, sponsored by General Motors, Jolson's image and name appeared in print ads, and he endorsed Chevrolet on the air.

E3) Colgate-Palmolive-Peet Company
    1942-43.
While on the radio for Colgate, Jolson's image and name appeared in print ads, and he endorsed various Colgate products on the air.

E4) Columbia Records
    1913-23.
During the years he recorded for Columbia, Jolson's image and name appeared in many Columbia print ads.

E5) Decca Records
    1945-50.
During the years he recorded for Decca, Jolson's image and name appeared in many Decca print ads, sometimes for his own recordings, occasionally endorsing other recordings in the Decca catalogue.

E6) Kraft Foods Company
1947-49.
While on the air with the *Kraft Music Hall*, Jolson's image and name appeared in print ads, and he endorsed various Kraft products on the air, most memorably exclaiming "Velveeta!" at the end of singing "She's a Latin From Manhattan."

E7) Kraft-Phoenix Cheese Corporation
1933-34.
Jolson opened the long-running *Kraft Music Hall* with this show, and while on the air, Jolson's image and name appeared in print ads, and he endorsed various Kraft-Phoenix products on the air.

E8) Lever Brothers Company
1936-39.
While hosting the *Al Jolson Lifebuoy /Rinso Show*, Jolson's image and name appeared in print ads, and he endorsed various Lever Brothers products on the air.

E9) Lucky Strike Cigarettes
1930.
Jolson's image and name appear in Lucky Strike ads at the time of the release of Jolson's film, *Mammy* (see F6).   The ads also plug Warner Bros-Vitaphone Pictures.

E10) Pepsi-Cola
1929.
Jolson's image and name appear in Pepsi-Cola print ads at the time of the release of his film, *Say It With Songs* (see F4).

E11) Schaefer Beer
1947.
Jolson's image and name appear in Schaefer print ads (including a photo of Jolson with a bottle of Schaefer beer) also plugging his forthcoming Decca recordings.

E12) Shell Oil
1935-36.
While on the air with the *Shell Chateau* radio show, Jolson's image and name appeared in print ads, and he endorsed various Shell products on the air.

E13) Stetson Shoes
1930.
Jolson's image and name appear in Stetson Shoes ads at the time of the release of Jolson's film, *Mammy* (see F6).

E14) Victor Records
1911-13.
While recording for Victor, Jolson's image and name appeared in print ads.

Title Index

This index of titles (films, stage shows, songs, acts) uses page numbers for material appearing in the biography and chronology of this book. Other sections are identified by entry letter and number. The letters used are C (cartoon), D (discography), F (film), R (radio), S (stage), SM (sheet music), and SS (stage show based on Al Jolson's life). The bibliographies are not indexed. Each letter is followed by a number for the appropriate entry.

"A-Tisket A-Tasket" (song), R4-74
"About a Quarter to Nine" (song), 24, D98, F11, F12, F18, R6-25, R6-37, R6-41, SM1, SM2, SM3
"After the Ball" (song), F18, R4-16, R6-21, R53, SM4
"After You've Gone" (song), D107, F20, SS4
"Ah, But It Happens" (song), SM5
"Ain't Love Grand" (song), SM6
"Ain't She Sweet" (song), SM7
"Ain't That a Grand and Glorious Feeling" (song), SM8
"Ain't We Got Fun?" (song), R6-66
"Ain't You Coming Back to Dixieland" (song), SM9
"Alabama Barbecue" (song), R4-18
"Alabamy Bound" (song), C11, R6-18, R82, R126, SM10, SS1, SS3
Al Jolson Colgate Show (radio show), 45, R5
Al Jolson, Jazz Singer (sheet music), SM407
Al Jolson Lifebuoy/Rinso Show (radio show), 25, 44, E8, R4
Al Jolson, Tonight (show), SS4
Al Jolson's Favorite Collection of Comedy Song Hits (sheet music), SM406

Al Jolson's Old Time Minstrel Show (sheet music), SM409
Alexander's Ragtime Band (film), 128
"Alexander's Ragtime Band" (song), D94, R4-16, R6-30, R6-37, R6-55, R40, R53, R83, R84, R85
Alice in Wonderland (cartoon), C15
"All Alone" (song), D70, R6-29, R6-38
"All By Myself" (song), R6-48, R85, R93, R126
"All God's Chillun Got Shoes" (song), F7
"All My Love" (song), D95, R6-1, R6-6, R87, SM11, SS1
"Almost Like Being in Love" (song), R6-5
"Along the Way to Waikiki" (song), SM12
"Always" (song), R2-2, R6-25, R84
"Always (You Can Come Back to Me)" (song), S26, SM13
"Am I Blue?" (song), R6-59
"American Boy" (song), R5-26
"American Patrol" (song), F18
"Among My Souvenirs" (song), R6-22
"An American in Paris" (song), F17
"Angel Child" (song), D40
"Annie Laurie" (song), R6-2, R6-11, R6-32, R6-60

"Anniversary Song" (song), D93, F18, R6-8, R6-14, R6-52, R80, R81, R98, R104, R137, SM14, SM15, SS1

"Any Bonds Today?" (song), C16

"Any Place Will Do With You" (song), S24, SM16

April Showers (or *Al Jolson in a Plantation Act*) (film), 15, 43, F27

"April Showers" (song), 2, 14, 15, 24, 30, C18, D38, D89, D90, F2, F12, F13, F18, F27, F35, N38, R1, R3-13, R4, R6, R6-22, R6-35, R7, R10, R28, R47, R69, R70, R71, R75, R77, R78, R79, R83, R86, R98, R113, R115, R121, R127, R135, R137, R138, S24, S29, SM17, SM18, SM19, SS1, SS4

"Arcady" (song), D57, S24, SM20

"Are You Happy?" (song), SM21

"Are You Lonesome Tonight" (song), D113

Artists and Models (show), 15, 42, S25, S26, S28

"As Long As I've Got My Mammy" (song), S25, SM22, SM23

"Asleep in the Deep" (song), D2

"At Long Last Love" (song), R4-74

"At Mammy's Fireside" (song), SM24

"At Peace With the World" (song), D78

"At Sundown" (song), R2-8, R6-10, R6-36, R6-62

"At the Candlelight Café" (song), R6-28

"At the Yiddish Cabaret" (song), SM25

"Auld Lang Syne" (song), R6-72

Avalon (film), 128

"Avalon" (song), 13, D33, D93, F13, F18, R1-8, R3-19, R4-32, R4-80, R6-14, R29, R71, R134, S23, SM26, SM27, SS1

"Ave Maria" (song), F18

"Baby Face" (song), D106, F20, R6-26, R6-33, R6-39, R124, R129, R135, SM28

"Back Home in Tennessee" (song), SM29, SM30

"Back in the Carolina You Love" (song), D7

"Back In Your Own Backyard" (song), D82, D96, F4, F20, R3-31, R6-11, R6-57, R11, R80, R124, R135, SM31

"Bagdad" (song), S23, SM32

"Bali 'H'ai" (song), R6-71

"Banks of the Wabash" (song), F18, R3-16, R6-7, R6-58, R82

"Barefoot Days" (song), SM33

"Beatrice Fairfax Tell Me What to Do" (song), SM34

"Beautiful Dreamer" (song), D114, R6-16

"Beauty and the Beast" (song), S23, SM35

"Bebe" (song), SM36

"Because I Love You" (song), SM37

"Bedalumbo, The" (song), S23, SM38

Belle Paree, La (show), 3, 11, 12, 41, S17

"Beloved" (song), SM39

Best Things in Life Are Free, The (film), 128, SS1

"Best Things in Life Are Free, The" (song), R1-15, R6-10, R89, R90

Big Boy (film), 17, 20, 43, F7, F34, S25

Big Boy (show), 14, 15, 20, 42, F7, S19, S25

"Billy, Billy, Bounce Your Baby Doll" (song), SM40

"Billy Used to Give Her Something Every Night" (song), SM41

"Billy's Melody" (song), SM42

"Bing Crosby Calypso: Bank of America's Joy" (song), R6-18

"Birth of the Blues" (song), R6-47

Black and White (film), F1

Black Magic (film), 15, 42, F1

"Blue Bell" (song), F18, SM43

"Blue Monday Blues" (song), F17

"Blue River" (song), D80

"Blue Skies" (song), F2, R2-2, R6-54, R87

Bombo (show), 14, 42, S24

"Boom! (The Merry Minstrel Men)" (song), F15

"Boots and Saddles" (song), R3-30

"Born and Bred in Old Kentucky" (song), S25, SM44, SM45

Bosko The Talk-Ink Kid (cartoon), C1

Box Car Blues (cartoon), C5

"Boyala" (song), SS2

"Brass Band Ephraim Jones" (song), D3

"Bright Eyes" (song), R6-44, R6-59

"Bring Along Your Dancing Shoes" (song), S21, SM46

"Bring Back Your Love" (song), S20

Broadway Highlights (film), F33

Broadway Through a Keyhole (film), 22

"Broken Doll, A" (song), D14

"Brother Bennie's Baking Buns for Belgians" (song), S21

Brother, Can You Spare a Dime? (film), 128

"Brother, Can You Spare a Dime?" (song), R1-2, R1-6, R1-15, R2-1, R6-55, R44, R109, R137

"Bumper Found a Grand" (song), F9

"Bundle of Love, A" (song), SM47

Burlesque (show), 24

"Buy American" (song), R1-9

"By a Waterfall" (song), R2-1, R2-5, R6-10

"By the Grand Canal" (song), S21

"By the Honesuckle Vine" (song), S23, SM48

"By the Light of the Silvery Moon" (song), D100, F18, R6-13, R6-22, R6-69, SM49

"Bye Bye Baby" (song), R131

Bye, Bye, Bonnie (show), 19

"Bylo Bay" (song), S24

"California, Here I Come" (song), 14, 24, 25, D60, D92, F12, F13, F18, F35, R1-8, R2-2, R3-11, R4-16, R6-9, R6-31, R6-35, R6-69, R11, R25, R28, R45, R47, R54, R56, R71, R75, R77, R84, R121, R131, S24, SM50, SM51, SM52, SS1, SS4

"Call of the Colors, The" (song), S21

"Call of the South, The" (song), F6, R1-10, R2-24

Can't Help Singing (book), 16

"Cantor on the Sabbath, The" (song), 21, R1-4, R1-14, R2, R26, SM53

"Carolina in the Morning" (song), 2, D97, F20, R6-16, R6-55, R126, R135, SM54

"Carolina Mammy" (song), SM55

Casino de Paree (film), F11

"Casino de Paree" (song), F11, SM56

Casino De Paris (film), F11

Cavalcade of the Academy Awards (film), F36

Ceiling Zero (film), F33

"Celito Lindo" (song), 24, F11

"Cellini's Dream" (song), S26

"Chazend'l Ohf Shabbes, A" (song), D88, D102, S28

"Cheek to Cheek" (song), R3-22

"Chicago" (song), F19, R6-22

"Chicken Reel, The" (song), SM57

"Chicken's Ball, The" (song), SM58

"Chidabee Ch Ch" (song), R6-12, R6-61

Children of the Ghetto (show), 9, 39, S3

"Chinatown, My Chinatown" (song), D107, F20, R6-29, R6-39, R6-63, R135, SM59

"Chloe" (song), D30, R1-12, S23, SM60

"Christmas Dreaming" (song), R6-10, R6-45

"Cinderella's Waltz" (song), S19

"Clap Yo' Hands" (song), F17

Clean Pastures (cartoon), C13

"Cleopatra" (song), S23, SM61, SM62

"Coal Black Mammy" (song), D49

Colleen (film), 22

"Come Along My Mandy" (song), D1

"Come Back to Me" (song), S18

"Come Josephine in My Flying Machine" (song), F19

"Come On and Play" (song), S25

"Come To Me, Bend To Me" (song), R6-2, R6-11, R6-32, R6-60

"Concerto in F" (song), F17

"Coney Island" (song), R3-16, R3-22

"Confidentially" (song), R4-78

Congo Jazz (cartoon), C4

"Coo-Coo" (song), D42, SM63

"Cookies and Bookies" (song), S25

"Cotton Blossom Lullaby" (song), SM64

"Covered Wagon Days" (song), R3-19

"Crazy Rhythm" (song), SS4

"Cuban Overture" (song), F17

"Cuddle Up a Little Closer" (song), R6-24

"Curse of the Aching Heart, The"

(song), F13
Curtain Razor (cartoon), C18

"Daddy, You've Been More Than a Mother to Me" (song), F19
Dainty Duchess, The (show), 10, S8
Dames (film), 22
"Dames" (song), R2-24
"Dance From Down Yonder, The" (song), S25, SM65, SM66
"Dance of the Dying Flamingo" (song), S28
Dancing Around (show), 12, 13, 41, S21
"Dancing the Blues Away" (song), SM67
"Dardanella" (song), F19
"Darn That Dream" (song), SS4
"Dark Eyes" (song), F10, R1-9, R6-8, R6-61, SM68
"Darktown Strutters Ball" (song), R6-22, R6-35, SS3
"Dat Lovin' Touch" (song), S17, SM69
Day at Santa Anita, A (film), 24, 44, F11, F34
"Day I Rode for Half Fare, The" (song), S25
Day of Atonement, The (story), 15, F2
"De Camptown Races" (song), D115, F15, R6-63, R46, R70
"De Cleanin' Man" (song), SM70
"Dear June" (song), F9
"Delicious" (song), F17
"Dinah" (song), R6-49, R31, SS4
"Dinah Might -- Dynamite" (song), SM71
"Ding-A-Ring A-Ring" (song), D35
Dinner at Eight (film), F7
"Dirty Hands, Dirty Face" (song), 17, D83, F2, R1-2, R1-14, R2-6, R6-29, R6-45, SM72
"Dixie Rose" (song), S23, SM73
"Dixie's Land" (song), F7
"Do I? (Do I? Do I Love Her?)" (song), D44
Dockstader's Minstrels, Lew (show), 11, 40, S14
Dogway Melody, The (film), 128
Don Juan (film), F2
"Don't Be a Sailor" (song), S22, SM74
"Don't Cry, Swanee" (song), SM75

"Don't Forget the Boys" (song), D24, SM76
"Don't Get Careless, Honey Dear" (song), SM77
"Don't Let It Get You Down" (song), R6-27, R6-35, R6-52, S29, SM78, SS4
"Don't Say Goodnight" (song), F10, SM79
"Don't Send Your Wife to the Country" (song), SM80
"Don't Write Me Letters" (song), D13
"Down Among the Sheltering Palms" (song), D104, R6-42, R6-49, SM81
"Down in Bom-Bombay" (song), SM82
"Down in Waterloo" (song), SM83
"Down Old Harmony Way" (song), SM84
"Down on the Old Dude Ranch" (song), S29
"Down South" (song), R1-1, S24, SM85
"Down Where the Swanee River Flows" (song), D10, S22, SM86
"Down Where the Tennessee Flows" (song), S20, SM87
"Down Yonder" (song), SM88
"Dream Kisses" (song), SM89
"Du Host A Liebes Punim" (song), SM90
Duchess at Home, The (show), S8
"Dullest Couple in Scarsdale" (song), SS3
"Dusty Shoes" (song), R1-11

"Easter Parade" (song), R2-10, R6-26, R6-65, R85, R132
"Eeny Meany Miney Moe" (song), D9
"Edinboro' Wiggle, The" (song), S17, SM91
"Egg and I, The" (song), SM92
"Elizabeth (My Queen)" (song), S28, SM93
"'Ello Hengland 'Ello" (song), SS3
"Embraceable You" (song), F17, R6-30, R6-66
Emperor Jones, The (show), 22
"Evangeline" (song), SM94
"Ev'ry Day Can't Be a Sunday" (song), SM95
"Every Morning She Makes Me Late" (song), SM96

"Every Rose Must Have a Thorn" (song), SM97

"Everybody Rag With Me" (song), S21, SM98

"Everybody Snap Your Fingers With Me" (song), D6

"Every Little Movement" (song), R6-24

"Ev'ry Little While" (song), D14

"Faces" (song), SS1

"Falena" (song), SS2

"Far From Cayuga's Water" (song), R6-5

"F.D.R. Jones" (song), R4-92

"Feeling the Way I Do" (song), D61

"Fellow Needs a Girl, A" (song), R6-7, R6-19

Flirtation Walk (film), 22

"Florida Moon" (song), SM99

Footlight Parade (film), 22

"For Me and My Gal" (song), 2, D97, F20, R6-3, R6-20, R6-41, R65, R68, R107, R132, SM100

"For Old Times Sake" (song), SM101

"Forgive Me" (song), SM102

42nd Street (film), 22

"Forty-Second Street" (song), SM103

"Four Walls" (song), D81, R11, S27, SM104

Freud (film), 32

"Friend Highball" (song), SM105

"From Here to Shanghai" (song), D15

"Fugitive From Justice" (song), R1-6

Funny Girl (film), F13

"Gaby Glide, The" (song), SM106

"Gee, I Wish I Had a Girl" (song), SS4

"Get Outa Town" (song), R4-87. R4-93

"Girl Has a Sailor in Every Port, A" (song), S24

"Give Me a Good Old Mammy Song" (song), SS2

"Give Me My Mammy" (song), D38, S24, SM107

"Give Me the Hudson Shore" (song), S20, SM108

"Give My Regards to Broadway" (song), D108, F20, R4-29, R6-31, R6-66, R34, R134, SM109, SS1

"Go Ahead and Dance a Little More" (song), S22, SM110

"Go Down, Moses" (song), F7

Go Into Your Dance (film), 6, 22, 23, 24, 44, C11, F11, F18, F33, F34, S28

"Go Into Your Dance" (song), 22, 23, 24, C11, F11. SM111

"Goblin's Glide, The" (song), S17, SM112

"God's Country" (song), D110, SS1

"Goil Like Me, A" (song), SS1

Goin' to Heaven on a Mule (cartoon), C10

"Goin' to Heaven on a Mule" (song), 22, C10, F10. SM113

Gold Diggers of 1933 (film), 22

"Golden Gate" (song), 18, D81, D98, F3, R1-1, R3, R6-6, R11, S27, SM114

Golden Twenties, The (film), F21

Gone With the Wind (film), 18

"Good-bye Boys" (song), S20, SM115

"Goodbye, G.I. Al" (song), SM116

"Good Days Coming" (song), R1-11

"Good Evening, Friends" (song), R3, S28, SM117

Goodfellas (film), 128

"Good Guy Always Gets the Girl, The" (song), SS2

"Good Old Fashioned Cocktail, A" (song), F11, SM118

Gorman Specialty Company, J.M. (show), S7

"Got to Get Some Shut Eye" (song), R4-93

"Graceful Exit, A" (song), SS3

Grand Hotel (film), F10

Grapes of Wrath, The (film), F10

Great Al Jolson, The (film), F42

"Green Pastures" (song), R3-14

"Grieving For You" (song), SM119

Guys and Dolls (show), 25

Hallelujah, I'm a Bum (film), 21, F8, F9

"Hallelujah, I'm a Bum" (song), 21, 43, D88, F9, R1-4, SM120

Hallelujah, I'm a Tramp (film), F9

"Hang On to the Rainbow" (song), F5

Hannah and Her Sisters (film), 128

"Hannah in Savannah" (song), R6-17

Happy Go Lucky (film), F9

"Happy Hottentots" (song), S22, SM121

"Hard Luck in Society" (song), S19

"Harding, You're the Man For Us" (song), SM122

Harlow (film), 128

Harum Scarum (film), S8

"Hatikvoh" (song), D103

Heart of New York, The (film), F9

"Hebrew and the Cadet, The" (skit), 10, 40

"He'd Have to Get Under-Get Out and Get Under (To Fix His Automobile)" (song), S20, SM123

"Hello Central! Give Me No Man's Land" (song), D20, R29, SM124

"Hello, My Baby" (song), R6-23, R6-42, R6-58, R53, SS4

"Hello 'Tucky!" (song), D72, D73, R3-20, R4-87, R6-8, R6-56, R106, S25, S26, SM125, SM126, SS1

"Henrietta" (song), SS3

"Her Danny" (song), D26, SM127

"Here Comes My Daddy, Oh Pop! Oh Pop! Oh Pop!" (song), SM128

"Here I Am" (song), D79

"Here Lies Love" (song), R1-7

"Here We Are" (song), F6

"Here We Are Again" (song), SS3

"Here's Looking at You" (song), F12

"Hey! Young Fella" (song), R1-9

"Hi-Ho Lack-A-Day, What Have We Got to Lose" (song), SM129

"Hip-Hip-Hip-noa-tized" (song), S16

"His Majesty the Baby" (song), R3-17

"Hitchy Coo" (song), SM130

Hold On to Your Hats (show), 3, 26, 27, 44, 45, S29

"Hold On to Your Hats" (song), S29

Hollywood and the Stars (television show), 46

Hollywood Cavalcade (film), 25, 26, 44, F14

Hollywood Girl (film), F5

Hollywood Revue of 1929, The (film), 128

"Hollywood Rose" (song), SM131

Hollywood's Famous Feet (film), F40, F42

"Home in Pasadena" (song), D62, D64

Honeymoon Express, The (film), F24

Honeymoon Express, The (show), 41, F24, S20, S21

Honky-Tonk (film), F3

"Hooray For Baby and Me" (song), F7, SM132

"Hot, Hot, Honey" (song), S27

"Hot Time in the Old Town Tonight, A" (song), R6-30

"How Deep Is the Ocean" (song), R1-15, R6-43

"How I Love You" (song), SM133

"How You Gonna Keep 'Em Down on the Farm" (song), SS4

"How'd 'Ya Like to Be a Kid Again?" (song), SM134

"How'd You Like to Be My Daddy?" (song), SM135

"Hula Hula Love" (song), SM136

Hunting the Ferocious and Extinct Cuckoo (film), 41, F25

"I Can't Give You Anything But Love" (song), R3-30, R6-13

"I Can't Stand It" (song), SM137

"I Could Not Get Along Without a Song" (song), SS1

"I Dream of Jeanie With the Light Brown Hair" (song), D115, F15

"I Feel a Song Coming On" (song), R3-21

"I Gave Her That" (song), D28, S23, SM138

"I Got Rhythm" (song), F17

"I Got You, Steve" (song), SM139

"I Gotta Get Back to New York" (song), 21, F9, R1-4, R6-31

"I Gotta Perform" (song), SS3

"I Hail From Cairo" (song), S23, SM140

"I Live the Life I Love" (song), R39

"I Love Her. Oh! Oh! Oh!" (song), S20, SM141

"I Love My Steady, But I'm Crazy For My Once-In-A-While" (song), SM142

"I Love the Heart of Dixie" (song), SM143

I Love to Sing-A (cartoon), C12

"I Love to Sing-A" (song), 24, C12, F12, SM144

"I Never Knew Heaven Could Speak" (song), F13, SM145

"I Only Have Eyes for You" (song), D105, F20, R6-5, R6-31, R6-44, R6-58, R23, R125, R135, SM146

"I, Pagliacci" (song), D66

"I Promise You" (song), R4-91

"I See Your Face Before Me" (song), R39

"I Sent a Letter to Santa Claus" (song), SM147

"I Sent My Wife to the Thousand Isles" (song), D11, SM148

"I Still Love You" (song), SM149, SS1

"I Want a Girl" (song), D100, F18, R6-52, SM150

"I Want a Toy Soldier Man" (song), S20

"I Want the Strolling Good" (song), S20

"I Want to Be in Norfolk" (song), S21

"I Want to Go Home" (song), SM151

"I Want You to Want Me to Want You" (song), F19

"I Was Born in Virginia" (song), R6-61, S14

"I Wish I Could Sing Like Jolson" (song), SM152

"I Wish I Had a Girl" (song), D101, R6-12, R90

"I Wish I Had My Old Gal Back Again" (song), D77

"I Wonder If It's True" (song), S18

"I Wonder What's Become of Sally" (song), D69, R6-5, R6-45, R6-58, SM153

"I Wonder Who's Kissing Her Now" (song), SS4

"I Wonder Why She Kept on Saying Si-Si-Si-Si-Senor?" (song), D21, S23, SM154

"Ida" (song), R51, R81, SS4

"(I'd Climb the Highest Mountain) If I Knew I'd Find You" (song), D77, R6-27

"I'd Do It Again" (song), F9, SM155

"I'd Love to Take Orders From You" (song), R3-23, R2-26

"I'd Rather Listen to You Eyes" (song), R3-23

"If I Could Be With You (One Hour Tonight)" (song), R6-67

"If I Only Had a Five Cent Piece" (song), R1-5

"If I Only Had a Match" (song), D99, R6-4, R6-15, R6-29, R96, SM156, SS4

"If It Wasn't For You" (song), SS2

"If We Can't Be the Same Old Sweethearts" (song), R6-40, R6-59

"If You Knew Susie" (song), R4-5, R81, S25, SM157, SS1, SS4

"If You Were the Only Girl in the World" (song), R6-54

"Il Barbiere di Siviglia" (song), D66

"I'll Be Seeing You" (song), R6-7, R6-42, R6-67

"I'll Build a Stairway to Paradise" (song), F17

"I'll Get By" (song), R6-21, R6-44

"I'll Say She Does" (song), D22, S23, SM158, SM159

"I'll See You In My Dreams" (song), R3-26, R6-29

"I'll Sing You a Song About Dear Old Dixie Land" (song), SM160

"I'll Stand Beneath Your Window Tonight and Whistle" (song), D43

"I'll Tell the World" (song), S23, SM161

"I'm a Fugitive From a Chain Letter Gang" (song), SM162

"I'm All Bound 'Round With the Mason-Dixon Line" (song), D17

"I'm Always Chasing Rainbows" (song), R6-24, R6-62, R92, SM163

"I'm Crying Just for You" (song), D105, R6-22, R6-36, R6-53, R115, SM164

"I'm Down in Honolulu Looking Them Over" (song), D13

"I'm Falling in Love" (song), S28

"I'm Forever Blowing Bubbles" (song), R4-88, R6-23

"I'm Glad I'm Spanish" (song), S24

"I'm Glad My Wife's in Europe" (song), SM165

"I'm Goin' Back to Old Nebraska" (song), SM166

"I'm Goin' South" (song), D58, D60, S24, SM167

"I'm Gonna Tramp! Tramp! Tramp!" (song), D71

"I'm in Seventh Heaven" (song), 19, D85, F4, R16, SM168

"I'm Just Wild About Harry" (song), D108, F13, F20, R4-91, R6-19, R6-28, R6-42, R6-54, R135, SM169, SS3

"I'm Ka-Razy For You" (song), F4, SM170

"I'm Looking Over a Four-Leaf Clover" (song), D106, F20, R6-24, R92, SM171

"I'm on My Way to Mandalay" (song), S20

"I'm Saving Up the Means to Get to New Orleans" (song), D12

"I'm Seeking for Siegfried" (song), S21

"I'm Sitting on Top of the World" (song), 18, D76, D96, F3, F18, R1-15, R2-7, R5-14, R6-4, R6-21, R6-49, R79, R87, R107, R128, S26, SM172, SS1, SS4

"I'm Sorry I Made You Cry" (song), F13, SM173

"I'm Tellin' the Birds" (song), SM174

"I'm the Human Brush" (song), S17, SM175

"I'm the Very Next Girl I See" (song), S24

Immortal Jolson, The (book), 6, 46

Impatient Years, The (film), 128

"In a Curio Shop" (song), S24

"In Ev'ry Nook and Corner You Are Missing" (song), SM176

"In Old Grenada" (song), S24, SM177

In Old Kentucky (show), S25

"In Old Kentucky" (song), R2-1

"In Our House" (song), D105, R6-39, R6-45, SM178

"In Sweet September" (song), D32

"In the Evening By the Moonlight" (song), R82

"In the Good Old Summertime" (song), R6-22, R6-28

"In the Morning" (song), F6

"In the Shade of the Old Apple Tree" (song), R6-26

"In the Way Off There" (song), S24, SM179

"Indian River Trail" (song), SM180

"International Rag, The" (song), R40

Into Your Dance (cartoon), C11

"Ireland Must Be Heaven Because My Mother Came From There" (song), F19

"Irish Tango, The" (song), SM181

"Is It True What They Say About Dixie?" (song), D104, D108, F20, R6-13, R6-38, R6-50, R27, R95, R126, R135, SM182, SM183

"Is She My Girl Friend" (song), SM184

"Isle of Youth" (song), S23

"Isn't This a Lovely Day" (song), R3-21, R3-25

"Israel" (song), D103, R6-37, R100, SM185

"It All Depends on You" (song), 15, 18, D106, D108, F3, F20, R1-10, R2-8, R6-30, R6-35, R10, R107, S25, SM186, SS4

"It's a Great Idea" (song), SS2

"It's Been a Long, Long Time" (song), R6-49

It's Got Me Again (cartoon), C9

"It's Wonderful" (song), S23, SM187

"It's You" (song), SM188

"I've Got a Song in Me" (song), SS2

"I've Got My Captain Working For Me Now" (song), D27

"I've Got My Eye On You" (song), F5

"I've Got My Love to Keep Me Warm" (song), R4-4

"I've Got Plenty of Nothin'" (song), R35

"I've Got to Get Back to New York" (song), SS1

"I've Got to Sing a Torch Song" (song), R2

"I've Heard That Song Before" (song), R5-28, R112

"Ja Da" (song), F13

Jacob's Ladder (film), 128

"Japanese Sandman" (song), R4-91

"Jazz a la Russe" (song), S26

Jazz Fool, The (cartoon), C2

Jazz Singer, The (film), 3, 4, 5, 6, 15, 16, 17, 18, 25, 43, A13, C2, F2, F3, F4, F7, F12, F14, F18, F31, F37, N14, N33, S27

"Jazzadaroo" (song), S24, SM189

"Jeepers Creepers" (song), R4-92

Joelson Brothers, The (act), 10, 40, S9

Joelson, Master, and Fred E. Moore (act), 9, 10, 40, S5

Joley. A Musical About the Life and Times of Al Jolson (show), SS3
"Jolie's Back in Town" (song), SS2
Jolson (show), SS1
"Jolson Medley" (song), SS4
Jolson, Palmer and Jolson (act), 40, S10
Jolson Sings Again (film), 7, 32, 45, A7, A10, F20, N21
Jolson Songs (sheet music), SM408
Jolson Story, The (film), 7, 8, 28, 29, 30, 31, 32, 45, A11, F6, F11, F18, F20, F39
Judy Garland.World's Greatest Entertainer (book), 1
"Just One of Those Things" (song), R6-40
"(Just One Way to Say) I Love You" (song), D109

"Kangaroo Court" (song), F9
"Keep Smiling at Trouble" (song), 14, 18, D72, D73, D95, F3, R1-3, R2-3, R4-32, R4-91, R6-20, R87, S25, SM190, SM191
"Keep That Hi-De-Ho in Your Soul" (song), F12
Kings of the Turf (film), F32
"Kissing Rock, The" (song), SS3
"Knights of the Road" (song), F6
"Kol Nidre" (song), 16, 25, D102, F2, F14, R87
"Koo-Kee-Koo" (song), SM192
Kraft Music Hall (radio show), 21, 22, 31, 44, 45, E6, E7, R2, R6

"Lackawanna" (song), S25, SM193, SM194
"Lady, Be Good" (song), F17
"Lady in Red, The" (song), R3-14
Lady Play Your Mandolin (cartoon), C7
"Last Night on the Back Porch" (song), SM195
"Last Round-Up, The" (song), R3-19
"Laying the Cornerstone" (song), F9
"Lazy" (song), D63, R6-46, R83, R85
Lazy Bones (film), F9
"Lazy Bones" (song), R2-5
"Lead 'Em On" (song), S25
"Learn to Croon" (song), SM196

"Lenox Avenue" (song), S28, SM197
Leon Schlesinger Presents Bugs Bunny (cartoon), C16
"Let the Little Joy Bell Ring" (song), SM198
"Let Me Sing a Berlin Song" (song), R40
"Let Me Sing and I'm Happy" (song), 20, D99, F6, F18, R1-3, R6-6, R6-32, R6-63, R80, R127, SM199, SM200, SM201
"Let's Go West Again" (song), D110
"Life Is a Gamble" (song), S24
"Life Is Just a Bowl of Cherries" (song), R1-2
"Life Was Pie for the Pioneer" (song), S29
"Lily Pool, The" (song), S26
"Limehouse Blues" (song), R4-86, R4-92
"Little Bit Bad, A" (song), SM202
"Little Bit of Every Nationality, A" (song), S23
"Little Bundle From Heaven, A" (song), R3-15
"Little Girl" (song), R6-45
Little Pal (film), 19
"Little Pal" (song), 20, D85, F4, R1-8, R6-46, R16, R17, SM203
"Little Sammy" (song), SS2
"Little Sunshine" (song), F7, SM204
"Little Things You Used to Do, The" (song), 24, F11, SM205
"Liza" (song), 19, 43, D86, D97, F18, R6-2, R6-24, R92, R98, SM206, SS4
"Liza Lee" (song), 20, F7, SM207
"Lonely Mothers on Parade" (song), SM208
"Longing" (song), SM209
"Look For the Silver Lining" (song), R6-15, R6-69, R6-71
"Look Me Over, Dearie" (song), SM210
"Looking at You" (song), D87, F6, SM211
"Lost: A Wonderful Girl" (song), D45
"Love Ahoy" (song), S23
"Love Is Just Like a Punch in the Nose" (song), SM212
"Love Is On the Air Tonight" (song), R4-29

"Love Walked In" (song), F17
Lucky Boy (film), F3
"Lucky Day" (song), R2-8
"Lucky in the Rain" (song), R6-47, R6-55, R6-70
"Lullaby of Broadway" (song), R134, SM213

"Ma Blushin' Rosie" (song), D91, F18, R6-9, R6-52, R34, R69, R71, R75, R78, R89, R98, R112, R134, SM214, SM215, SS1
"Ma, She's Makin' Eyes at Me" (song), R6-48, R6-67, R93, SS1
"Ma Mere" (song), R1-1, R1-4, S28, SM216
Magic of Jolson, The (show), SS1
"Maid of the Milky Way" (show), S26
Main Circus, Walter L. (show), 9, 39, S2
"Makin' Whoopee" (song), SS1
"Mama" (song), SS3
"Mama Loves Papa" (song), D56
Mammy (film), 17, 20, 43, E9, E13, F3, F6
"Mammy, I'll Sing About You" (song), 6, 24, F11, F33, R3-1, R24, SM217
Mammy's Boy (film), F1
"Mammy's Little Coal Black Rose" (song), SM218
"Man I Love, The" (song), F17
"Mañana" (song), R128
"Mandalay" (song), D65
"Mandy" (song), R6-18, R6-44, R40, R113
"March Winds and April Showers" (song), R3-13
"Marcheta" (song), R6-23, R6-36, R6-57
"Margie" (song), R6-25, SS4
"Mary's a Grand Old Name" (song), R6-19, R6-61
"Massa's in De Cold, Cold Ground" (song), D114
"Maxim's" (song), R6-19
"Me and My Shadow" (song), SM219
"Melons" (song), SS3
Memorial to Al Jolson (film), F41
"Memories" (song), R6-20, R6-51
"Mem'ries of One Sweet Kiss" (song), D85, F4, SM220

Merry Monahans, The (film), 128
"Miami" (song), D74, D75, D76, S25, SM221, SM222
"Mighty Lak A Rose" (song), 16, R3-18, R6-16, R6-58
"Mimi" (song), R6-9
"Mine" (song), F17
Minstrel Days (film), F35
"Minstrel Days" (song), S22, SM223
Mistah Jolson (book), 7
Mister Bones (show), F6
"Molly Dear, It's You I'm After" (song), SM224
"Moonlight and Magnolias" (song), R3-14, R3-24
"More Than You Know" (song), R6-41
"Morning Will Come" (song), D50, D51, SM225
Mother Carey's Chickens (film), 22
"Mother Macree" (song), R6-15, R6-50
"Mother of Mine, I Still Have You" (song), D80, F2, R1-3, R1-9, SM226
Mother's Boy (film), F3
"Mothers of the World" (song), S26
"Mother's Sitting Knitting Little Mittens for the Navy" (song), SM227
"Movin' Man, Don't Take My Baby Grand" (song), D4
"Mr. Radio Man" (song), D62, D64
"Mrs. Ulysses" (song), SS3
"My Blue Heaven" (song), R3-25, R6-14, R6-51, R6-70, R126, SS4
"My Buddy" (song), R1-12, R2-3, R5-1, SM228
"My Cocoa-Cola Belle" (song), S20
"My Dixie" (song), SM229
"My Gal Sal" (song), F2, R2, R3-16, R4-16, R6-9, R6-68, R53
"My Guiding Star" (song), S24
"My, How This Country's Changed" (song), F12
"My Kid" (song), SM230
My Lady's Dress (show), S21
"My Lou" (song), S18
"My Mammy" (song), 2, 13, 16, 17, 22, 24, 25, 33, C5, D83, D91, F2, F6, F12, F13, F15, F18, F27, F38, R1-15, R2-9, R4-16, R10, R11, R17, R29, R32, R53, R54, R56, R65, R71, R75, R77, R82, R98, R137, S23, S27, S28, S29, SM231, SM232, SM233, SS1, SS4

My Man (film), F3
"My Man" (song), 14, F13, SM234
"My Melancholy Baby" (song), R3-24, R6-13, R6-51, R6-70, R26
"My Mother's Rosary" (song), D110, D111, SM235
"My Old Kentucky Home" (song), D114, F15, R2-7, R46, R70, R134
"My Pal Bumper" (song), F9
"My Papa Doesn't Two Time No More" (song), D63
"My Pirate Lady" (song), S22, SM236
"My Raggyadore" (song), S20
"My Rainbow Beau" (song), S21
"My Rose of Spain" (song), S27
"My Sin" (song), F5
"My Sumurun Girl" (song), D3, SM237
"My Sweet Moana" (song), SM238
"My Tom Tom Man" (song), SM239
"My Walking Stick" (song), R4-74
"My Wild Irish Rose" (song), R6-15, R6-56
"My Yellow Jacket Girl" (song), D5, S20, SM240

"Nature Boy" (song), R6-31, R6-33
"N' Everything" (song), 16, D18, S23, SM241, 242
"Near You" (song), R6-13, R95, R97
"Nearest Thing to Heaven" (song), R6-18, R6-34, R6-54, SM243
"Never Again" (song), D60
"Never Trust a Soldier Man" (song), S21
New York (film), F9
New York Nights (film), F8
"Night and Day" (song), R2-3, R3-25
Night in Spain, A (show), 18, 43, S27
"Night in the Orient, A" (song), S23
Night With the Pierrots, A (show), S19
"Nightingale" (song), SM244
"No More Worryin'" (song), SM245
No, No, Nanette (show), 26, S28
"No One Loves a Clown" (song), S24
"No Sad Songs for Me" (song), D113, SM246
No Time For Tears (film), F22
"Nobody But Fanny" (song), D74, D75, S25, S26, SM247, SM248
"Nobody Do Me Like My Daddy Do

Me" (song), SS2
"Not For All the Rice In China" (song), R2-10
Not Quite Decent (film), F3
"Now He's Got a Beautiful Girl" (song), D10, S22, SM249

"Oh! Donna Clara" (song), 21, R1-2, R1-7, R1-9, S28, SM250
"O-hi-o" (song), D34, SM251, SM252
"Oh, Dem Golden Slippers" (song), F6
"Oh! How I Wish I Could Sleep Until My Daddy Comes Home" (song), SM253
"Oh! Oh! Columbus" (song), SM254
"Oh! Shush" (song), SM255
"Oh! Susannah" (song), 26, D115, F15, R3-13, R3-21, R46, R52, R70, R82
"Oh Suzanna, Dust Off That Old Piano" (song), R3-6
"Oh! What a Night" (song), SM256
Oh, You Beautiful Doll (film), F19
"Oh, You Beautiful Doll" (song), F19, R4-88, R6-57, SS3
"Oh! You Girls" (song), SM257
"Old Black Joe" (song), D114, F15
"Old Fashioned Girl" (song), R106, SM258, R46, R51, R70
"Old Folks at Home (Swanee River)" (song), 26, F15
"Old Kitchen Kettle Keeps Singing a Song, The" (song), R1-6, SM259
"Old Piano Roll Blues, The" (song), D112
"Old Timer" (song), S29
"Olga From the Volga" (song), S18
"Ol' Man River" (song), D82, R1-7, R1-15, R2-2, R6-8, R6-28, R6-48, R96
"On Cupid's Green" (song), S23
"On the Banks of the Wabash" (song), SM260
"On the Mississippi" (song), SM261
"On the Road to Calais" (song), D23, S23, SM262
On the Town (film), 128
"On the Z.R.3." (song), SM263
"One I Love Belongs to Somebody Else, The" (song), D60, R6-20, R6-46, R78, R113, R126
"One In a Million" (song), R3-15

"One O'Clock Baby" (song), S25, SM264

"Oogie Oogie Wa Wa" (song), D41

Optimists, The (show), F9

"Our Ancestors" (song), S23, SM265

"Our Little Cabaret Up Home" (song), S20

"Outdoor Life" (song), SM266

"Over There" (song), 13, S23

"Page Miss Glory" (song), R3-13, R3-15, R3-25

Pagliacci (opera), 13

Pal Joey (show), F9

Palmer and Jolson (act), S11

"Pardon Me Porter" (song), SS3

"Paree, Gay Paree" (song), S18

"Paris Is a Paradise for Coons" (song), S17, SM267

"Paris Wakes Up and Smiles" (song), D109

"Pastels" (song), S26

"Peg O' My Heart" (song), F19, R6-3,

Penny Arcade (show), 19

"People Will Say We're In Love" (song), R6-18, R6-37, R6-47, R6-71, R64

"Pettin' on the Old Porch Swing" (song), SS3

Phar Lap (film), 128

"Pickaninnies Heaven" (song), R1-6

"Plain Old Me" (song), R3-22

Plaza Suite (show), 32

"Poi Ball" (song), S26

"Poor Butterfly" (song), R3-24, R6-9, R6-32, R6-38, R26

Porky in Wackyland (cartoon), C15

"Pray for Sunshine" (song), D15

Presenting Al Jolson (radio show), 21, 44, E2, R1

"Pretty Baby" (song), 25, D106, F13, F20, R6-20, R6-38, R6-70, R129, SM268

"Pretty Girl Is Like a Melody, A" (song), R6-11, R6-63, R27, R83, R89

"Pretty Little Leader of the Band, The" (song), SM269

"Pretty Little Mayflower Girl" (song), S22, SM270

"Pretty Little Milliners" (song), S17, SM271

"Promenade Walk, The" (song), S26

"Pullman Porters on Parade" (song), D6

Purple Heart Diary (film), F22

"Put On Your Old Grey Bonnet" (song), R6-9, R6-43

"Put Your Arms Around Me, Honey" (song), R6-49, R6-68

"Question, The" (song), SS2

"Race Is Over, The" (song), S25

"Raggin' the Baby to Sleep" (song), D4, SM273

"Rag Lad of Bagdad, The" (song), S23, SM272

"The Rag Time Express" (song), S20

Rainbow Man, The (film), F3

"Ramona" (song), R6-25

"Raz-Ma-Taz" (song), S23, SM274

Ready, Willing and Able (film), 22

"Real Piano Player, A" (song), R6-67, R115, R122

Reeves' Famous Big Company, Al (show), 10, 40, S6

"Remember" (song), R6-21, R6-33, R6-60

"Remember Mother's Day" (song), D110, R6-32, R6-69, R133

"Revival Day" (song), D7

Rhapsody in Blue (film), 27, 28, 45, F17, F23

"Rhapsody in Blue" (song), F17

Rich and Hoppe's Big Company of Funmakers (show), 9, 39, S1

"Ring de Banjo" (song), F15

"Road Is Open Again, The" (song), R2-7

"Robert E. Lee Cakewalk" (song), SS3

"Robinson Crusoe" (song), S22, SM275

Robinson Crusoe, Jr. (show), 12, 41, S22

"Rock-A-Bye Your Baby With a Dixie Melody" (song), 2, 13, 15, 24, 25, D19, D89, D92, F12, F13, F18, F20, F27, R1-1, R1-9, R2-7, R6-47, R23, R29, R80, R87, R135, S23, S26, SM276, SM277, SM278, SS1, SS3, SS4

"Rosalie" (song), R6-12, R90

"Rosary, The" (song), R4-9

"Rose In Her Hair, The" (song), R3-16, R3-18

"Rose of Spain" (song), S24

Rose of Washington Square (film), 25, 44, F13, F16

"Rose of Washington Square" (song), F13, SM279

"Roses of Picardy" (song), R6-44

"Rosie" (song), SS4

"Rotisserie Number" (song), S26

"Row, Row, Row" (song), S19, SM280

"Ruby" (song), SS3

"Rum Tum Tiddle" (song), D2, S18, SM281

Sanford's Players, Walter (show), 10, 40, S13

"Santa Claus Is Coming to Town" (song), R107

"Save Me Sister" (song), C13, F12, R29, SM282

"Say It Isn't So" (song), R6-47, R6-56, R6-65

Say It With Songs (film), 17, 19, 43, E10, F3, F4

"Say No More" (song), SM283

"Scandinavia" (song), D36

Screen Snapshots (film), F29, F30, F39, F40, F41, F42

See America First (film), F31

"September in the Rain" (song), C17, R4-18

"Shanghai Lil" (song), R2-5

"She Came, She Saw, She Can-Canned" (song), S29

"She Don't Wanna" (song), SM284

"She Is Ma Daisy" (song), R6-50

"She Knows It" (song), D37, SM285

"She Used to Be the Slowest Girl in Town" (song), SM286

Shell Chateau (radio show), 24, 44, F33, R3

"She's a Latin From Manhattan" (song), 24, E6, F11, F18, R3-17, R6-27, R6-42, R6-53, SM287, SM288

"S-h-i-n-e" (song), R4-93

"Shine on Harvest Moon" (song), R6-26, R6-43

Show Boat (show), S17

Show Business at War (film), F38

Show Girl (show), 19, 43, F18

Show Girl In Hollywood (film), F5

Showgirl in Hollywood, The (film), F5

Show of Shows, The (film), 128, S26

"Shubert Serenade" (song), SS3

"Shuffling Shivaree, The" (song), S21

Sidewalks of New York, The (show), S27

"Simple Life" (song), S22, SM289

Sinbad (show), 13, 14, 41, 42, F17, F26, S23, S28

"Sinbad Was In Bad All the Time" (song), SM290

"Sing Trovatore" (song), S17, SM291

Singing Fool, The (film), 4, 6, 17, 19, 43, C1, C2, F3, F4, F7, S27

Singing Kid, The (film), 23, 24, 25, 44, C12, C13, F12, F34, F35

Singin' in the Rain (film), 128

Sinkin' in the Bathtub (cartoon), C3

"Sister Susie's Sewing Shirts for Soldiers" (song), D8, S21, SM292

"Sittin' in a Corner" (song), SM293

"Sleeping Beauty" (song), F9

"Smiles" (song), R6-51

"Smoke Gets In Your Eyes" (song), R3-26, R6-36, R6-48, R93

"Snap Your Fingers" (song), D3, S19, SM294

Snow White and the Seven Dwarfs (film), 18

"So Help Me" (song), R4-80

"So Long Mary" (song), R6-57

"So Long, Mother" (song), SM295

"Soft Shoe" (song), SS4

"Some Beautiful Morning" (song), D25, SM296

"Some Enchanted Evening" (song), D109, R6-70

"Some of These Days" (song), D46, F33

"Somebody Loves Me" (song), F17, R6-33

"Someone Else May Be There While I'm Gone" (song), D13, D101, R6-23, R6-34, R6-43, R6-54

"Something for Nothing" (song), S25

"Something Seems to Tell Me" (song), S28, SM297

"Song of the Immigrant Mothers" (song), SS3

"Song's Gotta Come From the Heart, The" (song), R6-61

Sonny Boy (film), F3

"Sonny Boy" (song), 18, 19, 20, 24, 30, C1, C2, C6, D84, D92, F3, F7, F12, F20, F28, F35, R1-4, R1-10, R1-15, R2, R3-26, R4-1, R5-15, R6-1, R6-55, R6-59, R13, R17, R29, R45, R53, R71, R75, R109, R115, R121, R137, S28, S29, SM298, SS1, SS3

South Bank Show, The (television show), 46

"Spaniard That Blighted My Life, The" (song), 12, D5, D94, F3, F18, R1-2, R29, S20, SM299, SM300, SM301, SS4

"Spanish Shawl, A" (song), S27

Stars and Stripes (film), 33, 46

"Stella" (song), D52, SM302

"Steppin' Out" (song), D61

Story of Will Rogers, The (film), F23

Streets of New York, The (show), 19

"Sugar" (song), SM303

"Summertime" (song), F17, R6-14, R6-57

Sumurun (show), S19

"Sunbonnet Sue" (song), R89

"Swanee" (song), 2, 13, 24, 27, 33, D31, D90, F12, F17, F18, F23, F35, R1-14, R4-16, R5-28, R6-35, R6-68, R29, R35, R36, R47, R53, R54, R71, R75, R78, R81, R98, R121, R125, R129, R137, R138, S23, S29, SM304, SM305, SM306, SS1, SS3

Swanee River (film), 26, 44, F15

"Swanee River" (song), R2-7

"Swanee River Trail" (song), SM307

"Swanee Rose" (song), SM308

"Sweet Georgia Brown" (song), R4-78

"Sweet One" (song), SM309

"Sweet Singer" (song), SS1

Sweetheart of the Campus (film), 22

"Sweetie Mine" (song), SM310

"Swing Low, Sweet Chariot" (song), R3-14, R52

"S'Wonderful" (song), F17

Swooner Crooner (cartoon), C17

"Syncopatia Land" (song), S20

Take It Or Leave It (film), F16

"Take Me Out to the Ballgame" (song), R6-27

"Take Me To That Swanee Shore" (song), SM311

"Tallahassee" (song), SM312

"Tap the Toe" (song), S25

"Tappin-G-Minor" (song), SS2

"Tell Me (Why Nights Are Lonely)" (song), D29

"Tell Me With Smiles" (song), SM313

"Tell That to the Marines" (song), D21, SM314

"Tennessee, I Hear You Calling Me" (song), SM315

"Thank You Father" (song), R3

"Thanks For Everything" (song), R4-86

"That Barber in Seville" (song), S24, SM316

"That Big Blond Mama" (song), D54

"That Certain Party" (song), R6-46, R6-53

"That Devlin' Rag" (song), SM317

"That Gal of Mine" (song), S20

"That Haunting Melody" (song), D2, S18

"That Little German Band" (song), D6, R6-65, SM318

"That Lovin' Traumerei" (song), D4, R6-17, R112, S17, SM319

"That Lullaby of Long Ago" (song), SM320

"That Mesmerizing Mendelssohn Tune" (song), D1

"That Old Gang of Mine" (song), R6-31

"That Wonderful Girl of Mine" (song), R6-68, R6-70, SM321

"That Wonderful Kid From Madrid" (song), D31

"That's All Right For Mulligan" (song), SM322

"That's Nice" (song), SM323

"That's What I Like About the South" (song), R2-3

Theatre Opening (film), 43, F28

"Then You Were Never in Love" (song), S29

"There Ain't No Color Line" (song), R1-5

"There's a Broken Heart For Every Light On Broadway" (song), D9, F19

"There's a Great Day Coming Mañana" (song), S29, SM324

"There's a Lump of Sugar Down in Dixie" (song), D18, SM325

"There's a Rainbow 'Round My Shoulder" (song), 2, 18, D84, D99, F3, F18, R1-6, R6-10, R13, SM326, SM327

"There's a Tear For Every Smile in Hollywood" (song), F5

"There's Only One Mary in Maryland" (song), SM328

"There's Something About You" (song), SM329

"They Come Back to California" (song), SM330

"They Can't Fool Me" (song), SM331

"They Didn't Believe Me" (song), R6-48, R93

"Things Look Brighter For You and Me" (song), R2-6

"Things You Left in My Heart, The" (song), R6-30

This is the Army (film), N9, N51

"This is the Life" (song), R40, S20, SM332

"This Time" (song), SS3

"This Year's Kisses" (song), R4-16

"Thousand and One Arabian Nights, A" (song), S23, SM333

"Through the Mist" (song), S24

"Tie That Binds, The" (song), SM334

Tiger by the Tail (film), 32

"Tillie Titwillow" (song), D16, S22

"Times Sqaure" (song), SS3

Tin Pan Alley (film), F8

"To My Mammy" (song), D87, F6, R1-11, SM335

"Toddlin' the Todalo" (song), S20

"Tomale (I'm Hot For You)" (song), SM336

"Tomorrow Is Another Day" (song), 20, F7, SM337

"Tonight's My Night With Baby" (song), D78

"Toot, Toot, Tootsie!" (song), 14, 17, 25, D96, F2, F13, F16, F18, F20, R1-2, R1-10, R4-29, R5-18, R6-1, R6-16, R6-34, R6-41, R11, R27, R29, R60, R81, R87, R98, R124, R129, R133, R135, S24, SM338, SM339, SM340, SS1, SS3, SS4

"Toot Your Horn, Kid, You're in a Fog" (song), SM341

"Trav'lin All Alone" (song), R1-7, R1-14, SM342

"Tree in the Meadow, A" (song), R6-39

"True Love" (song), S25

"Try a Little Tenderness" (song), SM343

"Twelve O'Clock at Night" (song), D59

Twinkle, Twinkle, "Killer" Kane (film), 128

"Uncle Sammy" (song), D4

"Under Southern Skies" (song), SM344

Untitled (film), F26

Ups 'N Downs (cartoon), C6

"Used to You" (song), 19, D85, F4, R16, SM345

"Vamp, The" (song), F13, SM346

Vanities (film), F33

"Venetia" (song), S21

Vera Violetta (show), 11, 12, S18

"Vera Violetta" (song), 41, S18

"Very Next Girl I See, The" (song), SM347

Victoria Burlesquers (show), 10, 40, S4

"Villain Still Pursued Her, The" (song), D3, SM348

Villanova Burlesque Company (show), 9, 40

"Virginia Lee" (song), SM349

"Vive La France" (song), F10, SM350

Voice That Thrilled the World, The (film), F37

"Voodoo Maiden" (song), S22

Vunderbar (show), S28

"Wah-Hoo!" (song), R3-30

"Waiki-Ki-Ki Lou" (song), SM351

"Wait Until My Ship Comes In" (song), S24

"Waitin' for the Evening' Mail" (song), D53

"Waiting for the Robert E. Lee" (song), 12, 33, D98, F2, F18, R4-86, R6-2, R6-50, R6-60, R6-72, R80,

R117, R125, R127, R131, S19, SM352, SM353, SM354, SS4

"Walkin' Along, Mindin' My Business" (song), S29

"Wanita" (song), D49

"War Babies" (song), SM355

"Water Boy" (song), R6-20

"Way Down Yonder in New Orleans" (song), D112, R6-59

"Way Out West Where the East Begins" (song), S29

"Wedding Bells" (song), D17

"Welcome Home" (song), S25

"We'll Never Know" (song), R4-88

"We're Gonna Make Sure There'll Never Be Another War" (song), R5-16

"We're Not Too Poor For That" (song), R1-3

"We're Only Here For a Day" (song), SS2

"Wetona" (song), S24, SM356

"What Do You Say?" (song), SM357

"What Do You Want With Money?" (song), F9, SM358

"What Does It Matter?" (song), R10

"What Will I Tell Her To-night?" (song), SM359

"What'll I Do?" (song), R6-17, R6-35, R6-66

What's Up Doc? (cartoon), C19

"When an Englishman Marries a Parisian" (song), S21

"When Day Is Done" (song), R4-78, R6-49

"When Gaby Did the Gaby Glide" (song), S20

"When I Get You Alone Tonight" (song), F19

"When I Leave the World Behind" (song), 2, 12, D101, R1-5, R2-6, R3-20, R5-17, R6-4, R6-53, S21, SM360

"When I Lost You" (song), 16, R6-38

"When Irish Eyes Are Smiling" (song), R6-19, R6-25, R6-56, R6-62

"When Sunday Comes to Town" (song), SM361

"When the Grown Up Ladies Act Like Babies" (song), D8, S21, SM362, SS4

"When the Honeymoon Stops Shining" (song), S20

"When the Little Red Roses Get the Blues for You" (song), C4, D87

"When the Red, Red Robin Comes Bob, Bob Bobbin' Along" (song), 15, D79, D101, F20, F27, R6-11, R6-36, R6-38, R6-47, R6-65, R105, R125, SM363

"When You and I Were Young, Maggie" (song), F6

"When You Get Yourself Married" (song), SS2

"When You Were Sweet Sixteen" (song), D98, F18, R6-1, R6-6, R6-34, R6-50, SM365

"When You're Starring in the Movies" (song), S22, SM364

"Where Did Robinson Crusoe Go With Friday on Saturday Night" (song), 13, D10, R6-15, S22, SM366, SS1

"Where Is My Wandering Boy Tonight?" (song), SM367

"Where the Black-Eyed Susans Grow" (song), 13, D96, R5-17, S22, SM368

"Where Would Cinderella Be?" (song), F34

"Which Shall I Choose?" (song), S19

"Which Switch Is the Switch, Miss, For Ipswich?" (song), SM369

"While They Were Dancing Around" (song), S20, SM370

Whirl of Society, The (show), 12, 41, S19, S20

"Whispering" (song), R6-28, R26, R131

"White Christmas" (song), R6-12, R6-50

"Who and Where" (song), R6-14, R6-46, SM371

"Who Cares?" (song), D47, D48, R6-51, S24, SM372

"Who Needs Love" (song), SS2

"Who Paid the Rent for Mrs. Rip Van Winkle" (song), 12, 20, F6, F19, R80, S20, SM373

"Who Said Dreams Don't Come True?" (song), SM374

"Who Says That Dreams Don't Come True?" (song), 128

"Who Wants a Bad Little Boy?" (song), D67, D68, S26

"Who Was Chasing Paul Revere?"

(song), S25, SM375, SM376

"Who Will Be With You When I'm Far Away" (song), R6-27

"Who-oo! You-oo! That's Who!" (song), SM377

Whoopee (show), 19

"Who's the Swingin'est Man in Town?" (song), F12

"Why Can't I Be Happy Too?" (song), SS2

"Why Can't You?" (song), D85, F4, R1-2, R16, R17, SM378

"Why Can't You Behave?" (song), R6-56, R6-65, R6-72, R128

"Why Do I Dream Those Dreams?" (song), F10, SM379

"Why Do They All Take the Night Boat For Albany?" (song), 20, F6, S23, SM380

Wilkerson's "Minstrels of Today", I.P. (show), 11, 40, S15

"Winder, The" (song), SM381

"Without a Song" (song), R6-19, R6-27, R6-41, R6-63

Wizard of Oz, The (film), F9

Wonder Bar (film), 22, 23, 44, C10, F10

Wonder Bar, The (show), 12, 21, 22, 43, S28, S29

"Wonder Bar" (song), F10, SM382

"Wond'rous Eyes of Araby" (song), SM383

Woods Are Full of Cuckoos, The (cartoon), C14

"World Is In My Arms, The" (song), S29, SM384

"World Is Waiting For the Sunrise, The" (song), R3-26

"World War II Medley" (song), SS3

"Would You Be So Kindly" (song), S29, SM385

"Yaaka Hula Hickey Dula" (song), D9, R6-17, R6-23, R6-32, R6-43, R6-52, R131, S22, SM386

"Yahrzeit" (song), F2

"Yankee Doodle Blues" (song), F17, F18, R1-3, R5-1, SM387

Yankee Doodle Dandy (film), 7, 27, F37

"Year From Today, A" (song), F8, SM388

"Yes, Sir, That's My Baby" (song), 16, R129

"Yes, We Have No Bananas" (song), 20, F6, R2-8, R3-24

"Yoo-Hoo" (song), D39, R5-15, R7, SM389

"You Ain't Heard Nothing Yet" (song), D28, SM390, SS1

"You Ain't See Nothin' Yet" (song), SS3

"You Ain't Talkin' to Me" (song), S14, SM391

"You Are the Someone" (song), S20

"You Are Too Beautiful" (song), 21, D88, F9, R1-11, SM392

You Are What You Eat (film), 128

"You Call Everybody Darling" (song), R6-40

You Don't Know What You're Doin' (cartoon), C8

"You Flew Away From the Nest" (song), D76

"You Forgot to Remember" (song), D76

"You Go In, Mister Friend of Mine, I'll Stay Out Here" (song), SM393

"You Let Me Down" (song), SS4

"You Little Mischief Maker" (song), R3-17, R3-19

"You Made Me Love You" (song), 2, D6, F18, R1-5, R2-6, R6-34, R6-41, R29, R47, R75, R77, R79, R80, R86, R98, S20, S29, SM394, SM395, SM396, SS1

"You'd Never Know That Old Home Town of Mine" (song), SM397

"You'll Always Be Beautiful" (song), R6-61, R6-68, SM398

"You'll Call the Next Love the First" (song), S20

"You'll Have to Gallop Some" (song), S22, SM399

"You'll Never Know" (song), R13, SM400

"You Must Have Been a Beautiful Baby" (song), R4-88

"Young and Healthy" (song), R1-14

"You're a Better Man Than I Am, Gunga-Din" (song), SM401

"You're All I Need" (song), R3-18

"You're the Coaxinest Man I Ever Knew" (song), SM402

"You're the Cure For What Ails Me" (song), 24, 25, F12, SM403

"You're a Dangerous Girl" (song), D11, SM404

"You're the Most Wonderful Girl" (song), SM405

"You've Simply Got Me Cuckoo" (song), D55

Name Index

This index of names uses page numbers for material appearing in the biography and chronology of this book. Other sections are identified by entry letter and number. The letters used are A (awards), C (cartoon), D (discography), F (film), N (newsreels), R (radio), S (stage), SM (sheet music), and T (television). The bibliographies are not indexed. Each letter is followed by a number for the appropriate entry.

Abbott and Costello, A8
Abrahams, Maurice, D6, D8, D15, SM123, SM255, SM256, SM362, SM405
Ager, Milton, D47, D48, D69, D77, SM7, SM21, SM102, SM149, SM153, SM184, SM284, SM357, SM372, S77
Ahlert, Fred E., D24, D25, SM76
Akst, Harry, D44, D52, D95, D106, D110, D113, F38, N30, SM11, SM28, SM92, SM116, SM246, SM283, SM302, SM374
Alberte, Charles S., D10, SM86
Alda, Robert, F17
Alexander, John, F18
Allen, Gracie, 14, 23, 30, 31, 32, A12, R2, R4-98, R6-43, R38, R79, R129, R132
Allen, Steve, R121
Allison, Wilmer, R3-25
Allyson, June, A11
Ameche, Don, 26, 44, F14, F15, N40, N41, R46
Amos 'N' Andy, R77
Andrews Sisters, The, D112, R6-59
Angel, Heather, R3-23
Aristophanes, S19
Arlecchino, 5
Arlen, Harold, 24, F12, SM144,

SM196, SM282, SM403
Armen, Kay, A6
Arnaz, Lucie, F2
Arnheim, Gus, D65
Arnstein, Nick, F13
Arthur, Jean, 128
Arthur, Robert, F23
Astaire, Adele, 14
Astaire, Fred, 5, 14, 23, F11, N17
Ates, Roscoe, R3-21
Atteridge, Harold, D5, D16, D21, D24, F7, S18, S19, S20, S21, S22, S23, S24, S25, S26, S27, SM16, SM32, SM35, SM38, SM74, SM76, SM108, SM110, SM121, SM140, SM161, SM177, SM179, SM187, SM223, SM236, SM240, SM254, SM265, SM270, SM272, SM274, SM275, SM289, SM314, SM316, SM333, SM347, SM356, SM364, SM399
Auer, Mischa, R4-83
Autry, Gene, F40, R4-93

Bacall, Lauren, A11, F39
Bacon, Lloyd, 19, F3, F4, F10
Baer, Abel, D56
Baer, Buddy, R3-1
Baer, Max, F33, R3-1
Bainter, Fay, R4-86

Baker, Phil, F16, S26, S27
Ball, Lucille, 34, R5-35, R6-17
Barnett, J., SM369
Barrat, Robert, F10
Barrett, Sheila, R3-6
Barrymore, Diana, R5-13, R5-34
Barrymore, John, F2, R3-4, R3-34, R4-48, R4-64
Barrymore, Lionel, R3-20, R3-37
Barthelmess, Richard, R3-14
Bartholomew, Freddie, R4-87
Baskette, Billy, D53
Basserman, Albert, F17
Bates, Blanche, S3
Bayes, Nora, D1
Bayha, Charles A., SM344
Beatles, The, 34
Beckett, Scotty, F18
Beda, SM250
Beery, Noah, F6, F7
Beery, Noah, Jr., F7
Beery, Wallace, F8
Behler, Aggie, 9, 40, S4
Behrman, S.N., 21, F9
Benchley, Robert, R5-14, R5-17
Bendix, William, R6-5
Bennett, Constance, R3-2, R4-50
Bennett, Leo, SM69
Bennett Sisters, The, SM134
Benny, Jack, 23, 31, 32, 34, 46, A8, A11, C19, F33, F41, N7, R2, R86, R133
Benson, Jerry, D43
Bergen, Edgar, 31, F40, R6-1, R97
Bergman, Ingrid, A11, F39
Berkeley, Busby, 22, 24, F10, F12
Berle, Milton, 3, 34, R71
Berlin, Irving, 8, 20, C16, D1, D6, D7, D13, D15, D27, D63, D70, D76, D78, D87, D94, D99, D101, D109, D110, F6, N51, R40, SM37, SM199, SM200, SM201, SM211, SM332, SM335, SM360
Bernard, Barney, S17, S18, S19
Bernie, Ben, R1-7, R4-31, R24, R37, R48
Besserer, Eugenie, F2
Bibo, Irving, D35
Biese, Paul, D47, D48
Binder, A.W., D88, D102, SM53
Bischof, Sam, F11

Blackton, Jay, D95
Blahoe, Julie, F17
Blake, Eubie, D108, SM169
Bloch, Ray, R5
Blondell, Joan, 19, R3-15
Blore, Eric, R4-66
Bogart, Humphrey, 31, A11, F39, R6-6
Boland, Mary, R4-65, R4-89
Bolton, Guy, S29
Bond, Ward, F11
Bordon, Betty, R3-23
Bordoni, Irene, R3-10
Boswell, Connee, R4-80
Bosworth, Hobart, F6
Bowman, Lee, 128
Boyer, Charles, 31, R6-8, R6-21, R6-29
Braddock, James J., R3-2
Bradley, Vi, R3-34, R3-37
Brady, Alice, R4-71
Brayton, Margaret, R3-19
Brenda and Cobina, R5-29
Brennan, James A., SM33
Bressart, Felix, F15
Breuer, Ernest, SM181
Brice, Fanny, 2, 5, 12, 14, 19, 25, F3, F13, F33, R3-24, S19, S20
Bring, Lou, D102, R6
Brockman, James, D104, SM81
Bromberg, J. Edward, F14
Bronson, Betty, F3
Brooks, Matt, S29
Brooks, Norman, 128
Brooks, Shelton, D46, SM391, SM393
Broun, Heywood, 49
Brown, Anne, F17
Brown, Fleta Jan, SM383
Brown, Joe E., N40
Brown, Lew, 18, 128, D77, D79, D84, D85, D106, D108, SM97, SM133, SM168, SM174, SM186, SM195, SM203, SM264, SM298, SM345, SM378
Brown, Nacio Herb, SM192
Brown, Russ, S29
Bruce, Carol, 27, R5
Bryan, Alfred, D18, D23, D80, S27, SM40, SM61, SM62, SM83, SM143, SM262, SM325, SM361, SM373
Bryer, Audrene, 29

Buchman, Sidney, F18, F20
Buck, Gene, SM367
Burke, Joe, D67, D68, D87
Burns, Bob, R4-77, R4-97
Burns, George, 3, 5, 6, 14, 23, 30, 32, A12, R2, R4-98, R6-43, R38, R79, R129, R132
Burtnett, Earl, D65
Butternuth, Bobby, D78
Butterworth, Charles, R4-78
Byers, Hale N., D26, SM127

Caesar, Irving, 21, D31, D78, D90, D104, D108, F9, S28, SM73, SM93, SM117, SM162, SM180, SM182, SM183, SM197, SM208, SM216, SM250, SM297, SM304, SM305, SM306, SM307, SM308, SM387, T4
Cagney, James, 19, 22, 23, R3-12
California Motion Picture Corporation, F25
Callahan, J. Will, D29
Calloway, Cab, 24, F12, R3-30
Campbell, Jimmy, SM259, SM343
Cantor, Eddie, 3, 5, 12, 13, 14, 16, 19, 23, 30, 31, 32, 49, A12, C19, F2, F23, F35, R4-5, R31, R40, R51, R81, R95, R104, R113, S25
Canzoneri, Tony, R3-9
Cardell, Carlton, R5
Carnovsky, Morris, F17
Carpenter, Ken, R6
Carrillo, Leo, R4-44
Carroll, Earl, F33
Carroll, Harry, S21, SM24, SM82, SM163, SM261, SM290
Carroll, Madelaine, R6-14
Caruso, Enrico, 13, S23
Cavanaugh, Hobart, F13
Chamlee, Mario, R4-67
Chaplin, Charlie, 3, 5
Chaplin, Saul, D93, D95, SM14, SM15, SM398, T4
Charlot, 5
Chase, Ilka, R5-20
Chatterton, Ruth, R3-17
Chevalier, Maurice, 3, 23
Chief Little Wolf Man, R3-12
Christy, E.P., 26
Claire, Sidney, D77, F42
Claney, Howard, R1, R2

Clark, Buddy, N49
Clark, Dutch, R3-29
Clarke, Grant, D7, D10, D11, D41, D62, D64, D80, D83, SM34, SM72, SM123, SM136, SM226, SM249, SM404, SM405
Clayton, Kay, SM152
Clayton, Lou, 19
Clesi, N.J., SM173
Cliff, Laddie, D49
Clive, E.E., R4-63
Cobb, Irwin S., R3-19
Coburn, Charles, 128, F17
Cohan, George M., 7, 13, 19, 27, D2, D108, F18, S23, SM109
Cohen, Cy, D112
Cohn, Harry, 28, 29, 30
Colbert, Claudette, A11
Colligan, Billy, SM134
Collins, José, S18, S19
Columbia Pictures, 28, 30, 32, 45, 128, F18, F20, F22, F29, F30, F39, F40, F41, F42
Como, Perry, 30, A12
Compton, Joyce, F11, F13
Conklin, Al, SM77
Conklin, Chester, F9, F14
Conley, Larry, SM202
Connelly, Reginald, SM259, SM343
Connolly, Bobby, 24, F11, F34, F35
Connolly, Walter, R3-36, R4-53
Connor, Edgar, F9
Conrad, Con, D50, D51, D61, D74, D75, D76, SM6, SM75, SM188, SM225, SM247, SM248, SM316
Considine, Bob, N33
Cooper, Gary, F33
Cooper, Jackie, R4-85
Cooper, Joe, SM42, SM84
Coots, J. Fred, S26
Corcoran, Red, R4-79
Corrigan, Douglas "Wrong Way", R4-74
Cortez, Ricardo, 22, F10, R3-25
Coslow, Sam, D49, R3-19, SM36
Costello, Johnny "Irish", 19
Cotten, Joseph, T3
Crain, Jeanne, A11
Creamer, Henry, D107, D112, SM160
Crosby, Bing, 4, 23, 31, 33, 46, C18, C19, D94, R6-3, R6-16, R78, R80,

R82, R85, R89, R124, R125, R126, R130, R131, R134

Crosland, Alan, F2, F7

Cummings, Irving, 128, F14

Curtis, Alan, F14

Curtiz, Michael, F6, F23

Dale, Dorothy, R3-28

Daley, Cass, R107

Daly, Joseph M., SM57

Darewski, Hermann, D8, SM227, SM292, SM369

D'Arrast, Harry, F9

Darro, Frankie, F3

Darwell, Jane, F10

Dash, Irwin, SM230

David, Worton, SM369

Davis, Benny, D40, D45, D52, D106, F42, SM28, SM188, SM202, SM283, SM302, SM323, SM374

Davis, Bette, F34, R3-18, R3-27

Davis, Eddie, S29

Davis, Joan, 31, R6-58, R128

Davis, Jr, Sammy, 6

Dawn, Alice, R3-19

Day, Dennis, R6-48, R6-56, R6-69

Day, Doris, R6-51, R6-68

Day, Edith, S21

Day, Oscar F.G., SM70

Dazey, Charles T., S25

Dean, Daffy, R3-6

Dean, Dizzy, R3-6

DeCamp, Rosemary, F17

DeCosta, Harry, D12

Dell, Claudia, F7

Dell, Floyd, 21, F9

Delmar, Ethel, see Ethel Delmar Jolson

Del Rio, Dolores, 22, F10, R3-21, R4-96

Demarest, William, 29, 32, F2, F18, F20

Dempsey, Jack, F33

Dennison, Jo-Carroll, F18

Deslys, Gaby, 11, 12, F24, S18, S20

De Sylva, B.G. "Buddy", 18, 128, D18, D22, D28, D30, D33, D38, D39, D50, D51, D57, D60, D61, D71, D72, D73, D74, D75, D76, D79, D84, D85, D89, D90, D92, D93, D95, D108, R25, S25, SM6, SM10, SM17, SM18, SM19,

SM20, SM22, SM23, SM26, SM27, SM44, SM45, SM47, SM48, SM50, SM51, SM52, SM63, SM65, SM66, SM73, SM75, SM80, SM85, SM96, SM97, SM107, SM125, SM126, SM138, SM157, SM158, SM159, SM168, SM186, SM190, SM191, SM193, SM194, SM203, SM221, SM222, SM225, SM241, SM242, SM247, SM248, SM264, SM266, SM298, SM308, SM312, SM320, SM331, SM345, SM375, SM376, SM378, SM387, SM389, SM390

Devine, Andy, R4-55

Diamond, Neil, 5, F2

Dillon, William, D100, SM150

Disney, Walt, C2, R4-68

Dixon, Mort, D69, D106, SM171

Doakes, Joe and Cynthia, R3-34

Dockstader, Lew, 11, 40, 41, F18, S14

Dodd, Claire, F12

Donahoo, Puss, SM71

Donaldson, Walter, D38, D61, D63, D83, D91, D97, SM6, SM29, SM54, SM80, SM85, SM107, SM228, SM231, SM232, SM233, SM397

Donath, Ludwig, 29, 32, F18, F20

Doner, Kitty, S21, S22, S23

Donnelly, Ruth, 23, F10

Dooley, Ray, R3-11

D'Orsay, Fifi, F10

Dowling, Bill, R3-14

Dowling, Eddie, R3-11

Downey, Morton, F3

Dragon, Carmen, D90

Dresser, Louise, 20, F3, F6

Dresser, Paul, SM260

Dreyer, Dave, D81, D82, D84, D85, D96, F8, SM30, SM31, SM104, SM114, SM170, SM219, SM220, SM326, SM327, SM388

Dreyfus, Max, F17

Dubin, Al, 24, D87, D96, D105, F10, F11, SM1, SM2, SM3, SM56, SM79, SM103, SM111, SM118, SM146, SM205, SM213, SM217, SM230, SM287, SM288, SM350, SM379, SM382

Duning, George, F20

Dunn, Josephine, F3

Dunne, Artie, R3-13

Dunne, Irene, 5
Dunnock, Mildred, F2
Durante, Jimmy, 3, 19, 32, A6, A8, R6-12, R6-27, R6-61, R6-67, R96, R115, R122
Dustin, Eddie, SM402
Dutra, Olin, R3-18
Dykes, Jimmy, R3-37

Earhart, Amelia, 24, R3-7
Early, Stephen T., A10
Eddy, Nelson, 23
Edwards, Gus, D100, SM49
Egan, Raymond, SM9, SM218, SM295, SM320
Ehrlich, Sam, SM401
Elbright, Ky, R3-14
Eldridge, Al, SM202
Ellis, Melville, S20, S21
Epstein, Louis "Eppy", 29
Erdman, Ernie, D44, D96, SM338, SM339, SM340
Erskine, Chester, F9
Evans, Dale, R6-62
Evans, Madge, F9
Eysler, Edmund, S18

Fagan, Barney, SM58
Fain, Sammy, F42, SM176
Fairbanks, Douglas, Jr., F4-61
Falkenburg, Jinx, R5-37, R72, R76, R136, S29
Farkas, Karl, S28
Farley, Ed, R3-31
Farrell, Glenda, F11
Farrell, Jimmy, N43
Fassio, A., SM68
Fay, Frank, R4-33
Faye, Alice, 25, 26, 44, F13, F14, F16, R3-12
Fazenda, Louise, 23, F10, R4-47
Fenton, Carl, D69, D72, D73, D76, D77, D78, D79
Ferber, Edna, S17
Fetchit, Stepin, 6, F35
Fields, Arthur, SM261
Fields, Sidney, R5-21
Fields, W.C., 5, 14
Fischer, George, R111
Fisher, Eddie, 3
Fisher, Fred, D6, D9, D67, D68, F19,

SM40, SM67, SM318, SM373
Fisher, Harry, S17
Fitzgerald, Ella, 4
Flick, Pat C. "Patsy", R3-20
Flippen, Jay C., F19
Fonda, Henry, R3-24
Forbes, Ralph, R3-23
Forbstein, Leo, R102
Foster, Phil, A6
Foster, Stephen, 26, D114, D115, F15
Four Hits & a Miss, D107
Fox, Harry, S20
Fox Studios, F6
Foy, Bryan, F16
Francis, Kay, 22, F10, R5-20
Franklin, Arthur, SM400
Franz, Eduard, F2, F19
Frawley, William, F13
Freedland, Michael, T4
Fried, Martin, D105, SM178, SM371
Friend, Cliff, D25, D56, D62, D64, SM133, SM174, SM198, SM296, SM313, SM351
Froos, Sylvia, R3-13
Fudd, Elmer, C19
Fulton, Jack, R2

Gaal, Franciska, R4-60
Gable, Clark, 23
Galbraith, Erle Chennault, see Erle Galbraith Jolson
Gallop, Sammy, D105, SM321
Galt, Edith Bolling, S21
Gamble, Albert, D18
Gardiner, Peggy, R3
Gardiner, Virginia, R3-39
Gardner, Ed 'Archie", R6-19
Garland, Judy, 1, 3, 4, 5, 27, 31, 34, R4-73, R6-38
Garrett, Betty, 28, 29, 32
Garroway, Dave, 119
Gay, Byron, SM346
Gay, Charles, R3-32
Gensler, Lewis, D72, D73, D95, SM190, SM191
Gershwin, George, 27, 43, 45, D31, D86, D90, D97, F17, R35, R36, SM73, SM206, SM304, SM305, SM306, SM308, SM387
Gershwin, Ira, D86, D90, D97, SM206
Gibson, Joe, SM119, SM329

Gilbert, L. Wolfe, D3, D98, F42, SM42, SM88, SM128, SM130, SM255, SM273, SM311, SM352, SM353, SM354

Gill, Frank, R3-14

Gillespie, Haven, D110

Gleason, Jackie, 34

Gleason, James, F23

Glendinning, Ernest, S20

Gluskin, Lud, R4

Godfrey, Jeff, SM315

Goetz, Coleman, SM165

Goetz, E. Ray, D9, D97, SM100, SM386

Gold, Joe, SM119

Golden, Ernie, D14

Goldman, Herbert G., 3

Goldwyn, Samuel, 23

Gomez, Lefty, R3-3

Goodelle, Niela, R3-11

Goodman, Al, F27, S23, S26

Goodwin, Bill, F18, F20

Goodwin, Joe, D3, D6, SM318, SM344

Gordon, Bert, S29

Gordon, Kitty, S17

Gordon, Mack, SM145

Gorman, J.W., S7

Gottler, Archie, D41, SM132, SM165, SM204

Grable, Betty, F16, N16, N41, N50

Grafton, Gloria, R3-9

Grand Duchess Marie of Russia, R4-92

Grant, Bert, D13

Grant, Cary, 31, R6-23

Gray, Barry, R75

Green, Alfred E., F18

Green, Bonnie, T4

Green, Bud, SM10, SM207, SM337

Green, Robert, F27

Greene, Richard, R4-90

Greenwood, Charlotte, F19

Greer, Jesse, D55

Grey, Clifford, S26

Gribble, Harry Wagstaff, S26

Griffith, D.W., 15, 42, F1, F14

Guinan, Texas, 19

Gumble, Albert, SM83, SM325

Hagan, Walter, R3-27

Hager, Clyde, R3-37

Hajos, Mitzi, S17

Hale, Alan, R4-72, R4-73

Hale, Barbara, 32, F20

Hale, George, S29

Hale, Louise Closser, F7

Hall Johnson Choir, The, F15, R3-33

Hammerstein, Oscar, II, D82, D109

Hampden, Walter, R3-8

Handman, Lou, D59, D113

Hanley, James F., D45, D72, D73, S22, S25, SM22, SM23, SM44, SM45, SM65, SM66, SM74, SM110, SM121, SM125, SM126, SM193, SM194, SM221, SM222, SM236, SM270, SM275, SM279, SM289, SM355, SM364, SM375, SM376, SM399

Harburg, E.Y. "Yip", 24, 26, 44, F12, S29, SM78, SM144, SM282, SM324, SM384, SM385, SM403

Hare, Ernest, S18, S19, S23

Harding, Warren G., N31

Haring, Robert, D86

Harlow, Jean, 128

Harris, Charles K., SM4, SM70, SM101, SM334

Harris, Phil, R6-60

Harris, Sam, F33

Hart, Lorenz, 21, 43, D88, F9, SM120, SM155, SM358, SM392

Haughton, William P., A3

Haver, June, F19

Hawley, Bill, SM71

Healy, Eunice, S29

Healy, Peggy, R2

Healy, Ted and Betty, S27

Heatherton, Ray, R4-34

Hecht, Ben, 21, F9

Heindorf, Ray, F17

Heller, Louis B., A9

Henderson, Ray, 18, 128, D69, D76, D79, D84, D85, D92, D96, D106, D108, SM10, SM168, SM172, SM186, SM298, SM345, SM378

Henie, Sonja, F16, R4-36

Henry, Ted, SM77

Herbert, Hugh, 23, F10, F34

Herbert, Joseph W., S20

Herczeg, Geta, S28

Herne, James A., S3

Herscher, Louis, SM90

Hess, Cliff, SM310

Hess Sisters, S17
Hickman, Darryl, F17
Hildegarde, 30, A12
Hinckley, Irving, SM142
Hirsch, Louis A., D3, S19, SM106, SM237
Hirsch, Walter, D55, SM313
Holden, William, A11
Holloway, Sterling, R3-39
Holmes, Frank "Pansy", 29, S20, S21, S22, S23, S24
Holmes, Philip, R3-7
Holtz, Lou, A8
Holzman, Abe, D4
Hope, Bob, 30, A8, A12, N10, R84
Hopkins, Jewel, R3-31
Horton, Edward Everett, F12, R3-26, R3-29, R4-39, R4-49, R6-24
Howard, Eugene, S19
Howard, Leslie, R4-91
Howard, Richard, D61
Howard, Willie, S19, R3-16
Hueston, Billy, SM41
Huffman, J.C., S17, S18, S19, S21, S22, S23, S24, S25
Hughes, Jackie, R3-24
Hughes, John B., F17
Hughes, Lloyd, F7
Hughes, Rush, R4
Hull, Henry, R3-16
Huston, John, 32
Huston, Walter, R3-10
Hutchens, John, 6

Imber, Nahtali Herz, D103
Irving, Margaret, S29
Irwin, Stuart, F14
Ivanovici, SM14, SM15

Jackson, Eddie, 19
Jackson, Tony, D106, SM268
Jacobs, Jacob, D105, SM321
James, Billy, SM55
Janis, Elsie, 15, F27
Jarman, Claude, Jr., A11
Jason, Sybil, 24, 25, 27, 33, F12, F34
Jeffries, James J., R3-15
Jenkins, Allen, F12, F34, R3-25
Jenkins, Gordon, D111, D113, D114, D115, R5
Jerome, Maurice K., F42, SM89

Jerome, William, D3, D107, SM29, SM59, SM115, SM280, SM348
Jessel, George, 3, 7, 14, 15, 16, 24, 30, 31, 33, 49, A12, F2, F3, F8, F19, F27, F39, N36, R3-18, R4-29, R4-35, R5-38, R6-44, R6-63, R34
Johnson, Arnold, SM342
Johnson, Arthur, D99, SM156, SM323
Johnson, Howard, D9, D12, SM67, SM165, SM397
Johnson, Mrs. Martin, R4-63
Jolson, Al (Asa Yoelson), (awards) 283-285; (bibliography) 209-268; (blackface) 4-6; (Broadway heyday) 11-14; (cartoons) 279-282; (chronology) 39-46; (comeback) 28-33; (death) 33-34; (discography) 129-149; (early life) 8-9; (endorsements) 287-288; (enigmas of personal life) 6-7; (film heyday) 14-26; (films) 83-127; (newsreels) 273-278; (radio and television) 151-175; (sheet music) 177-208; (show business beginnings) 9-11; (significance as an artist) 1-4, 7-8; (stage shows) 49-81; stage shows based on Jolson's life) 269-272
Jolson, Al, Jr. (adopted son with Ruby Keeler), 24
Jolson, Asa, Jr. (adopted son with Erle Galbraith), A4, A9, N8, N24
Jolson, Erle Galbraith (fourth wife of Al Jolson), 7, 28, 32, 44, 46, A4, A9, N7, N8, N12, N24, N45
Jolson, Ethel Delmar (Alma Osborne) (2nd wife of Al Jolson), 14, 15, 42, 46
Jolson, Harry (Hirsch Yoelson) (brother of Al Jolson), 7, 9, 10, 29, 39, 40, 46, S9, S10, SM90
Jolson, Henrietta Keller (first wife of Al Jolson), 10, 14, 40, 42, 46
Jolson, Maurice (cousin of Al Jolson), 8
Jolson, Ruby Keeler (third wife of Al Jolson), see Ruby Keeler
Jones, Isham, D60, D61, D62, F42
Judels, Charles, S27
Judge, Virginia, R4-12

Kahal, Irving, SM176
Kahn, Gus, D18, D22, D28, D44, D60, D86, D96, D101, D106, SM12,

SM39, SM46, SM54, SM64, SM96, SM98, SM131, SM137, SM158, SM159, SM206, SM228, SMSM239, SM241, SM242, SM245, SM268, SM293, SM295, SM320, SM338, SM339, SM340, SM390
Kalmar, Bert, D4, D6, D76, SM92
Kandel, Aben, S28
Kane, Helen, S27
Kaplan, Teresa Flax Goode (niece of Al Jolson), 14, 30
Karloff, Boris, R3-22, R6-13
Katscher, Robert, 21, S28, SM93, SM117, SM297
Katzman, Sam, F22
Kaufman, George S., 13
Kaye, Danny, 27, A8
Keaton, Buster, F14
Keeler, Marjorie (sister of Ruby Keeler), R3-21
Keeler, Ruby (third wife of Al Jolson), 7, 19, 22, 23, 24, 25, 26, 27, 29, 43, 44, 45, 46, A5, C14, F5, F6, F11, F34, N2, N19, N35, N39, N47, R4-1, R4-45, R20, R21, R27, R38, S27, S28, S29
Keighley, William, F12
Keller, Henrietta, see Henrietta Keller Jolson
Kelley, George, R4-12
Kelly, Gene, T3
Kelly, Patsy, 21, 24, F11, R3-29, R4-52, S28
Kelly, Paul, N30
Kennedy, Merna, F10
Kent, Barbara, R3-39
Kent, Walter, SM5
Kern, Jerome, D82, S17, SM91, SM112, SM175, SM210, SM257, SM267, SM269, SM271, SM291, SM294, SM317, SM322
Keyes, Evelyn, 29, 30, F18, T4
Keystone Kops, The, F14
Kibbee, Guy, 23, F10, R4-70
Kimm, Nancy, N26
King, Alexander, 26
King, Charles, S20
Kirkwood, Jack, R6-66, R6-71, R107
Kirsten, Dorothy, R6-30, R6-33, R6-35, R6-37, R6-42, R6-60, R6-71
Klein, Arthur, 11, 41

Klickman, F. Henri, D4
Knight, Evelyn, A8
Kolker, Henry, F10
Kortlander, Max, D29
Kraft Choral Club, R6-26, R6-50
Krasna, Erle, see Erle Galbraith Jolson
Krasna, Norman, 33, 46
Kroll, H., SM13
Krone, Truck, 29
Kruger, Otto, R3-13
Kuchel, Thomas H., A4

Lackaye, Wilton, S3
Ladd, Alan, A11
LaGuardia, Fiorello, R58
Lahr, Bert, R2, R3-9
Laine, Frankie, 3
Lamb, Arthur, D2
Lamb, Gil, S29
Lamour, Dorothy, R6-9
Landi, Elissa, R3-3, R3-35
Landis, Carole, R5-36
Lane, Burton, 26, 44, S29, SM78, SM324, SM384, SM385
Lanfield, Sidney, F15
Langdon, Harry, 21, F9
Langford, Frances, F22
Lasky, Jesse, Jr., F17
Laughton, Charles, R6-20
Layton, J. Turner, D107, D112, SM160
LeBoy, Grace, D101, SM46, SM98
Lederer, Frances, R3-28
Lederer, Otto, F2
Lee, Davey, 18, F3, F4
Lee, Dixie, R3-14
Lee, Gypsy Rose, R5-10
Lee, Peggy, F2, R6-47, R6-57
Lee, Sam, R3-17
Lee, Tisha, R3-24
Leeds, Andrea, 26, 44, F15
Leftwich, Alexander, S25, S26
Le Gallienne, Eva, R3-6
Leigh, Rowland, S28
Leonard, Eddie, 40
Leoncavallo, R., D66
Lerner, Sammy, D104, D108, SM162, SM182, SM183
Le Roy, Hal, 22, F10
LeRoy, Mervyn, F5

Leslie, Edgar, D8, D10, D32, D41, D62, D64, D83, D97, SM72, SM100, SM123, SM249, SM362, SM405
Leslie, Joan, F17
Lessy, Ben, F22
Levant, Oscar, F17, R6
Levin, Henry, F20
Levinson, Nathan, F17
Lewin, Peter, SM90
Lewis, Ada, F24, S20
Lewis, Buddy, 128
Lewis, Eddie, SM209
Lewis, Elliot, R6-60
Lewis, Jerry Lee, 4
Lewis, Joe E., R3-32, R3-38
Lewis, Maxine, R3-22
Lewis, Mitchell, F6
Lewis, Sam M., D10, D17, D19, D20, D21, D25, D44, D76, D83, D89, D92, D96, D110, D111, SM69, SM124, SM135, SM154, SM172, SM231, SM232, SM233, SM235, SM253, SM276, SM277, SM278, SM366, SM380
Lewis, Ted, A8
Liebling, Leonard, S18
Lillie, Beatrice, F33, R4-41, R4-81
Livadary, John P., F18
Logan, Ella, R3-8
Lombardo, Guy, D89
Lord, Robert, F10, F11
Lorre, Peter, R4-88, R5-12
Louis, Joe, R3-35
Lowe, John, 26
Loy, Myrna, 16, F2
Lum 'N' Abner, R4-40
Lyman, Abe, D65, D67, D68, D83
Lynn, Diana, N16
Lyon, William, F18

MacArthur, Douglas, 33
MacDonald, Ballard, D31, F8, SM24, SM82, SM261, SM279, SM355, SM388
MacDuff, Allan W.S., SM142
Macgowan, Kenneth, F15
MacGregor, Edgar, S29
MacKenna, William, SM105
MacLane, Barton, F11
Madden, Edward, D2, D100, S17, SM43, SM49, SM91, SM112, SM175, SM210, SM257, SM267, SM269, SM271, SM281, SM291, SM294, SM317, SM322, SM355
Main, Walter L., 9, 39, S2
Malneck, Matty, D107
March of Time, The, F21, F38
Markham, Pigmeat, 6
Marks, Clarence J., SM285
Marks, Gerald, D104, D108, SM162, SM182, SM183
Marks, Hilliard, 32
Marlow, June, R3-25
Marshall, George, A9, N24
Marshall, Herbert, R3-30
Marshall, Tully, F6
Martin, Tony, A8
Martinelli, Giovanni, 15
Marx Brothers, The, F40
Marx, Chico, N50, N53
Marx, Groucho, 31, R6-4, R6-32, R6-45, R6-53, R6-65, R6-72
Massow, Marjorie, F16
Mast, Gerald, 16
Mature, Victor, R6-46
Matthews, Joyce, S29
Maxwell, Eddie, SM116
Maxwell, Elsa, F17
Mayer, Louis B., N41
Mayhew, Stella, S17, S18, S19
Mayo, Archie, 24, F11
McAvoy, May, F2
McCarron, Charles, D10, SM86, SM286
McCarthy, Charlie, 31, F40, R97
McCarthy, Clem, R3-5, R3-34
McCarthy, Joseph, D6, D91, D105, SM34, SM40, SM67, SM141, SM163, SM164, SM318, SM370, SM394, SM395, SM396
McClellan, Jack, R3-31
McConnell, Lulu, R3-7, R3-28
McCormick, Myron, F20
McCrary, Tex, R72, R76, R136
McDaniel, Hattie, F12
McDowell, Roddy, R5-19
McEvoy, J.P., F5
McGee, Fibber, R4-95
McGee, Foghorn, R3-17
McHugh, Frank, F34, N34, R3-25
McHugh, Jimmy, D43, F42, SM134, SM230
Melchior, Lauritz, R5-11, R6-2

Melvin, Arthur C., SM41
Menjou, Adolphe, R4-37, R4-46, R4-94, R5-9
Menuhin, Yehudi, R6-11
Merman, Ethel, R40
Merry Macs, The, R4-82
Merson, Billy, D5, D94, SM299, SM300, SM301
Meyer, George W., D3, D10, D97, D99, D110, D111, SM100, SM132, SM156, SM204, SM208, SM235, SM366
Meyer, Joseph, D60, D72, D73, D78, D80, D81, D92, D98, S25, SM22, SM23, SM44, SM45, SM50, SM51, SM52, SM65, SM66, SM114, SM125, SM126, SM193, SM197, SM221, SM222, SM266, SM293, SM375, SM376
Mickey Mouse, C2
Milestone, Lewis, 21, F8, F9
Miljan, John, F5
Millay, Edna St. Vincent, 34
Miller, Marilyn, 14
Miller, Milena, R6
Miller, Ray, D70, D71
Mills Brothers, The, D104
Mills, Jay, SM245
Mitchell, Greenwood, R1-13
Mitchell, Sidney, SM132. SM204, SM229, SM303, SM310
Mittenthal, Joseph, SM57
Mix, Tom, F40
Mollison, William, S28
Monroe Family Singers, The, F7
Monaco, James V., D6, D11, D32, D54, D83, D92, D105, SM34, SM72, SM136, SM141, SM164, SM280, SM370, SM394, SM395, SM396, SM404
Moore, Fred E., 9, 10, 40, S4, S5, S8
Moore, Victor, 31, R6-7, R6-31, R6-54, R6-70
Moran, Ed P., D11, SM141, SM148
Moran, Lois, F6
Moran, Polly, R3-4
Moret, Neil, SM238
Morgan, Frank, F9
Morgan, Helen, 24, F11
Morgan, Henry, R6-34
Morosco, Walter, F6

Morris, Lee, D99, SM156
Morrison, Patricia, N34
Morrone, Josephine, R3-10
Morse, Dolly, SM43
Morton, Ed, SM139
Morton, Lewis, S18
Moss, Arnold, S29
Muir, Lewis F., D3, D98, SM25, SM128, SM130, SM255, SM256, SM273, SM311, SM352, SM353, SM354
Mulhall, Jack, F5
Murphy, George, 5
Murphy, Stanley, SM290
Murray, Charlie, R3-15
Myers, Carmel, R3-20

Nathan, George Jean, 15
Nazarro, Cliff, R4-96
Nazimova, Alla, R3-11
Negulesco, Jean, F37
Nelson, Harmon, F34
Nelson, Ivan, R3-30
Newman, Alfred, D75
Niblo, Fred, R3-336
Niven, David, R6-22
Nixon, Marian, F3, F4
Nolan, Bob, SM349
Norman, Adele, R6-72
North, Robert, F5
Norworth, Jack, D1

Oberon, Merle, N34
O'Brien, Pat, R3-39, R4-76
O'Connell, Helen, R5-22, R5-23, R5-24, R5-25
O'Connor, Donald, 5, 128
O'Day, June, R3-3
O'Keefe, Walter, R6-18
Oland, Warner, F2
Oldfield, Barney, R3-33
Oliver, Edna May, R4-56, R4-75
Olivier, Laurence, F2
Olman, Abe, D34, D104, SM81, SM251, SM252
Olsen and Johnson, R3-5, R4-79
Olshanetsky, Alexander, D105, SM321
O'Neill, Eugene, 1, 22
Oppenheimer, Dave, SM84
Osborne, Nat, D31, SM401

Palmer, Joe, 10, 40, S10, S11
Paramount Pictures, F33
Parks, Larry, 28, 29, 30, 31, 32, F18, R6-52
Parks, Sam, Jr., R3-11
Parkyakarkus (Harry Einstein), 26, R4, R5
Parsons, Louella, R74, R138
Patrick, Gail, R4-80
Patricola, Tom, F17
Paulist Choristers, R3-3
Pearl, Jack, R2
Pemberton, Brock, F33
Penner, Joe, R3-23, R4-32
Perkins, Osgood, F33
Perkins, Ray, D36
Perry, Margaret, F33
Pershing, General John J., R8
Peterburshi, J., SM250
Pether, Henry E., SM224
Petrie, H.W., D2
Phillips, Eddie, F7
Pichel, Irving, R3-19
Pickens, Slim, F23
Pigeon, Walter, F5
Pilcer, Harry, F24, S18, S20, SM106
Pinchon, Edgecomb, R4-20
Pinkard, Maceo, SM229, SM303
Pinza, Ezio, 31, R6-36, R6-40
Pitts, Zasu, R4-43, R4-84
Plautus, S19
Pollock, Channing, SM234
Pollock, Lew, D77
Porter, Cole, SM151
Portway, Alf, SM152
Powell, Dick, 22, 23, A11, F10, R4-99
Powell, William, N16, R6-15
Power, Tyrone, 25, 44, F13, R40
Presley, Elvis, 3, 34
Price, Georgie, D40, D43
Prima, Louis, F13
Prince, Charles A., D6, D7, D8, D9, D10, D11, D12, D13, D14, D15, D16, D17, D18, D19, D20, D21, D22, D23, D24, D25, D26, D27, D28, D29, D30, D31, D32, D33, D34, D35, D36, D37, D38, D39, D40, D41, D42, D43, D44
Professor Quiz, R4-82
Puck, Harry, D6

Quine, Richard, F22

Radford, Dave, D96, SM368
Raft, George, N50, R3-32
Ralston, Mary, F34
Randolph, John, S29
Raphaelson, Samson, 15, 16, F2
Rapper, Irving, F17
Rathbone, Basil, R4-51
Ratoff, Gregory, F13, R4-6, R4-99
Raven, Carol, SM68
Raye, Martha, 26, 30, A12, R4, S29
Reeves, Al, 10, 29, 40, S5, S6
Reid, Carl Benton, F23
Reinhardt, Max, S19
Reis, Leo, R3-13
Revel, Harry, SM145
Rhodes, Harrison, S19
Ribaud, Joe, SM119, SM329
Rice, Florence, R4-54
Rice, Grantland, R4-54
Rickenbacher, Paul, R4
Riley, Mike, R3-31
Ritz Brothers, The, A8, F16, F40
RKO, 33
Robbins, Gale, F19
Robe, Harold A., SM315
Roberti, Lyda, R4-54
Roberts, Beverly, F12
Roberts, Luckieth, SM312
Robinson, Bill "Bojangles", R3-36
Robinson, Edward G., 23, F34, R4-34, R6-25, R6-39
Rockwell, Doc, R3-8
Rodemich, Gene, D63
Rodgers, Richard, 21, 43, D88, D109, F9, SM120, SM155, SM358, SM392
Rogers, Alex, SM312
Rogers, Ginger, F11, R3-26
Rogers, Roy, R6-62
Rogers, Walter B., D2, D3, D4, D5
Rogers, Will, 5, 10, 14, F23
Rogers, Will, Jr., F23
Roland, Gilbert, F8
Romberg, Sigmund, S21, S22, S23, S24, SM16, SM32, SM35, SM38, SM74, SM110, SM121, SM140, SM161, SM177, SM179, SM187, SM189, SM223, SM236, SM254, SM265, SM270, SM272, SM274, SM275, SM289, SM333, SM247, SM356, SM364, SM399
Roosevelt, Franklin D., 49, R20

Roscoe, Philip, F27
Rose, Billy, D54, D69, D81, D84, D96, D99, SM30, SM31, SM94, SM104, SM114, SM170, SM244, SM326, SM327, SM400
Rose, Jack, R9
Rose, Vincent, D33, D93, SM26, SM27
Rosenblatt, Cantor Josef, F2
Rosenbloom, Maxie, R3-13
Ross, Betty, R3-29
Ross, Shirley, A8
Rossini, G., D66
Roth, Abe, R3-39
Rubens, Maurie, S26
Rubin, Benny, F11
Ruby, Harry, D76, F42, SM92
Rudley, Herbert, F17
Ruffner, Tiny, R4
Ruggles, Charles, R3-38, R4-59
Rule, Bert L., SM87, SM166
Russell, Benee, D103, D105, SM185, SM243, SM371
Russo, Dan, D44, D96, SM338, SM339, SM340
Ruth, George Herman "Babe", 9, 24, R3-4
Rutherford, Ann, N16
Ryan, Ben, D110

Sakall, S.Z., F19
Sanders, Joe, SM39
Sanford, Walter, 10, 40, S13
Santley, Eddie, R3-3
Saunders, Willie, R3-8
Savoy, Harry, R3-26
Saxon, Grace, R3-33
Scharf, Walter, T4
Schenck, Joseph, 21, F8, F9
Schmidt, Erwin R., SM209
Schoen, Vic, D110
Schonberg, Chris, D26, SM127
Schraubstader, Carl, SM195
Schumann, Robert, SM319
Schuster, Ira, D35, D62, D64
Schwartz, Jean, D2, D5, D7, D17, D19, D20, D21, D23, D89, D92, D107, F42, S20, S27, SM59, SM124, SM143, SM240, SM262, SM276, SM277, SM278, SM281, SM314, SM380

Schwartz, Phil, D16
Scott, Hazel, F17
Seeley, Blossom, S19, S20
Seldes, Gilbert, 5, 12
Sennett, Mack, F14
Seven Dwarfs, The, R4-62
Sganarelle, 5
Shaw, Al, R3-17
Shaw, Wini, F12, R3-32
Shayne, Tamara, 29, 32, F18, F20
Sherman, Al, D49
Sherman, Lowell, F6
Sherwood, Ray, SM87, SM166
Shore, Dinah, 30, A12, R6-49
Shubert, Jacob J. "Jake", 11, S23
Shubert, Lee, 11
Shubert, Sam S., 11
Shubert Brothers, 11, 12, 13, 15, 18, 41, 42, S17, S18, S19, S20, S21, S22, S23, S24, S25, S26, S27, S28
Sidney, George, R3-15
Sieben, Pearl Goldberg, 7, S29, T3
Silver, Abner, D40, D58, D60, SM36, SM167
Silvers, Louis, D38, D80, D84, D85, D87, D89, D91, F15, R1, SM17, SM18, SM19, SM226, SM309
Silvers, Phil, F16
Silvers, Sid, R4, S26
Simon, Neil, 32
Simon Rady Chorus, D103
Sinatra, Frank, 3, 4, 30, A12, C18
Siskel, Gene, 6
Sissle, Noble, D108, SM169
Skelton, Red, 31, R6-10
Skinner, Otis, F33
Skolsky, Sidney, F18
Sleeper, Martha, R3-13
Smith, Al, R4-80
Smith, Alexis, F17
Smith and Dale, R3-2
Smith, Beasley, D110
Smith, C. Aubrey, R4-57
Smith, Edgar, D91, S17, S22, SM214, SM215
Smith, Kate, R4-81, R46
Snyder, Ted, D4, D10, D21, SM135, SM154, SM249
Snyder, William, F20
Sobel, Bernard, F33
Sparks, Ned, R4-58

Spencer, Herbert, SM383
Spitzer, Samuel E., N28
St. Clair, Malcolm, F14
St. Helier, Ivy, D49
Stahl, John M., F19
Stamper, Dave, SM367
Stander, Lionel, R4-8, R4-9, R4-10
Stange, Hugh Stanislaus, F8
Stanton, Jack, R3
Staub, Ralph, F39, F40, F41, F42
Stauffer, Aubrey, D4, SM319
Stein, Leo, S18
Steiner, Max, F17
Stept, Sam H., SM207, SM337
Sterling, Andrew B., D11, SM115, SM148
Sterling, Ford, F5
Stern, Jack, D37, SM285
Stevens, Mark, F17, F19
Stevenson, Charles, R3-28
Stewart, Jimmy, N50
Stoloff, Benjamin, F16
Stoloff, Morris W., D91, D92, D93, D94, D96, D97, D98, D99, D100, D101, D105, D106, D108, F18, F20
Stone, Alex, R3-24
Stoopnagle and Budd, R4-42
Stromberg, John, D91, SM214, SM215
Strong, Ken, R1-1
Sullivan, Alexander C., SM99
Swanson, Bob, R3-31
Sweet, Blanche, F5

Talbot, Lyle, F12
Talifierro, Mabel, S3
Talmadge, Norma, F8
Tamiroff, Akim, F11
Tanquay, Eva, 2
Taps, Joni, T4
Tate, Joseph W., D14
Taylor, Deems, R2
Taylor, Estelle, R3-18
Taylor, Irene, R3-16, R3-39
Teasdale, Veree, R3-37, R4-46, R4-94
Temple, Shirley, 5, F16
Terence, S19
Terris, Norma, S27
Terry, Lois, R3-23
Thomas, Danny, A6, F2
Thompson, Kay, R4-79
Thornton, James, D98, SM365

Tierney, Harry, SM61, SM62
Tone, Franchot, 23
Toones, Fred, F11
Tours, Frank, S17, SM91, SM112, SM175, SM210, SM257, SM267, SM269, SM271, SM291, SM294, SM317, SM322
Tracy, Spencer, 23
Treacher, Arthur, F11, R4-1, R4-66, R6-55, S28
Treen, Mary, F34
Troy, Helen, R3-30
Truex, Ernest, R3-10
Truman, Harry S, A9
Tucker, Sophie, 2, 5, F3, F33, R40
Turk, Roy, D59, D113
Turnbull, Irene, R3-16
Turner, Colonel Roscoe, R3-21
Twentieth Century-Fox, 25, 44, F13, F14, F15, F16, F19

Ulrich, Lenore, R3-9
United Artists, 21, 43, F8, F9
Uttal, Fred, R5

Vague, Vera, R6-28
Vallee, Rudy, F33, R5-28, R21
Van Alstyne, Egbert, D106, SM239, SM268, SM295
Van Upp, Virginia, 128
Velez, Lupe, R3-5
Venuta, Benay, R3, R3-36
Violinsky, Solly, D110
Vitagraph, F26
Vitaphone Corporation, F2, F3, F4, F5, F6, F7, F10, F11, F12, F17, F23, F27, F28, F32, F34, F35, F36, R13
Von Tilzer, Albert, D10
Von Tilzer, Harry, D3, D11, D100, SM86, SM115, SM148, SM150, SM348, SM361

Wald, Jerry, 33
Walker, James J., 30, A12
Walker, Joseph, F18
Walker, Raymond, SM286
Walsh, James, SM181
Warner, Albert, N9
Warner Bros., 3, 15, 16, 17, 18, 19, 21, 23, 24, 25, 27, 28, 43, 44, A13, C1, C3, C4, C5, C6, C7, C8, C9, C10, C11,

C12, C13, C14, C15, C16, C17, C18, C19, F2, F3, F4, F5, F6, F7, F10, F11, F12, F17, F23, F27, F28, F34, F35, F37, R13
Warner Choral Singers, F17
Warner, Harry, 16
Warner, Jack L., 16, 23, 25, F2, N9
Warner, Jack L., Jr., T4
Warner, Sam, 16
Warren, Harry, 24, D62, D64, D105, F10, F11, SM1, SM2, SM3, SM79, SM103, SM111, SM113, SM118, SM146, SM205, SM213, SM216, SM217, SM287, SM288, M350, SM379, SM382
Waters, Ethel, 3
Watson Sisters, The, R3-20
Watts, Reggie, R3-14
Wayburn, Ned, S20
Wayne, John, F40
Webb, Clifton, R6-26, S21
Weber, Lawrence, 10, S8
Wells, Jack, SM83
Wendling, Pete, D9, D32, SM253, SM386
West, Mae, S18
Westphal, Frank, D45, D46, D49
Weston, R.P., D8, SM227, SM292
Wethered, Joyce, R3-22
White, Alice, F5
White, George, F17, S18, S19
White, William Allen, F33
Whiteman, Loyce, R3-17
Whiteman, Paul, F17, F33, R2, R4-45
Whiting, Jack, S29
Whiting, Margaret, R6-66
Whiting, Richard A., D96, SM9, SM12, SM218, SM320, SM328
Wickes, Mary, F23
Wildhack, Robert, R3-33
Wiley, Lee, R3-15
Wiley, Noble J., Jr., N28
Wilfred, William, D62, D64
Wilkerson, I.P., 11, 40, S15
Willard, Jesse, R3-38
Williams, Bert, 5, 6, 14
Williams, J.O., SM402
Williams, Midge, R3-27
Wilson, Al, D35, SM33
Wilson, Marie, R4-78
Wilson, Marjorie, R4-96

Wilson, William J., S17, S18, S19
Wilson, Woodrow, 41, S21
Wilton, Eric, F18, F20
Winchell, Walter, 22, F33
Wirges, William F., D80, D81, D82
Wong, Anna May, R4-38
Woods, Harry, D58, D60, D71, D79, D101, D106, SM167, SM171, SM259, SM343, SM363
Woolley, Monty, R5, R5-14, R5-16
Wray, John, F8
Wyman, Jane, F23
Wynn, Ed, 23, R2

Yacht Club Boys, The, F12, R3-27
Yellen, Jack, D18, D34, D47, D48, D69, D77, SM7, SM8, SM21, SM89, SM102, SM149, SM153, SM184, SM196, SM251, SM252, SM284, SM357, SM372, SM377
Yoelson, Asa, see **Al Jolson**
Yoelson, Etta (sister of Al Jolson), 9
Yoelson, George (half-brother of Al Jolson), 9
Yoelson, Gertrude (sister of Al Jolson), 9
Yoelson, Hirsch, see **Harry Jolson**
Yoelson, Rose (sister of Al Jolson), 9, 14
Yoelson, Chyesa "Hessi" Yoels (stepmother of Al Jolson), 9, 39
Yoelson, Moshe Reuben (father of Al Jolson), 8, 9, 30, 39, 40, 45, S3
Yoelson, Naomi Cantor (mother of Al Jolson), 8, 9, 39
Young, J. Russell, A7
Young, Joe, D8, D9, D10, D15, D17, D19, D20, D21, D25, D44, D76, D89, D91, D92, D96, SM124, SM135, SM154, SM172, SM231, SM232, SM233, SM253, SM276, SM277, SM278, SM362, SM366, SM380, SM386
Young, Loretta, A11
Young, Roland, F9
Young, Victor, D88, D109, F33, R3, R4
Yvain, Maurice, SM234

Zaney, King, SM192
Zangwill, Israel, 9, 39, S3

Zanuck, Darryl F., F13, F14, F15
Ziegfeld, Florenz, 19, 25, 43, F13, F18
Zorina, Vera, R4-82
Zukor, Adolph, F33, N56

About the Author

JAMES FISHER is Associate Professor of Theater at Wabash College. He has written several books and a play. His many articles have appeared in journals such as *Modern Drama*, *Soviet and Eastern European Performance*, *New England Theatre Journal*, and *The Drama Review*. In addition, he has directed or acted in more than 200 performances, and is the book review editor for the *Journal of Dramatic Theory and Criticism*.

**Titles in
Bio-Bibliographies in the Performing Arts**

Milos Forman: A Bio-Bibliography
Thomas J. Slater

Kate Smith: A Bio-Bibliography
Michael R. Pitts

Patty Duke: A Bio-Bibliography
Stephen L. Eberly

Carole Lombard: A Bio-Bibliography
Robert D. Matzen

Eva Le Gallienne: A Bio-Bibliography
Robert A. Schanke

Julie Andrews: A Bio-Bibliography
Les Spindle

Richard Widmark: A Bio-Bibliography
Kim Holston

Orson Welles: A Bio-Bibliography
Bret Wood

Ann Sothern: A Bio-Bibliography
Margie Schultz

Alice Faye: A Bio-Bibliography
Barry Rivadue

Jennifer Jones: A Bio-Bibliography
Jeffrey L. Carrier

Cary Grant: A Bio-Bibliography
Beverley Bare Buehrer

Maureen O'Sullivan: A Bio-Bibliography
Connie J. Billips

Ava Gardner: A Bio-Bibliography
Karin J. Fowler

Jean Arthur: A Bio-Bibliography
Arthur Pierce and Douglas Swarthout

Donna Reed: A Bio-Bibliography
Brenda Scott Royce

Gordon MacRae: A Bio-Bibliography
Bruce R. Leiby

Mary Martin: A Bio-Bibliography
Barry Rivadue

Irene Dunne: A Bio-Bibliography
Margie Schultz

Anne Baxter: A Bio-Bibliography
Karin J. Fowler

Tallulah Bankhead: A Bio-Bibliography
Jeffrey L. Carrier

Jessica Tandy: A Bio-Bibliography
Milly S. Barranger

Janet Gaynor: A Bio-Bibliography
Connie Billips

James Stewart: A Bio-Bibliography
Gerard Molyneaux

Joseph Papp: A Bio-Bibliography
Barbara Lee Horn

Henry Fonda: A Bio-Bibliography
Kevin Sweeney

Edwin Booth: A Bio-Bibliography
L. Terry Oggel

Ethel Merman: A Bio-Bibliography
George B. Bryan

Lauren Bacall: A Bio-Bibliography
Brenda Scott Royce

Joseph Chaikin: A Bio-Bibliography
Alex Gildzen and Dimitris Karageorgiou

Richard Burton: A Bio-Bibliography
Tyrone Steverson

Maureen Stapleton A Bio-Bibliography
Jeannie M. Woods

David Merrick: A Bio-Bibliography
Barbara Lee Horn

Vivien Leigh: A Bio-Bibliography
Cynthia Marylee Molt

Robert Mitchum: A Bio-Bibliography
Jerry Roberts

Agnes Moorehead: A Bio-Bibliography
Lynn Kear

Colleen Dewhurst: A Bio-Bibliography
Barbara Lee Horn

Helen Hayes: A Bio-Bibliography
Donn B. Murphy and Stephen Moore

Boris Karloff: A Bio-Bibliography
Beverley Bare Buehrer

Betty Grable: A Bio-Bibliography
Larry Billman

Ellen Stewart and La Mama: A Bio-Bibliography
Barbara Lee Horn

Lucille Lortel: A Bio-Bibliography
Sam McCready

Noël Coward: A Bio-Bibliography
Stephen Cole

Oliver Smith: A Bio-Bibliography
Tom Mikotowicz

Katharine Cornell: A Bio-Bibliography
Lucille M. Pederson

Betty Comden and Adolph Green:
A Bio-Bibliography
Alice M. Robinson